POLITICS AND ECONOMICS OF THE MIDDLE EAST

IRAQ

RECONSTRUCTION LESSONS, POLITICS AND GOVERNANCE

POLITICS AND ECONOMICS OF THE MIDDLE EAST

Additional books in this series can be found on Nova's website under the Series tab.

Additional E-books in this series can be found on Nova's website under the E-book tab.

POLITICS AND ECONOMICS OF THE MIDDLE EAST

IRAQ

RECONSTRUCTION LESSONS, POLITICS AND GOVERNANCE

CONNOR E. SMITS
EDITOR

Copyright © 2013 by Nova Science Publishers, Inc.

All rights reserved. No part of this book may be reproduced, stored in a retrieval system or transmitted in any form or by any means: electronic, electrostatic, magnetic, tape, mechanical photocopying, recording or otherwise without the written permission of the Publisher.

For permission to use material from this book please contact us:
Telephone 631-231-7269; Fax 631-231-8175
Web Site: http://www.novapublishers.com

NOTICE TO THE READER

The Publisher has taken reasonable care in the preparation of this book, but makes no expressed or implied warranty of any kind and assumes no responsibility for any errors or omissions. No liability is assumed for incidental or consequential damages in connection with or arising out of information contained in this book. The Publisher shall not be liable for any special, consequential, or exemplary damages resulting, in whole or in part, from the readers' use of, or reliance upon, this material. Any parts of this book based on government reports are so indicated and copyright is claimed for those parts to the extent applicable to compilations of such works.

Independent verification should be sought for any data, advice or recommendations contained in this book. In addition, no responsibility is assumed by the publisher for any injury and/or damage to persons or property arising from any methods, products, instructions, ideas or otherwise contained in this publication.

This publication is designed to provide accurate and authoritative information with regard to the subject matter covered herein. It is sold with the clear understanding that the Publisher is not engaged in rendering legal or any other professional services. If legal or any other expert assistance is required, the services of a competent person should be sought. FROM A DECLARATION OF PARTICIPANTS JOINTLY ADOPTED BY A COMMITTEE OF THE AMERICAN BAR ASSOCIATION AND A COMMITTEE OF PUBLISHERS.

Additional color graphics may be available in the e-book version of this book.

Library of Congress Cataloging-in-Publication Data

ISBN: 978-1-62618-707-8

Published by Nova Science Publishers, Inc. † New York

CONTENTS

Preface   **vii**

Chapter 1   Learning from Iraq: A Final Report from the Special Inspector
General for Iraq Reconstruction   **1**

Chapter 2   Iraq: Politics, Governance, and Human Rights   **259**
Kenneth Katzman

Index   **313**

PREFACE

This book brings together a wealth of information and analysis to identify important lessons learned from the rebuilding program in Iraq; lessons that could help improve significantly the U.S. approach to future stabilization and reconstruction operations. Drawing from numerous interviews with past and present Iraqi leaders, senior U.S. policymakers and practitioners, members of Congress, and others who were involved with Iraq, this book lays out in detail the enormous U.S. reconstruction effort, which completed thousands of projects and programs since 2003, but in which there were many lessons learned the hard way. This book describes the challenges, encountered by the soldiers, diplomats, and other civilians who served in Iraq. The nine-year rebuilding program, expended about $60 billion in U.S. taxpayer dollars and billions more in Iraqi funds. Over $25 billion of that was committed to the training and equipping of Iraqi Security Forces, with the balance funding everything from major infrastructure construction in the electricity and water sectors to local governance programs and reconstruction projects.

Chapter 1 – *Learning From Iraq: A Final Report From the Special Inspector General for Iraq Reconstruction* culminates SIGIR's nine-year mission overseeing Iraq's reconstruction. It serves as a follow-up to their previous comprehensive review of the rebuilding effort, *Hard Lessons: The Iraq Reconstruction Experience.*

This study provides much more than a recapitulation of what the reconstruction program accomplished and what the author's office found in the interstices. While examining both of these issues and many more, *Learning From Iraq* importantly captures the effects of the rebuilding program as derived from 44 interviews with the recipients (the Iraqi leadership), the executors (U.S. senior leaders), and the providers (congressional members). These interviews piece together an instructive picture of what was the largest stabilization and reconstruction operation ever undertaken by the United States (until recently overtaken by Afghanistan).

The body of this report reveals countless details about the use of more than $60 billion in taxpayer dollars to support programs and projects in Iraq. It articulates numerous lessons derived from SIGIR's 220 audits and 170 inspections, and it lists the varying consequences meted out from the 82 convictions achieved through the authors' investigations. It urges and substantiates necessary reforms that could improve stabilization and reconstruction operations, and it highlights the financial benefits accomplished by SIGIR's work: more than $1.61 billion from audits and over $191 million from investigations.

Chapter 2 – Accelerating violence and growing political schisms call into question whether the fragile stability left in place in Iraq after the U.S. withdrawal from Iraq will collapse. Iraq's stability is increasingly threatened by a revolt—with both peaceful and violent aspects—by Sunni Arab Muslims who resent Shiite political domination. Sunni Arabs, always fearful that Prime Minister Nuri al-Maliki would seek unchallenged power, accuse him of attempting to marginalize them politically by arresting or attempting to remove key Sunni leaders. Sunni demonstrations have grown since late December 2012 over Maliki's moves against leading Sunni figures. Iraq's Kurds are increasingly aligned with the Sunnis, based on their own disputes with Maliki over territorial, political, and economic issues. The Shiite faction of Moqtada Al Sadr has been leaning to the Sunnis and Kurds and could hold the key to Maliki's political survival. Adding to the schisms is the physical incapacity of President Jalal Talabani, a Kurd who has served as a key mediator, who suffered a stroke in mid-December 2012. The growing rifts raise the potential for early national elections, originally due for 2014 but which could be advanced to coincide with provincial elections in April 2013.

The violent component of revolt is spearheaded by Sunni insurgents linked to Al Qaeda in Iraq (AQ-I), perhaps emboldened by the Sunni-led uprising in Syria. They have conducted numerous complex attacks against Shiite religious pilgrims and neighborhoods and Iraqi Security Force (ISF) members. The attacks are intended to reignite all-out sectarian conflict, but have failed to do so to date. There are concerns whether the ISF—which numbers nearly 700,000 members— can counter the violence now that U.S. troops are no longer in Iraq; U.S. forces left in December 2011 in line with a November 2008 bilateral U.S.-Iraq Security Agreement. The Iraqis refused to extend the presence of U.S. troops in Iraq, believing Iraq could handle violence on its own and seeking to put behind it the period of U.S. occupation and political and military tutelage.

Since the U.S. pullout, U.S. training for Iraq's security forces through an Office of Security Cooperation—Iraq (OSC-I) and a State Department police development program have languished. However, the Administration—with increasing Iraqi concurrence—has asserted that the escalating violence necessitates that Iraq rededicate itself to military cooperation with and assistance from the United States. Since August 2012, Iraqi officials have requested expedited delivery of U.S. arms and joint exercises and in December 2012 signed a new defense cooperation agreement with the United States.

Although recognizing that Iraq wants to rebuild its relations in the Arab world and in its immediate neighborhood, the United States is seeking to prevent Iraq from falling under the sway of Iran. The Maliki government is inclined toward close relations with the Islamic Republic, but the legacy of Iran-Iraq hostilities, and Arab and Persian differences, limit Iranian influence. Still, Iraq has aligned with Iran's support for Bashar Al Assad's regime in Syria and may be allowing Iranian arms supply flights to reach Syria by transiting Iraqi airspace. Some see Iraq instead to reestablish its historic role as a major player in the Arab world. Iraq took a large step toward returning to the Arab fold by hosting an Arab League summit on March 27-29, 2012.

In: Iraq: Reconstruction Lessons, Politics and Governance   ISBN: 978-1-62618-707-8
Editor: Connor E. Smits   © 2013 Nova Science Publishers, Inc.

Chapter 1

LEARNING FROM IRAQ: A FINAL REPORT FROM THE SPECIAL INSPECTOR GENERAL FOR IRAQ RECONSTRUCTION[*]

FOREWORD

To the Members of the United States Congress:

We commend to your attention *Learning From Iraq: A Final Report From the Special Inspector General for Iraq Reconstruction*. This important work brings together a wealth of information and analysis to identify important lessons learned from the rebuilding program in Iraq—lessons that could help improve significantly the U.S. approach to future stabilization and reconstruction operations (SROs). Drawing from numerous interviews with past and present Iraqi leaders, senior U.S. policymakers and practitioners, members of Congress, and others who were involved with Iraq, this report lays out in detail the enormous U.S. reconstruction effort, which completed thousands of projects and programs since 2003, but in which there were many lessons learned the hard way.

Learning From Iraq describes at length the challenges encountered by the soldiers, diplomats, and other civilians who served in Iraq. The nine-year rebuilding program, the second largest SRO in U.S. history (after Afghanistan), expended about $60 billion in U.S. taxpayer dollars and billions more in Iraqi funds. Over $25 billion of that was committed to the training and equipping of the Iraqi Security Forces, with the balance funding everything from major infrastructure construction in the electricity and water sectors to local governance programs and small Provincial Reconstruction Team projects.

We worked closely with Inspector General Bowen and his team during our time together in Iraq, and we found their oversight and reporting very useful in providing insights into the execution of our respective missions. While SIGIR's audits, inspections, and investigations addressed the rebuilding program's challenges, its lessons-learned reports, of which this is the ninth and last, also identified many of the important solutions that were developed.

---

[*] This is an edited, reformatted and augmented version of A Final Report from the Special Inspector General for Iraq Reconstruction, dated March 2013.

Of course, a lesson is not truly learned until it is incorporated in policies, practices, regulations, and, in some cases, laws. Now is the time to draw on the lessons from Iraq as we seek to improve the way the United States plans, executes, and oversees SROs.

We salute the Inspector General as he completes his mission, and we thank the members of the SIGIR team for their superb contributions to the effort in Iraq. Indeed, they were among the hundreds of thousands of great Americans, Coalition country members, and Iraqis who served so courageously, skillfully, and selflessly to help provide a new opportunity to the citizens of the Land of the Two Rivers. It was the greatest of privileges for us to serve with all of them.

Respectfully submitted,
General David H. Petraeus
United States Army (Retired)

Ambassador Ryan C. Crocker

PREFACE

Learning From Iraq: A Final Report From the Special Inspector General for Iraq Reconstruction culminates SIGIR's nine-year mission overseeing Iraq's reconstruction. It serves as a follow-up to our previous comprehensive review of the rebuilding effort, *Hard Lessons: The Iraq Reconstruction Experience.*

This study provides much more than a recapitulation of what the reconstruction program accomplished and what my office found in the interstices. While examining both of these issues and many more, *Learning From Iraq* importantly captures the effects of the rebuilding program as derived from 44 interviews with the recipients (the Iraqi leadership), the executors (U.S. senior leaders), and the providers (congressional members). These interviews piece together an instructive picture of what was the largest stabilization and reconstruction operation ever undertaken by the United States (until recently overtaken by Afghanistan).

The body of this report reveals countless details about the use of more than $60 billion in taxpayer dollars to support programs and projects in Iraq. It articulates numerous lessons derived from SIGIR's 220 audits and 170 inspections, and it lists the varying consequences meted out from the 82 convictions achieved through our investigations. It urges and substantiates necessary reforms that could improve stabilization and reconstruction operations, and it highlights the financial benefits accomplished by SIGIR's work: more than $1.61 billion from audits and over $191 million from investigations.

My office carried out an unprecedented mission under extraordinarily adverse circumstances. Hundreds of auditors, inspectors, and investigators served with SIGIR during that span, traveling across Iraq to answer a deceptively facile question: what happened to the billions of dollars expended to rebuild that country?

Our work became increasingly more difficult as the security situation deteriorated, the effect of which forced our mission to become quite literally oversight under fire. The collapse of order in Iraq caused an unacceptably high human toll: at least 719 people lost their lives while working on reconstruction-related activities. SIGIR suffered from this toll, with one auditor killed by indirect fire in 2008 and five others wounded the year before.

Construction official briefs the Inspector General on the status of construction at the Nassiriya Prison during an on-site inspection in 2008.

In late 2003, the burgeoning rebuilding program required more oversight: that was the Congress's view. Thanks to the vigilant efforts of Senator Russ Feingold of Wisconsin, Senator Susan Collins of Maine, and many others, the Congress created and undergirded an unprecedented inspector general office—the Coalition Provisional Authority Inspector General (later SIGIR)—with the power and resources sufficient to provide independent, cross-jurisdictional oversight.

The CPA-IG came into being through a November 2003 congressional act that also provided over $18.4 billion in taxpayer dollars for Iraq's reconstruction. Total appropriations for the rebuilding of Iraq eventually would crest $60 billion. In late January 2004, the Secretaries of Defense and State appointed me to lead the mission of auditing and investigating the CPA's programs and projects.

During my initial visit to Baghdad in early February 2004, I quickly became aware of the immense task before me. Walking the halls of the Republican Palace, a sprawling structure on the Tigris River constructed by Saddam Hussein and now housing the CPA, I overheard someone say: "We can't do that anymore. There's a new inspector general here." That offhand remark augured an oversight mission imbued with challenges of a scope well beyond what anyone then could have imagined.

I made several more trips to Iraq that year—the total would eventually tally to 34—deploying teams of auditors and investigators and engaging with leadership to address the fraud, waste, and abuse that we were uncovering. Pursuant to a presidential decision, the CPA closed its doors in late June 2004, with the Department of State assuming formal control of the rebuilding program. Although sovereignty passed back to the Iraqis, the U.S.-led reconstruction effort was just ramping up. The delays inherent in contracting out a sum as large as $18.4 billion meant that the CPA actually spent very little of it.

In mid-2004, the new U.S. Ambassador to Iraq, John Negroponte, assessed the troubled situation. He determined that about $3 billion should be reprogrammed to address the rapidly declining security situation. Thus began a stark shift away from the CPA's large civic infrastructure strategy to a course aimed at improving the country's military and police forces. This sea change in spending stemmed from the well-founded belief that Iraq's rule-of-law system required immediate and substantial aid. Creating the Multi-National Security Transition Command-Iraq bolstered the new approach, bringing Lieutenant General David Petraeus back to Iraq to lead it. Over the next eight years, MNSTC-I and its successors would oversee expenditures in excess of $24 billion to train, equip, and employ Iraq's security forces.

The earlier-than-expected end of the CPA triggered a statutory provision requiring my office to close by December 2004. Though barely having stood up, I now started to stand down. By October, my staff had dropped to 15, when the Congress acted again, passing a bill transforming the CPA-IG into SIGIR and expanding our mission to reach more of the rebuilding money. We reversed course and moved into an accelerated expansion mode.

In January 2005, SIGIR released a major audit exposing the vulnerabilities inherent in managing a multibillion-dollar rebuilding program in an unstable environment. The audit documented the poor controls over billions disbursed from the Development Fund for Iraq, which left that Iraqi money subject to fraud, waste, and abuse. Future SIGIR investigations revealed fraud in the use of the DFI, and people went to prison for it, but our subsequent audits showed that waste was the paramount problem. Ultimately, we estimate that the Iraq program wasted at least $8 billion.

In mid-2005, Ambassador Zalmay Khalilzad arrived to replace Ambassador Negroponte, who left to serve as the first Director of National Intelligence. Ambassador Khalilzad embraced SIGIR's oversight work, partnering with us in a way that would generally continue for the remainder of our mission. He agreed with our view that the cost-plus design-build contracts then in place were inappropriate for the mission and too wasteful. Ambassador Khalilzad asked the Department of Defense, which controlled those contracts, to terminate them and implement fixed-cost vehicles in their place. The challenges encountered in pushing this policy exposed interagency weaknesses within the Iraq program's ad hoc structure. Pursuant to a May 2004 presidential order, Defense managed the contracts, while State managed rebuilding policy. Given that the operators within these respective "stove-pipes" answered to different masters with different agendas, program and project discontinuities and disconnects became *de rigueur.*

Seeking to remedy these palpable weaknesses, Ambassador Khalilzad created the Provincial Reconstruction Team program, similar to one he developed in Afghanistan, where he previously served as Ambassador. Though desultory at inception, the PRT program picked up speed in 2006 and, along with the Commander's Emergency Response Program, eventually became a significant innovative effort. SIGIR's audits of the PRTs and the CERP exposed unsurprising weaknesses, but they also spotted effective progress achieved by both programs. We found that PRT success depended chiefly on the performance of the PRT leader, while CERP success required limited project scopes and continuity of oversight.

Worsening security problems ultimately swamped Ambassador Khalilzad's plans. Oil and electricity outputs sagged, while al-Qaeda in Iraq expanded, fomenting Sunni-Shia conflicts. By the spring of 2007, when Ambassador Ryan Crocker arrived as the new Chief of Mission, Iraq was in the throes of a virtual civil war. Foreign fighters flooded the country, and improvised explosive devices wreaked daily death and havoc. As Ambassador Crocker put it, we very nearly lost Iraq.

General Petraeus returned again to Iraq in early 2007 as Commanding General, Multi-National Force-Iraq, to implement a new strategy called the "surge." This comprehensive, multilayered approach entailed, among other things, a deeper engagement with restive Sunnis through reconciliation initiatives and the "Sons of Iraq" program, a stronger emphasis on CERP-funded local rebuilding projects that better met Iraqi needs, and the deployment of over 25,000 more troops into the country. While attacks and deaths initially spiked, the strategy succeeded in significantly suppressing violence.

Importantly, both General Petraeus and Ambassador Crocker, like Ambassador Khalilzad before them, believed in the value of SIGIR's oversight and teamed with us to target areas that most crucially needed it. SIGIR's in-country presence rose to more than 40 auditors and inspectors and more than 10 investigators. They worked out of the Republican Palace, which was subject to weekly, if not daily, rocket attacks.

By the fall of 2007, efforts to secure the Iraqi people, pursue extremists, and foster reconciliation had combined to improve conditions substantially. Expanding the "Awakening" movement to all of Anbar province, and then to wherever Sunni insurgents or Shia militia existed, catalyzed reconciliation efforts across the country. The Sons of Iraq program expended about $370 million in CERP funds to employ about 100,000 Sunni insurgents and some Shia militia, effectively removing them from the battlespace. A revised Iraqi-oriented reconstruction program, reflected in the Joint Contracting Command-Iraq's "Iraqi First" policy, fed economic potential into local towns and villages. CERP spending on reconstruction markedly increased, supporting a renewed "clear, hold, and build" program. The Embassy extended the reach of the PRT effort, implementing an "embedded PRT" initiative, which doubled the program's capacity. All of these infusions, expansions, and innovations strategically coalesced to roll back the deadly tide that had submerged Iraq.

Throughout this period, SIGIR produced an average of six audits and at least six inspections per quarter. My Assistant Inspector General for Inspections implemented innovative practices to good effect. Each of his teams included auditors and engineers, with every report examining a project's financial and structural aspects. This produced propitious results, including the discovery by SIGIR engineers of project defects, the correction of which yielded savings of taxpayer dollars. Our audit teams addressed issues crucial to the maturing program such as how to transfer projects to Iraqi control and how Iraq should sustain them thereafter.

In 2008, SIGIR's investigative branch boosted production. Thanks to the leadership of a new and highly experienced Assistant Inspector General for Investigations, our case inventory burgeoned, with indictments and convictions increasing. These positive results came about through several new programs, including coordinated efforts to trace funds through special means and the building of better partnerships with domestic and international law-enforcement agencies.

In 2009, we partnered with the Department of Justice to implement an unprecedented program dubbed the SIGIR Prosecutorial Initiative, or SIGPRO. It involved hiring our own prosecutors and placing them within DoJ's fraud section where they aggressively pursued SIGIR cases. SIGPRO proved great success, yielding a rapid rise in prosecutions and many more convictions. SIGIR's Investigations Directorate more than doubled its financial results, indictments, and convictions in just over two years.

Transition was the theme of 2010 and 2011. U.S. and Iraqi authorities focused on implementing the Security Agreement and the Security Framework Agreement. The former laid out a timeline for U.S. troop withdrawal, while the latter established a process for continuing bilateral cooperation on Iraq's reconstruction and recovery needs. The overarching challenge at this juncture involved transmogrifying a support system largely sustained by

Defense to one handled exclusively by State. SIGIR played a role in this process through audits of the Police Development Program, which revealed weaknesses in planning and coordination. From a taxpayer perspective, these reviews had good effect. State downsized the program to levels the Iraqis wanted, saving hundreds of millions of taxpayer dollars.

Taken together, the following seven chapters of *Learning From Iraq* provide the most comprehensive picture of the reconstruction program yet produced. Chapter 1 synopsizes the prodigious work SIGIR's auditors, investigators, and inspectors accomplished over the past nine years, providing best practices each directorate developed. The second chapter presents key primary source material on the effects of the rebuilding program drawn from interviews with Iraqis, U.S. senior leaders, and congressional members. They paint a telling tableau of a program fraught with challenge.

Chapters 3 and 4 describe the many ad hoc entities that managed the Iraq rebuilding program, denoting who did the actual work and detailing the varying funding streams that supported thousands of programs and projects. Chapter 5, the report's lengthiest, thoroughly lays out where the $60 billion in U.S. funds for Iraq went, with extensive explications of how the money was used to rebuild the country's infrastructure, security system, governance capacity, and economy, punctuated by project vignettes that provide brief but piquant looks into the program's wide scope. The penultimate chapter frames a short history of attempted reforms that sought to respond to management problems encountered during the Iraq program. *Learning From Iraq* concludes with seven final lessons that SIGIR's collective work points to and supports.

These seven lessons and our substantial body of work stand as our legacy. We saved money through audits, improved construction through inspections, and punished criminals through investigations. As pleased as I am with the SIGIR teams that achieved these important results, I view our lessons-learned reports, of which this is the last, as equally important.

Seven Final Lessons from Iraq

1. Create an integrated civilian-military office to plan, execute, and be accountable for contingency rebuilding activities during stabilization and reconstruction operations.
2. Begin rebuilding only after establishing sufficient security, and focus first on small programs and projects.
3. Ensure full host-country engagement in program and project selection, securing commitments to share costs (possibly through loans) and agreements to sustain completed projects after their transfer.
4. Establish uniform contracting, personnel, and information management systems that all SRO participants use.
5. Require robust oversight of SRO activities from the operation's inception.
6. Preserve and refine programs developed in Iraq, like the Commander's Emergency Response Program and the Provincial Reconstruction Team program, that produced successes when used judiciously.
7. Plan in advance, plan comprehensively and in an integrated fashion, and have backup plans ready to go.

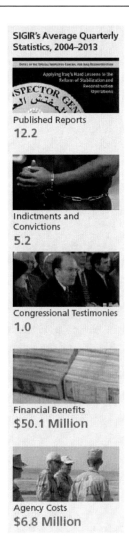

SIGIR most succeeded when it helped the relief and reconstruction mission improve. Our audits, inspections, and lessons-learned reports did that by identifying program challenges and offering recommendations for positive change. SIGIR's reporting points to a crucial bottom line: the United States must reform its approach to planning, executing, and overseeing stabilization and reconstruction operations.

Respectfully submitted,
Stuart W. Bowen, Jr. Inspector General

1. OVERSIGHT IN A WAR ZONE

When SIGIR began work in early 2004 as the Coalition Provisional Authority Inspector General, it was the only inspector general office within the U.S. government possessing oversight responsibilities encompassing several federal agencies. Over time, the Congress expanded SIGIR's mission so that, by 2008, its mandate required reporting on all reconstruction funds regardless of provenance. During most of its nine-year lifespan, SIGIR maintained the largest on-the-ground presence of any U.S. auditing or investigative agency operating in Iraq. In 2008, the number of SIGIR personnel in country exceeded 50. Three operational directorates accomplished the oversight work: Audits, Inspections, and Investigations. They had these common objectives:

- to deter the misuse of taxpayer dollars through the prevention and detection of fraud, waste, and abuse
- to promote improved economy, efficiency, and effectiveness in the Iraq reconstruction program

The Iraq reconstruction program provided a plethora of lessons about what happens when stabilization and reconstruction operations commence without sufficient systemic support in place. Among the most salient is the need to provide a robust in-country team of auditors, inspectors, and investigators from the operation's outset. A substantial IG presence will deter or detect fraud, waste, and abuse, improving mission efficiency and effectiveness. Fraud is the intentional wrongdoing by persons seeking to enrich themselves. Waste is the product of poor planning and weak controls. Abuse is bad management. The absence of a strong oversight force early in the Iraq program allowed too much of each to occur.

SIGIR Audits

Within a month of his appointment, the Inspector General completed 2 trips to Iraq: 32 more would follow. The urgent oversight needs identified during those initial visits led him to deploy two teams of four auditors each to Baghdad, along with investigative support. Those teams were on the ground and working by mid-March 2004, with the agency's first quarterly report to the Congress produced by the end of that month. SIGIR's auditing presence in Iraq rapidly expanded from 2005 to 2007. Buttressed by the development of innovative oversight practices, auditors focused on quickly producing performance reviews rather than slow-moving *ex post facto* financial audits. By forming the Iraq Inspectors General Council, which met quarterly for seven years, the Inspector General emphasized coordination among executive branch audit and investigative agencies working in Iraq. This improved the planning and execution of oversight activities.

At its peak in 2008, SIGIR had 35 auditors permanently stationed in Baghdad conducting audits to root out fraud, waste, and abuse. This in-country presence received steady support from audit managers based in Arlington, Virginia, who regularly traveled to Iraq to strengthen specific reviews.

SIGIR's audit plan sought to determine whether reconstruction managers effectively and efficiently oversaw programs and operations funded by the United States. Further, it aimed at promoting on-theground change through near-real-time reporting, producing audits at an average rate of six per quarter, usually within 90 to 120 days of an audit's announcement.

Best Practices for SRO Audit Programs

1. Focus early audit attention on contracting, quality-assurance, and quality-control resources dedicated to programs and projects.
2. Develop a systematic approach to reporting on the sustainability of projects.
3. Develop an integrated database of contracts, grants, and projects to keep track of what is procured and delivered.
4. Develop close working relationships with senior reconstruction managers to encourage improved program implementation.
5. Ensure that implementing agencies develop program goals, with measurable milestones and outcomes.
6. Provide strong oversight of programs involving cash payments to host-country contractors or officials.
7. Develop expertise in grants management to improve oversight of State and USAID programs.

Table 1.1. SIGIR Summary of Performance; As of March 2013

Audits	Cumulative
Reports Issued	220
Recommendations Issued	487
Potential Savings if Agencies Implement SIGIR Recommendations to:	
Put Funds to Better Use ($ Millions)	$973.62
Disallow Costs SIGIR Questioned ($ Millions)	$640.68
Inspections	
Project Assessments Issued	170
Limited On-site Assessments Issued	96
Aerial Assessments	923
Investigations	
Investigations Initiated	637
Investigations Closed or Referred	562
Open (Active) Investigations	75
Arrests	41
Indictments	104
Convictions	82
Sentencings	68
Monetary Results ($ Millions)	$191.2
Hotline Contacts	
Email	413
Fax	19
Mail	30
Referrals	26
SIGIR Website	200
Telephone	84
Walk-in	112
Total Hotline Contacts	884
Other Products	
Congressional Testimony	35
Lessons Learned Reports	9
Special Reports	3
Evaluation Reports	1
Quarterly Reports	35

From 2004 to 2013, SIGIR published 220 audit reports covering a wide variety of reconstruction issues, including contingency contracting, the promotion of democracy, the transfer and sustainment of completed projects, contract award fees, the management of programs and projects, and the development of Iraq's security forces.

SIGIR's audits questioned about $641 million in costs and identified an additional $974 million in funds to be put to better use—a combined potential financial benefit of $1.61 billion. As of September 2012, the actual savings to the government from renegotiated contracts, refunds, and operational savings resulting from SIGIR findings had reached nearly $645 million (see Figure 1.1).

Among others, SIGIR's audits effected these positive changes within the Iraq program:

- In October 2005, a report examining contract award fees found that none of the contracts reviewed contained the required criteria for awarding fees. Subsequent actions by Defense remedied the deficiency.
- In January and April 2006, three reports reviewed the transfer of completed construction projects to the GOI, finding that U.S. agencies had policies on asset transfer applicable at the local level, but none addressing the GOI ministries responsible for sustaining completed projects. The Congress responded by requiring U.S. agencies to certify that they had implemented an asset-transfer agreement that secured GOI commitments to maintaining U.S.- funded infrastructure.
- In January 2008, SIGIR issued a report on the Commander's Emergency Response Program, finding that an increasing amount of CERP funds was being spent on large projects rather than small-scale urgent projects, as required by CERP guidance. The Congress responded to SIGIR's finding in the National Defense Authorization Act for FY 2009, setting a limit of $2 million for any CERP project. In the Ike Skelton National Defense Authorization Act for FY 2011, the Congress acted further, requiring that program funds be used only for small-scale projects.
-

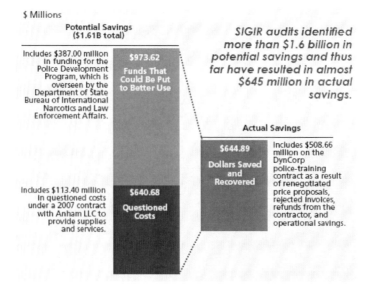

Figure 1.1. Potential and Actual Financial Accomplishments From SIGIR Audits $ Millions.

Our audit findings identified a number of critical deficiencies in reconstruction planning, implementation, and oversight, making recommendations for improvement.

These problems ranged from poor quality-control programs, ineffective quality-assurance programs, lack of sufficient in-country contracting officer representatives, inadequate invoice review procedures, and poor controls over funds such that vulnerabilities to fraud, waste, and abuse were significant.

Departmental responses almost always concurred with SIGIR's findings, usually agreeing to implement all recommended changes.

SIGIR Audit 11-022
The Anham Contract: Oversight Was an Oversight

In September 2007, Defense awarded a $300 million contract to Anham, LLC, to operate and maintain two warehouse and distribution facilities, one near Baghdad International Airport and the other at the Port of Umm Qasr.

Two years later, the contract had incurred obligations of approximately $119.1 million, with Anham subcontractors providing at least $55 million in supplies and services.

A SIGIR audit found weak contract oversight practices that left the government vulnerable to improper overcharges:

- The Defense Contract Audit Agency failed to review Anham's cost-estimating system.
- The Defense Contract Management Agency recommended approval of Anham's purchasing system, despite identifying significant gaps in documentation.
- Contracting officer's representatives failed to effectively review invoices.

SIGIR questioned almost 40% of the costs it reviewed. These overbillings by an Anham subcontractor were especially egregious:

- $900 for a control switch valued at $7.05 (a 12,666% markup)
- $80 for a small segment of drain pipe valued at $1.41 (a 5,574% markup)
- $75 for a different piece of plumbing equipment also valued at $1.41 (a 5,219% markup)
- $3,000 for a circuit breaker valued at $94.47 (a 3,076% markup)
- $4,500 for another kind of circuit breaker valued at $183.30 (a 2,355% markup)

SIGIR further found that there had been questionable competition practices, inappropriate bundling of subcontractor items, and close working relationships—with possible ownership affiliations—between Anham and its subcontractors.

In light of these many deficiencies, SIGIR questioned the entire contract and recommended that the U.S. military initiate a systematic review of billing practices on all Anham contracts in Iraq and Afghanistan.

At the time of SIGIR's review in 2011, Anham held about $3.9 billion in U.S. government contracts. That number has since increased.

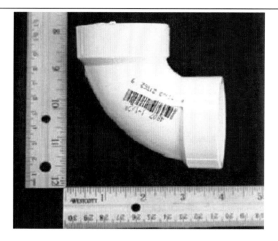

Anham billed the U.S. government $80 for this PVC plumbing elbow, 5,574% more than a competitor's offer of $1.41.

SIGIR PA-08-138 and Audit 08-019
Khan Bani Sa'ad Prison:
Waste in the Desert

Years of neglect, war damage, and looting left Diyala province's prisons in deplorable condition. In May 2004, the CPA awarded Parsons Delaware an $80 million task order to build the Khan Bani Sa'ad Prison, which would add 3,600 beds to the province's correctional capacity.

In February 2006, three months after the scheduled completion date, Parsons submitted notification that its new projected completion target was September 2008—a 990-day schedule slippage.

In June 2006, the U.S. government terminated the contract for "failure to make sufficient progress on the project" and "massive cost overruns."

Still believing the prison was wanted by the Iraqi Ministry of Justice, reconstruction managers awarded three successor contracts to complete the work.

In June 2007, the U.S. government terminated all work on the project for convenience, citing security issues.

At the time of termination, the United States had spent almost $40 million, but no building was complete.

Two months later, USACE unilaterally transferred the unfinished project to the GOI even though Ministry of Justice officials told USACE they did not plan to "complete, occupy, or provide security for" the poorly and partially constructed facility.

SIGIR visited the site in June 2008, finding it neither secured nor occupied by the GOI. SIGIR's assessment documented poor-quality workmanship by Parsons, including many potentially dangerous conditions.

Several sections were recommended for demolition. The site still sits dormant in Diyala and apparently will never be used.

The Khan Bani Sa'ad Prison was abandoned after the United States spent almost $40 million on it.

SIGIR Inspections

During his initial visits to Iraq in 2004, the Inspector General heard conflicting stories about U.S.-funded stabilization and reconstruction projects. On the one hand, U.S. agencies and private construction companies commonly reported construction projects as success stories. But many Iraqis and some U.S. military and civilian personnel privately registered strong complaints about the program. They pointed to unwanted projects and to equipment that was either too sophisticated for the Iraqis to use or of very poor quality.

SIGIR auditors began to discover inadequately designed projects, which were poorly constructed and unsustainable. With billions of taxpayer dollars at stake, the Inspector General took action to expand SIGIR's oversight capacity. In June 2005, he created the Inspections Directorate to assess and report on reconstruction work by visiting project sites.

Best Practices for SRO Inspection Programs

1. Provide reconstruction officials with near real-time reporting.
2. Team engineers with auditors.
3. Report on complex technical topics in accessible language.
4. Execute inspections rapidly.
5. Visit project sites in person.
6. Visit as many projects as possible early in the program.
7. Always consider sustainability in assessing reconstruction projects.

Over the next five years, inspection teams composed of experienced engineers and auditors traveled to sites all over Iraq. The Inspections Directorate selected projects for review from each reconstruction sector, covering large and small contractors, different geographical areas, each of the major U.S. agencies operating in country, and all funding sources.

The selection criteria asked the following questions:

- Was the request from a military commander or a State Department official?
- Was the project significant?
- Was there a likelihood of fraud or waste?
- Were there existing concerns about the project under consideration or its contractor?

In assessing construction projects, SIGIR asked the following questions:

- Was the project properly designed?
- Was the project built according to contract specifications?
- Was an adequate contractor-managed quality-control program and government-managed quality-assurance program in place?
- Was sustainability considered and planned for?
- Was the project likely to meet contract objectives?

As the program matured, the Inspections Directorate added project sustainment inspections into the mix, examining whether a completed project was operating as intended and whether the Iraqis were sustaining it through effective operations and maintenance.

Unstable conditions in Iraq sometimes prevented SIGIR's inspectors from conducting on-site assessments. Because of security threats, SIGIR had to cancel visits to 18 project sites between June 2005 and August 2008. In 2008, General David Petraeus, the Multi-National Force-Iraq Commanding General, authorized SIGIR's inspectors to travel under Defense Department authority, which subsequently ensured access and transport to all sites.

SIGIR's inspections commonly identified deficiencies in design, construction, quality control, quality assurance, and sustainability. The Directorate referred these to the appropriate relief and reconstruction agencies for corrective action. Indicators of potential fraud were referred to investigators for analysis, investigation, and possible Department of Justice action. For example, in 2008, SIGIR's inspectors at the Sarwaran Primary School and the Binaslawa Middle School discovered possible illegal activity by two Korean Army officers and a master sergeant who had authorized a contract requiring the use of prohibited Iranian parts. SIGIR's inspectors referred the matter to SIGIR investigators, who carried out an inquiry that led to the three individuals eventually being convicted by a Korean military court.

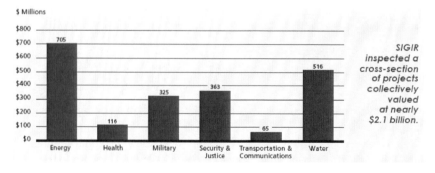

Figure 1.2. Contract Value of Projects SIGIR Inspected, by Reconstruction Sector.

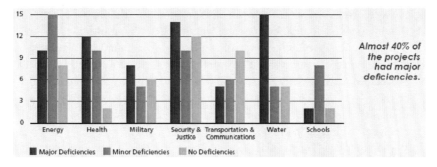

Figure 1.3. Deficiencies for Projects SIGIR Assessed, by Reconstruction Sector.

SIGIR's Inspections Directorate concluded operations in April 2010, just as major U.S. construction projects were winding down and as Iraq was assuming control of the rebuilding program. In all, SIGIR issued 170 inspection reports covering projects valued at nearly $2.1 billion (see Figure 1.2).

Of the 116 ongoing projects that SIGIR inspected, almost one-half did not meet contract specifications and had major deficiencies. Of the 54 completed projects that SIGIR inspected, more than threefourths had deficiencies, with 14 suffering major defects that, if left unaddressed, would place the survival of the project in jeopardy. In all, 40% of the inspected projects had major deficiencies (see Figure 1.3)

SIGIR Investigations
The Bloom-Stein Conspiracy: Life in a Free Fraud Zone

Following a whistleblower complaint, SIGIR auditors reviewed contracts that the CPA's regional office in Hilla had awarded to a contractor, Philip Bloom, for construction work. The auditors found inflated charges, the circumvention of regulations, false claims, and improper payments.

These fraud indicators caused the Inspector General to order a team of investigators to Hilla. It soon uncovered a sordid scheme involving bribery, money laundering, and the theft of millions of dollars of reconstruction money.

At the center of the conspiracy was Robert Stein, a convicted felon, who served as the CPA's comptroller in Hilla—a position entrusted with overseeing and disbursing hundreds of millions in reconstruction funds. From December 2003 to December 2004, Stein used a rigged bidding process to award approximately 20 contracts, collectively valued at more than $8.6 million, to Bloom's companies. In return, Bloom:

- provided bribes and kickbacks, expensive vehicles, business-class airline tickets, computers, jewelry, and other items
- laundered in excess of $2 million in cash stolen from the vault at CPA headquarters
- used Romanian and Swiss bank accounts to send stolen funds to co-conspirators

SIGIR's investigation led to eight convictions with combined sentencings totaling more than 26 years:

- Stein received nine years in prison and forfeited $3.6 million.
- Bloom received 46 months in prison and forfeited $3.6 million.
- U.S. Army Reserve Lieutenant Colonel Bruce Hopfengardner, a security advisor at the regional office, received 21 months in prison and forfeited $144,500.
- Steven Merkes, a DoD operational support planner, received 12 months in prison.
- Lieutenant Colonel Debra Harrison, the acting comptroller at the regional office, received 30 months in prison and forfeited $366,340.
- William Driver, Harrison's husband, received three years probation and six months of house arrest, and was ordered to pay $36,000 in restitution.
- Colonel Curtis Whiteford, the second-mostsenior official in the office, received five years in prison and was ordered to pay $16,200 in restitution.
- U.S. Army Reserve Lieutenant Colonel Michael Wheeler, the office's Deputy Chief of Staff, received 42 months in prison and was ordered to pay $1,200 in restitution.

The CPA gave $58.8 million in cash to Robert Stein, the South Central Regional Comptroller (and a convicted felon), to disburse for the benefit of the Iraqi people.

SIGIR Investigations

SIGIR investigators served in Iraq from 2004 to 2013, frequently under fire. The inherent disorder of life in a war zone—coupled with the challenges of starting up a new organization—meant that substantial investigative results came gradually. The incremental nature of this progress stemmed in part from the unpredictable character of the criminal investigative process, which is less structured than the audit or inspection processes.

But significant results did come, and their numbers stand as testimony supporting the need for robust oversight during SROs: 104 indictments, 82 convictions, and over $191 million in courtordered fines, forfeitures, restitution payments, and other monetary penalties (see Figure 1.4). SIGIR's investigative work also produced 114 debarments and 98 suspensions of contractors and government personnel for fraud or other corrupt practices.

> **Best Practices for SRO Investigation Programs**
>
> 1. Integrate law-enforcement efforts. Prior integrative planning must occur for law-enforcement agencies to function well together.
> 2. Begin oversight early. As soon as the planning for an SRO begins, the relevant investigative entities should develop joint investigative programs.
> 3. Deploy agents forward. A strong and widely noticed lawenforcement presence in theater will deter crime.
> 4. Intervene with education. All government and contractor personnel operating in an SRO need fraud-awareness training.
> 5. Use task forces. Investigative task forces improve the likelihood of success because pooled resources mitigate the lack of technical capacities in some law-enforcement offices.
> 6. Hire investigators with fraud experience. Investigators should have backgrounds in contract fraud, financial transactions, and asset tracing.
> 7. Dedicate specific prosecutors. SIGIR's hiring of its own prosecutors produced outstanding results.

Other SIGIR Oversight Work

Lessons Learned

In 2005, SIGIR developed a novel lessons-learned initiative to convert the findings derived from its oversight work into lessons for operators in theater. The initiative yielded nine reports, including this one.

The first three reports focused on human capital management, contracting and procurement, and program and project management. Published in 2006 and 2007, they contributed to a number of helpful changes in U.S. reconstruction policy. SIGIR's contracting report, for example, exposed the Defense Department's weak contingency contracting resources, practices, and procedures. The Congress responded in these ways:

- The John Warner National Defense Authorization Act required Defense to develop policies and procedures that defined contingency contracting requirements, identified a deployable cadre of contracting experts, and provided training in contingency contracting.
- The Congress further required contracting training for personnel outside the acquisition workforce because of the broad reach of contracting activities in Iraq, particularly regarding the CERP.
- The Accountability in Government Contracting Act of 2007 strengthened the federal acquisition workforce by establishing a contingency contracting corps and providing specific guidance to encourage accountability and limit fraud, waste, and abuse.

SIGIR's report on program and project management helped the development of an updated Emergency Acquisitions Guide issued by the Office of Management and Budget's Office of Federal Procurement Policy. The guide included a number of best practices that agencies should consider when planning for contingency operations.

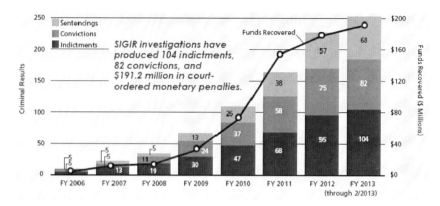

Figure 1.4. SIGIR Investigations Criminal Results and Funds Recovered, Cumulative to Date, by Fiscal Year.

In February 2009, SIGIR published its fourth lessons-learne report—*Hard Lessons: The Iraq Reconstruction Experience*—which provided a detailed primary-sourced narrative and analysis of the U.S. reconstruction program, presenting 13 lessons applicable to stabilization and reconstruction operations. After reviewing *Hard Lessons,* General David Petraeus concluded that the U.S. Central Command would apply 9 of the 13 lessons in Afghanistan.

Building on *Hard Lessons,* SIGIR issued its fifth lessons learned report in February 2010, *Applying Iraq's Hard Lessons to the Reform of Stabilization and Reconstruction Operations.* This study proposed an innovative solution to the question of who should be accountable for planning and executing stabilization and reconstruction operations.

Learning From Iraq further fleshes out this proposal. SIGIR's next three reports, published in 2011 and 2012, captured lessons from SIGIR's inspections, auditing, and investigative activities.

David Ricardo Ramirez was sentenced to more than four years in prison and forfeiture of real estate and the vehicles and boat shown here for stealing bulk cash while working as a Defense Department contractor in Iraq during 2006–2007.

Special Studies

To deepen insight into the Iraq reconstruction program, SIGIR accomplished these four focused studies:

- *Review of Major U.S. Government Infrastructure Projects in Iraq: Nassiriya and Ifraz Water Treatment Plants* (October 2010). To accomplish this evaluation, SIGIR visited two major water treatment plants, one in southern Iraq and the other in the Kurdistan Region. The evaluation assessed the local populations' perceptions of these plants, as well as the projects' contributions to U.S. reconstruction goals. SIGIR concluded that the northern project was a success, while the one in southern Iraq fell far short of its goals.
- *Reconstruction Leaders' Perceptions of the Commander's Emergency Response Program in Iraq* (April 2012). In this first Special Report, SIGIR surveyed U.S. Army and Marine Corps battalion commanders and civilian agency officials to obtain their views about the use of CERP funds in Iraq. Their revealing responses indicated weak interagency coordination on CERP projects.
- *The Human Toll of Reconstruction or Stabilization during Operation Iraqi Freedom* (July 2012). In this second Special Report, SIGIR sought to account for the number of personnel killed while specifically engaged in reconstruction activities in Iraq. The report concluded that at least 719 people (U.S., Iraqi., and third-country nationals) died working on reconstruction-related programs or projects.
- *Interagency Rebuilding Efforts in Iraq: A Case Study of the Rusafa Political District* (February 2013). In this third Special Report, SIGIR took a deep look into one geographic area—Baghdad's Rusafa Political District—to detail the collective U.S. investment. The report found that project tracking was very weak and thus the actual number of projects accomplished could not be precisely identified.

WHAT HAPPENED AND TO WHAT EFFECT

The two most common questions asked about the Iraq reconstruction program are "What happened to the money?" and "What effect did it have?" This report answers both queries, as well as many more detailed ones, such as which sectors received the most money, how was the reconstruction program managed, and was anyone convicted for fraud.

Answering "What happened to the money?" requires first answering "What money?" There were three primary sources of funding for the rebuilding program: Iraqi, U.S., and international. During the first year of reconstruction, the Coalition Provisional Authority obligated and expended money drawn from the Development Fund for Iraq. Comprising revenues from the sale of Iraq's oil and gas assets, the DFI was established in 2003 as an Iraqi account at the Federal Reserve Bank of New York. The stream of revenue flowing into the DFI account previously funded the United Nations Oil For Food Program.

During its existence, the CPA controlled over $23.4 billion in Iraqi funds composed of $20.7 billion from the DFI and $2.7 billion in seized and vested assets. In 2003 and 2004, more than $10 billion in DFI cash was flown to Baghdad on U.S. military aircraft in the form of massive shrink-wrapped bundles of $100 bills stored on large pallets. This money was not managed particularly well, either by the CPA or its successors, as SIGIR audits revealed. Iraqi funding, including DFI expenditures and Iraqi capital budgets, amounts to the largest single tranche of spending on rebuilding efforts over the past nine years (about $146 billion).[1]

Funding from the United States constitutes the next largest tranche. Since the spring of 2003, the Congress appropriated just over $60 billion for Iraq's reconstruction. Most of this money went into five funds:[2]

- the Iraq Relief and Reconstruction Fund ($20.86 billion)
- the Iraq Security Forces Fund ($20.19 billion)
- the Economic Support Fund ($5.13 billion)
- the Commander's Emergency Response Program ($4.12 billion)
- the International Narcotics Control and Law Enforcement account ($1.31 billion)

Deciding which of these funds provided the greatest benefit to Iraq is difficult to do, but each underperformed vis-a-vis expectations. Though the particular causes of the various shortfalls differ, security problems limited progress in every area. But the success of the Iraq Security Forces Fund in training and equipping the country's police and military forces stands out.

International funding, the third tranche of support for the program, was relatively muted. About $13.5 billion in grants and loans were promised in a multinational pact reached at Madrid in October 2003. These promises remained largely unfulfilled for years afterward.

But this does not mean that the international community failed to help Iraq. A highly beneficial financial boon came through the Paris Club debt-forgiveness agreement of 2004.[3] Iraq's total external debt at the end of 2003, estimated to be about $120 billion, significantly burdened the country's disabled economy. Thanks to negotiations led by former-Secretary of State and Treasury James A. Baker III, the Paris Club, comprising 19 of the world's largest economies, secured an agreement eventually canceling 80% of the Paris Club debt including $4.1 billion owed the United States and $12 billion owed Russia. The accord effectively amounted to a $32 billion gift to Iraq, with the potential of more to come, because the negotiations laid the groundwork for forgiveness of non-Paris Club debt.[4]

That answers the "What money?" question. Answering "What happened to that money?" has been SIGIR's mission for the past nine years. The details summarized in this report's succeeding chapters are pulled from the catalogue of our work: 220 audits, 170 inspections, 35 quarterly reports, 35 Inspector General testimonies, 8 lessons-learned studies, and hundreds of investigations. But fully answering what happened requires exploring *what effect* the massive expenditures had upon Iraq, an enquiry that only now can truly begin to be meaningfully answered. Exploring the program's effects is the crux of this chapter, which provides a body of new information culled from 44 interviews conducted by SIGIR with Iraqi leadership, U.S. senior leaders, and congressional members.

The interviews, which took place between September 2012 and February 2013, flowed from several questions put to each interviewee and were largely conducted in person by the Inspector General. The answers, which are encapsulated below, provide a bounty of useful and occasionally eye-popping insights into the effects and outcomes of the rebuilding program and the lessons learned from it.

The general belief across each group is that the relief and reconstruction program should have accomplished more, that too much was wasted, and that the lessons derived from the Iraq reconstruction experience should drive improvements to the U.S. approach to stabilization and reconstruction operations.

At a September 2008 ceremony, Iraqi Prime Minister Nuri al-Maliki and Chief Justice Medhat al-Mahmoud cut the ribbon to open the $12.5 million, U.S. constructed Rusafa courthouse in Baghdad. (USACE photo).

The Iraqis

Securing and stabilizing a new democracy in Iraq and helping its economy grow were the foundational rationales behind the massive U.S. assistance effort. But only now, after the reconstruction program has largely come to an end, could more comprehensive assessments be drawn and final lessons derived. To be meaningful, the views of the people the program was designed to help must shape those assessments and lessons.

The Inspector General interviewed the following Iraqi leaders, with most of the engagements occurring in September 2012 in Baghdad:

- Prime Minister Nuri al-Maliki
- Deputy Prime Minister for Energy Affairs Hussain al-Shahristani
- Speaker of the Council of Representatives Osama al-Nujaifi
- Minister of Finance Rafi al-Eissawi
- Minister of Justice Hassan al-Shimari
- Acting Minister of Interior Adnan al-Asadi
- Chief Justice Medhat al-Mahmoud
- President of the Board of Supreme Audit and Acting Governor of the Central Bank of Iraq Abdul Basit Turki al-Sae'ed
- Former Prime Minister Ayad Allawi
- Former Prime Minister Ibrahim al-Ja'afari
- Former Deputy Prime Minister Ahmed Chalabi
- Former Minister of Housing, Interior, and Finance Baqir Jabr al-Zubeidi
- Former Minister of Interior Jawad al-Bolani
- Former Commissioner of Integrity Judge Raheem al-Ugaili

In Erbil, the Inspector General interviewed these officials from the Kurdistan Regional Government:

- Falah Mustafa Bakir, Minister of Foreign Affairs
- Qubad Talabani, Minister, Department of Coordination and Follow-up
- Fuad M. Hussein, Chief of Staff to KRG President Massoud Barzani

What follows are concise summaries of what these senior Iraqi officials said, including relevant quotations that substantiate key points. The words speak for themselves, but these themes emerge:

1. The United States failed to consult sufficiently with Iraqi authorities when planning the reconstruction program.
2. Corruption and poor security fundamentally impeded progress throughout the program.
3. The overall rebuilding effort had limited positive effects.

Prime Minister Nuri al-Maliki

After spending 23 years in exile, Prime Minister al-Maliki returned to Iraq in 2003, serving on the Iraqi Governing Council, assisting in the drafting of Iraq's constitution, and participating in the implementation of de-Ba'athification reforms. In late 2004, he helped frame a broad coalition of Shia parties into the United Iraqi Alliance. Running for Prime Minister under its banner in the 2005 general election, he emerged victorious. In 2010, Prime Minister al-Maliki earned a second four-year term, eventually prevailing after a highly contested and controversial election.

The Prime Minister opened the interview with gratitude for the U.S. reconstruction effort but quickly descended into more dour tones, expressing his belief that the overall benefit to Iraq was small when compared with the size of the sums spent. He stated that "$55 billion could have brought great change in Iraq," but the positive effects of those funds were too often "lost."

Several critical factors limited the progress of reconstruction, including poor American knowledge about what Iraq needed. According to the Prime Minister, U.S. officials too often "depended on others" (local subcontractors), who frequently turned out to be ill-informed or dishonest. Thus, "there was misspending of money." Exemplifying this misspending, the Prime Minister recalled a small school refurbishment project for which the school's administrator requested $10,000, but the U.S. authorities insisted on providing $70,000—a needless waste. He also recollected that the United States built over a hundred healthcare centers at a cost far more than budgeted, while delivering much less than promised. The Prime Minister's memory was on point: a SIGIR audit of the primary healthcare clinic program found that it ultimately cost $345 million—more than 40% over budget. Prime Minister alMaliki complained that the Basrah Children's Hospital, a flagship project, was still not completely finished, despite expenditures that greatly outstripped the budget. Again, his observations were apt: a SIGIR audit of this project found it 200% over budget and four years behind schedule. Despite his litany of complaints, the Prime Minister concluded the interview gratefully, observing that the reconstruction program contributed to an ultimately successful U.S. effort to establish democracy in Iraq. "This money and the blood that was shed here is part of the price [paid by] the United States of America in cooperation with Iraq to fight terrorism...and establish the Strategic Framework Agreement."

Deputy Prime Minister for Energy Affairs Hussain al-Shahristani
Deputy Prime Minister al-Shahristani, a Shia Arab, served as Deputy Speaker of the Council of Representatives in 2005. He became Minister of Oil in 2006. In 2010, the Prime Minister appointed him Deputy Prime Minister for Energy Affairs.

Deputy Prime Minister al-Shahristani's assessment of the U.S. reconstruction program can be summed up in six words: well intentioned, poorly prepared, inadequately supervised.

After suffering through 25 years of Saddam's brutal dictatorship, including 3 wars, 13 years of a harsh trade sanctions, and continuous infrastructure neglect, the Deputy Prime Minister observed that virtually any rebuilding project accomplished in 2003 should have met some minimal need in a then-decrepit Iraq. But all too few of the projects the United States undertook at that time met this standard. There were some successes, he said, including the Port of Umm Qasr and the Baghdad and Basrah airports, but "there were a lot of unsuccessful rehabilitation projects in the fields of electric power generation, water and sewage treatment, roads and bridges, telecommunications, institution strengthening, school construction, and health." The Deputy Prime Minister listed these shortfalls of the rebuilding program:

- failure to consult with the relevant Iraqi ministries on project selection
- inefficient and unsuccessful execution of projects
- poor contractor selection

- award of contracts without review of a company's experience or financial profile
- use of unqualified contractors, many of which were simply shell companies that subcontracted work to others

Speaker of the Council of Representatives Osama al-Nujaifi

Speaker al-Nujaifi, a Sunni Arab, is the leader of Iraq's Council of Representatives (the National Parliament). After working in industry and agriculture for over a decade, he entered public service in 2005 as the Minister of Industry and Minerals. The following year, he was elected to the Council of Representatives as a member of the al-Iraqiya Party. He has been Speaker since 2010. Regarding the U.S. rebuilding effort, Speaker al-Nujaifi stated that the more than $50 billion spent on the Iraq reconstruction program did not "achieve the purpose for which it was launched. Rather, it had unfavorable outcomes in general." Given "the amounts that were allocated for the implementation," there should have been "better outcomes and more acceptable results." Speaker al-Nujaifi criticized the CPA's decisions to disband the army and impose a strict de-Ba'athification regime. "The decision to turn a work force of more than two million capable individuals into unemployed individuals because of two successive orders added more unemployment." The American administration implementing the occupation "was responsible for this issue." Going forward, "the best thing that the United States can do is invest in this work force through productive small or medium projects that would be of service to the society, helping it regain self-esteem and contributing to meeting basic needs, as well as creating economic stability in the country."

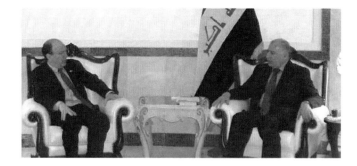

Minister of Finance Rafi al-Eissawi

Minister al-Eissawi, a Sunni Arab from Falluja in western Iraq, is an orthopedic surgeon. In 2005, he entered public life as a Minister of State in the Ministry of Foreign

Affairs. In 2008, Prime Minister al-Maliki elevated him to Deputy Prime Minister. Subsequent to the 2010 elections, Mr. al-Eissawi was named Minister of Finance.

Minister al-Eissawi criticized the rebuilding program's planning, citing a series of miscalculations that severely reduced the impact of the overall U.S. reconstruction effort.

Included in his bill of complaint were the following particulars:

- It was a mistake to launch a huge number of programs across numerous geographic and infrastructure sectors rather than devote resources to a finite number of worthy and well-focused projects. This critical error caused "thousands of projects" to be incomplete at the time they were transferred to the Government of Iraq, complicating efforts to finish them and substantially diminishing the impact of the overall reconstruction effort.
- There exists limited tangible evidence of any positive effects from the rebuilding program. Citing his hometown of Falluja as an example, Minister al-Eissawi stated that the residents there gratefully remember the British presence from the 1920s because of the Euphrates River Bridge, which still stands as a testament to the British program. He distinguished that salutary legacy from the U.S. program, represented by the Falluja Wastewater Treatment Plant, which was constructed at great cost but to little effect, at least in the eyes of Fallujans. Though the plant is complete, it serves but a fraction of those intended. Minister al-Eissawi commented that U.S. rebuilding managers governed "in a vacuum, so they were responsible for everything," to the exclusion, in his view, of meaningful Iraqi input.
- Early failures to stem the growth of militias within ministries created polarizing power centers that divided employee loyalties, weakened government institutions, slowed ministry decision making, and transformed corruption into a political agenda.
- Although the militias were largely stamped out, the legacy of their divisiveness lives on in the form of party committees within ministries whose sole job is to ensure that contracts go to party-controlled contractors. This kind of corruption is very difficult to suppress.
- An overly stringent de-Ba'athification program led to the dismissal of many competent government bureaucrats, even though they had little actual connection to the Ba'ath Party beyond perfunctory membership, which was largely required during Saddam's era as a prerequisite to entering government. This led to a post-CPA government populated by "amateur people."
- The wholesale dissolution of the Iraq Army, followed by a replacement force that he believed was less "national" and more politicized.
- The CPA's creation of the Iraqi Governing Council along sectarian lines, an error echoed, in his view, by the U.S. failure to support what Minister al-Eissawi called the "nonsectarian al-Iraqiya coalition" as it worked to form a government after winning a plurality of seats in the 2010 election.

Minister of Justice Hassan al-Shimari

Minister al-Shimari entered public service after the fall of Saddam's regime in 2003. He was a member of the Constitutional Drafting Committee, helped establish the authorities of the Council of Representatives, and became Minister of Justice in late 2010.

Declaring that the billions in U.S. reconstruction money had no tangible effect on Iraq, Minister al-Shimari said:

> We always wondered why the U.S. Army was in charge of making the choice on projects and how the money was spent. It was always personal relationships that determined who got the projects and how much was spent. Those [Iraqis] who had personal relationships [with the Army] got the projects.

The U.S. reconstruction program failed to meet its goals because of poor planning, indiscriminate priorities, and insufficient consultation with Iraqi authorities. "There was no real planning done, nor did they consult the Iraqis on what was really needed," the Minister asserted, adding that U.S. officials seemed to prefer smaller projects that could escape close scrutiny. "They pursued projects built close to U.S. bases to build goodwill with the local population and enhance security in the process." Consequently, many projects served U.S. short-term tactical goals rather than the longer-term needs of Iraq. The U.S. government was not solely to blame for poor outcomes. The Iraqis also lacked a clear set of reconstruction priorities. Further, the degraded security environment diminished the positive impact of reconstruction efforts. Focusing on one major infrastructure need, like electricity, would have been a better strategy than trying to improve every sector simultaneously. "If I were a government minister in 2004, I would have tried to give the Americans a vision," he said. "That's what was missing. Because there was no vision, there were no priorities."

Acting Minister of Interior Adnan alAsadi
After returning to Iraq in 2003, Minister al-Asadi was an alternate member of the Iraqi Governing Council. In 2004, he moved to the Ministry of Interior, serving first as Ministerial

Deputy for Administrative Affairs, then for Administrative and Financial Affairs before rising to the level of Senior Deputy Minister in 2008, and since 2010, as Acting Minister. He is also a member of the Council of Representatives.

The U.S. reconstruction program made three major mistakes:

- overpayment of contractors and subcontractors such that projects ending up costing double or triple their actual worth
- absence of meaningful cooperation and coordination between U.S. authorities and the GOI during project completion and transfer
- tolerance of rampant corruption that occurred on both the Iraqi and U.S. sides

There is little visible evidence of the program's effects, notwithstanding nine years of rebuilding activity and tens of billions in U.S. dollars expended. "With all the money the U.S. has spent, you can go into any city in Iraq and you cannot find one building or project [built by the U.S. government]," Minister al-Asadi observed. "You can fly in a helicopter around Baghdad or other cities, but you cannot point a finger at a single project that was built and completed by the United States."

The Minister cited three examples of project failure, including two buildings he tracked as acting minister: the Baghdad Police Academy and an office building constructed in the International Zone for processing weapons licenses. The roof at the processing facility leaked when it rained, requiring another contractor to install a new roof, doubling the structure's cost. At the police academy, raw sewage leaked through ceilings, requiring replacement of all pipes and ceilings. SIGIR's inspection of the Baghdad Police Academy substantiates Minister al-Asadi's complaint.

In the third example, the Minister highlighted a shortfall that directly affected his work: a contract to provide the MOI with computer servers and software. He was told by U.S. officials that the already-paid-for materials were sitting at the U.S. Embassy, even though the project was ostensibly complete.

The greatest example of poor U.S.-Iraqi coordination was the development of the multibillion-dollar Police Development Program in 2011, which carried overhead costs of around 80%. Minister alAsadi publicly decried the program, declaring that Iraq did not need it. After spending over a billion dollars and wasting about $200 million, the United States downsized the program by 90% to fit GOI desires.

Chief Justice Medhat al-Mahmoud

Chief Justice al-Mahmoud, a Shia Arab, was named Minister of Justice in June 2003 and Chief Justice and head of the Higher Judicial Council in 2004.

The Chief Justice expressed appreciation for U.S. reconstruction efforts, saying "we believe that history will judge those programs based on the achieved benefits gained by the Iraqi people... Among these projects, there were noticeable positive outcomes that will be left as clear proof for history." U.S.-funded electricity and water-treatment plants helped meet Iraq's needs, especially in areas of the country that previously lacked basic services. But, for the amount of funds spent, the results should have been greater than what was received. Moreover, the United States should have included the Central Bank of Iraq in overseeing the use of the Development Fund for Iraq.

These factors contributed to reconstruction shortfalls:

- Some contractors lacked the capacity to implement projects awarded to them.
- Some contractors lacked integrity.
- The absence of Iraqi input led to the failure in meeting goals set for project maintenance.

Support from the United States, especially the Department of Justice, enabled Iraq's judiciary to become "completely independent." The Chief Justice expressed satisfaction with support for the strengthened security arrangements established in the wake of an extended assassination campaign against members of the judicial branch. Looking to the future, the United States could have the biggest impact on Iraq's growth and prosperity by continuing to assist in arming and training the Iraqi Security Forces and encouraging U.S. companies to invest in Iraq. "Financial corruption" is the main cause for the unsettled conditions that continue to burden Iraq's government. Recognizing that money laundering plagues the country, the Chief Justice acknowledged that no system was yet in place to deal effectively with the problem, and that the GOI had failed to "put the right person into the right position." There exists an urgent need for greater transparency within the GOI, improved personnel decisions, and "more complete" oversight of financial transactions. Effecting these changes could reduce the level of corruption by 80%.

President of the Board of Supreme Audit and Acting Governor of the Central Bank of Iraq Dr. Abdul Basit Turki al-Sae'ed

Dr. Basit, a Sunni Arab, became BSA President in October 2004, after his predecessor was assassinated. He has since played an important role in the oversight of the GOI, supervising many politically sensitive audits. He was appointed Acting Governor of the CBI in October 2012. The U.S. reconstruction program inadvertently fostered a "triangle of political patronage," involving political parties, government officials, and sectarian groups. This lethal axis fomented a brew of terrorism and corruption that poisoned the country. Dr. Basit asserted that the unrestrained growth of corruption allowed it to become an "institution unto itself in Iraq." This substantially diminished the potential for reconstruction efforts to have a positive effect.

The GOI institutions established by the United States to fight corruption are weak, with the Commission of Integrity having lost its impartiality and the IGs proving vulnerable to politicization. "If they keep working in this way, they will be eliminated." Several key operational weaknesses caused the rebuilding program to fall short of its goals, including poor record keeping, inadequate communication, ineffective consultation, and the absence of a coordinated set of reconstruction priorities. "The way that the Americans spent [reconstruction] money was sometimes undocumented and sometimes irresponsible," Dr. Basit noted. Too many projects were awarded at inflated prices, while others were undertaken despite offering little benefit to Iraq. "Some projects were built without asking the Iraqis if it was proper to build such projects." When the GOI assumed responsibility for these usually incomplete projects, it had little interest in providing funds to finish or maintain them.

Dr. Basit asserted that the Ministry of Finance never enforced a 2005 agreement with the United States requiring the provision of all documentation related to reconstruction projects. A dearth of reliable data on the U.S. and Iraqi sides alike significantly impeded oversight of the rebuilding effort.

Former Prime Minister Dr. Ayad Allawi

Dr. Allawi served on the Iraqi Governing Council in 2003 and 2004. The Council elected him Prime Minister in May 2004, and he served in that post from June 2004 to May 2005. In the 2010 parliamentary elections, Dr. Allawi's al-Iraqiya party won a plurality of seats. Subsequent wrangling over the outcome left succession in doubt until December 2010, when the disputing parties came to an agreement that allowed Prime Minister al-Maliki to continue in office.

The reconstruction program in Iraq suffered from these weaknesses:

- insufficient planning and unclear priorities
- poor oversight of projects
- grave insecurity and political instability
- unqualified contractors receiving contracts
- corruption affecting the entire effort

The most significant planning shortfall was the weak consultation and coordination between U.S. reconstruction managers and Iraqi leaders. Dr. Allawi tried to remedy this issue by creating the Construction Council in 2004 led by Deputy Prime Minister Barham Salih. It included the Planning Minister, the Housing and Construction Minister, the Electricity Minister, the Industry and Minerals Minister, and the Finance Minister. The Commission sought to address corruption by increasing the review of contracts. In Dr. Allawi's view, the failure to address corruption early in the program "was one of the United States' biggest mistakes." Additionally, the politicized de-Ba'athification order and the dissolution of the army and related Iraqi security institutions at the beginning of the CPA were significant errors, complicating the remainder of the rebuilding program. On the positive side, there were a number of successful projects in the electricity and education sectors.

Former Prime Minister of Iraq Dr. Ibrahim al-Ja'afari
Dr. al-Ja'afari, a Shia Arab, served as Prime Minister from May 2005 to May 2006. His tenure was marked by a period of intense unrest in Iraq, including the February 2006 bombing of Shia al-Askari Mosque in Samarra, which many point to as a flashpoint in the Sunni-Shia violence that pervaded Iraq that year. Dr. al-Ja'afari said that American political support for the GOI was of "unique importance" to the success of democracy in Iraq— even more important than military aid. However, he attributed Iraq's many continuing economic problems to failures within the U.S. reconstruction program. For example, the country's oil wealth was gravely mismanaged and thus subject to corrupt disposition such that the

condition of the average Iraqi has improved little since 2003. This mismanagement contributed to substandard public services, including declines in the country's once-admired educational and medical care systems, and a power-generating sector that remains unable to meet the country's demand for electricity. Dr. al-Ja'afari observed that these weaknesses, together with the twin plagues of security and corruption, caused economic inequities and high unemployment, leaving the average Iraqi quite poor, despite the country's growing oil wealth and visible progress in infrastructure restoration. Corruption in Iraq is now "routine."

Former Deputy Prime Minister Dr. Ahmed Chalabi

Dr. Chalabi, a Shia Arab, is a member of the Council of Representatives. He served as President of the Iraqi Governing Council in September 2003, as interim Minister of Oil during April–May 2005, and as Deputy Prime Minister from May 2005 to May 2006. In 2007, Prime Minister al-Maliki appointed him to lead the Prime Minister's Services Committee to improve the provision of public services. He was elected to the CoR in 2010. According to Dr. Chalabi, creating a regency to rule Iraq was "the first big mistake by the United States." By August 2003, there was significant support for a sovereign government in Iraq. "The Coalition Provisional Authority failed in its role as the provisional government of Iraq in 2003–2004." The United States reconstruction program managers did not consult adequately with Iraq in developing the rebuilding effort. "The U.S. personnel knew what to do and viewed all Iraqi ideas as useless, but the U.S. approach was wasteful, using design-build contracts to accomplish simple construction projects." Offering an example of how too much money was paid under these contracts, Dr. Chalabi said: "a square meter of concrete should cost 4,000 Iraqi dinar. The United States paid 16,000." The infrastructure reconstruction efforts provided limited benefits to Iraq. Dr. Chalabi offered these lessons from the Iraq rebuilding programs:

- Ensure the existence of a coherent structure that is responsible for planning and executing relief and reconstruction operations before you start spending money. It was counterproductive in Iraq to spend so much development money without a sensible management structure in place.
- Ensure that strong oversight is in place from the beginning of stabilization and reconstruction operation or corruption will run rampant. Dr. Chalabi said that corruption in Iraq today is "very dangerous and everywhere present from the top levels of government to the bottom."

Dr. Chalabi said "significant amounts of GOI money are leaving the country under false pretenses." He estimated that "15% of all GOI revenues are lost to money laundering."

Former Minister of Housing, Interior, and Finance Baqir Jabr al-Zubeidi

A member of the Council of Representatives, Mr. al-Zubeidi, a Shia Arab, joined Iraq's first post-invasion cabinet in September 2003 as Minister of Housing and Reconstruction and went on to serve as the GOI's Minister of Interior (2005– 2006) and Minister of Finance (2006–2010). Mr. al-Zubeidi offered a generally positive assessment of the U.S. reconstruction program, saying that U.S. efforts in 2006–2007 had saved Iraq from becoming a failed state. Police training was especially important because, from a security perspective, the country started "from nothing" after the CPA disbanded the Iraqi Army. The United States provided critical training to the police through the Multi-National Security Transition Command-Iraq, but the failure to arm them adequately proved a problem. Recalling a visit to Babylon in November 2005 with Ambassador Khalilzad, Mr. al-Zubeidi remembered that just a quarter of the Iraqi police present carried weapons. The two biggest challenges that daunted the reconstruction program were security and corruption. Poor security conditions constrained reconstruction efforts, especially when terrorists started targeting prime-contractor representatives at project sites. Killings or kidnappings would force work to stop. Mr. al-Zubeidi observed that "corruption today is worse than ever. It's a disaster." He expressed specific concerns about money laundering, calling it a major problem for the government. When asked what the United States could do to help Iraq, he suggested assistance on fighting money laundering as a crucial need and hoped that U.S. expertise in this area could help stem the illegal flight of money from Iraq.

Former Minister of Interior Jawad alBolani

Mr. al-Bolani, a Shia Arab, served in the Iraqi Governing Council and the Council of Representatives before being named Minister of Interior in June 2006, a post he held until

December 2010. His tenure began during the most violent period of the post-war era, and he ended it as a failed candidate for Prime Minister.

Mr. al-Bolani recognized the sacrifices and resources expended during the reconstruction effort. He assigned blame for the shortcomings of U.S. programs on the Americans and the Iraqis. "U.S. reconstruction programs failed to implement important strategic projects, but they were able to accomplish small projects to create job opportunities for locals in some areas, avert attacks on U.S. forces by armed insurgents, and gain intelligence for U.S. forces."

U.S.-Iraqi cooperation accomplished some successes in the areas of training and security. Mr. al-Bolani offered the example of a U.S.- funded passport systems program that continued to produce good results after the Ministry of Interior took control of the program.

One of the biggest mistakes was assigning the CPA full governance authority over Iraq, with insufficient Iraqi inclusion. This policy contributed to a lack of oversight on money spent and a lack of follow-up on project execution. The existence of militias, al-Qaeda gangs, and the reliance of Americans on certain Iraqi political parties caused the emergence of sectarian controversies that hindered Iraqi governance. Sectarian groups became embedded in most of the country's ministries and institutions, impeding progress. Additionally, foreign interference in Iraq's matters weakened the national political stance, resulting in a country that lacked a free political administration focused on the needs of the Iraqi people.

Former Commissioner of Integrity Judge Raheem al-Ugaili

Judge al-Ugaili was appointed in 1997 as a judge in the al-Karada district court in Baghdad and served there until he was appointed Acting Commissioner of the Commission on Public Integrity in 2004. He became Deputy Commissioner in May 2005, and he was appointed by the Council of Ministers as the COI's Commissioner in January 2008. He resigned that post in late 2011, apparently under pressure to do so, after releasing a controversial report on corruption in Iraq. History will determine that the U.S. reconstruction program failed for two major reasons: (1) the U.S. government excluded Iraqis from the process of establishing reconstruction priorities, and (2) the reconstruction effort left very little visible impact on the ground. "Vast amounts of money were wasted without attaining actual intended results," Judge al-Ugaili said. The reconstruction program failed to establish a governance system of reliable integrity. Sketching out a grim picture of Iraq's anticorruption institutions in full retreat, the judge asserted that the level of kickbacks to GOI officials and the volume of money laundering continue to grow. The Commission of Integrity, he said, had been "totally kidnapped," and was now operating under executive-branch control. The COI's

Investigations Department, once one of the strongest and most active within the Commission, had been "severely reduced," and the number of corruption-related arrests in 2012 was 35% of the 2011 level. The GOI plans to reduce sharply or perhaps eliminate completely the system of inspectors general set in place by the United States in 2004 to control corruption in the government. It has not filled an IG vacancy in over two years. Some in government whose job it was to fight corruption and other white-collar crimes became targets for criminal charges simply because they did their jobs. For example, the Judge noted that he has had at least 10 charges leveled against him, stemming from actions taken during his years at the COI. He claimed that most of the charges were related to routine decisions made in his capacity as Commissioner.

Minister Falah Mustafa Bakir

Between 1996 and 1999, Minister Bakir served as a public relations officer for the Kurdistan Democratic Party and then entered public service with the KRG in 1999 as Deputy Minister of Agriculture and Irrigation. In 2002, he was named a senior advisor to Prime Minister Nechirvan Barzani, and two years later, he became Minister of State. He also served as the KRG's liaison officer with the CPA in 2003. Minister Bakir established the KRG's Department of Foreign Relations, which he has led since its inception in 2006.

The lack of planning, coordination, and sufficient resources on the part of the U.S. government made the failure of the rebuilding program inevitable. "The biggest problem was that the White House, the Department of Defense, the Department of State, and the CIA were all carrying out different strategies. From the day after the invasion, they were not able to win the peace," Minister Bakir observed.

Another factor contributing to failure was the Americans' poor grasp of Iraqi culture. "For example, men were searching Iraqi women and entering into private quarters of homes unannounced." Minister Bakir contrasted the U.S. actions with those of Korean military forces, who studied Kurdish culture and used Kurdish expressions in their arrival statements. "The U.S. spent a lot of money, but that didn't translate into making friends" in Iraq.

After relying on the Kurds in the months prior to the 2003 invasion, the United States neglected them during the reconstruction period. The Kurdistan Region received less than 3% of all reconstruction dollars spent in Iraq. According to Minister Bakir, the United States looked at Erbil as little more than a transit point between Baghdad and Turkey. Though the Region offered a more stable and safer investment climate than southern Iraq, the KRG was not included in any high-level Washington meeting on investment and reconstruction opportunities.

On the security front, Minister Bakir expressed what he said was a widely held concern within the KRG about the U.S. sale of F-16 military aircraft to the GOI, asserting that there was grave concern that the aircraft would be "misused" against the Kurds.

Minister Qubad Talabani

Minister Talabani leads the Department of Coordination and Follow-up in the Kurdistan Regional Government's Office of the Prime Minister. He is the son of Iraqi President Jalal Talabani. In 2003, he worked closely with the Office of Reconstruction and Humanitarian Assistance and the Coalition Provisional Authority.

The U.S. decision to devote modest amounts of reconstruction money to the Kurdistan Region, while spending heavily in non-Kurdish provinces, constituted a fundamental strategic failure. "You think if you throw money at a problem, you can fix it. It was just not strategic thinking," Minister Talabani said. His point is buttressed, to a certain extent, by SIGIR's inspections work, which found most Kurdish projects in good order, while most non-Kurdish projects were below par. Instead of focusing on where it was wise to work, reconstruction authorities looked at projects "as if they were going to happen in a vacuum." Minister Talabani singled out the Commander's Emergency Response Program as a successful initiative, calling it "one of the things that worked," because it funded tangible projects in areas where work could be done. He cited inflexibility as a crucial systemic weakness within the reconstruction program. "There was usually a Plan A, but never a Plan B," to rely on when things went wrong. Instead of adjusting to adversity when the program began to fail, the United States resorted to blank reassurances that "everything was fine."

Dr. Fuad Hussein

Dr. Hussein serves as Chief of Staff to KRG President Massoud Barzani. In 2003, he was appointed by Office of Reconstruction and Humanitarian Assistance Director Jay Garner as a member of the Iraqi Reconstruction and Development Council. He then became an advisor to the CPA's Ministry of Education. From November 2004 to February 2005, Dr. Hussein served as Senior Consultant to the Iraqi National Communications and Media Commission.

Dr. Hussein described two reconstructions programs in Iraq: one very large effort in the 15 provinces in the south, from which much money disappeared and few benefitted, and the other in the Kurdistan Region, which, though far smaller, was far more successful on a per capita basis.

Two large wastewater treatment plants testify to the difference: the one in the south at Nassiriya cost $277 million and was widely viewed as a failure, while the other at Ifraz, near Erbil, cost $185 million and was a huge success. Dr. Hussein attributed Ifraz's success to the input of local residents, who were involved in the project from the start. The U.S. authorities simply poured money into the Nassiriya project without much consultation or coordination with local officials or residents.

Dr. Hussein criticized the lack of coordination among the various U.S. government agencies involved in reconstruction, noting that the consequent discord diminished program effectiveness. "Not only was there no coordination between the Department of State, the Pentagon and the CPA, they were fighting each other. I had two advisors—one from the State Department, the other from the Defense Department; they didn't talk to one another. The lack of local knowledge coupled with the U.S. decision to maintain total control over key ministries also proved to be damaging. "The policy was to control the Ministries of Oil, Interior, and Defense completely, but if you know nothing about the culture you're trying to control, the result is chaos."

If the U.S. reconstruction authorities had begun in the Kurdistan Region, using it as an example of what was possible, many of the failures that occurred in the rest of Iraq could have been avoided.

The U.S. Senior Leaders

The Department of Defense, Department of State, and United States Agency for International Development chiefly managed the reconstruction effort in Iraq, with the Departments of Justice, Treasury, and Agriculture making notable contributions. The Coalition Provisional Authority reported to the Department of Defense.

SIGIR's previous comprehensive report on Iraq's reconstruction, *Hard Lessons*, was built upon interviews with those chiefly responsible for planning and managing the early and middle phases of the program.

To capture the insights and understanding of those who led the later phases, the Inspector General interviewed the following U.S. senior leaders:

- Secretary of Defense Leon Panetta
- Deputy Secretary of State William Burns
- Deputy Secretary of State Thomas Nides
- USAID Administrator Rajiv Shah
- Former Under Secretary of Defense (Comptroller) and Member of the Commission on Wartime Contracting in Iraq and Afghanistan Dov Zakheim

July 11, 2011: Secretary of Defense Leon E. Panetta and General Lloyd J. Austin III, commander of U.S. Forces-Iraq, fly by helicopter over Baghdad on their way to meetings with Iraqi Prime Minister Nuri al-Maliki and President Jalal Talabani. (DoD photo).

- General David Petraeus
- General Raymond Odierno
- General Lloyd Austin III
- Lieutenant General Thomas Bostick
- Lieutenant General Robert Caslen
- Ambassador Ryan Crocker
- Ambassador Christopher Hill
- Ambassador James Jeffrey
- Senior Deputy Assistant USAID Administrator Christopher Crowley
- USAID Mission Director Thomas Staal

Secretary of Defense Leon Panetta

Secretary Panetta was sworn in on July 1, 2011, almost six months before the withdrawal of all U.S. ground forces from Iraq. He previously served as President Obama's Director of the Central Intelligence Agency, as President Clinton's Director of the Office of Management and Budget and White House Chief of Staff, and as a representative from California for 16 years. He was a member of the Iraq Study Group in 2006.

The reconstruction program's early phases revealed "a lack of thought" with regard to the initial rebuilding plan. From the Secretary's perspective, there did not appear to be a sustained strategic vision of how reconstruction should be conducted following the invasion. "The U.S. military was in Iraq to fight a war. They were not USAID," he said. "That's not their role."

The decision to give battalion commanders control of reconstruction money under the auspices of the Commander's Emergency Response Program produced mixed results, with some commanders making good use of the money but others falling short in carrying out their duties. The number of convictions SIGIR secured stemming from the abuse of the CERP substantiates this point.

Highlighting a singularly positive example of reconstruction leadership, the Secretary pointed to the work of General Peter Chiarelli, who served several tours in Iraq, including as Commander, Multi-National Corps-Iraq in 2006. General Chiarelli's broad vision improved interagency coordination. Others, the Secretary said, sometimes had a limited understanding how the CERP could complement the overall rebuilding effort.

Secretary of Defense Panetta talks to U.S. troops in Baghdad in July 2011. (USF-I photo).

Secretary Panetta emphasized the importance of military-civilian cooperation in Iraq, noting that when the senior U.S. military commander and the State Department's Chief of Mission "served together, they created a strong force" that could persuade Prime Minister al-Maliki to back away from "bad decisions" and prevent him from "going off a cliff."

According to the Secretary, the inability to negotiate a basis for a continuing U.S. military presence in the post-2011 Strategic Framework Agreement left the United States without important leverage in Iraq. This weakened American capacity to push for greater change within the GOI.

Deputy Secretary of State William Burns

Deputy Secretary Burns, a Career Ambassador, served as Assistant Secretary of State for the Bureau of Near Eastern Affairs from 2001 to 2005, Undersecretary of State for Political Affairs from 2008 to 2011, and Deputy Secretary of State since 2011.

When we entered Iraq in 2003, the United States failed to establish a strong working relationship with the Iraqis.

Deputy Secretary Burns said this greatly hindered the rebuilding program, both at the national and local levels. Further, advancing an ambitious reconstruction agenda amid a growing insurgency proved unwise.

Early on, the United States poorly prioritized programs and projects, failing to make realistic evaluations as it forged forward while security conditions collapsed.

Program managers tended to do too much too fast, pushing too much money out the door too quickly.

A key lesson learned from Iraq is that the United States should not enter an SRO expecting to "do it all and do it our way." We must share the burden better multilaterally and engage the host country constantly on what is truly needed.

This is both a planning and an executory responsibility. Meeting immediate needs is where "we can best add value." Starting small on the rebuilding front makes sense as a rule of thumb.

In future SROs, the United States must balance better its national security interests with the host nation's interests. In Iraq, the large U.S. footprint "wore out our welcome" rather quickly, with the CPA overreaching through out-sized plans and programs. A more modest approach could obviate this problem.

The continual review of assumptions is also key to SRO success. Hard questions need to be regularly asked and answered. Otherwise, hard lessons will ensue.

When the military was present in Iraq (through 2011), it was reasonably possible to execute programs and projects across the country. After it departed, movement limitations set in. We should have then asked "what is it that really needs to be accomplished."

The Embassy tried to fill the security training void left by the military's departure. But the military and the State Department operate differently with different responsibilities and goals. State is much more constrained in what it can do.

Regarding interagency reform, Ambassador Burns cited State's new Bureau of Conflict and Stabilization Operations led by Assistant Secretary Rick Barton as a good start. But a broader interagency capacity is needed to promote improved coordination among State, USAID, and the Pentagon.

Deputy Secretary of State Thomas Nides

Deputy Secretary Nides took office on January 3, 2011, after distinguished careers on Capitol Hill and in investment banking. Charged with overseeing the management at the State Department, he guided transition planning in Iraq from a predominantly military environment to one now run by State.

Many predicted that State would fail in executing the 2011 transition, Deputy Secretary Nides recalled, "but it did not. To the contrary, we achieved a successful transition from a military controlled environment to one managed by civilians and controlled exclusively by the Department of State."

There were difficult challenges: "The Embassy was too large after transition." But State has been in the process of implementing reductions, and more will continue until it "achieves a normal Embassy presence by the end of 2013."

"Consultation is key," said the Deputy Secretary. "If the Iraqis don't want it, don't give it to them. This approach is not just good diplomacy; it saves taxpayer dollars."

He said relations with Iraq substantially changed with the departure of the military. State moved toward "a more bilateral engagement like we have with other regional partners. It is important to give Iraq room to be completely sovereign while maintaining a strong diplomatic presence."

Deputy Secretary Nides' three most important lessons from Iraq:

1. Bigger is not better.
2. Plan more strategically (in five-year, not one-year, increments).
3. Ensure good oversight (you need to keep asking hard questions or you will lose focus).

"Those in Iraq who developed and implemented the rebuilding program intended well, but good intentions don't always produce good results. You have to have systems that work and strong oversight." The Deputy Secretary concluded by noting that "SIGIR provided a good service in that regard, helping to save taxpayer dollars."

USAID Administrator Rajiv Shah

Administrator Shah has led USAID since January 2010, in which capacity he has overseen the gradual drawdown of USAID's operations in Iraq. He previously served as an Under Secretary at the Department of Agriculture.

Administrator Shah offered several pertinent lessons drawn from USAID's experience in Iraq:

- Stabilization and reconstruction operations are civilian-military enterprises, and "we must do a lot better in planning them." Defense, State, and USAID should develop joint planning mechanisms for future stability and reconstruction operations. These mechanisms must prepare for all scenarios: crisis and post-crisis.
- Cost-sharing with the host country is key to gaining buy-in to a rebuilding program. The amount the Iraqis are contributing to cost sharing continues to grow, both in cash and participation. This development deepened Iraqi engagement on project sustainment.
- Addressing corruption is crucial. The Administrator emphasized the importance of focusing on fighting corruption credibly and consistently.

Former under Secretary of Defense (Comptroller) and member of the Commission on Wartime Contracting in Iraq and Afghanistan Dr. Dov Zakheim

Dr. Zakheim was Under Secretary of Defense (Comptroller) as well as the Defense Department's Chief Financial Officer from 2001 to 2004. Later, he served as a member of the Commission on Wartime Contracting in Iraq and Afghanistan, which formed in 2008 and presented its final report in August 2011. The effects of the U.S. reconstruction program were "mixed." Dr. Zakheim cited poor sustainability as a paramount weakness. "We built projects with the unstated assumption that our military would stay on, that it would be there to deal not just with the reduced security threat but also to keep the projects going that we built. That did not happen." The departure of U.S. forces (in December of 2011) complicated the sustainability problem: their absence made the local environment more dangerous, making it harder for Iraqis to keep projects going. Moreover, the Iraqis had neither the technical knowledge nor the motivation to carry out the maintenance required to ensure project sustainability. The CERP morphed from its proper role as a tactical commander's tool to finance quick-impact projects into a program that funded far larger ones, transforming the military into what Dr. Zakheim called "USAID in uniform." This problematic development led to waste and poor project outcomes. Another mistake was permitting a vast but largely invisible number of subcontractors to work on reconstruction projects with little oversight or control. "What worked were projects that were thought through, were manageable, and had Iraqi buy-in. When we did consult (with the Iraqis), a project usually worked; when we didn't, it didn't." As examples, Dr. Zakheim cited a 500 MW expansion of the Qudas power plant near Baghdad and smaller CERP projects. He criticized long-term design-build contracts with extension options that were "all but automatic." He also criticized the use of undefinitized contracts (which authorize contractors to begin work before all contract terms have been settled) that were still undefinitized more than six months after the start of the reconstruction program. "If you can't figure it out in six months, you'll not figure it out at all." These are three biggest lessons learned from the Iraq experience:

- An empowered civilian agency is needed to deal effectively with SROs. USAID is ill-equipped for the mission. Its Office of Transition Initiatives has been suggested as an option, but its staff is too small. But USAID should establish a career path for those involved in contingency operations. It should be modeled on the military's Special Operations Forces/Special Operations Command and lead to an office of deputy director of USAID for contingency operations.
- The military is a limited reconstruction partner. The CERP was an effective idea, but only when jobs are kept small and contracts short. Let the civilian agencies do most projects.
- Subcontractors must be held more accountable. Acceptance of U.S. regulatory and legal jurisdiction must be made a contractual condition in all subcontracting work given to foreign subcontractors.

Dr. Zakheim supports establishing an independent office to plan for and oversee SROs, but to work it must not be "an orphan child." To avert this requires ensuring support from the Departments of State, Defense, and other agencies. Creating assistant secretaries for stabilization operations at the Departments of State, Defense, Justice, Agriculture, and Commerce could ensure that support.

General David Petraeus

A 1974 graduate of the United States Military Academy at West Point, General Petraeus served in a variety of leadership positions during the U.S. engagement in Iraq. As Commander of the 101st Airborne Division, he led the division during the fight to Baghdad and then in northern Iraq during the first year of Operation Iraqi Freedom. From June 2004 to September 2005, he established and commanded the Multi-National Security Transition Command-Iraq and the NATO Training Mission-Iraq; from February 2007 to September 2008, he served as Commanding General, Multi-National Force-Iraq, implementing the "surge;" from October 2008 to June 2010, he served as Commander, U.S. Central Command. He subsequently served as Commander of the NATO International Security Assistance Force and U.S. Forces in Afghanistan and later as Director of the Central Intelligence Agency.

The three big lessons General Petraeus took from Iraq are these:

- Ensure a comprehensive, detailed understanding of the target country before an SRO begins, including deep knowledge of political, economic, business, and cultural conditions, in addition to the security conditions. This knowledge must include a nuanced appreciation of governance and the rule of law at the national, provincial, district, and local levels. It is also crucial to understand how cultural factors, such as tribal loyalties, local customs, and national histories, influence governance and society. This array of knowledge is "imperative" to success in an SRO.
- Develop a comprehensive, civilian-military strategy and campaign plan, in consultation with host-nation leaders. The strategy must avoid policies that alienate populations or institutions, something that was missed early on in Iraq. "When you fire the military without giving those in it a future, or fire the first four tiers of Ba'athist Party membership, they will have no interest in helping you reach your goals. In fact, the opposite is true. Such actions only give them incentives to oppose what we were trying to do." (In fact, one should ask of each contemplated operation or policy, "Will this action take more bad guys off the battlefield than it creates?" If the answer to that question is, "No," then it should be reconsidered.)
- Implement a civilian-military campaign, using existing institutions wherever possible. Avoid creating new ad hoc institutions. If no existing institution fits, then find existing models and adapt organizations from them. Instead of creating a CPA element to oversee reconstruction, we should have used an existing U.S. Army Corps of Engineers division or created one that could use an existing organization and be guided by USACE policies, regulations, and practices. Examples of good adaptation in Iraq were the USACE Gulf Region Division, the PRTs, the Joint Contracting Command, and SIGIR.

Unlike (until very late in) Afghanistan, the United States did "get it right" in Iraq within four years of intervening. He said the right resources, the right ideas, and the right organizational structures were eventually deployed; however, it was very costly, in blood and treasure, and it became a very manpower-intensive experience. The Iraq experience proved the value of oversight; SIGIR, the U.S. Army Audit Agency, and DoD Office of Inspector General made particularly important contributions. General Petraeus repeatedly requested inspections by outside agencies to assist with oversight of various programs.

The reconstruction program brought "colossal benefits to Iraq." "Over time, we got the electricity infrastructure running and the oil industry working again, and, thanks to these efforts, the country began generating significant oil revenues." Beyond those critical efforts, the program touched every aspect of Iraq's society, from the economy to education to health care to governance. Perhaps most significantly, thanks to a very robust U.S.-led train-and-equip program, Iraq's security forces were able progressively to take over the mission of securing the country, with some one million total Iraqi security force members in uniform by the departure of U.S. forces at the end of 2011.

Serious violence in Iraq had risen a bit since the departure of American military forces in late 2011, but it still remains 90%–95% lower than the levels of violence reached in 2006–2007, and it has not stopped the country from functioning and improving various segments of its economy, most significantly the oil sector.

General Raymond Odierno

A 1976 graduate of the United States Military Academy at West Point, General Odierno serves as Chief of Staff of the U.S. Army. He commanded the 4th Infantry Division during Operation Iraqi Freedom between March 2003 and April 2004; he served as Commanding General, Multi-National Corps-Iraq, from November 2006 to February 2008; and he served as Commanding General, Multi-National Force-Iraq, and the U.S. Forces-Iraq, from September 2008 through September 2010.

With regard to reconstruction efforts, the United States made two poor assumptions during the early phases of Operation Iraqi Freedom. First, it underestimated the societal devastation that Iraq suffered during the 25 years of Saddam's oppressive rule and thus miscalculated how incapacitated the country would be following the invasion. Second, the United States tried to execute a full-scale reconstruction program too early and consequently found itself working with a weak and uncertain Iraqi government in an insecure environment. "It would have been better to hold off spending large sums of money until 2008, 2009, and 2010," by which time the country had stabilized.

Against the backdrop of this troubled start, General Odierno picked out the Commander's Emergency Response Program and the training of the Iraqi Security Forces as "good investments—successes when compared with some of the other programs." The security force training programs did not start well, he said. But once the correct formula was developed, they worked very effectively. General Odierno strongly supports the use of the CERP for smaller-scale projects in future operations, describing the program as a "useful tool" for tactical and operational commanders that saves lives. But he recommended that Defense review the CERP program to understand its successes and see where it can be improved. He noted that the CERP should not be used to finance larger projects, and it should have a better training program to ensure its effective use in theater.

Major lessons learned include these:

- Across all agencies, we must formalize what we have learned from the Iraq experience to include sustaining civil-military relations, training, planning, and sharing lessons. It is important that we not lose or forget what we have gained. Due to the complexity and uncertainty in the strategic environment, we must consider a more comprehensive whole-of-government approach going forward.
- One of the most encouraging lessons is the tremendous adaptability that we exhibited in Iraq—our ability to "figure it out" while in contact. But we must develop greater flexibility and versatility in our post-conflict management systems. "We need a

coherent civil-military structure in place before we begin Phase IV stabilization operations, which would allow for greater adaptability."
- Fully understand the conditions on the ground, including security, governance, and economic factors—as well as host-nation capacity—before embarking on reconstruction and recovery efforts.

General Lloyd Austin III

A 1975 graduate of the United States Military Academy at West Point, General Austin is the Vice Chief of Staff of the Army. As of late February 2013, his nomination as Commanding General, U.S. Central Command was pending Senate confirmation. He commanded the 10th Mountain Division in Afghanistan before coming to Iraq, where he served as Commanding General, Multi-National Corps-Iraq, during 2008–2009, and as the last Commanding General of U.S. Forces-Iraq during 2010–2011. General Austin recalled that, after the 2003 invasion:

> The decision to disband the Iraqi Army alienated the Sunnis and contributed to the birth of the insurgency. Early on there was no coherent Iraqi government at the federal and local levels. Coalition forces sought to build local and state governments while at the same time trying to increase security and stand up the Iraqi Security Forces. In the beginning, there was no leadership and nonexistent Iraqi security forces. The Iraqi police were not respected. There was no Iraqi governmental structure. The country was ravaged by fighting. These factors combined to impede our ability to pursue reconstruction efforts.

Eventually, the reconstruction program made progress. "Now look at Iraq. There is cause for some optimism. The local governments are functioning. The country is pumping over three million barrels of oil each day. Electricity distribution has improved dramatically. All of these improvements are because of the U.S. program. It is not perfect. But it is much better [than when we began our efforts in 2003]." Among the critical lessons learned, General Austin cited the need to develop a system for "effective interagency operations" as perhaps the most important. Initially, there was no coherent working relationship between Defense and State at a time when it was crucial that they work well together. "Phase IV was not thought through," he said. "Each organization was working on its own projects" without any synchronization of effort. But, "as we progressed we were able to create systems and begin working together as an integrated team." Learning to use the CERP properly was an important lesson. The CERP "empowered the commander on the ground and helped to increase security. It gave the locals confidence to work on their own." General Austin echoed a key lesson: you "must provide security in order to carry out reconstruction activities. You should not undertake major reconstruction work until security is established. It is difficult to get contracting done in dangerous areas." Recognizing the importance of oversight to mission success, General Austin closed by noting that, "with the increase in the amount of money in Iraq, enhanced oversight was needed. SIGIR provided the necessary help in this area."

Lieutenant General Thomas Bostick

A 1978 graduate of the United States Military Academy at West Point, Lieutenant General Bostick is the Chief of Engineers, United States Army. He served in Iraq as the first Commander of the U.S. Army Corps of Engineers Gulf Region Division. In that capacity, he oversaw the start up of reconstruction operations. It was "a bad assumption" on the part of the United States to believe that post-invasion Iraq would provide a permissive environment within which large-scale reconstruction programs could proceed without hindrance. This mistake meant that a significant amount of reconstruction money had to be diverted to security programs, money that was lost to the rebuilding effort. Lieutenant General Bostick said the Provincial Reconstruction Teams provided a positive dimension to the rebuilding program through their efforts to involve local Iraqi officials in programs and projects. Some oil-sector projects were also a success, though they were not completed as quickly as hoped. Smaller water and electricity projects made positive contributions because Iraqis could see that these projects put people to work and delivered services. The top lessons from the Iraq program are:

- Develop a contingency Federal Acquisition Regulation to facilitate contracting during stabilization and reconstruction operations.
- Do not rely on an "ad hoc team," with limited contracting and rebuilding experience whose members serve short tours.
- Put less emphasis on large infrastructure projects and more focus on smaller ones anchored at the local level.
- Choose the correct set of metrics to measure success. (Washington measured the success of reconstruction by the amount of money obligated and spent, which clashed directly with the need for what Lieutenant General Bostick called "strategic patience" in a contingency operation.)
- Include capacity development at all levels in the early stages of reconstruction effort.

Lieutenant General Robert Caslen

A 1975 graduate of the United States Military Academy at West Point, Lieutenant General Caslen served two tours in Afghanistan before coming to Iraq in 2008 to take command of the Multi-National Division-North. Following 15 months as Commandant of the U.S. Army Command and General Staff College at Fort Leavenworth, he was named the first Commander of the Office of Security Cooperation-Iraq in July 2011. As of February 2013, he was slated to be the next Superintendent of West Point.

Successful efforts to beat the insurgency in Iraq had a common thread: interagency and intergovernmental coordination and cooperation. But this kind of cooperation was too often missing, and the lessons drawn from it should serve as a basis for reforming the U.S. approach to stabilization and reconstruction operations.

As a division commander, Lieutenant General Caslen partnered with local governors and provincial councils to build credible governance, providing security, essential services, and the rule of law. This consultative process yielded an array of benefits: it strengthened the credibility of U.S. commanders among the local population and its elected leadership, it helped U.S. commanders better understand the local Iraqi environment and culture, and it produced governance that was credible in the eyes of local Iraqis. These actions helped bring stability and improved security. "It was a true partnership. That's why it worked."

The Provincial Reconstruction Team program provided examples of agencies succeeding by partnering; but the degree of success within individual PRTs depended heavily on the personalities involved. That is, good leaders brought success. PRTs approached problems in a holistic manner, requiring military and civilian members to integrate strategies and cultures. When this happened, the PRTs achieved leverage with their Iraqi interlocutors in the provincial councils and decent project outcomes resulted.

Recalling one coordination success, Lieutenant General Caslen cited a brigade commander in Diyala province who dedicated his artillery battalion to the local PRT to provide personnel for staff, coordination of programs and security, which added substantially to the team's mobility—and thus its effectiveness—in a very unsettled area. "That was one of the best examples of integration I saw." The PRT concept is "something we have to continue. That is one of the huge takeaways from this experience."

In contrast, Defense's Task Force for Business and Stability Operations was not sufficiently coordinated with local, provincial, or regional initiatives. According to General Caslen, the program was "dropped on local military commanders," who had little idea how to integrate it into their areas of responsibility or into economic programs they were already developing. Although the TFBSO commendably sought to stimulate free enterprise and economic growth, it failed to integrate its ambitious initiatives into the ongoing work under his command. This is a "lesson learned for the future" that applies not just to military programs but to all future SROs.

Ambassador Ryan Crocker

Ambassador Crocker, a Career Ambassador, served as Chief of Mission in Iraq from 2007 to 2009. He previously had two other assignments to Baghdad, first as a junior Foreign Service Officer at the U.S. Embassy in the late 1970s and later as the CPA's Director of Governance for a short span in 2003. He was named Ambassador to Afghanistan in July 2011. On leave of absence as Dean of the Bush School of Government and Public Service at Texas A&M University, Ambassador Crocker is the Kissinger Senior Fellow at Yale University. The U.S. reconstruction programs in both Iraq and Afghanistan provide a number of significant lessons learned, the most notable of which is that major infrastructure projects in stabilization and reconstruction operations must be approached with extreme care and assiduous planning. Undertaking such in unstable zones presents what Ambassador Crocker termed "huge complications," and the normal cost estimate for projects should be multiplied by a factor of ten to arrive at the true end price.

A major shortcoming of the Iraq program was the failure early on to obtain "genuine" Iraqi buy-in on major projects before U.S. funds were committed to building them. Although the Iraqis would occasionally give a "head-nod" to a project, they usually were not paying much attention because they were not footing the bill. Once work was completed, however, U.S. officials frequently found that there was no will on the Iraqi side to accept or maintain the projects. Ambassador Crocker took these lessons with him to Afghanistan, where the United States did a better job of securing local buy-in. But sustainment problems persisted there too. For example, there is no Afghan budget to maintain the new roads built with reconstruction money. "We're already seeing them crumbling," he said. Operations and maintenance issues were especially complicated in Iraq. The U.S. program produced projects built to U.S. specifications, without taking into account Iraqi capacity to maintain them. The Iraqis erroneously assumed that the United States would be there to provide support. After transfer occurred, Iraq often found it impossible to sustain the projects. As a general rule, Ambassador Crocker said, when it comes to a major project "dumb it down." The Ambassador supports the idea of a unified contingency office to plan and execute stabilization and reconstruction operations. But he said that such a structure must have a clear and concise chain of command to guard against the kind of State-Defense tensions that plagued the Iraq experience and obviate what Ambassador Crocker called "a second Rumsfeld era."

Ambassador Christopher Hill

Ambassador Hill served as Chief of Mission in Iraq from April 2009 to August 2010. He previously served as Ambassador to Poland, the Republic of Macedonia, and the Republic of Korea. He is the Dean of the Korbel School of International Studies at the University of Denver. The U.S. reconstruction program was much too large, well beyond the scale of anything State or USAID had ever done. Calling it the "largest ever foreign aid program," Ambassador Hill emphasized the many differences between the Iraq rebuilding program and the post-World War II Marshall Plan for Europe's reconstruction. The latter was chiefly loan-based, and the target countries provided a foundation on which U.S. funding could effectively build. In Iraq, the United States attempted to build an American-shaped reconstruction program on a fundamentally incompatible foundation with an entirely grant-based program. There was a bureaucratic clash of cultures in Iraq among U.S. government agencies; its ill effects weakened the reconstruction effort.

For example, the State Department faced problems that arose when USAID programs, which are designed with maximum controls, sought to follow up on projects carried out through the military's CERP program, implemented with less-developed controls. This particular collision of philosophies exemplified the many departmental differences that caused shortfalls in Iraq. A Defense-State rebuilding rivalry, in part driven by spending rates, took a toll on the reconstruction effort. Ambassador Hill observed that, as U.S. forces prepared to leave Iraq and State positioned itself to assume responsibility for the complete U.S. mission there, the measurement of accomplishment became departmental "spend rates." As a result, "State spent too much and took on too much." Ambassador Hill stressed the need for what he called "a holistic approach" that should go well beyond simply an agglomeration of USAID, State, or military capacities. He supports forming a new office with clear responsibilities to manage SROs, modeled along the lines of USAID's Disaster Assistance Response Teams and possessing a broad mandate, interagency jurisdiction, and sufficient resources. Shortcomings in the State Department's defunct Office of the Coordinator for Reconstruction Stabilization and its successor, the Bureau of Conflict and Stabilization Operations, reveal that an integrated solution to managing SROs has yet to be established. These are the three paramount lessons from Iraq:

- Don't take on a program you don't have the capacity to complete.
- Don't ask institutions to do what they are incapable of doing.
- Set an exit date.

Ambassador James Jeffrey

Ambassador Jeffrey, a Career Ambassador, served initially in Iraq in 2004 to bridge the transition from CPA to State and subsequently as Deputy Chief of Mission at the Embassy in Baghdad. He continued to focus on Iraq in subsequent assignments as the Secretary of State's Senior Advisor on Iraq, as Principal Deputy Assistant Secretary of State for Near Eastern Affairs, and as Deputy National Security Advisor. He returned to Iraq as Ambassador in 2010, serving into 2012.

After U.S. forces removed Saddam Hussein in 2003, Iraq's "government was totally nonfunctional." The CPA had to rebuild not just power and water plants, but also the most basic elements of governance, recalled Ambassador Jeffrey. This was a scenario for which no plan existed.

Although the United States put tens of thousands of Iraqis to work through its reconstruction program, "the question can be asked whether this money spent by the United States was cost effective." In the Ambassador's view, "the U.S. reconstruction money used to build up Iraq was not effective. There were many development problems, and we didn't get much in return for the $50 billion-plus that we spent."

The reasons were manifold. To begin with, there were questions as to whether the U.S. effort was a nation-building effort or a counterinsurgency program. Regardless of definition, Iraq required enormous assistance to recover not just from the war but also from Saddam's 25 years of reckless neglect. "The money spent on improving health care was needed, including the money spent on hospitals. Money was needed to be spent on oil-field production, the electricity production and the grid, and drinking water."

Consultation with the Iraqis was a problem during the CPA period. "On most of this work, there was no Iraqi buy-in. There was never an impression that the Iraqis were included in any decision process."

Although "too much money was spent with too few results," there were a number of positive effects: "Iraq ended up, nine years after the U.S. invasion, with: (1) more than 2.7 million barrels per day of oil being exported, (2) expanded availability of electricity and cell phones, and (3) a capable Iraqi military."

Moreover, "the United States defeated the insurgency and got Iraq on its feet. Overall, our efforts were a success."

The three biggest weaknesses in the Iraq program were these:

- not realizing how much work needed to be done to get the Iraqi government functioning
- not determining whether the United States was conducting a counterinsurgency or a nation-building program
- operating under U.S. contracting rules that were so "goofy" that they debilitated those trying to execute the program

"What happened in Iraq was the military versus State and USAID, all of it occurring in the middle of an insurgency and nation-building mess. The U.S. Army Corps of Engineers was in USAID's lane, placed in a very confusing role." The military's expansion into the rebuilding sectors perhaps went a bit too far: "The role of the U.S. military was to fight and secure the population. It [was not expected to have a] role in the reconstruction of Iraq. Its job was to defend the people. It did not have a plan for political or economic development."

Senior Deputy Assistant USAID Administrator Christopher Crowley

Mr. Crowley is USAID's Senior Deputy Assistant Administrator for the Middle East. He served as USAID Mission Director in Iraq from 2007 to 2010, longer than any other Mission Director. A Middle East specialist, with a career at USAID spanning 40 years, Mr. Crowley's assignments included tours in Egypt, Syria, the West Bank, and Gaza.

Mr. Crowley said the failure to engage much earlier in effective capacity development programs was a "key gap" in the reconstruction effort. "We knew that the capacities of local governments and GOI ministries had been weakened over time, but the impact of Iraq's isolation, the negative effects of Saddam's rule, and the draining of good people from the country all made the task of capacity development much more difficult." The GOI's weak budget execution capacity was a key example. "We'd have teams go to a ministry to de-bottleneck a problem for them, but the real problem was that the people working the system didn't even know the most basic steps of how to execute a budget."

The $32 million project to implement the Iraq Financial Management Information System for the GOI failed because the Iraqis did not want it and thus had no interest in learning how to use it. In contrast, when USAID hired Arabic speakers—either local Iraqis or residents of other Middle East countries—to help implement ideas, projects succeeded because we were able more effectively to incorporate Iraqi priorities into programs.

The three principal lessons learned from the Iraq experience were these:

- Look beyond the title of a U.S. government department before assigning it an overseas mission. Some of these agencies sent people to Iraq who had no experience abroad at all, much less in the Middle East.
- Define what's needed for sustainability from the start.
- Find the right people before deploying them to a contingency operation and then keep them there. The one-year tour limit was an obstacle to sustainability and continuity.

USAID Mission Director Thomas Staal

Mr. Staal's career at USAID has spanned 25 years, with many spent on Middle East issues. During 2003–2004, he served with the CPA in Basrah as USAID's representative in southern Iraq. He then served as the head of USAID's Middle East office. In 2012, he returned to Iraq as the USAID Mission Director, based in Baghdad.

According to Director Staal, the early U.S. reconstruction program was insufficiently planned. There was no strategic thinking about a longer and larger rebuilding program before the invasion. Although USAID had formulated a 3-year plan for Iraq's reconstruction and rehabilitation, the official U.S. government position was that we would be out within six months. The goal was to repair as much as we could in that time and then leave. But that policy changed with the advent of the CPA, which developed an $18 billion reconstruction program, devised in the summer of 2003 and approved by the Congress that fall.

Leading the CPA's effort was the Project Management Office. The projects requested for each ministry were put forward to the PMO by American ministerial advisors. The program "was not a plan; it was a wish list. Further, it had no capacity building, no real training initiatives. We didn't come with a holistic approach." Another shortcoming was a lack of understanding among those leading the U.S. reconstruction program of what three major wars and a decade of international sanctions had done to the country's infrastructure and to the spirit and psyche of the Iraqi people. "It wasn't just the 2003 invasion that had subdued Iraq; it was the wars of repression waged by Saddam that had beaten down the people's spirit." The collective effect of these varying calamities left Iraq in need of much more help than was initially recognized. The U.S. government made the mistake of focusing on fixing everything rather than getting Iraqis involved in setting priorities on what most needed repair. "We said 'let's just get everything fixed' and failed to do enough to develop capacities within the Iraqi society so that they could do a lot of these things themselves and then take them over and run them themselves."

The Congress

The fuel for the Iraq reconstruction program—billions in taxpayer dollars—came from decisions made and votes cast in the chambers of the U.S. Congress. Overseeing how these billions were used ultimately was executed in Senate and House committee rooms.

SIGIR provided numerous testimonies over the past nine years to congressional committees, making a variety of recommendations for improvement, some of which found their way into law. As the authorizing body for the agencies that manage stabilization and reconstruction operations, the Congress possesses the ultimate constitutional responsibility for implementing reforms drawn from the lessons of Iraq. To obtain congressional insights and judgments about the Iraq program, the Inspector General interviewed:

- Senator John McCain
- Senator Susan Collins
- Senator Claire McCaskill
- Representative Howard "Buck" McKeon
- Representative Adam Smith
- Representative Stephen Lynch
- Representative Michael McCaul
- Representative Peter Welch
- Representative Jason Chaffetz
- Former Representative Christopher Shays
- Former Representative Bill Delahunt
- Former Representative Jim Marshall

Senator John McCain III (R-Arizona)

Senator McCain is a member of three of SIGIR's reporting committees: the Senate Foreign Relations Committee, the Senate Homeland Security and Government Affairs Committee, and the Senate Armed Services Committee. A Vietnam War hero, Senator

McCain was a consistently strong supporter of the U.S. military mission in Iraq, strongly backing the troop surge in 2007 and making numerous trips to the country over the past nine years.

Senator McCain pointed to two crucial shortcomings that undercut the U.S. reconstruction program: inadequate program and project oversight and insufficient security. If those challenges had been resolved early, the reconstruction effort could have "made a lot of progress." Instead, the program unfolded as security conditions deteriorated, aggravating an already weak management system and causing massive shortfalls and waste.

The Defense and State Departments and the Congress all failed to fulfill their oversight responsibilities regarding Iraq's reconstruction. Senator McCain recounted how he was "stunned" when, during one of his many visits to Iraq, a general told him that project oversight of a contractor's work was being conducted by drone aircraft. Defense and State were unprepared to take on the challenges of so large an effort, and congressional oversight was "out the window" for a while. In the early phases of the program, the United States Congress appeared to have a "laissez faire" attitude toward the expenditure of U.S. tax dollars in Iraq. The paramount lesson from the Iraq rebuilding experience is the need for a complete overhaul of the U.S. approach to stabilization and reconstruction operations. Contingency contracting procedures were a particular weakness that such an overhaul should address. In addition, Senator McCain raised concerns about the failure of the government departments and agencies involved in SROs to conduct integrated operations and maintain accountability. He supports the idea of a consolidated office to plan, execute, and oversee future stabilization and reconstruction operations. Finally, Senator McCain generously observed that the SIGIR team of auditors, investigators, and inspectors had provided a crucial public service, identifying areas in the rebuilding effort needing improvement and highlighting opportunities for saving taxpayer dollars. The lesson here, he stressed, is that an IG should be present on the ground in an SRO "as the situation first evolves."

Senator Susan Collins (R-Maine)

As a member of three of SIGIR's reporting committees (Appropriations, Armed Services, and Homeland Security and Government Affairs), Senator Collins was the most consistent congressional supporter of oversight in Iraq during the past nine years, sponsoring legislation to strengthen SIGIR's mandate, leading hearings on the Iraq program, and regularly meeting with the Inspector General and his staff. While the U.S. reconstruction program in Iraq produced "some success," many rebuilding projects failed to meet their goals because of poor planning, a deteriorating security situation, and weak program and project oversight. "The level of fraud, waste, and abuse in Iraq was appalling." Senator Collins was especially angry when she learned that some reconstruction money found its way into the hands of insurgent groups. The CERP was a program especially subject to fraud. The lesson there is that the CERP should have been limited to small-scale projects. With regard to appropriations, Senator Collins initially favored a loan-based reconstruction program for Iraq, but President Bush had "no interest" in such and insisted on "no-strings-attached" funding. In retrospect, pursuing a program that included a loan-based component would have made economic sense for the U.S. taxpayer. Ensuring effective security and strong oversight are keys to success in a stabilization and reconstruction operation. Regarding oversight, the on-the-ground presence of SIGIR auditors, inspectors, and investigators was essential. The reason the special inspector general idea first surfaced was that the Congress was not getting the necessary oversight from departmental inspectors general. The decision to create SIGIR was a wise one.

Senator Claire McCaskill (D-Missouri)

Senator McCaskill, a former prosecutor and State Auditor of Missouri, serves on two of SIGIR's reporting committees: Armed Services and Homeland Security and Government Affairs. In 2007, she co-sponsored legislation for an independent, bipartisan Commission on Wartime Contracting, which offered numerous recommendations for reforming overseas contingency operations. Many of her proposals for contingency contracting reform became law with the passage of the PY 2013 National Defense Authorization Act. According to Senator McCaskill, the vast majority of U.S. reconstruction funds in Iraq were wasted. While detailed research would be required to determine precisely which programs worked and which ones failed, it is likely the best program the United States ran in Iraq was one that paid its enemies to switch sides. (The Sons of Iraq Program spent $370 million in CERP funds to pay mostly Sunnis to stay off the battlefield and perform other work.[5]) A central cause of U.S. reconstruction program's shortcomings was what Senator McCaskill called "an utter, abject failure" of the various U.S. agencies and departments to coordinate with each other. Instead, they worked at cross-purposes, creating "a circular firing squad" that guaranteed program failure. The CERP was initially a useful tool that enabled local commanders to fund projects quickly and effectively. The early projects were often "so simple and straightforward that they didn't need a contracting officer." Later, however, CERP projects grew too large, and the program "just got out of hand." These were the three most important lessons from the Iraq experience:

- Small projects are better than big ones, especially in unstable settings.
- Make realistic assessments about the sustainability of projects constructed as part a stabilization and reconstruction operation.
- Ensure strong accountability for those managing rebuilding programs and projects. The constant turnover in personnel produced a system where no one was held accountable for failure.

Representative Howard "Buck" McKeon (R-California)

Representative McKeon is the Chairman of the House Committee on Armed Services, one of SIGIR's reporting committees. He regularly traveled to Iraq over the past nine years.

Chairman McKeon said that the substantial U.S. investment in Iraq since 2003 was successful in bringing improved security. But, "although we won the war, we have not won the peace."

The United States sacrificed a lot but dropped the ball by failing to protect our investment in Iraq. Based on meetings with senior Iraqi officials, Chairman McKeon believed there had been an ongoing dialogue in 2011 between the United States and Iraq aimed at reaching an agreement to keep about 20,000 U.S. troops in Iraq after December 2011. He was told that if the United States asked the Iraqis to permit such, the Iraqis would agree. Unfortunately, the negotiations did not succeed.

An ongoing troop presence would have allowed the United States to exert more leverage over Iraq in 2012 and beyond. We have a large number of contractors performing missions that might have been performed at a lesser expense and with better effect by U.S. troops.

The U.S. reconstruction program was initiated without sufficient planning or strategic direction. As a result, significant sums of U.S. tax dollars were wasted in Iraq. Chairman McKeon's oversight trips to Iraq enabled him to visit a few reconstruction projects. At one project to rebuild a large electricity generation plant, the Iraqi chief engineer told him of the deteriorated condition of the plant, which the engineer had managed to keep going with a series of "patches." He explained that, under Saddam Hussein's rule, Iraqi officials would tell the leaders what they wanted to hear, rather than the truth, about issues such as the plant's condition.

The effort led by the U.S. military to improve Iraq's security forces produced the most lasting, positive impact of our reconstruction dollars. That impact could be lost, however, because of the withdrawal of U.S. troops. As the Chairman put it, we will be unable to influence the course of Iraq's future, and the security forces may deteriorate, be misused, or both.

Representative Adam Smith (D-Washington)
Representative Smith is the ranking member of the House Armed Services Committee, having served on the committee since 1997. He has maintained a strong interest in the oversight of the reconstruction program since its inception.

The funds for rebuilding Iraq's infrastructure were, on the whole, not well spent. The United States went through a period in which its goal was to rebuild Iraq "from whole cloth," and those involved in the effort failed to realize the serious problems that plagued the program. We tried to do too much "on the fly."

Representative Smith cited as a success the U.S. ability to leverage the "Anbar Awakening," noting that when program decision making became more locally driven, the rebuilding strategy became more successful. The United States did "an okay job" of reconstituting and training the Iraqi Special Operations Forces.

The biggest mistake was the de-Ba'athification decision. While a move to diminish the Ba'athist influence and its grip on power was necessary, problems arose because too many highly-skilled, experienced people were excluded from office by the severe deBa'athification process. "The overarching problem" was the U.S. attempt to enforce a political structure on the Iraqis that had too little Iraqi input.

The biggest lesson from Iraq is that the U.S. government must develop better capabilities to respond to SROs. Bureaucratic rivalries between the State and Defense Departments hurt the program. You don't have to wait until there is another SRO," he added. "You can fix things in advance."

Representative Stephen Lynch (D-Massachusetts)
Representative Lynch serves on one of SIGIR's reporting committees (Oversight and Government Reform). He traveled to Iraq 14 times, visiting reconstruction sites with SIGIR's inspectors. Representative Lynch derived these lessons from the Iraq reconstruction program:

- Strong oversight must be present from the start of a stabilization and reconstruction operation. "We did not have that at the beginning." SIGIR provided it later, but "a lot of money went out the door" before SIGIR arrived in Iraq in the spring of 2004.
- An established coherent management structure is crucial to executing SROs effectively. "We did not have that in Iraq." Instead, a number of temporary entities were created to fill the planning and execution gaps.
- The CERP was a success when used properly. Battalion commanders that used CERP money to execute wisely targeted, quick-turn-around projects helped the mission succeed. Those who spent it on large-scale rebuilding efforts, like the Baghdad Enterprise Zone, missed the mark.

Emblematic of the oversight problem, Representative Lynch recalled a hearing in late 2004 involving the Defense Contract Auditing Agency, at which the DCAA Director was testifying. The Director stated, in response to a query from Representative Lynch, that DCAA had "no boots on the ground in Iraq" but was performing oversight from Virginia. Representative Lynch told him that was unacceptable; DCAA soon thereafter had auditors in Iraq. SIGIR succeeded because it had a significant on-the-ground presence. Representative Lynch recalled trips to Sadr City and the Rusafa Courthouse in Baghdad with SIGIR's inspection teams. He also recalled a meeting with the GOI's Council of Ministers in 2011 at which a Sadrist pointed at him, saying "Congressman, you never told us democracy would be so hard." For Representative Lynch, that criticism was a sign of progress.

Representative Michael McCaul (R-Texas)

Representative McCaul was elected in 2004 and serves on one of SIGIR's reporting committees, the House Committee on Foreign Affairs. He also serves as Chairman of the Homeland Security Committee. He previously was Deputy Attorney General of Texas, Chief of Counter Terrorism and National Security in the U.S. Attorney's office, Western District of Texas, and a federal prosecutor in the Department of Justice's Public Integrity Section in Washington, D.C.

The United States rebuilding program accomplished a lot. "For the most part, we can be proud of what our soldiers and diplomats achieved," said Chairman McCaul. The comprehensive strategy that comprised the "surge" reached the goals that it set: a reduction in violence allowing the rebuilding program to move forward and the democracy to stabilize.

The most significant errors occurred during the CPA's tenure:

- the de-Ba'athification order, which effectively fired about 30,000 government employees
- the dissolution of the Army, which dismissed about 500,000 members of Iraq's military without pay or pension

There were significant areas of waste throughout the Iraq program that SIGIR identified; the causes of it serve as lessons learned for the next stabilization and reconstruction operation. One example cited by Chairman McCaul was $200 million spent on the construction of facilities for the Police Development Program that were never used for their intended purposes. Iraq has significant wealth from its oil reserves and growing exports. The U.S. reconstruction program built the foundation for the growth of that wealth. At the time of the departure of U.S. troops in 2011, Iraq was in a stable position, with a growing economy and a much-improved security situation, enabling it to move forward as an ally of the United States in the Middle East. But many challenges remain.

Representative Peter Welch (D-Vermont)

Representative Welch was first elected to represent Vermont in 2006, and developed a great interest in Iraq's reconstruction from his membership on the House Oversight and Government Reform Committee. Previously, Mr. Welch served in Vermont's State Senate.

The personnel system used to support work in Iraq weakened the program by allowing incessant turnover, which attenuated program management and project oversight. Further, the limitations imposed by the security situation prevented the effective execution of programs and projects. According to Representative Welch, Iraq teaches that security must be established before undertaking substantial reconstruction efforts during an SRO.

With regard to the execution of stability and reconstruction operations, he said, "We should not have the military doing it. It is not their job. Some of the mistakes lie with Congress. We were not disciplined in directing what organization and structure we should have been using in Iraq."

Representative Welch emphasized the importance of SIGIR's work, thanking the staff for its excellent productivity. Without the audits, investigations, and inspections that SIGIR executed, little would have been known of the challenges that persistently dogged the rebuilding of Iraq.

Representative Jason Chaffetz (R-Utah)

Representative Chaffetz was first elected in 2008 and serves on the House Oversight and Government Reform Committee. As Chairman of the Sub-Committee on National Security, Homeland Defense, and Foreign Operations, Mr. Chaffetz has held a number of hearings addressing Iraq's reconstruction operations at which SIGIR has testified. Some public works projects constructed during the Iraq program were effective and had a positive impact. Representative Chaffetz said, "they helped the country get back on its feet." But too much reconstruction money was wasted on projects that failed for lack of sustainment because the United States did not sufficiently consult with the Iraqis. Once given control of projects, Iraq frequently had little interest in maintaining them chiefly because they were never consulted.

The top three lessons learned from the Iraq experience were:

- When entering stabilization and reconstruction operations, seek out trustworthy local partners and make sure they are actively engaged in the reconstruction process and "have skin in the game."
- Make certain that reconstruction programs during SROs have strong oversight. People will behave if they are watched.
- Improve interagency coordination. This was a major weakness.

Representative Chaffetz believes the management systems for SROs must be reformed—a difficult task because Defense and State have conflicting agendas and a history of not communicating well with each other. This reflects the problem of "stove-piped" operations within U.S. departments and agencies involved in SROs.

Former Representative Christopher Shays (R-Connecticut)

Mr. Shays served in the Congress from 1987 to 2008 and was a member of the House Committee on Oversight and Government Reform, a SIGIR reporting committee. He traveled to Iraq over 20 times, more than any other Representative, and demonstrated a deep interest in

SIGIR's work, leading a number of hearings as Chair of the Subcommittee on National Security and Foreign Affairs. He later served as Co-Chairman of the Commission on Wartime Contracting in Iraq and Afghanistan from 2008 to 2011, before which SIGIR testified several times.

Mr. Shays estimated that "close to half" of all reconstruction money for Iraq was wasted. He cited the cause as insufficient coordination between and among the U.S. government agencies that designed projects and the private civilian contractors that implemented them. "Contractors played an important role because they freed up the military to address their mission; they have to have a seat at the table during project planning," he said.

He named these as the top lessons from Iraq:

- U.S. agencies must bear a greater responsibility for the money they spend. Because funds for Iraq's reconstruction were not directly linked to departmental budgets, agencies felt little ownership of the money and thus engaged in imprudent spending practices.
- Public revenues must be raised (through taxes or fees) to pay for SROs; otherwise, there may be a perception that such operations are effectively without cost. If the public actually feels the burden of funding SROs, then there will be public pressure on the government to exercise greater spending discipline over the billions in tax dollars spent abroad.
- Civilian contractors must be used more effectively. In Iraq, lax oversight and poor communication led to too much waste.

Former Representative Bill Delahunt (D-Massachusetts)

Bill Delahunt is a former Representative from Massachusetts, who represented the 10th District from 1997 through 2011. As a member of the House Committee on Foreign Affairs, Mr. Delahunt demonstrated a consistent interest in and focus on Iraq's reconstruction, conducting numerous hearings as Chairman of the Subcommittee on Oversight and International Organizations at which the Inspector General testified.

According to Mr. Delahunt, the failure to plan properly for the invasion's aftermath caused disastrous results. "We should never go into combat operations again without doing the kind of planning that's needed to deal with what comes next in Phase IV. The lack of preparation for dealing with post-invasion Iraq was a tragedy." A key lesson is the need for a permanent planning agency designed specifically for contingency operations. Such an agency would integrate U.S. policy into an action plan, doing the kind of preparation and oversight necessary to succeed in an SRO. If such an entity existed 10 years ago, then what happened in Iraq would have unfolded very differently. The biggest single concern for Mr. Delahunt is that the lessons of Iraq will go unlearned and unapplied. "We had hearing after hearing, but people didn't listen. My concern is that people will look back and ask why we didn't pay more attention. We continue to make mistakes. We're missing an opportunity now; we should apply a lesson from Iraq by creating an office that would actually be primarily responsible for planning, executing, and overseeing SROs." Mr. Delahunt said that SIGIR was "one of the success stories from Iraq."

Former Representative Jim Marshall (D-Georgia)

Mr. Marshall served in the Congress from 2003 to 2011, during which time he was a member of the House Armed Services Committee (one of SIGIR's reporting committees) and traveled to Iraq many times. A decorated combat veteran of the Vietnam War, Mr. Marshall is a member of the U.S. Army Ranger Hall of Fame. He now serves as President and CEO of the U.S. Institute of Peace. Mr. Marshall's first exposure to the U.S. reconstruction plan in Iraq occurred in August 2003, when he traveled there on the first of more than 15 trips he would make to Iraq over the next 8 years. He accompanied Chairman Ike Skelton, and, during a meeting with Coalition Provisional Authority Administrator Paul Bremer, Commander of U.S. forces Lieutenant General Rick Sanchez, and Project Management Office Director Dave Nash, Mr. Marshall asked what plans the CPA had to address the security problems that inevitably would arise. The response he got was: "You cannot plan for that." Incredulously, Mr. Marshall replied that they could "count on it" and expect that perhaps 25% of the reconstruction money would be spent on security and post-attack repairs. Events later proved his prognostication correct. Significant audit risk is acceptable when using CERP funds to accomplish projects that promote or secure tactical gains. The CERP helped commanders in Iraq to build relationships with locals, which reduced battlefield casualties. This truth should allow for a balancing of oversight rules when it comes to auditing the CERP in these situations. But it must not support large infrastructure projects. Auditors rightly challenged CERP's use in Iraq for such purposes. Like the CERP, the Provincial Reconstruction Teams suffered weaknesses from having been "built in flight." For example, PRT managers should have recruited and relied more heavily on local nationals, which would have improved security and reduced costs. PRT personnel needed more training; the United States should have established an in-country "PRT University." And more experienced leadership coupled with a more stable team of advisors could have built better local relationships and improved interagency operations. By contrast, the PRTs played a more effective role in Afghanistan. Mr. Marshall drew these lessons from the reconstruction program in Iraq:

1. Planners should expect everything to cost more than first estimates indicate.
2. The host government must credibly commit to providing project security, sustainment, and maintenance after project transfer.
3. Small projects are better than large; local projects are better than national.
4. The U.S. Army Corps of Engineers should have had the reconstruction lead in Iraq from the start. It trains to operate in a contingency environment.
5. Implementing effective quality-assurance programs produces better results; that is, project oversight personnel who are present at the project site are crucial to project success.

NATION (RE)BUILDING BY ADHOCRACY

The nine-year U.S.-led reconstruction effort in Iraq was extraordinarily difficult. Optimistic pre-war expectations for a limited humanitarian relief and recovery program quickly gave way to post-invasion realities that ultimately required a prolonged effort and the expenditure of tens of billions of dollars. The program faced an array of daunting challenges, pushing up costs in blood and treasure and pushing out the timeline for departure. Those challenges included a deteriorating security situation, conflicting departmental approaches, poor unity of command, weak unity of effort, and a parade of ad hoc management entities that came and went with little accountability. Reconstruction managers and contracting authorities faced complicated decisions, unprecedented challenges, and limiting restrictions as they planned, executed, and oversaw multifarious efforts to create a free, sovereign, and democratic Iraq. A succession of diverse, largely improvised entities ultimately managed more than $60 billion in U.S. appropriations and billions more in Iraqi funds to execute more than 90,000 contracting actions.[6]

When Iraq's reconstruction began, the U.S. government relied on—in the words of former Secretary of Defense Rumsfeld—"quickly assembled, ad hoc efforts"[7] to coordinate the resources of departments long used to working independently. The lead agencies—the Department of Defense, the Department of State, and the U.S. Agency for International Development—sometimes coordinated but rarely integrated their operations: "stovepiping" is the apt descriptor. Early on, in particular, there were few effective mechanisms for unifying their diverse efforts. Figure 3.1 shows the many handoffs of reconstruction authority and program management that took place during the rebuilding effort. Experience improved interagency coordination along the way. A necessary shift from an early focus on large infrastructure projects to a program centered on security and capacity-building bolstered interagency engagement because it required deeper involvement by government officials, as opposed to contractors. But these hard-won alliances, driven as they were by white-hot circumstances, have yet to yield the kind of systemic institutional reform within the U.S. government that would forestall future agency "stovepiping" during stabilization and reconstruction operations. The relatively limited transfer of lessons from Iraq to its contingency cousin in Afghanistan testifies to this truth.

Who Was in Charge?

The old cliché, money is power, could prove a useful touchstone in arriving at a first answer to this question. Defense controlled the contracting for the Iraq Security Forces Fund ($20.19 billion), the Commander's Emergency Response Program ($4.12 billion), and the bulk of contracting for the Iraq Relief and Reconstruction Fund ($20.86 billion). Thus, it held decisive sway over $45 billion (87%) of the roughly $52 billion allocated to the five major rebuilding funds that supported Iraq's reconstruction—most of which addressed security priorities through 2008 (see Figure 3.2).[8] In Iraq, if money was power, and power determined who was in charge, then Defense was in charge. Some say people are power. The formula plays out similarly. Defense's presence in Iraq peaked at over 170,000 personnel supported by an even larger contractor contingent. True, they were predominantly combat troops, but the CERP put combat troops into the rebuilding business, and the ISFF put them into the security-training business. The CERP funded thousands of civil reconstruction projects, almost all overseen and executed by battalion commanders, and the ISFF paid for the training of Iraq's security forces (army *and* police), overseen and executed chiefly by "green-suiters." So if people are power, then in Iraq, Defense was in charge.[9] In Washington, policy is power. In January 2003, thanks to the persuasive arguments of the Secretary of Defense, the President signed National Security Presidential Directive 24, putting Defense formally in the lead for post-war rebuilding. With the stroke of a pen, this ended what had been a fairly fervid interagency debate about post-conflict strategy. If policy is power, then—again—Defense was in charge in Iraq, at least for the first year. Clarifying the answer to the "who's in charge" question is crucial for future stabilization and reconstruction operations. Three successive organizations bore responsibility for providing the U.S. reconstruction program with strategic oversight and tactical direction: the Office of Reconstruction and Humanitarian Assistance, the Coalition Provisional Authority, and the U.S. Mission-Iraq. ORHA and the CPA both fell under the aegis of the Defense Department; the U.S. Mission-Iraq is a Department of State entity. Each organization developed successive, differentiated reconstruction strategies to respond to the evolving environments they faced in Iraq and to coordinate the work of multiple agencies and other implementing partners in country and back in Washington.[10]

ORHA—Initiating the Program (January 2003–April 2003)

On January 20, 2003, NSPD 24 consolidated responsibility for the reconstruction program under the Defense Department and established ORHA as its implementing authority. With no staff and barely integrated into Defense's command structure, ORHA's leader, retired Lieutenant General Jay Garner, set out to build an organization from scratch just two months before the invasion.[11] Lieutenant General Garner consulted experts and explored workaround solutions for staffing and contracting to gear up for what was expected to be a relatively short-term endeavor aimed at ameliorating expected humanitarian crises and potential man-made disasters, such as oil-field fires.[12] He received few responses from U.S. agencies to his staffing requests, marking the first instance of inadequacy in U.S. attempts to provide civilian personnel for Iraq.[13]

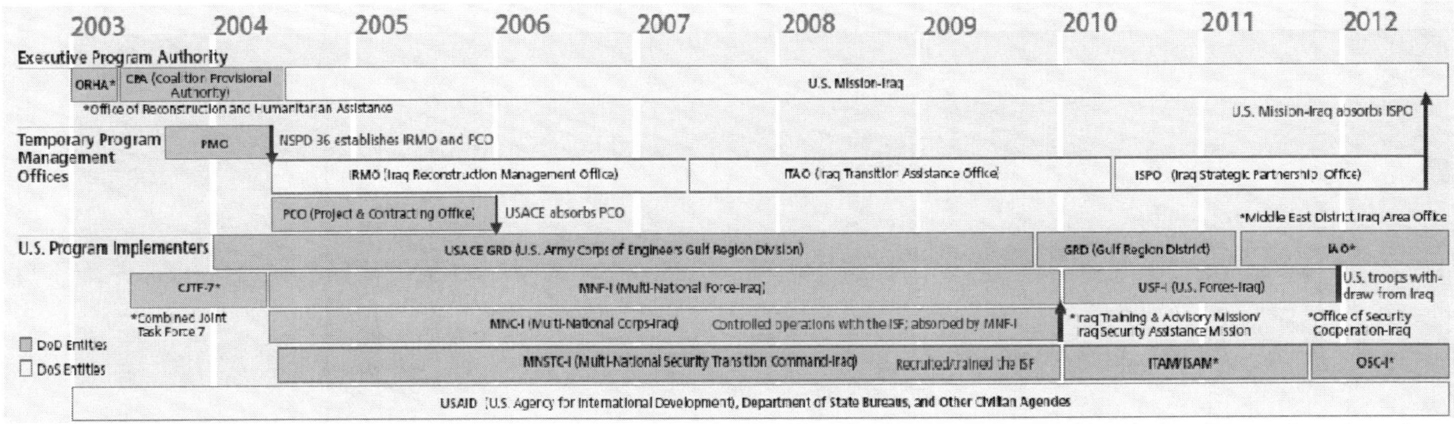

Iraq Reconstruction Program Execution, 2003–2012

2003	2004	2005	2006	2007	2008	2009	2010	2011	2012

Executive Program Authority

ORHA* | CPA (Coalition Provisional Authority)
*Office of Reconstruction and Humanitarian Assistance
U.S. Mission-Iraq
U.S. Mission-Iraq absorbs ISPO

Temporary Program Management Offices

PMO
ISPO 36 establishes IRMO and PCO
IRMO (Iraq Reconstruction Management Office)
ITAO (Iraq Transition Assistance Office)
ISPO (Iraq Strategic Partnership Office)
PCO (Project & Contracting Office)
USACE absorbs PCO
*Middle East District Iraq Area Office

U.S. Program Implementers

USACE GRD (U.S. Army Corps of Engineer's Gulf Region Division)
GRD (Gulf Region District)
IAO*
CJTF-7* *Combined Joint Task Force 7
MNF-I (Multi-National Force-Iraq)
USF-I (U.S. Forces-Iraq)
U.S. troops withdraw from Iraq
MNC-I (Multi-National Corps-Iraq) Controlled operations with the ISF; absorbed by MNF-I
*Iraq Training & Advisory Mission/Iraq Security Assistance Mission
*Office of Security Cooperation-Iraq
MNSTC-I (Multi-National Security Transition Command-Iraq) Recruited/trained the ISF
ITAM/ISAM*
OSCI*

Legend:
- DoD Entities
- DoS Entities

USAID (U.S. Agency for International Development), Department of State Bureaus, and other Civilian Agencies

Although State had executive authority over reconstruction by the second year, Defense implementers oversaw the majority of the work performed.

Figure 3.1. Iraq Reconstruction Program Execution, 2003–2012.

ORHA moved into Baghdad in April 2003, lacking sufficient capacities for obtaining acquisition support. It worked with the Defense Contracting Command-Washington to award $108.2 million to execute the Iraqi Free Media Program and establish the Iraq Reconstruction Development Council, which sought to fold Iraqi leaders into project decision making. The Defense Department's Office of Inspector General later determined that ORHA's contracting practices circumvented proper procedures but cited a lack of contracting personnel and extreme time constraints as extenuating circumstances.[14]

USAID mobilized for humanitarian aid and disaster relief operations. From February through May 2003, it awarded eight major contracts, worth $1.3 billion, constituting the largest short-term burst of contracting in the agency's history. After the invasion, its Office of Foreign Disaster Assistance moved a 65-person Disaster Assistance Response Team in from Kuwait—the largest ever deployed—with the Office of Transition Initiatives providing 24-hour support.[15] The DART applied "creative contracting mechanisms," including the issuance of cooperative agreements to non-governmental organizations up to a maximum of $4 million each.[16]

These early contracting actions provided a start to relief and reconstruction operations shortly after U.S. forces had prevailed in Iraq. But an enduring hangover from prewar disagreements on post-war strategy as well as controversial decisions about mission leadership hampered progress in mid-2003. The most controversial early decision, one that would affect the program's entire trajectory, was the superseding of ORHA by the CPA in late April.

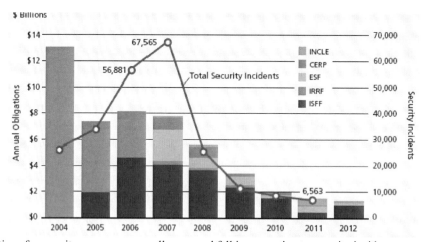

Obligations for security programs generally rose and fell in proportion to security incidents.

Figure 3.2. Annual Obligations, by Funding Source vs. Security Incidents, 2004–2012.

Coalition Provisional Authority—Re-initiating the Program (April 2003–June 2004)

Two weeks after ORHA arrived in Baghdad, President Bush announced the appointment of Ambassador L. Paul Bremer III as the Coalition Provisional Authority Administrator.[17] Concomitantly, the Congress created the IRRF, appropriating $2.475 billion, approximately

74% of which was allocated to USAID.[18] The allocation of IRRF 1 reflected what many expected the post-invasion situation in Iraq to require: rapid relief efforts, minimal reconstruction, and some support for economic development.[19]

The Defense Department's planning anticipated that Iraq would soon assume sovereignty through an elected interim government and then begin to shoulder the responsibility for rebuilding the country. Defense presumed that Iraq's governance capacity could manage reconstruction programs and projects, but this projection proved off the mark.[20]

Trying to Bring Order

Ambassador Bremer arrived in May 2003 to find that neither the military nor the civilian leadership were responding effectively to the disintegration of Iraq's government and the consequent loss of law and order. The CPA's first two orders—de-Ba'athification and disbanding the Army—further complicated the chaos.[21]

In the summer of 2003, Defense opened the Head of Contracting Activity office in Baghdad to provide acquisition support to the CPA, starting with just three contracting officers to execute a rapidly growing backlog of contracts. The HCA expanded to 50 people within a year, but this represented just 50% of the personnel required to administer the thousands of contracting actions the CPA requested.[22]

The White House provided support by facilitating a Joint Manning Document, which determined that the CPA would need a staff of at least 1,200 people. Throughout its tenure, however, the CPA operated with about one-third fewer people than necessary, and turnover was constant. Moreover, the length of duty for various agencies ranged from 3 to 18 months, with military and civilian rotations not synchronized.[23]

Attempting Iraq's Recovery

The CPA sought to spur Iraq's recovery through large infrastructure projects focused on the electricity and water sectors. Ambassador Bremer hoped these efforts would energize the economy and supply Iraqis with much-needed essential services.[24]

The CPA developed its program in haste, missing opportunities to integrate adequately the views of Iraqis—a fact borne out in this report—and alienating USAID, whose arguments for early capacity-building programs went largely unrecognized.[25] By the fall of 2003, Iraqi and U.S. government leaders became increasingly impatient with the slow pace of recovery, prompting the United States to announce, on November 15, 2003, that sovereignty would transfer back to Iraq by June 30, 2004. This immediately increased pressure to amplify and accelerate the rebuilding program, but the CPA did not yet have IRRF 2 money to spend, and it would not until toward the end of its tenure.[26]

Establishing what would be the first of several ad hoc organizations to manage reconstruction, the CPA created the Program Management Office in the summer of 2003. Initially, USACE provided a handful of staff to support the new entity. Over the course of its 10-month lifespan, the PMO had only half of the 100 people it needed to manage the CPA's programs.[27]

A Slow Start

Several issues limited the initiation of the IRRF 2 program. First, Washington concluded that the CPA's spend plan lacked sufficient detail. The Office of Management and Budget thus withheld the allocation of some funds through the winter of 2004, pending more specific information, which slowed action on contracts then in the process of being competitively bid.[28]

Defense sent an acquisition assessment team to Baghdad to review the CPA's practices and determine the resources necessary for effective IRRF contract administration. It found weaknesses in staffing and processes that SIGIR would echo in later audit findings. In response, the HCA took immediate steps to increase staff, create a management team to advise the PMO on contract requirements, establish a board for prioritizing contracts, develop an automated contracting data system, and end the unauthorized procurement of goods and services. But these changes were never fully realized.[29]

Prime Minister Ayad Allawi, Ambassador L. Paul Bremer, and Iraqi President Ghazi Mashal Ajil al-Yawar leave a ceremony celebrating the transfer of full governmental authority to the Iraqi Interim Government in June 2004. (DoD photo).

In the spring of 2004, ongoing projects began to suffer as security deteriorated, with some seeing cost increases of up to 20%.[30] At its end, 14 months after its creation, the CPA had barely begun to use the IRRF 2 for reconstruction. Ambassador Bremer funded most of the CPA's early projects, as well as Iraqi government operations, from the Development Fund for Iraq. By April 2004, the HCA had awarded 1,988 contracts, grants, and purchase and delivery orders—1,928 of which were funded by the DFI.[31]

U.S. Embassy—Re-evaluating the Program (June 2004–June 2005)

In May 2004, just after Coalition forces reorganized as the new Multi-National Force-Iraq, the President signed NSPD 36, assigning responsibility for Iraq's reconstruction to State. On June 28, 2004, when the Iraqi Interim Government gained sovereignty, the U.S. Mission-Iraq, under new Ambassador John Negroponte, assumed the nominal lead of the rebuilding program.[32]

NSPD 36 established the Iraq Reconstruction Management Office to manage the reconstruction program's strategic direction. Its senior advisors provided support and technical assistance to Iraqi ministers. Meanwhile, another ad hoc Defense entity called the Project and Contracting Office subsumed the PMO, and it took over managing most construction contracts.[33]

The ambiguities created by having two ad hoc reconstruction offices—IRMO and PCO—reporting to two different U.S. agencies—State and Defense—made it difficult to achieve unity of effort. A third ad hoc entity, the Multi-National Security Transition Command-Iraq, took charge of ISF training and equipping. Meanwhile, USAID maintained control of its own programs. This diffusion of activities limited Ambassador Negroponte's ability to integrate reconstruction activities, weakened management insight, and fed interagency tensions, all of which impeded progress.[34]

In the summer of 2004, Ambassador Negroponte ordered a review of reconstruction priorities, which led to the reprogramming of substantial IRRF 2 funds from the water and electricity sectors into the security and economic development sectors.[35] This contributed to a "reconstruction gap"—the difference between the number of projects that the U.S. government told the Iraqis it would build and the number of projects that it would ultimately complete. The gap marred Iraqi expectations, attenuating their trust, but security problems demanded the change.[36]

A rising insurgency in Iraq required the revamping of reconstruction funding allocations. In May 2005, the Congress provided more than $700 million for the CERP and $5.49 billion for the new Iraq Security Forces Fund created chiefly to equip and train the ISF. Over the course of its life, the ISFF received $20.19 billion, nearly matching the IRRF.[37]

The U.S. Mission-Iraq began moving away from using expensive design-build contracts with large companies to direct contracting with Iraqi firms. But the PCO director cautioned against shifting large amounts of funding away from contracts that had been awarded under full and open competition. Hundreds of firms were active across the country, employing tens of thousands of foreign contractors and an estimated 180,000 Iraqis.[38]

Project management systems remained problematic. In mid-2005, the U.S. Mission-Iraq still could not match projects with the contracts that funded them, nor could it estimate how much they would cost to complete. Further, completed projects were failing after being turned over to Iraqis who could not properly maintain and operate the facilities.[39] SIGIR reported on all of this, making recommendations for improvements.

Ambassador John Negroponte was the first U.S. Chief of Mission to serve in Iraq after the second Gulf War. (DoS photo).

U.S. Mission-Iraq—Executing the Program Amid Growing and Then Descending Violence (June 2005–August 2010)

The U.S. reconstruction strategy continued to evolve during the tenure of Ambassador Zalmay Khalilzad, who arrived in Baghdad in June 2005.[40]

At that time, the U.S. government began to recognize that the GOI lacked sufficient capacity—both at the national and provincial levels—to manage the infrastructure projects provided through the IRRF.[41]

Reconstruction managers identified sustainment as a problem. Ambassador Khalilzad thus shifted the reconstruction effort's focus to smaller projects at the local level designed to provide jobs and improve the delivery of services.[42]

Zalmay Khalilzad served as the U.S. Ambassador to Afghanistan prior to taking over as the Chief of Mission in Iraq in June 2005. (DoD photo).

SIGIR Audits 06-036, 10-006, 10-014, 10-020, 12-001, 12-008 12-013, 13-003
Documenting the DFI:
Transparency and Accountability 101

During its 14-month regency, the Coalition Provisional Authority possessed authority over about $23.4 billion in Iraqi funds: $20.7 billion in Development Fund for Iraq money and $2.7 billion in Iraqi seized and vested assets.

It directed DFI distributions totaling $14.1 billion, most of which went to Iraqi ministries and the Kurdistan Regional Government to pay salaries, pensions, and operating costs.

It also spent about $2.4 billion in seized and vested assets by the time its mission ended on June 28, 2004.

When the CPA concluded operations, it had $6.6 billion in DFI funds on hand. The Administrator transferred almost all of it to the Central Bank of Iraq.

Defense kept control over $217.7 million in cash in the Republican Palace vault.

Later, the GOI provided Defense $2.8 billion in DFI funds to pay bills from contracts the CPA awarded prior to its dissolution.

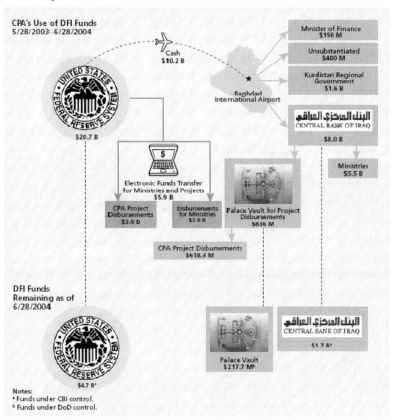

SIGIR audits made the following findings about the use of the DFI:

- Of the $14.1 billion used by the CPA, about $5.9 billion involved electronic fund transfer payments made for Iraqi ministry expenses and for a variety of items and services such as petroleum products, firearms and ammunition, vehicles, firefighting equipment, and military equipment. SIGIR found most of the required financial documents supporting payments for items and services purchased in 2003, but documents for payments made in 2004 were largely missing. The largest portion of the DFI, more than $10 billion, was provided to the Iraqi ministries and the KRG in 2003 and 2004 to pay for salaries, pensions, and operating costs. SIGIR found poor controls, weak accountability, and limited documentation supporting the use of funds.
- Of the $2.8 billion in DFI provided to the Defense Department by the GOI, Defense could not produce documents supporting the use of approximately $1.7 billion, including $1.3 billion in fuel purchases. Instead of using the required receiving reports to document fuel purchases, Defense officials maintained a fuel delivery log book. When SIGIR audited these funds, the log book could not be found.
- Defense spent $193.3 million of the $217.7 million in cash that was in the Republican Palace vault, but it could not locate documentation supporting $119.4 million of these expenditures.

Reaching out to the Provinces

To extend capacity-building efforts beyond Baghdad, Ambassador Khalilzad deployed Provincial Reconstruction Teams across Iraq, adapting a concept he developed during his time as Ambassador to Afghanistan. The PRT program established a novel system in which military and civilian personnel sought to work as an integrated team, rather than as a coordinative partnership. Its mission encompassed not only capacity-development efforts to support provincial and local governments but also projects that supported the counterinsurgency effort and stability operations. Although funded primarily from U.S. sources, PRT activities also received Coalition support, as well as help from nongovernmental organizations, donor nations, and the Iraqis.[43] On November 11, 2005, the first PRT opened in Mosul.[44] Originally conceived as a smaller two-phase program, the United States expanded and extended the effort to support the 2007 "surge." By the time Ambassador Khalilzad's replacement arrived in the spring of 2007, the United States led seven PRTs, with other Coalition nations leading another three.[45]

Surging Ahead

Throughout 2006, Iraq fell further into deadly chaos. The February 2006 bombing of the "Golden Mosque" in Samarra eventually sparked a chain of retaliatory killings, kidnappings, mosque attacks, and street fighting. For the rest of the year and into the next, sectarian violence worsened, decimating mixed Sunni-Shia neighborhoods in Baghdad and spreading its lethal effects across the country.[46]

General David Petraeus assumed command of MNF-I in February 2007, and Ambassador Ryan Crocker became Chief of Mission the following month. Together, they implemented a new comprehensive, civilian-military campaign plan that brought more than 25,000 additional U.S. troops into Iraq and a smaller, but complementary, contingent of civilian personnel to staff "ePRTs" (PRTs embedded in brigade combat teams). The new strategy also focused on securing the people by locating with them, emphasized implementation of CERPfunded projects, and supported reconciliation with Sunni insurgents and Shia militia members (including funding the "Sons of Iraq" program to employ Sunnis and some Shia who might otherwise have continued to take up arms against the Coalition) .47

The complementary leadership that General Petraeus and Ambassador Crocker brought to bear at this crucial moment achieved something that their respective institutions could not: integrated civilian-military operations. The new approach turned the tide, tamping down sectarian violence, relentlessly targeting Sunni insurgent leaders, and compelling Muqtada al-Sadr, leader of the Mahdi Army, to declare a cease-fire in August 2007. Al-Sadr's forces ultimately would be defeated in April 2008 in the Battles of Basrah and Sadr City. By summer's end, attacks had significantly decreased, and they would continue to do so for the balance of the year.[48]

In September 2007, the United States had more than 170,000 combat personnel in Iraq as part of the counterinsurgency operation, with more than 171,000 contractors supporting the mission.[49] There were 15 new "ePRTs" operating across Iraq, staffed chiefly by U.S. government civilians and overseen by the new Office of Provincial Affairs at the Embassy (see Figure 3.3). The ePRTs supported the counterinsurgency mission in unstable, yet strategically significant, areas such as Baghdad, Anbar, and Babylon provinces.[50]

Although the civilian surge provided much-needed personnel for the dispersed capacity-building efforts that began to dominate reconstruction, the coordination of an expanding U.S.

Mission-Iraq became much more complicated. As the organization chart for 2007 visually reveals, it was difficult to manage funding and programs (see Figure 3.4).

U.S. Ambassador Ryan Crocker, Iraqi President Jalal Talabani, and Deputy Secretary of State John Negroponte attend the dedication of the new U.S. Embassy in Baghdad on January 5, 2009. (DoS photo).

SIGIR Audit 06-045
Building Capacity to Sustain Projects: Too Little, Too Late

In the spring of 2003, Iraq's governance capacity was shattered. Thirty years of centralized control had debilitated the government's core functions, and post-invasion looting and the de-Ba'athification order aggravated matters. System failures became acutely apparent when Iraq could not maintain transferred facilities constructed by the United States. Although the Congress encouraged U.S. agencies receiving reconstruction funds to provide capacity-building support to the GOI, SIGIR found a dearth of efforts on this front during the rebuilding program's early stages.

SIGIR's inspection of the Hai Musalla Primary Healthcare Center revealed that U.S. funded equipment was not being used because Iraqi staffs had not been trained to operate it.

Turnover of personnel across several interim Iraqi governments hampered efforts to assess GOI competencies and capacities. Exacerbating this weakness, U.S. agencies failed to share information garnered from GOI engagements in an integrated fashion. Without a clear understanding of Iraq's abilities and needs, program managers initiated projects driven by parochial understandings and particular preferences.

Symptoms of this ad hoc approach lingered. For example, by 2007, the U.S. Mission had yet to designate a lead office to direct coordinated capacity-development efforts.

Moreover, Embassy officials indicated that they lacked the legal authority to integrate interagency activities. Unity of effort was missing, weakening sustainment and putting reconstruction projects at risk.

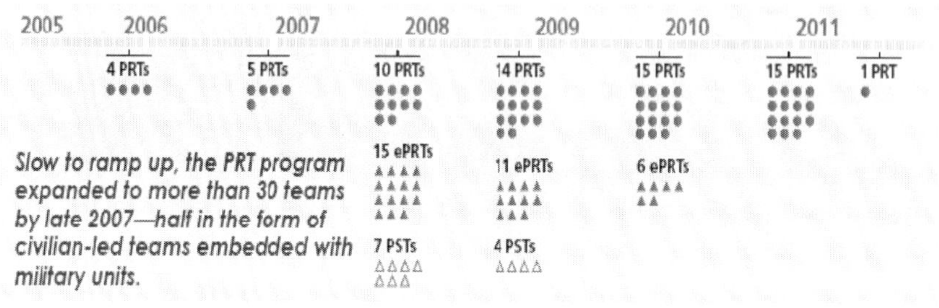

Figure 3.3. U.S. Provincial Reconstruction Team Footprint, 2005–2011.

SIGIR Audit 09-005
Private Security Contractors: Iraq Amok

Private security contractors provided protection in Iraq for U.S. government and contractor personnel, facilities, and property. These services included guarding bases and work sites, escorting individuals and convoys, and providing security advice and planning.

In an October 2008 report, SIGIR identified 77 companies that provided such services since 2003. But the number of personnel deployed by these companies was more difficult to pin down.

In August 2008, the Congressional Budget Office estimated that number to be 25,000– 30,000. But an October 2008 Government Accountability Office report stated that complete and reliable data was unavailable, and thus it was impossible to determine the precise number.

The security contractor phenomenon brought serious problems. A September 2007 incident in Baghdad, involving State's security contractor Blackwater, resulted in the deaths of 17 Iraqi civilians. This tragedy forced Defense and State to improve oversight of PSCs, producing, among other things, the following improvements:

- MNF-I established an Armed Contractor Oversight Division to monitor PSCs and serve as the prime point of contact on PSC policies.
- MNF-I published comprehensive guidance for PSCs, assigning military units more responsibility for overseeing PSC missions, managing incidents, conducting investigations, and executing contract management.

- A memorandum of agreement defined State and Defense authorities and responsibilities for overseeing PSC operations in Iraq. In addition to establishing common rules regarding the use of force, serious incident investigation, and report preparation, the agreement spelled out prudential control procedures for PSC missions, requiring liaison officers to monitor them.

Iraqi security forces stand guard at the April 2008 re-dedication ceremony at the newly refurbished King Faisal Bridge. Four years earlier, the bodies of four Blackwater security contractors were hung from the bridge. (USMC photo).

Three years of ISFF investment into training and equipping the ISF began to pay dividends.[51] Iraqi forces played important security roles in the "surge." By the same token, Iraqis began to take leadership in funding and managing reconstruction projects. At the end of 2007, the GOI had drawn even with the United States in funding reconstruction, and, in 2008, Iraq provided more than $19 billion or almost four times the amount provided by the United States.[52]

During this period, SIGIR expressed concerns about the process for transferring completed projects to the GOI, citing the lack of a definitive bilateral asset-transfer agreement.

The absence of such caused many projects to be unilaterally transferred to Iraqi control without formal acceptance, increasing the risk that the U.S. investment in Iraq would be wasted.[53] Additionally, as the IRRF program closed out, the CERP increasingly served as a vehicle to finish ongoing IRRF projects,[54] with new CERP projects growing larger in size—a trend that eventually became a serious problem.[55]

When the last "surge" brigade left Iraq in July 2008, the transfer of security responsibilities to Iraq was well underway, with the ISF in the lead in 10 of Iraq's 18 provinces. The "surge" helped drop average daily security incidents to 2004 levels and reduced Iraqi civilian deaths by 75%.[56]

Preparing for Transition

In April 2009, Ambassador Christopher Hill inherited the mammoth challenge of preparing for the withdrawal of U.S. troops. The November 2008 Security Agreement required all U.S. troops to leave Iraq by the end of 2011. After final withdrawal, the new Strategic Framework Agreement would drive U.S.-Iraq relations.[57]

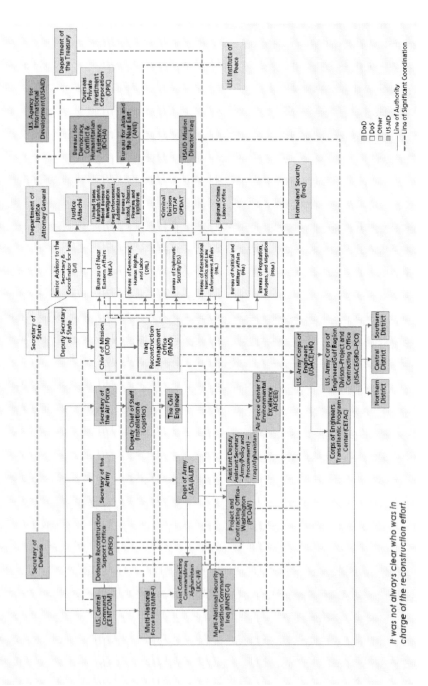

Figure 3.4. U.S. Embassy-Baghdad Organization Chart During 2007.

In December 2009, President Obama announced that the U.S. combat mission in Iraq would conclude by August 31, 2010. On January 1, 2010, five major MNF-I command groups merged under a single command—the U.S. Forces-Iraq—which would manage the drawdown in coordination with State.[58] The Iraq Training and Advisory Mission assumed responsibility for activities that had been under MNSTC-I, including police training conducted by 574 international police advisors.[59]

The Iraq Security Assistance Mission took over administering the Foreign Military Sales program, with contracting support from the Defense Security Cooperation Agency.

Among its many responsibilities over the two years leading up to the final troop withdrawal, the Defense Department was responsible for determining the disposition of more than 3 million pieces of U.S. military equipment, including items valued collectively at $1.1 billion that transferred to the GOI's security forces.[60]

When USACE's Gulf Region Division deactivated on October 23, 2009, it reported having completed 4,697 U.S.-funded projects at a combined cost of $7.3 billion. Two smaller districts overseen by the USACE Transatlantic Division continued work in Iraq until April 10, 2010, when operations merged into a single Gulf Region District.[61]

U.S. Mission-Iraq continued efforts to "right-size" U.S. Embassy-Baghdad operations and State's presence in the provinces. Upon expiration of its authority in May 2010, the Iraq Transition Assistance Office transferred most program management responsibilities to the Iraq Strategic Partnership Office, a third successive ad hoc agency. ISPO continued oversight of construction projects and grants. Another ad hoc entity, the Office of Provincial Affairs, coordinated PRT/ PRDC projects and played an increasing support role in prioritizing and administering CERP projects through the PRTs.[62]

U.S. Embassy—Transitioning to Traditional Assistance (August 2010– October 2012)

In August 2010, the U.S. combat mission formally concluded, and Ambassador James Jeffrey returned to Iraq to take over as Chief of Mission.[63] The slow march to full U.S. military withdrawal spanned 15 months. The CERP in Iraq closed out in September 2011,[64] and almost all of the $20 billion in ISFF was obligated when the final authority to obligate expired a year later.[65] The Office of Security Cooperation-Iraq continued ISAM's mission, coordinating continuing security assistance for the ISF with funding chiefly from the FMS program. Defense transferred its police training advisors to State's new Police Development Program and prepared to hand off its limited counterterrorism and training support activities to OSC-I in October 2011.[66]

The PDP saw State's Bureau for International Narcotics and Law Enforcement Affairs resume responsibility for police training, a mission it had led early on in the reconstruction program. Although INL continued to execute and fund small anticorruption and rule-of-law efforts, most INCLE funds now supported the police development efforts.[67]

In October 2011, ITAM transferred full responsibility for police training to INL's planned five-year, multibillion-dollar program. One year later, however, State scaled back the PDP dramatically because of an internal INL assessment and SIGIR audit findings. Slashing hundreds of millions of dollars from the program, State reduced the number of police advisors to 35—a tenth of the original requirement.[68]

The total number of personnel dropped when USACE's Iraq Area Office subsumed GRD in March 2011, and the PRT program closed its doors that summer. But personnel numbers rose slightly in early 2012 as State prepared to operate at several Embassy satellite locations, OSC-I hubs, and training sites. As long-running USAID programs closed and the scope of U.S. involvement in Iraq narrowed through 2012, U.S. Mission-Iraq again moved to decrease civilian and contractor personnel. ISPO's three remaining staff members transferred to U.S. Embassy sections when that office closed in August 2012.[69]

U.S. Ambassador Christopher Hill (second from right) and GOI officials visit the Qudas Power Plant, one of the largest U.S.-funded power-generation projects, in 2009. (DoS photo).

Ambassador Robert Beecroft took over as Chief of Mission in September 2012. State's role in Iraq still transcended the traditional boundaries of diplomacy and development assistance, requiring Ambassador Beecroft to manage a sprawling mission of unprecedented size and unrivaled complexity amid a still-volatile Iraq. At the end of 2012, the Mission's personnel totals still exceeded 10,000, with programs coordinated out of 11 sites (see Figure 3.5).[70]

Who Did the Work?

As the Executive Agent for most reconstruction funding, the Defense Department directed programs covering more than 75% of U.S. funds allocated for Iraq's reconstruction.[71]

USAID directed almost 15% of money in the five major funds. Its programs initially addressed the restoration of critical public services and then transitioned to capacity-development efforts in the governance and economy sectors funded by the IRRF 2 and the ESF.[72]

Although State bore responsibility for the strategic direction of the program starting in May 2004, it implemented less than 10% of the obligations from the five major funds. Approximately three-fourths of all State-led efforts addressed rule-of-law programs, supported by the INCLE, ISFF, and IRRF. The remainder provided technical support to Iraq's ministries and funded projects to build capacity at the local level, mainly through the PRT/PRDC program.[73]

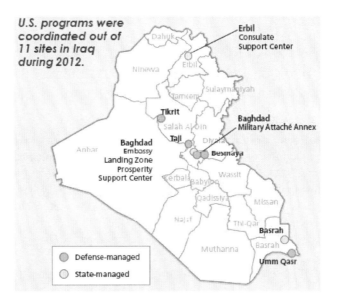

Figure 3.5. State- and Defense-managed Sites in Iraq, as of 12/2012.

Department of Defense Programs

Construction Services

USACE, through its Gulf Region Division (activated in January 2004), served as the primary construction manager of U.S.- and Iraqi-funded construction projects in every reconstruction sector. NSPD 36 authorized the establishment of the PCO a few months later to provide additional reconstruction management oversight. By December 4, 2005, GRD and PCO merged, and by October 14, 2006, GRD became the successor to PCO, which closed its Washington office several months later. USACE oversaw military construction services provided through Iraqi-funded FMS cases and implemented an additional $2.4 billion in DFI-funded projects contracted by the CPA, almost all of which supported contracts for the Task Forces to Restore Iraqi Oil and Iraqi Electricity. USACE implemented many types of U.S.-funded construction, including these:[74]

- IRRF and ESF projects overseen by ISPO and its predecessors
- projects funded through Defense allocations of the IRRF to USACE and through interagency agreements with other agencies to build or refurbish schools, hospitals, medical clinics, government buildings, water and waste supply and treatment facilities, oil and electrical infrastructure, police stations, border forts, prisons, courthouses, and much more
- "pseudo-FMS" projects funded by the ISFF to build and refurbish ISF bases and facilities

- INL-funded police training facilities and other projects to support the ISF
- at least $1.65 billion in Army Operations and Maintenance projects to build facilities and install security measures on bases occupied by U.S. military forces, such as overhead protection for dining halls and barracks facilities

As of September 2012, USACE reported completing more than 5,000 projects since March 2003, funded by at least $8.27 billion of the major U.S. reconstructions funds (see Figure 3.6). It had 44 ongoing or planned projects with a collective contract value of $639.1 million, the majority of which were FMS cases.[75]

Rebuilding the ISF

Defense directed more than $25 billion in projects and programs to recruit, train, equip, and sustain MOI police forces and MOD military forces through September 2012.[76] Prior to 2004, Combined Joint Task Force-7 led U.S. efforts to begin rebuilding the ISF, including initial projects utilizing Iraqi funds such as the DFI and CERP. When MNF-I assumed command and control of military operations in April 2004, its subordinate command MNSTC-I took over the role of rebuilding the ISF.[77] Under MNSTC-I, these elements carried out programs:[78]

- **Coalition Military Assistance Training Team**—CMATT supported the Ministry of Defense and Joint Headquarters Transition Team in building the ranks of Iraqi Army, Air Force, and Navy units throughout Iraq.
- **Civilian Police Assistance Training Team**—CPATT coordinated with INL, DoJ, and IRMO to train, equip, organize, mentor, and develop MOI forces.
- **Coalition Air Force Transition Team**—CAFTT worked to build Iraq's military air capability, and coordinated with two other MNSTC-I teams assigned to work with the MOD and MOI to improve command and control and develop law-enforcement capacity.

The Air Force Center for Engineering and the Environment supported MNSTC-I's contracting. In January 2010, ITAM subsumed MNSTC-I's various CMATT and CPATT teams, continuing certain specialized teams to support Iraq's security forces.[79]

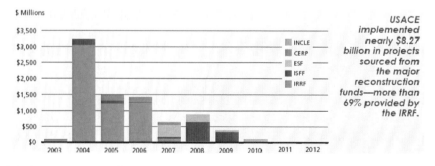

Figure 3.6. Contract Amount of USACE-managed Projects, by Year of Award and Funding Source.

Security Assistance Through the FMS Program

The FMS program facilitated contracting for the purchase of military equipment sales and construction services in Iraq since 2005. Through September 2012, the FMS program executed 496 separate cases valued at $12.79 billion—237 FMS cases funded by the GOI for about $9.44 billion and 259 pseudo-FMS cases funded by the United States through the ISFF for about $3.35 billion.[80]

Notable cases included the purchase of 140 M1A1 tanks, 36 F-16s and associated training, and a fleet of 35-meter and 60-meter coastal patrol boats.[81] Supported first by the Multi-National Corps-Iraq with help from DSCA, the program transitioned to the responsibility of the Iraq Security Assistance Mission in January 2010. When the last U.S. combat troops left Iraq in December 2011, the Office of Security Cooperation-Iraq assumed responsibility for administering FMS cases as well as those funded through Foreign Military Financing.

U.S. Agency for International Development Programs

USAID's Office of Foreign Disaster Assistance supported Iraq reconstruction ahead of the invasion, using creative cooperative agreements with non-governmental organizations to get projects started quickly. By September 30, 2012, when OFDA ended its operations in Iraq, it had spent more than $450 million on its programs to provide humanitarian assistance, including $261 million in International Disaster Assistance Funds.[82]

USAID's Bureau for the Middle East supported Iraq programs overseen by USAID Mission/Iraq, headquartered in Baghdad. Contractors, grantees, and United Nations implementing partners executed USAID's project and program activities, with support over time from these five ad hoc entities: the CPA, IRMO, ITAO, ISPO, and GRD.

From February through May 2003, USAID awarded eight contracts under less than full and open competition to meet pressing requirements funded by IRRF 1 signed in mid-April 2003.

The largest went to Bechtel National for the Restore Economically Critical Infrastructure Program. USAID received only $2.98 billion of the IRRF 2, predominantly for infrastructure projects, after its funding requests for capacity-building and democracy programs went ignored.[83]

During FY 2006–FY 2012, USAID programs received $2.92 billion from the Economic Support Fund and focused on capacity building, economic growth, and democracy and governance initiatives. As of September 2012, remaining USAID programs were valued at approximately $685 million.[84] Figure 3.7 provides a snapshot of major USAID programs, including their funding sources and duration.

Department of State Programs

State had responsibility for civil reconstruction efforts in Iraq, including Defense-funded projects executed through the Project and Contracting Office and USACE's Gulf Region Division.

SIGIR affirmed that mandate in an October 2005 legal opinion prepared in response to a request from IRMO, the first ad hoc program management office to report to State.

IRMO (and its ad hoc successors, ITAO and ISPO) provided overall strategic direction for the reconstruction program, while the PCO continued oversight of most construction contracts. Since 2003, the following State entities provided humanitarian relief and served as implementing partners for programs funded by almost every major U.S. reconstruction fund (see Appendix B for details):

- Bureau of International Narcotics and Law Enforcement Affairs
- Bureau of Population, Refugees, and Migration
- Bureau of Democracy, Human Rights, and Labor
- Bureau of Political-Military Affairs
- Office of Export Control Cooperation

State personnel working in Embassy sections provided advisory support to the Iraqi government. Expenses for the bureaus overseeing programs came out of State's operating funds. State relied on the support of implementing partners for program and project execution through interagency agreements. For example, USACE provided technical construction expertise and program management for $618 million in PRT/PRDC projects funded through obligations of the ESF, and INL funded rule-of-law programs conducted by the Department of Justice.[85]

Other Civilian Agency Programs

From the earliest days of reconstruction, civilian detailees from U.S. agencies served ORHA, the CPA, and U.S. Mission-Iraq. Several major agencies established Attaché offices to support U.S. Embassy-Baghdad sections and oversee a variety of reconstruction programs (see Appendix B for details). The salaries and operating expenses for these offices were provided through the budgets of the agencies. Funding for most programs, however, was provided through interagency agreements with State and Defense using IRRF, ESF, CERP, and INCLE funds. These agencies included:

- Department of Justice
- Department of Homeland Security
- Department of the Treasury
- Department of Transportation
- Department of Commerce
- Department of Agriculture
- Department of Health and Human Services
- Export-Import Bank
- Overseas Private Investment Corporation
- U.S. Institute of Peace

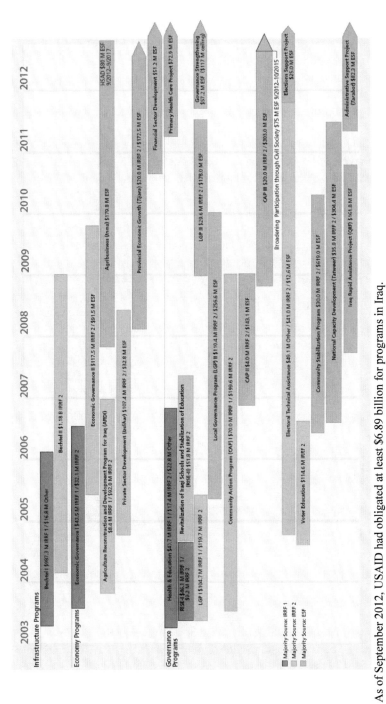

As of September 2012, USAID had obligated at least $6.89 billion for programs in Iraq.

Figure 3.7. Major USAID Programs, 2003–2012.

Contractors

Although U.S. government agencies managed the reconstruction program in Iraq, contractors performed the bulk of the work on the ground. Throughout the Iraq reconstruction effort, contractors trained police, constructed facilities, provided technical assistance to the Iraqi government, executed capacity-building programs, guarded critical infrastructure and reconstruction sites, and provided personal security and other support services for Iraqi, U.S., and Coalition entities. Many died doing so.[86]

Determining the number of contractor personnel in Iraq proved a challenge. In 2008, the Secretary of Defense, Secretary of State, and USAID Administrator entered into a memorandum of understanding to identify roles and responsibilities and establish procedures for the coordination and movement of contractors. It designated the Synchronized Pre-Deployment and Operational Tracker as the database system for tracking all contractor information.[87]

To support accurate and timely contractor tracking, a SPOT-generated letter of authorization was required for contractors receiving government support, which prompted a substantial increase in registered contract personnel. Not all contractors required government support, and agencies continued to use different systems to track personnel. Although the SPOT offered the most comprehensive picture of contractor and grantee personnel working in Iraq, it was far from complete.[88]

In August 2009, Defense reported that almost 174,000 contractor personnel were working in Iraq.[89] By April 2011, according to SPOT data, that number had been cut in half, and it continued to drop in conjunction with the withdrawal of U.S. troops (see Figure 3.8).[90]

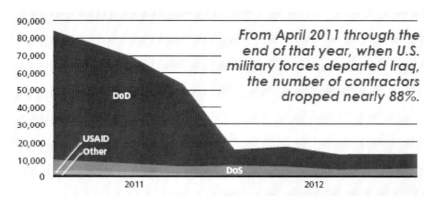

Figure 3.8. U.S.-funded Contractor and Grantee Personnel in Iraq, as Reported by SPOT Database, by Quarter, 4/2011–10/2012.

Contract Administration

Effectively implementing programs begins with strong acquisition support that prepares and conducts solicitations, writes contracts, and provides financial controls. SIGIR found that the lack of sufficient contracting personnel in Iraq weakened acquisition support, hampering project outcomes.

As the volume of contracting actions mounted, an overwhelmed cadre of acquisition staff could not provide sufficiently detailed statements of work, resulting in contract changes, delays, and higher project costs. Contracting officers did not always check invoices against goods and services received, which created opportunities for fraud. Ultimately, SIGIR determined that contracting processes and personnel improved over time, but the U.S. government lacked the right regulations and sufficient personnel to support a large-scale stabilization and reconstruction operation.[91] Defense designated the U.S. Army as Executive Agent for most of the major funds used in Iraq. The Army transitioned this contracting authority through six different organizations over the course of the program (see Figure 3.9).[92] State controlled the ESF and INCLE, with contract administration provided through the State and USAID Offices of Acquisition.[93]

SIGIR Investigations
The Cockerham Conspiracy: Contracting and Kickbacks

The Cockerham case was the most significant criminal conspiracy case uncovered during the Iraq reconstruction program. The investigation found widespread fraud that, by the end of 2012, led to the conviction of 22 individuals, the recovery of $67.7 million, and the suspension or debarment of 57 companies and individuals. The Cockerham case was fraught with intrigue: one military officer who received bribes committed suicide after being caught; another key player was murdered. Occurring at the principal supply hub for the Iraq reconstruction program located at Camp Arifjan, Kuwait, the criminal conspiracy arose from the actions of former U.S. Army Major John Cockerham. Between June 2004 and December 2005, Cockerham served as the base contracting officer responsible for soliciting and reviewing proposals for bottled-water contracts and other ongoing program-support needs for Iraq. Cockerham's crimes were simple but lucrative: he received more than $9 million in kickbacks from companies or individuals in return for contract awards. He brought his wife, sister, and a niece into the conspiracy. Several other officers participated, including a lieutenant colonel who chaired the selection board for an annual $12 million contract to build and operate DoD warehouses in Iraq. The Cockerham Task Force drew agents from SIGIR, the Defense Criminal Investigative Service, the U.S. Army Criminal Investigation Command's Major Procurement Fraud Unit, and other U.S. government investigative agencies to produce these and other convictions:

- Cockerham received 17.5 years in prison and was ordered to pay $9.6 million in restitution.
- Melissa Cockerham, his wife, received 3 years and 5 months in prison.
- Carolyn Blake, his sister, received 5 years and 10 months in prison.
- Nyree Pettaway, his niece, received 12 months and 1 day in prison and was ordered to pay $5 million in restitution.
- Levonda Selph, the former lieutenant colonel who chaired the selection board, received
- 12 months in prison and was ordered to pay a $5,000 fine and $9,000 in restitution.
- Derrick Shoemake, a former Army major who worked with Cockerham on contracts for the purchase of bottled water, received 41 months in prison and was ordered to pay $181,900 in restitution and forfeit $68,100.

- Major Christopher Murray, a contracting specialist at Camp Arifjan, received 4 years and 9 months in prison and was ordered to pay $245,000 in restitution.
- Terry Hall, a contractor, received 39 months in prison and was ordered to forfeit $15.8 million, real estate, and a motorcycle.
- Tijani Saani, a former DoD civilian employee, received 110 months in prison and was ordered to pay a $1.6 million fine and $816,485 in restitution.
- Eddie Pressley, a former U.S. Army major and contracting official, received 12 years in prison and was ordered to forfeit $21 million, real estate, and several automobiles.
- Eurica Pressley, his wife, received 6 years in prison and was ordered to forfeit $21 million, real estate, and several cars.

John Cockerham received more than $9 million in kickbacks for which he was convicted and sentenced to 17.5 years in jail.

The core IRRF 2 infrastructure program had two main components: design-build construction contracts and program-management contracts. The PMO planned for 12 design-build, cost-plus contracts to execute projects in six primary construction sectors (see Figure 3.10).

In addition, the PMO planned for seven program-management contracts to support oversight—one to provide management of the entire program and six to provide supervisory management for the six sectors.[94]

USACE provided additional construction management and contracting support through GRD, which was activated in January 2004.[95]

Before the design-build contracts were competed in the spring of 2004, the PMO requested and received approval in December 2003 from the U.S. Air Force to execute "bridge" contracts through the Worldwide Environmental Restoration and Construction contract administered by AFCEE. By January 2004, AFCEE had awarded four task orders, totaling $191.1 million, predominantly to meet the urgent requirements for rebuilding New Iraqi Army facilities.

By May 2004, AFCEE awarded 11 additional task orders totaling $290.1 million. However, SIGIR auditors found that some task orders were outside the scope of the WERC contract.[96]

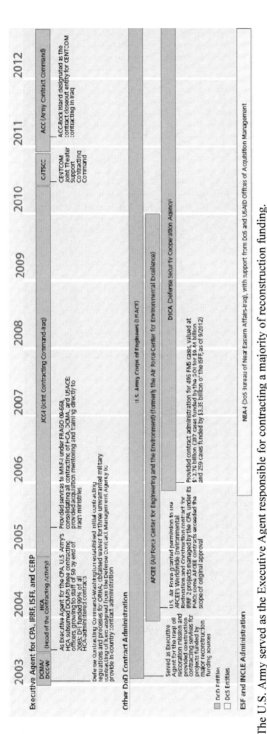

Figure 3.9. Contracting Authorities for Major Iraq Reconstruction Funds, 2003–2012.

The U.S. Army served as the Executive Agent responsible for contracting a majority of reconstruction funding.

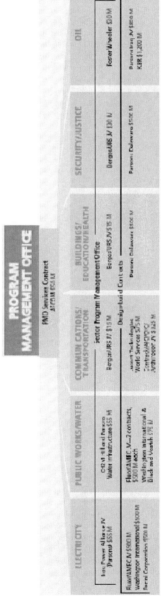

The PMO had two tiers of support through the design-build program—AECOM's contract to manage the prime contractors across all sectors and six prime contractors to manage construction in each sector.

Figure 3.10. IRRF 2 Design-build Program Management Structure.

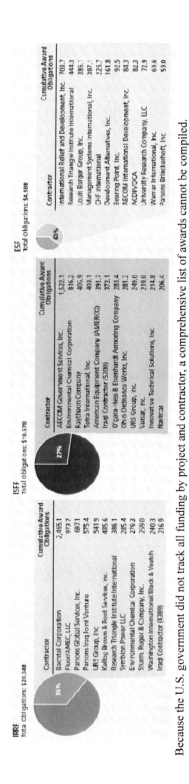

Because the U.S. government did not track all funding by project and contractor, a comprehensive list of awards cannot be compiled.

Figure 3.11. Selected Major Contractors: IRRF, ISFF, and ESF.

USAID awarded a bridge contract in early January 2004: the $1.8 billion Bechtel II contract to provide engineering, procurement, and construction services as a follow-on to its IRRF 1 infrastructure contract.

The PMO issued only four task orders under Bechtel II, amounting to $180 million of work, before the remaining 10 design-build sector contracts and 7 program-management contracts were awarded in March 2004.[97]

Task orders for the IRRF 2 contracts awarded in March took several months to be issued, while contractors charged costs waiting for work.[98] SIGIR audits reported on USAID and USACE contracting challenges that led to project delays and, ultimately, charges for overhead with no work being carried out.[99]

Indefinite-delivery indefinite-quantity contracts facilitated quick start-up, allowing the scope of work to be defined as project requirements were definitized.

These early contracts has provisions allowing the U.S. government to convert to firm-fixed pricing once a set percentage of design work had been completed, but SIGIR found that the government failed to exercise these options.[100]

Moreover, SIGIR auditors found that the government failed to enforce deadlines for definitization, increasing costs and wasting money. Award fees to motivate contractor performance were also poorly managed; a SIGIR audit reported that failing contractors still received substantial fees. SIGIR also reported that poor oversight of contractor invoices caused waste and created vulnerabilities to fraud.[101]

Major Contracting Firms

A complete project-by-project accounting of funds, including contractor details, is not available through the U.S. government's database of record—the Iraq Reconstruction Management System.

However, for a list of selected major contractors and the cumulative amounts awarded to them from the IRRF, ISFF, and ESF, see Figure 3.11.[102]

HOW MUCH MONEY WAS SPENT

From 2003 through 2012, the United States provided $60.64 billion for the relief and reconstruction of Iraq. As of September 2012, the United States had obligated at least $55.19 billion and expended at least $53.26 billion.

During the nine-year Iraq rebuilding program, U.S. expenditures averaged more than $15 million per day.

The expenditure rate generally decreased over time. In 2005, for example, the U.S. government spent more than $25 million per day; by 2012, the rate had dropped to less than $7 million (see Figure 4.1).[103]

More than 85% of the appropriations, amounting to $51.62 billion, went to these five major funds:

- **Iraq Relief and Reconstruction Fund**—With $20.86 billion, this was the largest fund. The Congress created it in 2003, allocating IRRF money to a variety of project sectors that covered activities ranging from security and law enforcement to

infrastructure and health care. By virtue of decisions made early in the program, the Department of Defense controlled the contracting and expenditure of most of the IRRF.
- **Iraq Security Forces Fund**—With $20.19 billion, the ISFF, created in 2005, supported the U.S. military's efforts to develop Iraq's security forces. These funds supported the training of Iraq's police and soldiers, purchased enormous amounts of equipment, and provided mentoring in operations and maintenance. Defense controlled the fund. The Iraqis deemed it the most effective source of support from the reconstruction program.[104]
- **Economic Support Fund**—With $5.13 billion, the ESF, a long-standing account at State, served as the primary civilian-implemented funding stream. State and the U.S. Agency for International Development managed the obligation and expenditure of ESF money, which met a great many needs within the democracy, capacity-building, and economic-development areas. The ESF's significance as a funding source grew as the rebuilding program matured.
- **Commander's Emergency Response Program**—With $4.12 billion, the CERP provided military commanders across Iraq with a funding source to address urgent relief and reconstruction needs in areas such as water and wastewater, education, electricity, security, rule of law, and protective measures, including the Sons of Iraq program. The CERP's importance diminished as the program evolved and security improved.
- International Narcotics Control and Law Enforcement—With $1.31 billion, the INCLE, another State Department account, helped train Iraq's police forces and supported rule-of-law programs. Its largest expenditures came later in the rebuilding effort for the Police Development Program.

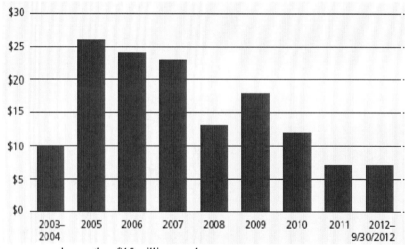

Expenditures averaged more than $15 million per day.

Figure 4.1. Average Daily Expenditure of U.S. Funds, by Year, 2003–2012.

Table 4.1. U.S. Funding for Iraq Reconstruction, as of 9/30/2012
$ Millions

	Appropriated	Obligated	Expended
Major Funds			
Iraq Relief and Reconstruction Fund (IRRF 1 and IRRF 2)	20,864	20,343	20,076
Iraq Security Forces Fund (ISFF)	20,194	19,569	18,762
Economic Support Fund (ESF)	5,134	4,578	4,199
Commander's Emergency Response Program (CERP)	4,119	3,728	3,728
International Narcotics Control and Law Enforcement (INCLE)	1,313	1,155	989
Subtotal	51,624	49,373	47,754
Other Assistance Programs			
Migration and Refugee Assistance (MRA) and Emergency Refugee and Migration Assistance (ERMA)	1,501	1,494	1,339
Foreign Military Financing (FMF)	850		
Natural Resources Risk Remediation Fund (NRRRF)	801	801	801
Iraq Freedom Fund (Other Reconstruction Activities)	700	680	654
P.L. 480 Food Aid (Title II and Non-Title II)	395	395	395
International Disaster Assistance (IDA) and International Disaster and Famine Assistance (IDFA)	272	261	261
Democracy Fund (DF) and Human Rights and Democracy Fund (HRDF)	266	266	262
U.S. Contributions to International Organizations (CIO)	179		
Iraq Freedom Fund (TFBSO)	174	86	65
Nonproliferation, Anti-terrorism, Demining, and Related Programs (NADR)	163	62	62
Department of Justice (DoJ)	133	121	119
Child Survival and Health Programs Fund (CSH)	90	90	90
Education and Cultural Exchange Programs	46		
Overseas Humanitarian, Disaster and Civic Aid (OHDACA)	27	27	10
International Affairs Technical Assistance	16	16	14
International Military Education and Training (IMET)	11	9	6
U.S. Marshals Service	9	9	9
Alhurra-Iraq Broadcasting	5	5	5
Subtotal	5,638	4,323	4,093
Reconstruction-related Operating Expenses	2,937	1,152	1,085
Reconstruction Oversight	445	340	333
Total	60,644	55,187	53,265

The Congress made more than 80% of the dollars allocated to these five funds available through "supplemental appropriations," that is, outside the perennial budgeting process (or "off book").[105] It also appropriated an additional $9.02 billion through several smaller funding streams. SIGIR classified these into three categories:[106]

- other assistance programs ($5.64 billion)
- reconstruction-related operating expenses ($2.94 billion)
- reconstruction oversight ($445 million)

See Table 4.1 for a summary of U.S. appropriations supporting Iraq reconstruction, including the status of these funds through FY 2012. Iraqi funds controlled by the CPA accounted for most of the money spent during the program's first year, while U.S. funding chiefly supported rebuilding efforts from 2005 through 2007 (see Figure 4.2). Since 2008,

Government of Iraq capital budgets funded most reconstruction activities. As of September 2012, about $220.21 billion had been made available for Iraq's relief and reconstruction:[107]

- $145.81 billion in Iraqi funds: the Development Fund for Iraq, seized and vested assets, and Iraqi capital budgets (66% of the total)
- $60.64 billion in U.S. funding (28% of the total)
- $13.75 billion in international commitments of assistance and loans from non-U.S. sources (6% of the total)

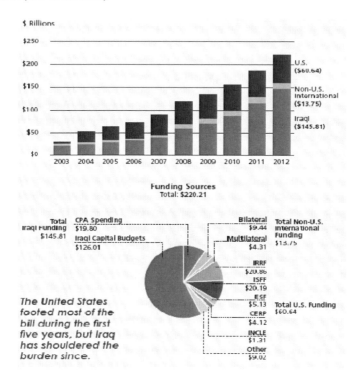

Figure 4.2. Cumulative U.S., Iraqi, and Non-U.S. International Support for Reconstruction, 2003–2012.

Major U.S. Funds

By September 2012, reconstruction managers had obligated $49.37 billion (96%) and expended $47.75 billion (93%) of the $51.62 billion appropriated to the five major U.S. funds. There remain $2.25 billion in unobligated funds and $1.62 billion in unexpended obligations (see Figure 4.3).[108] Cumulative obligations for the five major funds through September 2012 are shown in Figure 4.4.

Iraq Relief and Reconstruction Fund

The IRRF was the first and the largest U.S. reconstruction fund for Iraq. The Congress appropriated money to the IRRF in two separate bills:

- **IRRF 1**—The April 16, 2003, bill provided $2.48 billion for "humanitarian assistance" and "rehabilitation and reconstruction in Iraq." The Congress identified 12 sectors for fund use, with the Office of Management and Budget apportioning the money. USAID received approximately 74% of IRRF 1.[109]
- **IRRF 2**—In November 2003, the Congress appropriated another $18.4 billion to the IRRF.[110] Pursuant to the CPA's request, the Congress allocated 70% of this new appropriation for large infrastructure projects, including electricity, water resources and sanitation, oil, transportation, telecommunications, and roads and bridges. The legislation imposed greater controls and more oversight, giving the CPA limited authority to make adjustments and creating the Office of the CPA Inspector General.[111] A majority of the IRRF 2 was apportioned to Defense.[112]

The most active years for the IRRF were FY 2004 and FY 2005, with obligations averaging $25.9 million per day in 2004 and expenditures averaging $21.4 million per day in 2005. Reconstruction managers obligated 90% of the IRRF by March 2006, with 90% expended by June 2007 (see Figure 4.5). As of September 2012, total IRRF obligations equaled $20.34 billion, and total expenditures equaled $20.08 billion (see Table 4.2).[113]

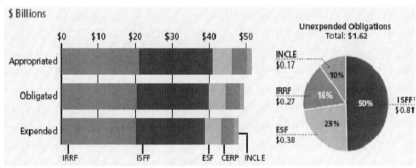

Almost $52 billion was provided through five major U.S. funds.

Figure 4.3. Status of Five Major U.S. Funds, as of 9/30/2012.

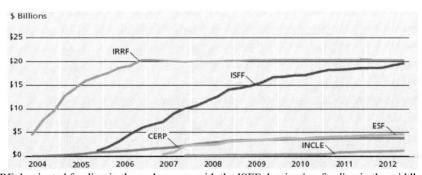

The IRRF dominated funding in the early years, with the ISFF dominating funding in the middle years.

Figure 4.4. Cumulative Obligations from Five Major Funds, 1/2004–9/2012.

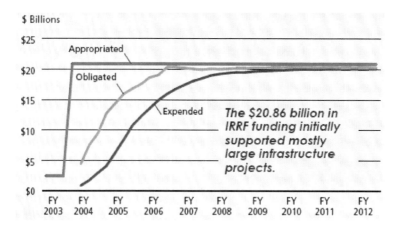

Figure 4.5. IRRF: Cumulative Appropriations, Obligations, and Expenditures, FY 2003–FY 2012.

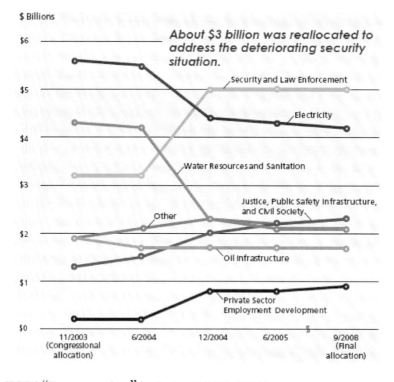

Figure 4.6. IRRF 2 "Reprogrammings" by Sector, 11/2003–9/2008.

Changing priorities in Iraq caused by the rise in violence in 2004 prompted numerous reprogrammings of funds. A key provision in the IRRF 2 legislation that enabled the reprogrammings permitted reallocation of up to 10% of any sector's funding.[114] During its life, the IRRF underwent over 250 reprogramming actions.[115] The most significant occurred in December 2004, when $3 billion in funds for the electricity and water sectors shifted to the security, justice, and employment-development sectors (see Figure 4.6).[116]

Learning from Iraq

Table 4.2. IRRF Obligations and Expenditures, by Appropriation and IRRF Sector, as of 9/30/2012
$ Millions

Appropriation	IRRF Sector	Obligated	Expended
IRRF 1	Subtotal	2,227.7	2,227.7
IRRF 2	Security & Law Enforcement	4,918.4	4,892.3
	Electric Sector	4,125.5	4,089.1
	Justice, Public Safety Infrastructure, & Civil Society	2,310.0	2,218.3
	Water Resources & Sanitation	1,965.0	1,961.4
	Oil Infrastructure	1,596.8	1,593.4
	Private Sector Development	860.0	830.0
	Health Care	808.6	805.4
	Education, Refugees, Human Rights, Democracy, & Governance	515.9	447.7
	Transportation & Telecommunications Projects	469.8	469.8
	Roads, Bridges, & Construction	280.9	280.7
	Administrative Expenses	219.5	217.9
	ISPO Capacity Development	44.9	42.3
	Subtotal	18,115.3	17,848.4
Total		20,343.0	20,076.0

Iraq Security Forces Fund

From 2005 through 2011, the Congress appropriated $20.19 billion to the ISFF, enabling the Multi-National Force-Iraq and then the U.S. Forces-Iraq to help Iraq's Ministry of Defense and Ministry of Interior grow, equip, and train the ISF.[117] During each of its seven years of appropriations, the ISFF's expenditures comprised at least one-third of all U.S. assistance to Iraq.[118] The ISFF grew out of the impetus underlying IRRF 2's reprogrammings. The fund's implementer, the Multi-National Security Transition Command-Iraq, prepared the first ISFF request, and MNSTC-I ensured that funding for ISF development remained consistent over the ensuing years.[119] The shift in sourcing security spending from the IRRF to the ISFF exponentially expanded support to Iraq's military and police forces, improving them greatly. The process was not without challenge. In 2005, the first ISFF appropriation of $5.49 billion severely strained the security assistance bureaucracy. The ISFF's earlier years saw larger appropriations that annually averaged $4.68 billion from 2005 to 2007. From 2008 through 2011, appropriations dropped to an average of $1.54 billion per year. During the seven-year period that the Congress funded the ISFF, supplemental appropriations were almost triple the size of regular appropriations—$14.84 billion versus $5.36 billion (see Figure 4.7 and Appendix B).[120] ISFF obligations and expenditures rose annually from 2005 to 2009, each averaging almost $1 billion per quarter (see Figure 4.8). The obligation and expenditure rates thereafter slowed as the military focused on transition and departure. As of September 2012, military managers had obligated about $19.57 billion (97%) of the ISFF and expended about $18.76 billion.[121] See Table 4.3 for a summary of cumulative ISFF obligations as of the end of FY 2012. From FY 2005 through FY 2012, quarterly ISFF obligations averaged $652 million, and quarterly expenditures averaged $625 million. Obligations were highest in FY 2006, when they reached $13.1 million per day, with expenditures topping out at $10.4 million per day in FY 2008.[122] Similar to the other Iraq reconstruction funds, ISFF obligations demonstrated predictable cyclical propensities. A disproportionate share of obligations perennially occurred in the fiscal year's final quarter (see Figure 4.9). This reflected the rush to commit and spend at fiscal year's end.[123]

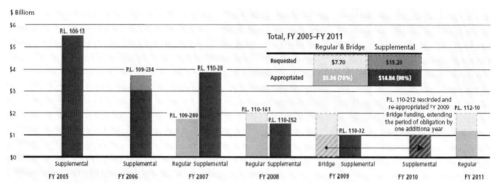

Almost three-fourths of the ISFF was provided through supplemental appropriations.

Figure 4.7. ISFF: Regular, Bridge, and Supplemental Appropriations.

As of September 2012, $18.71 billion (93%) of the ISFF had been obligated to support the MOD and MOI in four major sub-activity groups: equipment and transportation, infrastructure, sustainment, and training. An additional $859 million (4%) was obligated to "related activities," which supported programs benefiting both ministries, particularly through the ISFF "quick response fund." The remaining funds—$625.4 million (3%)—expired.[124]

Almost $12.02 billion of the ISFF went to support the MOD, with more than 44% of those obligations spent on equipment and transportation.[125] For the status on the ISFF by year of appropriation, as of the end of FY 2012, see Figure 4.10. When the U.S. military departed Iraq in December 2011, it transferred responsibility for administering the final tranche of the ISFF to the Office of Security Cooperation-Iraq.[126] Although staffed by U.S. military personnel, OSC-I falls under the authority of the U.S. Ambassador to Iraq. This money chiefly supported the Foreign Military Sales program. In FY 2012, the Foreign Military Financing program and INCLE functionally replaced the ISFF as U.S. security funding sources supporting Iraq.[127] The FMF and INCLE are U.S. accounts used worldwide to provide civil and military security assistance. This transition fit within broader efforts to normalize Embassy operations.

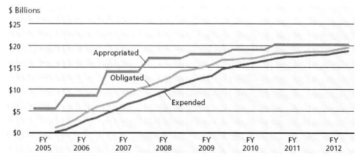

From FY 2005 to FY 2009, ISFF obligations and expenditures each averaged almost $1 billion per quarter.

Figure 4.8. ISFF: Cumulative Appropriations, Obligations, and Expenditures, FY 2005–FY 2012.

Table 4.3. ISFF Obligations and Expenditures, by Ministry and Program, as of 9/30/2012; $ Millions

	Obligated	Expended
MOD Equipment and Transportation	5,327	5,227
Infrastructure	3,075	2,972
Sustainment	2,894	2,620
Training and Operations	723	698
Subtotal	12,018	11,518
MOI Equipment and Transportation	2,026	1,945
Infrastructure	1,347	1,260
Sustainment	663	623
Training and Operations	2,656	2,592
Subtotal	6,692	6,420
Related Activities	859	825
Total	19,569	18,762

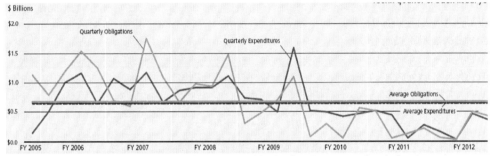

A disproportionate share of ISFF obligations occurred in the fourth quarter of each fiscal year.

Figure 4.9. ISFF: Obligation and Expenditure Rates, FY 2005–FY 2012.

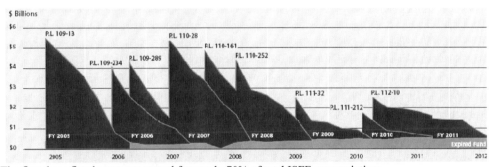

The first three fiscal years accounted for nearly 70% of total ISFF appropriations.

Figure 4.10. Unobligated ISFF Appropriations.

Economic Support Fund

From FY 2006 through FY 2012, the Congress appropriated about $5.13 billion to the ESF to enable State and USAID to improve Iraq's infrastructure, strengthen security, promote democracy, empower civil society, support capacity building, and promote economic development.[128] Quarterly obligations from FY 2006 through FY 2012 averaged about $164 million, and quarterly expenditures averaged about $150 million. During the first two years of its use, almost 70% of the ESF was obligated and more than 50% was expended (Figure 4.11). Obligations were highest in FY 2007, averaging $6.2 million per day, and expenditures peaked at $4.5 million per day in FY 2008. As of September 2012, the United States had obligated about $4.58 billion of the total appropriations and expended $4.20 billion.[129]

The $5.13 billion in ESF allocations for Iraq comprised about 75% of the $6.89 billion in Administration requests. Most ESF money in Iraq was made available through the supplemental funding process, with the size of these requests and regular appropriations declining after 2007 (see Figure 4.12 and Appendix B).[130] Supplemental appropriations in FY 2006 and FY 2007 were obligated more quickly than appropriations in later years. For example, in the fourth quarter of FY 2007, the United States obligated the ESF at a rate of nearly $15.7 million per day.[131] Average expenditures across all years peaked at an average $6.7 million per day during the fourth quarter of FY 2008, as obligations of the FY 2006–FY 2007 appropriations were liquidated. See Figure 4.13 for the status of obligations, by year of appropriation. As of September 2012, $379 million of obligated ESF funds remained unexpended. An additional $556 million remained unobligated, with $260 million expired. Expired funds cannot be obligated to new projects but can be used to modify existing ones. $296 million remains for new obligations.[132] For the status of each ESF program as of the end of FY 2012, see Table 4.4.

SIGIR Audit 09-006
ESF Spending: Low and Slow

A long-standing account at the Department of State, the ESF was the chief source of funding for non-military programs during the latter stages of the rebuilding effort. Its obligation and expenditure cadence in Iraq was lower and slower than other funds for two reasons:

- The fund has a two-year appropriation cycle. Its money remains available for deobligation and subsequent reobligation for a period of four years after the appropriation expires. This means that the end-of-fiscal-year pressures that pushed up spending rates for other funds did not affect the ESF.
- State treats ESF funds as "obligated" when it executes an agreement to commit the money to a program. Contracts for specific projects come later. Other funds in Iraq treated money as "obligated" when it was put under contract. The ESF "obligation" practice obviated pressures to spend funds and led to slower expenditure rates. For example, a SIGIR audit showed that, in 2008, a party to an ESF agreement had yet to award contracts for 15% of 2006 ESF funds and 58% of 2007 ESF funds.

USACE expected to complete ESF-funded construction of the Missan Surgical Hospital by the end of 2012. (USACE photo).

Learning from Iraq 99

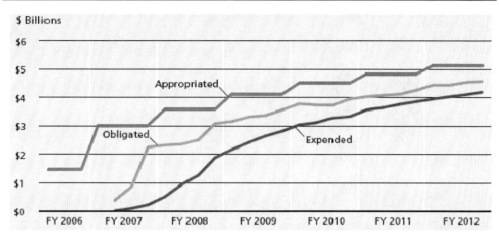

More than $5 billion in ESF funds were provided to State and USAID to improve Iraq's infrastructure, strengthen security, promote democracy, empower civil society, support capacity building, and promote economic development.

Figure 4.11. ESF: Cumulative Appropriations, Obligations, and Expenditures, FY 2006–FY 2012.

USAID implements most ESF programs worldwide. Given the reconstruction program's early emphasis on infrastructure, generally outside of USAID's métier, State executed special agreements to execute ESF in Iraq.

As of September 2012, $4.58 billion of the ESF had been obligated as follows:[133]

- $2.90 billion (63%) for USAID projects
- $1.14 billion (25%) for projects implemented by the U.S. Army Corps of Engineers
- $536 million (12%) for projects implemented by State through the Bureau of Democracy, Human Rights, and Labor and the Bureau of Population, Refugees, and Migration, as well as U.S. Embassy-Baghdad organizations

Under the ESF-funded Infrastructure Security Program, the United States supported construction of secured corridors to protect oil pipelines from insurgent attacks. The program contributed to an almost 12-fold increase in northern exports from 2006 to 2008.

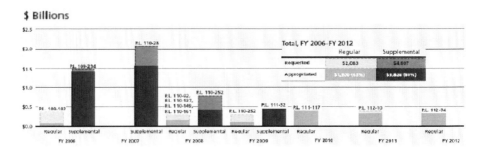

The largest tranche of ESF funding came in the FY 2007 supplemental appropriation.

Figure 4.12. ESF: Regular and Supplemental Appropriations.

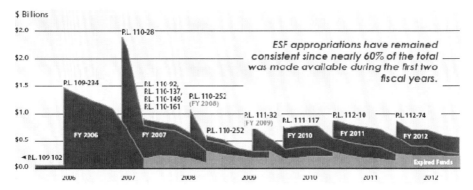

Figure 4.13. Unobligated ESF Appropriations.

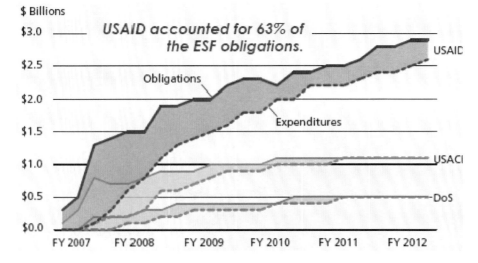

Figure 4.14. ESF: Cumulative Obligations and Expenditures, by Agency, FY 2007–FY 2012.

Table 4.4. ESF Obligations and Expenditures, by Implementing Agency and Program, as of 9/30/2012
$ Millions

	Agency Program	Obligated	Expended
USAID	Community Stabilization Program	619	615
	Community Action Program	450	448
	Local Governance Program	435	434
	Tatweer National Capacity Development	309	309
	Inma Agribusiness Development	180	162
	Tijara Provincial Economic Growth	173	144
	Agency Program	Obligated	Expended
	PRT Quick Response Fund	162	161
	Democracy and Civil Society	88	71
	Economic Governance II, Policy and Regulatory Reforms	84	84
	Tarabot Administrative Reform	82	30
	Primary Health Care	73	13
	Governance Strengthening	57	10
	Financial Sector Development	51	24
	Elections Support	40	22
	Izdihar Private Sector Development	33	32
	Personnel Support	21	9
	Primary Education Strengthening	19	
	Monitoring and Evaluation	14	10
	Harmonized Support for Agriculture	10	
	Education, Health and Social Services	4	3
	Subtotal	2,904	2,579
USACE/ GRD	PRT/PRDC Projects	618	591
	O&M Sustainment	276	275
	Infrastructure Security Protection	194	194
	Plant-Level Capacity Development & Technical Training	50	50
	Subtotal	1,138	1,110
DoS/ Embassy	Democracy and Civil Society	177	172
	PRT Quick Response Fund	125	122
	Iraqi Refugees	95	95
	Ministerial Capacity Development	45	40
	Regime Crimes Liaison Office	33	29
	Targeted Development	60	52
	Ambassador's Fund	1	
	Subtotal	536	510
Total		4,578	4,199

For details on ESF program obligations and expenditures, by agency, see Figure 4.14 and Chapter 3 of this report. For details on program and project activities, see Chapter 5 of this report.

Commander's Emergency Response Program

The CERP enabled U.S. military commanders to respond to urgent humanitarian relief and reconstruction requirements. Established by the CPA in 2003 with $177 million in Iraqi funds from the DFI and seized and vested assets,[134] the CERP addressed acute local needs that, in the judgment of U.S. military commanders, called for immediate action.

On November 6, 2003, the first U.S. funding for the CERP provided $140 million.[135] The Congress made 11 more appropriations to the CERP over the next seven years, amounting to $3.98 billion.[136]

In addition, the GOI provided $270 million in DFI funds for a joint U.S.-Iraqi program called I-CERP, under which the U.S. military implemented reconstruction projects through CERP processes using these Iraqi funds.[137]

From 2004 through 2011, the Congress appropriated $4.12 billion to the CERP for Iraq.[138] The fund officially closed (for Iraq) on September 30, 2011.

USF-I and its predecessors obligated and expended $3.73 billion of CERP funds.[139] The remaining $391 million expired,[140] but, under certain conditions, it could be used for other Defense activities, such as for CERP projects in Afghanistan.[141]

From FY 2004 through FY 2011, quarterly CERP obligations and expenditures both averaged $116 million.

FY 2008 was the CERP's most active year, with an average of $2.8 million obligated and expended each day. Ninety percent of total CERP funds used in Iraq had been obligated by December 31, 2008, and expended by December 31, 2009 (see Figure 4.15).[142]

From the military's perspective, the advantage of CERP projects was their quick execution and highly visible results, which had counterinsurgency effects. The Defense Department's *Financial Management Regulation* (FMR) and the *Money as a Weapon System (MAAWS)* manual provided CERP regulations.[143]

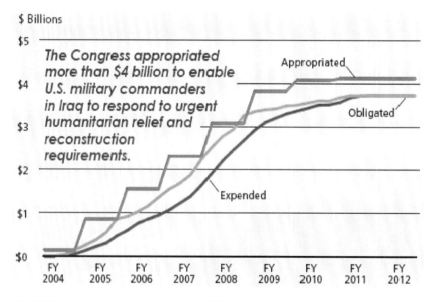

Figure 4.15. CERP: Cumulative Appropriations, Obligations, and Expenditures, FY 2004–FY 2012.

Throughout the CERP's life, there were tensions between the need for centralized direction to ensure program results and the dispersed authorities necessary for quick execution. CERP projects sometimes duplicated the efforts of other U.S. agency programs.[144]

In 2006, the Congress expressed concerns that increasingly large project sizes indicated a shift away from the CERP's intent.

In 2007, the House Committee on Appropriations expressed similar concerns about the growth of high-dollar CERP projects.[145]

After the Congress put controls in place, obligations for large projects decreased to 15% of total obligations in FY 2008. The downward trend continued, and the percentage gradually decreased to zero for FY 2011 (see Figure 4.16).[146]

The Congress ended support for the CERP in Iraq in FY 2012, providing a limited extension of budget authority through November 18, 2011.[147]

Defense ended up reallocating most of the $100 million appropriated in FY 2011 for other purposes. Ultimately, it only obligated $44 million of this funding.[148]

CERP record keeping was inadequate. SIGIR could not provide a thorough accounting of the final disposition of all projects executed under the program. USF-I's CERP project tracker—Defense's only systemic database—was only updated through the end of the fiscal year in which the funds were appropriated. If a project was not completed during that fiscal year, there were no records in the system indicating when it was eventually completed.

The Army Budget Office prepared financial reports detailing the total number of outstanding projects and the sum of unliquidated obligations by fiscal year, but it did not track projects on an individual basis.

SIGIR found that financial data maintained by the Army Budget Office and CERP project data reported by USF-I differed substantially. USF-I generally over-reported CERP obligations, while under-reporting CERP expenditures (see Table 4.5).[149]

No Defense Department office has a comprehensive picture of what the program actually accomplished in Iraq. The best available CERP data provides a rough approximation of actual activities. This renders suspect commander narratives, academic studies, and other analyses that claim success based on that data.

SIGIR Audit 11-020
Strategic Drift in the CERP:
Project Cost Up, CERP Stock Down

The Commander's Emergency Response Program was a key innovation in Iraq. Formalized by a CPA order in the summer of 2003, the CERP provided about $4 billion in assistance to the rebuilding program over the next eight years.

The program's original intent aimed to support urgent small-scale projects that met local needs. Most of the early projects cost less than $25,000.

As CERP matured, SIGIR found evidence of strategic drift. That is, it began to fund higher-cost projects far afield from the program's mandate.

SIGIR audits questioned using CERP money to fund multimillion-dollar infrastructure projects or to support civil capacity-development programs. CERP's ethos had a counterinsurgency core; these capacity-building programs departed from it.

The Congress acted at various points to rein in overreaches, but Defense never established a formal program office to oversee the program.

Instead, it created a three-tier "oversight structure" comprising a CERP Steering Committee, a CERP Management Cell, and a CERP Working Group.

The United States spent $4.2 million in CERP funds to build the Caravan Hotel at Baghdad International Airport.

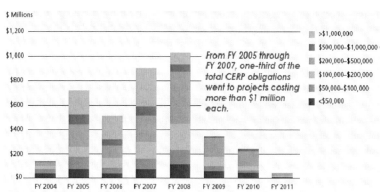
Figure 4.16. CERP Obligations, by Project Size, FY 2004–FY 2011.

In a $10.2 million, CERP-funded project completed in three phases, USACE installed 1,200 solar-powered street lights along 35 kilometers of roadway in and around Falluja. (USACE photo).

Table 4.5. CERP Obligations and Expenditures, by Project Category, as of 12/31/2011
$ Millions

	Project Category/Fiscal Year	Obligated	Expended
Status of Funds, by Project Category, According to the USF-I CERP Project Tracker	Water & Sanitation	673.8	227.8
	Protective Measures	490.6	268.1
	Electricity	444.7	134.5
	Education	428.8	180.1
	Transportation	386.1	150.0
	Civic Cleanup Activities	240.9	117.6
	Other Urgent Humanitarian or Reconstruction Projects	224.5	84.9
	Agriculture	208.5	76.2
	Economic, Financial, and Management Improvements	183.4	77.7
	Health Care	152.5	61.7
	Rule of Law & Governance	113.4	46.2
	Civic Infrastructure Repair	67.5	23.9
	Repair of Civic & Cultural Facilities	62.9	27.4
	Civic Support Vehicles	58.5	33.7
	Condolence Payments	50.8	35.5
	Telecommunications	39.6	10.2
	Temporary Contract Guards for Critical Infrastructure	35.6	35.3
	Battle Damage Repair	23.8	18.0
	Food Production & Distribution	21.2	8.2
	Non-FMR	5.8	
	Detainee Payments	1.0	0.6
	Iraqi Hero Payments	0.7	0.7
	Subtotal	3,914.4	1,618.1
Difference between ABO Financial Data and USF-I CERP Project Tracker, by Fiscal Year	2004	-5.8	133.6
	2005	-49.2	404.4
	2006	136.7	499.8
	2007	-181.5	324.2
	2008	-91.6	513.5
	2009	-9.5	116.2
	2010	14.2	118.0
	2011		
	Subtotal	-186.6	2,109.7
Total, According to ABO Financial Data		3,727.9	3,727.8

International Narcotics Control and Law Enforcement Affairs

From FY 2006 through FY 2012, the Congress appropriated $1.31 billion to the INCLE for use in Iraq by State to support rule-oflaw activities.[150] Although modest by comparison to the ISFF, CERP, and ESF, appropriations to the INCLE became a significant portion of U.S. reconstruction funding after FY 2009. The Congress allocated INCLE to 12 programs in four areas: criminal justice, corrections, counternarcotics, and program development and support. The criminal justice sector received the majority of obligations through FY 2012 (see Table 4.6).[151] In February 2010, the Administration requested $832 million and received $765 million in FY 2010 supplemental and FY 2011 regular appropriations for the INCLE to prepare for the transition of police-training responsibility from Defense to State.[152] The two appropriations accounted for nearly 60% of the cumulative funding appropriated from FY 2006 through FY 2012.[153] From November 2005 through September 2012, INCLE quarterly obligations averaged $41 million, while quarterly expenditures averaged $35 million. FY 2011 was the INCLE's most active year, with $1.6 million obligated and $1.5 million expended each day. As of September 2012, at least $1.16 billion of the total INCLE appropriations had been obligated and $989 million had been expended (see Figure 4.17).[154]

The Administration's proposed uses of the INCLE in Iraq evolved.

Cadets are trained at the Baghdad Police Academy.

Table 4.6. INCLE Obligations and Expenditures, by Sector and Program, as of 9/30/2012
$ Millions

Sector	Program	Obligated	Expended
Criminal Justice	Police Advisors	710.2	620.6
	Courts	109.3	86.1
	Public Integrity	31.7	25.9
	Rule of Law Advisors	26.1	18.9
	Major Crimes Task Force	13.5	11.9
	Justice Integration	6.8	6.3
	Justice Programs	9.5	4.7
	Legal Framework	2.5	2.5
	Subtotal	909.6	777.0
Corrections	Construction	83.7	83.3
	Advisors	98.2	81.6
	Corrections	13.2	10.9
	Subtotal	195.1	175.8
Other	Program Development & Support	**47.3**	**35.8**
Counternarcotics	Counternarcotics	**3.5**	**0.2**
Total		**1,155.4**	**988.8**

Early requests focused on corrections, but later they shifted to judicial capacity building and security.[155] Requests to support the transition of police training responsibility to State began with the FY 2009 supplemental appropriation and increased in FY 2010–FY 2011 (see Figure 4.18 and Appendix B).[156]

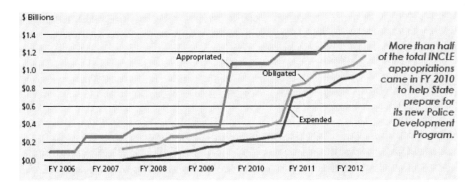

Figure 4.17. INCLE: Cumulative Appropriations, Obligations, and Expenditures, FY 2006–FY 2012.

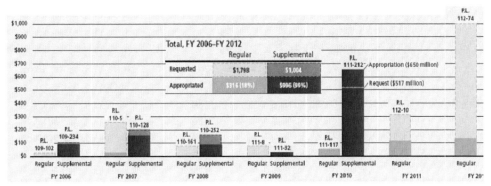

The Congress responded much more positively to supplemental requests than to regular requests for INCLE funding.

Figure 4.18. INCLE: Regular and Supplemental Appropriations.

Flow of the Major Funds

The Congress allocated almost all U.S. funding for relief and reconstruction initially to DoD, USAID, and DoS. The agencies passed on some of these funds to others to implement programs in Iraq. Defense and State transferred amounts ranging from a few thousand dollars to more than a billion through interagency agreements, which allowed the legal transfer of funds to programs run by other U.S. government agencies or United Nations organizations. Figure 4.19 shows how appropriations flowed first to the agencies and then to four broad reconstruction areas.

Smaller U.S. Funding Streams

Other Assistance Programs

The Congress provided about 85% of appropriations for Iraq's reconstruction through the five major funds addressed above. Several smaller funding streams also proved crucial to the program. Almost $5.64 billion was made available through these smaller funds, including $1.50 billion for the Migration and Refugee Assistance and Emergency Refugee and Migration Assistance funds.[157] Curiously, the FMF program received $850 million, but none was obligated or expended as of the end of FY 2012.[158] See Appendix B for details on all other assistance programs, including the total amount appropriated by fiscal year. For a brief description of selected programs, see Table 4.7.

Operating Expenses

Since 2003, the Congress made at least $2.94 billion available for reconstruction-related operating expenses. This included expenses totaling $908 million incurred by the CPA in FY 2004. Other entities that reported substantial operating expenses were the Project and Contracting Office ($830 million), OSC-I ($524 million), and USAID ($446 million.)[159] For more detail, including total amounts appropriated by fiscal year and agency, refer to Appendix B.

Oversight Expenses

The Congress made at least $445 million available for reconstruction oversight since 2003. This included $246 million for SIGIR's work during FY 2004 through FY 2013 (yearly average of about $25 million).[160] Other agencies reporting oversight expenses included the Defense Contract Audit Agency ($111 million), Department of State Office of Inspector General ($35 million), USAID OIG ($29 million), and the Department of Defense OIG ($26 million).[161] While SIGIR funding data covers the entire cost of doing business, including personnel costs, the funding data for the other oversight agencies does not. Total oversight expenses were under-reported. For more details, including total amounts appropriated by fiscal year and agency, refer to Appendix B.

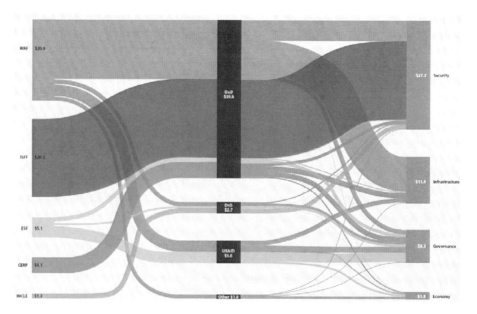

Figure 4.19. Flow of Major U.S. Reconstruction Funds to Agencies and Reconstruction Areas; $ Billions.

Table 4.7. Selected Other Assistance Programs, by Implementing Agency

Fund (Amount Appropriated)	Purpose
Department of Defense	
Foreign Military Financing (FMF) ($850 million)	First made available to Iraq in FY 2012 when the Congress made no new ISFF appro-priations; FMF is intended to support the continued development of the Iraqi military.
Natural Resources Risk Remediation Fund (NRRRF) ($801 million)	NRRRF was used for early reconstruction of the oil sector. USACE reported that all funds were fully expended as of September 30, 2008.
Iraq Freedom Fund (IFF) ($700 million)	The IFF was established by P.L. 108-11 to fund additional expenses for ongoing mil-itary operations in Iraq and elsewhere. It allows the Secretary of Defense to transfer funds to finance combat, stability operations, force reconstitution, and other war-related costs. Once funds are transferred, they "take on the characteristics" and are subject to the same rules and restrictions as the receiving fund or account.
Overseas Humanitarian, Disaster, and Civic Aid (OHDACA) ($27 million)	OHDACA provides basic humanitarian aid and services to populations in need. According to the Defense Security Cooperation Agency, which oversees OHDACA, these funds build indigenous capabilities and cooperative relationships with allies and potential partners and improve access to areas not otherwise available to U.S. forces.
Department of State	
Migration and Refugee Assistance (MRA) and Emergency Refugee and Migration Assistance (ERMA) ($1,501 million)	MRA and ERMA are administered by the Bureau of Population, Refugees, and Migra-tion and used to fund contributions to international organizations that benefit Iraqi refugees, internally displaced persons, and other conflict victims; funding is also pro-vided to non-governmental organizations that fill gaps in the multilateral response.
Democracy Fund and Human Rights Democracy Fund ($266 million)	The Democracy Fund is allocated by the Bureau of Democracy, Human Rights, and Labor to support democracy-promotion programs of organizations such as the National Democratic Institute and the International Republican Institute.
Nonproliferation, Anti-Terrorism, Demining, and Related Programs (NADR) ($163 million)	NADR supports security and humanitarian-related initiatives, including humanitarian demining, antiterrorism, and small-arms destruction.
International Military Education and Training (IMET) ($11 million)	IMET is intended to strengthen alliances and promote military professionalism through training and education for students from allied and friendly nations. The program is administered jointly with DoD.
Educational and Cultural Exchange Programs (ECA) ($46 million)	ECA supports education, democracy, civil society, and cultural heritage activities in Iraq through educational and cultural exchanges.
U.S. Agency for International Development	
International Disaster Assistance (IDA) and International Disaster and Famine Assistance (IDFA) ($272 million)	The USAID Office of Foreign Disaster Assistance is responsible for IDA and IDFA. These funds allow the U.S. government to respond to disasters in foreign countries through famine relief, cash food aid, and related programs.
P.L. 480 Food Aid (Title II and Non-Title II) ($395 million)	P.L. 480 Title II Food Aid, or Food for Peace, provides for the donation of U.S. agri-cultural commodities to meet food needs in other countries.
Child Survival and Health (CSH) ($90 million)	USAID's Bureau of Global Health is responsible for CSH, which funds maternal, newborn, and child health programs implemented by voluntary organizations and NGOs.
U.S. Treasury	
International Affairs Technical Assistance ($16 million)	The Department of the Treasury is responsible for International Affairs Technical As-sistance, which is funded in Iraq by State under a reimbursable agreement. Technical Assistance advisors work with foreign governments to improve their financial systems.

WHERE THE MONEY WENT

Planning to Spend

Shortly after the September 11, 2001, terrorist attacks, Department of Defense and National Security Council officials began exploring preliminary plans for the possible invasion of Iraq. *Hard Lessons: The Iraq Reconstruction Experience* covers much of what happened regarding reconstruction planning during this period. As detailed there, significant differences unfolded among the departments about the appropriate post-war rebuilding strategy.[162]

The prevailing preference among Defense Department planners was to "liberate and leave." That is, Coalition forces would topple the Saddam Hussein regime, stabilize the country, transfer power to an interim governing authority, and allow the Iraqis to manage the country's recovery and pay for its relief and reconstruction. Policymakers viewed this general strategy as having worked reasonably well in Afghanistan. Defense sought to replicate it in Iraq.[163]

Defense planners expected to provide some post-conflict humanitarian and reconstruction assistance. The April 2003 $2.475 billion Iraq Relief and Reconstruction Fund appropriation embodied this provision. No one at Defense planned for a lengthy occupation or a large relief and reconstruction program. The program in place in the early spring of 2003 anticipated a limited U.S.-funded rebuilding effort, a quick transfer of sovereignty, and the departure of U.S. troops from Iraq by September.[164]

As *Hard Lessons* recounts, planners from the Department of State and the U.S. Agency for International Development had a less sanguine view. They envisioned a protracted U.S. involvement, requiring the considerable commitment of U.S. resources. To that end, USAID's *Vision for Post-Conflict Iraq* concluded that the "complete reconstruction [of Iraq's] economic and institutional capacity...will require years of public investment." The January 2003 National Security Presidential Directive 24 largely ended the pre-war debate, putting the Department of Defense in charge of managing post-war Iraq.[165] NSPD 24 created the Office of Reconstruction and Humanitarian Assistance, which would operate under Defense Department auspices, charging it to plan relief and reconstruction programs. Retired Army Lieutenant General Jay M. Garner led ORHA for its short life. When Garner subsequently told Secretary of Defense Rumsfeld that the United States might need to spend "billions of dollars" to rebuild Iraq, the Secretary responded, "if you think we're going to spend a billion dollars of our money over there, you are sadly mistaken."[166]

Shortly after Saddam fell, the Iraq Relief and Reconstruction Fund came into play. Its initial $2.475 billion supported rebuilding in the following areas:[167]

- water/sanitation infrastructure
- feeding and food distribution
- relief efforts for refugees, internally displaced persons, and vulnerable individuals, including assistance for families of innocent Iraqi civilians who suffered losses as a result of military operations
- electricity
- health care

- telecommunications
- economic and financial policy
- education
- transportation
- governance and the rule of law
- humanitarian demining
- agriculture

Lieutenant General Garner never employed these funds. The creation of the Coalition Provisional Authority truncated his tenure in late April 2003. This leadership change marked a major policy shift: "occupy and rebuild" replaced "liberate and leave," a development not yet fully in focus and certainly not then embraced by Defense. The CPA quickly formulated an ambitious program for the country's large-scale recovery, relief, and reconstruction. This new plan was substantially larger than any previously anticipated.[168]

On September 17, 2003, less than six months after Saddam was deposed, President Bush asked the Congress for $20.3 billion for the relief and reconstruction of Iraq, stating that these funds were "essential to secure the transition to self-government and to create conditions for economic growth and investment."[169] After brief debate, the Congress provided more than 90% of the request,[170] and thus began an unprecedented nine-year rebuilding campaign, for which congressional appropriations eventually would top $60 billion.

You Break It, You Own It?

When Coalition forces entered Iraq, they found the country in much worse condition than pre-war planners anticipated. Indeed, it is not a stretch to say that Iraq was broken before the invasion. But already decrepit conditions severely worsened in April and May 2003, aggravated by looting, insecurity, and a couple of arguably errant decisions by the CPA.

Immediately following the invasion, U.S. Army Corps of Engineers teams quickly assessed Iraq's civil infrastructure, finding it in grievous disrepair. The Iran-Iraq War and the 1991 Gulf War left pockets of weakness, which the invasion aggravated. United Nations sanctions imposed in the 1990s, effecting as they did an international trade embargo, constrained Iraq's access to spare parts, limiting the country's capacity to sustain and maintain its infrastructure. Saddam's neglect, corruption, and mismanagement exacerbated every shortfall. It soon became clear in mid-2003 that a much larger investment was required.[171]

The widespread looting following the invasion devastated the country's infrastructure. Looters ransacked government buildings, stole munitions from military depots, robbed and destroyed banks, ravaged oil-sector facilities, ripped apart electrical systems, and incapacitated most of Iraq's 192 state-owned enterprises. This indiscriminate pillaging caused billions of dollars in damage, provided weapons for insurgents, and destroyed hopes that Iraq's public institutions and critical infrastructure could quickly resume operations.[172]

What the looters did to Iraq's government buildings, some argue the CPA did to its government's bureaucracy. CPA Order 1, issued on May 16, 2003, banned members of Saddam's Ba'ath Party above certain levels from serving in Iraq's public sector. Lieutenant General Ricardo Sanchez, Commander of Coalition forces in Iraq from June 2003 to June 2004, later stated that this order "essentially ... eliminated the entire government and civic capacity of the nation. Organizations involving justice, defense, interior, communications, schools, universities, and hospitals were all either completely shut down or severely crippled because anybody with any experience was now out of a job."[173]

A growing insurgency followed the looting, fueled in part by CPA Order 2, which, among other things, abolished Iraq's Ministry of Defense and disbanded the army, putting 500,000 men out of work without pay or pension. As General Petraeus told SIGIR, this action "created tens of thousands, if not hundreds of thousands, of additional enemies of the Coalition."[174]

In mid-2003, Iraq had no capacity for self-government, no functioning security forces, an almost useless electricity system, virtually no oil exports, and no ongoing revenue stream to pay the costs of rebuilding.[175] Iraq was broken; the United States "owned it."

Defining and Redefining: Moving Goals and Benchmarks

Pre-war planning identified areas that would need post-war relief and reconstruction. But reconstruction managers did not define specific goals, objectives, measures, and metrics until very late in the planning process. The relevant documents included:

- **USAID's** *Vision for Post-Conflict Iraq*—This February 2003 paper established a set of milestones, ranging from 60 days to 18 months after the fall of Saddam and reaching many sectors, including health, water and sanitation, electricity, transportation, telecommunications, and agriculture/rural development.[176]
- **ORHA's** *A Unified Mission Plan for Post-Hostilities Iraq*—This April 2003 paper defined the desired "end state" as "a stable Iraq, with its territorial integrity intact, and a broad-based government that renounces WMD development and use and no longer supports terrorism or threatens its neighbors." It set forth benchmarks that defined the desired end state.[177]
- **CPA's** *Achieving the Vision*—This July 2003 plan defined the desired end state as "a unified and stable, democratic Iraq that provides effective and representative government for the Iraqi people, is underpinned by new and protected freedoms and a growing market economy; is able to defend itself but no longer poses a threat to its neighbors or international security." The CPA's program focused on these four general areas:[178]
  - **Security**—establishing a secure and safe environment
  - **Essential services**—restoring basic services to an acceptable standard
  - **Economy**—creating the conditions for economic growth
  - **Governance**—enabling the transition to transparent and inclusive democratic governance

Obligations and Expenditures: An Incomplete Story

The November 2003 law appropriating $18.4 billion for the IRRF established the requirement that agencies report quarterly to the Congress on their use of U.S. funds on a "project-byproject" basis.[179] The departments involved in reconstruction attempted to meet this requirement; but, as of the end of 2012, no reliably complete source of information existed showing what U.S reconstruction funds accomplished. SIGIR issued numerous reports documenting the limitations of the applicable data systems, but little improvement occurred. Thus, the full story on the use of billions of U.S. dollars for reconstructing Iraq will forever remain incomplete.

For the past nine years, SIGIR provided comprehensive reports to the Congress every quarter. In so doing, SIGIR gathered a mountain of data on the use of reconstruction funds. This chapter draws from SIGIR's 35 *Quarterly and Semiannual Reports* and our independent audit analyses of agency reconstruction data, classifying U.S.-funded programs into four categories that correspond to the CPA's four core areas. Because of the questionable quality, accuracy, and completeness of the project records, SIGIR often had to make a judgment call when assigning costs to programs and projects. Moreover, their effects are based largely on what the agencies reported to SIGIR.

Table 5.1 shows how much the United States obligated and expended from the five major U.S. reconstruction funds in each of these areas through September 2012.

SIGIR Audit 13-006
Accounting for Project Costs: Caveat Lector

The Congress mandated U.S. agencies to submit quarterly reports detailing how they used reconstruction funds on a project-byproject basis. It also required that SIGIR's quarterly reports include "a project-by-project and program-by-program accounting of the costs incurred to date for the reconstruction of Iraq." Using data reported by the State and Defense Departments, USAID, and other agencies, SIGIR has consistently accounted for obligations and expenditures at the program level. But pinning down the costs of specific projects has been more difficult. Among the problems are these:

- **No commonly understood and applied definition of "project"**—A single record in a database might represent the entire turnkey cost of completing a facility, the cost of building just one component or phase of the facility, the cost of work that was unsatisfactory and had to be redone by another contractor, or the cost of similar work performed at multiple facilities.
- **Inaccurate and incomplete cost data**— SIGIR identified numerous cases in which the costs reported for individual projects did not match across databases and internal agency records. In the case of the Iraq Reconstruction Management System (the $50 million system developed to support the project-by-project reporting requirement), the recorded costs are the estimated contract values, not the actual expenditures. In another database, SIGIR found multiple instances where the total amount expended for a contract was reported as the amount expended for each individual project funded by that contract, resulting in a dramatic overreporting of project costs.
- **Missing data**—15% of the IRRF obligations were not accounted for in agency databases. SIGIR could not determine if the missing obligation and expenditure data resulted from data-entry problems or something more, such as fraud. Resolving this issue would entail a close review of every IRRF-funded contract, a task that exceeded SIGIR's resources.

Because of these deficiencies in record keeping, the disposition of billions of dollars for projects remains unknown because the U.S. government agencies involved in the relief and reconstruction effort did not maintain project information in any uniform or comprehensive manner.

The Falluja Waste Water Treatment System project, on which the United States spent $100 million in U.S. funds, is not listed as a single project in the Iraq Reconstruction Management System. Instead, IRMS has 49 separate records, including records for project activities funded from the IRRF, CERP, and ESF. (U.S. Army photo).

Table 5.1. Obligations and Expenditures of Major U.S. Reconstruction Funds, by Area of Use, as of 9/30/2012
$ Billions

Area	Sector	Obligated	Expended
Security and Rule of Law	Ministry of Defense Support	14.41	13.90
	Ministry of Interior Support	9.73	9.35
	Related Activities	1.12	1.08
	Justice	0.77	0.68
	Infrastructure Security	0.67	0.63
	Corrections	0.53	0.46
	Anticorruption	0.07	0.06
	Subtotal	27.30	26.16
Infrastructure	Electricity	5.45	5.36
	Water and Sanitation	2.78	2.71
	Oil and Gas	1.76	1.76
	Transportation and Communications	1.31	1.25
	General Infrastructure	0.58	0.58
	Subtotal	11.88	11.66
Governance	Public Services	3.06	2.55
	Capacity Development	2.45	2.27
	Democracy and Civil Society	1.91	1.82
	Humanitarian Relief	0.89	0.84
	Subtotal	8.32	7.48
Economy	Private Sector Development	0.98	0.87
	Economic Governance	0.84	0.78
	Subtotal	1.82	1.65
Total		49.32	46.96

Infrastructure

Three wars, international sanctions, massive looting, and Saddam's reckless neglect devastated Iraq's capacity to provide essential services.[180] A senior official told SIGIR that the "invasion seemed to have occurred just as the condition of the entire infrastructure teetered on the edge of the cliff of disaster."[181]

The CPA made the delivery of basic services a major priority, setting these goals:[182]

- reconstituting the power infrastructure
- improving water-resource management
- ensuring food security
- improving health care—quality and access
- rehabilitating key transport infrastructure
- improving education and housing—quality and access
- reconstructing the telecommunications system

The early phase of reconstruction spending emphasized large capital projects.[183] Almost $1.64 billion (66%) of the IRRF 1 appropriation was spent on large projects: $1.1 billion executed by USAID and $518 million by Defense.[184]

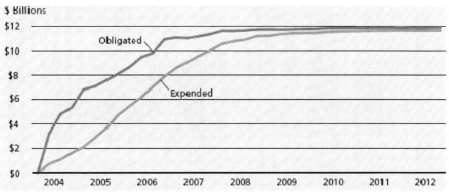

90% of the money for infrastructure projects was obligated before the end of 2006.

Figure 5.1. Infrastructure: Cumulative Obligations and Expenditures, FY 2004–FY 2012.

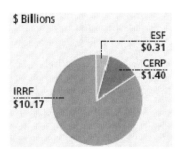

Figure 5.2. Infrastructure: Cumulative Obligations, by Fund, as of 9/30/2012.

Over the next nine years, the amount allocated to programs to repair and develop Iraq's critical infrastructure sectors grew to $12.32 billion. As of September 2012, the United States had obligated $11.88 billion had and spent $11.66 billion. Almost 70% of this money was obligated within the first two years of the reconstruction effort, and more than 85% of the total obligations came from the IRRF (see Figures 5.1 and 5.2).[185]

Escalating violence in Iraq severely affected the rebuilding program. Attacks on contractors caused high rates of worker absenteeism, disrupted logistics, delayed countless projects, escalated security and project costs, and forced projects to shut down (see Figure 5.3).[186]

Project management personnel commonly could not visit work sites because of dangerous conditions, diminishing oversight and causing poor results. The U.S. government awarded contracts and task orders containing unrealistic cost estimates and impossible-to-meet completion dates, leading to a parade of change orders that scaled down projects, foreshortened outcomes, and contributed to a trove of complaints that SIGIR heard from Iraqis about the transfer of semi-complete projects.[187]

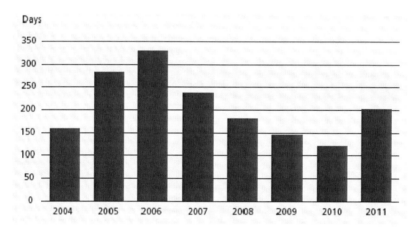

Figure 5.3. Average Slippage in Completion of USACE Infrastructure Projects Valued at More than $1 Million, by Year of Award, 2004–2011.

Electricity

During the 1980s, average electricity production from Iraq's power plants increased from about 1,200 megawatts to 3,100 MW, generally keeping pace with rising demand. During the 1991 Gulf War, air attacks severely damaged Iraq's electricity infrastructure, causing production to drop below 2,200 MW.[188]

Supplies could not to meet the country's demand during the 1990s. Although repairs to the system boosted average production to more than 3,600 MW by 2002, the 2003 invasion, postwar looting, and insurgent sabotage quickly drove levels down, hitting a low of 711 MW in mid-April 2003.[189]

Increasing Iraq's electricity production became a paramount priority. CPA and Iraqi officials recognized that rebuilding the power sector was key to reviving Iraq's economy, energizing the infrastructure, improving well-being, and gaining local support for the Coalition's presence.[190]

In July 2003, the CPA established the goals of increasing generating capacity to 4,000 MW by October 2003, to 5,000 MW by January 2004, to 7,000 MW by 2005, and to 14,000 MW by 2009.[191] That same month, the CPA made a more ambitious prediction: electricity supply would be back to prewar levels of 4,400 MW by October 2003.[192]

To reach these goals, USACE deployed Task Force Restore Iraqi Electricity, which used three contractors—Perini Corporation, Fluor International, and Washington Group—for numerous projects to repair electrical infrastructure across the country. Working under its IRRF 1 contract with USAID, Bechtel supported the push, assessing power facilities and making numerous repairs.

This collective effort achieved temporary success: on October 6, 2003, Iraq produced more than 4,500 MW of electricity. But the grid was fragile, and it could not hold the increase. Outputs quickly fell, with the promised level of 6,000 MW not sustainably reached until 2009.[193]

As part of a $174 million U.S.-funded project that began in August 2003, a 600-ton, 260 MW combustion turbine is delivered to a substation near Kirkuk in April 2005, after a trip through the Middle East that took more than a year. (USACE photo).

In November 2003, the CPA developed a list of 110 high-priority generation, transmission, and distribution projects. To support them, the Congress allocated $5.56 billion—30% of the entire IRRF 2 funding. Each of the three RIE contracting firms eventually won a $500 million IRRF 2 contract from Defense to help rebuild Iraq's electricity sector.[194] Separately, USAID awarded Bechtel another contract, valued at $1.8 billion and funded by the IRRF 2.[195]

In all, the U.S. government obligated more than $5.45 billion and expended more than $5.36 billion through September 2012 to increase electricity generation, transmission, and distribution, including the rehabilitation of power plants and transmission lines, the construction of new substations, and the training of Iraqis.[196] Almost 76% of the funding came from the IRRF 2. That share would have been higher but for a $1.3 billion reduction effected by reprogrammings that moved funds to meet security needs.[197]

The United States completed the last IRRF-funded electricity project in April 2011, involving the construction of a $29.1 million substation in Ramadi. Seven other electricity projects finished after that required $21.7 million in ESF funds.[198]

Table 5.2. Major U.S.-funded Electricity Projects
$ Millions

| Project Name | Province | Contractor Name | Contract Award Date | Completion Date | | Fund | U.S. Cost |
				Original	Actual		
Kirkuk Substation Combustion Turbines	Tameem	Bechtel National, Inc.	2/7/2003	10/31/2005	11/29/2005	IRRF 1	205.2
Baghdad South New Generation Ph II; Equipment	Baghdad	Bechtel National, Inc.	1/5/2004	10/1/2004	8/14/2006	IRRF 2	189.4
Qudas Gas Turbine Expansion	Baghdad	Uruk-Baghdad Joint Venture	8/31/2006	9/13/2007	5/4/2009	IRRF 2	169.5
Baghdad Distribution Substations	Baghdad	Bechtel National, Inc.	3/1/2004	6/15/2005	2/28/2006	IRRF 2	137.2
Buzurgan New Power Generation	Missan	Fluor/AMEC, LLC	3/25/2005	6/1/2006	6/15/2005	IRRF 2	125.1
Khor Az Zubair Power Generation	Basrah	Fluor/AMEC, LLC	9/14/2004	12/29/2005	1/6/2006	IRRF 2	110.9
Power Plant Maintenance Program	Various	Bechtel National, Inc.	3/4/2004	12/31/2004	3/22/2007	IRRF 2	92.7
Doura Power Plant Units 5 and 6	Baghdad	Bechtel National, Inc.	2/7/2003	4/30/2004	6/15/2005	IRRF 1	90.8
Mansuria Natural Gas Development for Power Generation	Various	Bechtel National, Inc.	6/23/2004	7/6/2005	1/31/2006	IRRF 2	62.7

The largest electricity sector undertakings rehabilitated and expanded power plants. In 2003, thermal plants provided most of Iraq's electricity. But U.S. investment focused on providing combustion-turbine facilities, which are both more technologically advanced than thermal plants and easier to construct.[199]

By the beginning of 2008, output from combustion-turbine units accounted for the largest share of the power supply.[200] Table 5.2 lists some of the largest U.S.-funded electricity projects.

In 2009, after the completion of most U.S.-funded electricity-generation projects, production from Iraq's government-run power plants averaged about 4,780 MW, 30% more than in 2004. Production at these plants grew by an additional 400 MW over the next three years, averaging roughly 5,175 MW during the first nine months of 2012.[201]

Cumulative supply on Iraq's grid in 2012, drawn from all sources, averaged about 8,400 MW, which was 3,225 MW higher than the total output from government power plants (see Figure 5.4).[202] Two-thirds of the increase from 2004 to 2012 came from these other sources:

- **Private power plants in the Kurdistan Region**—The Kurdistan Regional Government turned to independent power producers to build and operate power plants in the Region's three provinces. These facilities collectively produced 1,950 MW in the late summer of 2012, almost all of which the Region consumed. The GOI's Ministry of Electricity considered making similar arrangements, even soliciting bids from independent power producers, but it subsequently canceled the plan.[203]
- **Powerships in Basrah**—In 2010, the first of two floating "powerships" owned by a Turkish company docked in Basrah. By 2012, they produced an average of about 220

MW. (The two Basrah powerships and the Kurdish private power plants provided about one-fourth of the country's electricity in 2012).[204]

- **Imports**—In 2004, Iraq imported 136 MW of electricity. By 2012, imports increased to about 1,000 MW (12% of Iraq's total supply), almost all of which came from Iran.[205]

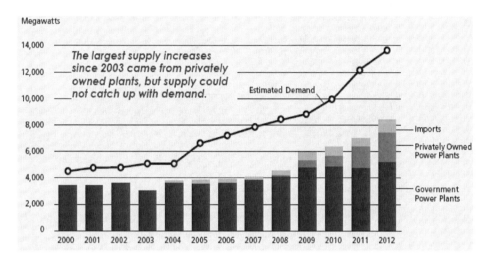

Figure 5.4. Average Electricity Supply on Grid vs. Estimated Demand, 2000–2012.

SIGIR PA-07-101 and PA-07-104
Shock and Audit: Inspecting an Electricity Plant

SIGIR assessed two large electricity projects in 2007. The projects planned to restore and expand generating capacity at the Qudas Power Plant in Baghdad. SIGIR inspections produced a number of "good news stories," and this was one, at least with regard to execution.

The two projects were adequately designed and properly completed or progressing satisfactorily.

The Qudas work was an important part of the rebuilding program's strategic commitment to improve Iraq's electricity production. It involved the installation or rehabilitation of combustion turbines. These units run best when fueled by natural gas, of which Iraq has enormous reserves.

The country's gas infrastructure in 2003 was vastly underdeveloped. Thus, there was no choice but to burn crude oil or low-grade fuel oil in the combustion turbines at the Qudas plant. But this reduced the generating units' capacity, increased downtime, and limited long-term productivity.

By late 2011, a solution appeared to be in the offing. The Ministry of Oil signed an agreement with Royal Dutch Shell to form a joint venture to capture and make productive use of natural gas from Iraq's southern fields.

This opened the door to more efficient power plants, assuming the Ministries of Oil and Electricity could learn to work well together.

The United States spent more than $250 million restoring the Qudas Power Plant under several different projects. (USACE photo).

Although the total supply of electricity more than doubled from 2004 through 2012, estimated demand increased at an even faster pace. The causes for this rocketing rise included a modernizing infrastructure, a post-sanctions flood of energy-consuming products, and the ineffective enforcement of electricity fees.[206]

The gap between supply and demand meant that Iraqis continued to endure power outages. Most households supplemented the public supply with power from "backyard" or neighborhood generators. According to a 2011 survey, the government-run grid provided households about 7.6 hours of electricity per day, with 9 out of 10 relying on off-grid generators to fill the gap. Respondents who used both public and private sources said they had an average of 14.6 hours of electricity per day. Almost 80% rated electricity service as "bad" or "very bad."[207] In June 2010, when temperatures exceeded 120 degrees Fahrenheit in southern Iraq, the shortages of electricity and potable water spurred violent protests, forcing the Minister of Electricity's resignation.[208]

Access to modern sewer facilities remains a problem for many Iraqi families.

As of September 2012, the GOI's Ministry of Electricity had 41 power plants under construction. These new plants could increase generating capacity to 22,000 MW by the end of 2015.

Assuming no delays, the International Energy Agency estimated that Iraq's grid-based electricity generation would catch up to peak demand by 2015.[209]

Water and Sanitation

In the early 1990s, Iraq had a well-developed water and sanitation sector: 95% of the urban population and 75% of the rural had access to potable water. Sewerage and wastewater coverage was high, particularly in urban areas, where 75% of the population had a sewer or septic tank connection. Public-health indicators were good, with minimal water- and sanitation-related diseases.[210]

But by 2003, this sector had experienced a devastating decline. Water distribution lines deteriorated from age, and the corroded system allowed contaminants in, causing a sharp rise in disease rates. The United Nations Children's Fund estimated that 25% of all children's deaths in Iraq in 2002 were caused by waterborne bacteria.[211]

In light of this grave public health crisis, the CPA requested $3.71 billion from the Congress to restore and expand Iraq's water and sanitation infrastructure.

In November 2003, the Congress exceeded that request, allocating $4.33 billion in IRRF 2 money for the water sector,[212] making it the second-highest infrastructure priority behind electricity.[213] The CPA's strategic plan outlined these water and sanitation sector goals:[214]

- Increase potable water access to 90% of Iraqis.
- Increase sewerage access to 15% of Iraqis.
- Reduce water distribution network losses from 60% to 40%.

SIGIR EV-10-002
Evaluating Water: Contracts in Contrast

The CPA's two largest water projects—among the very largest in the Iraq program—were the $277 million Nassiriya Water Treatment Plant in Thi-Qar province in southern Iraq and the $185 million Ifraz Water Treatment Plant near the Kurdistan Region's capital city, Erbil.

The Nassiriya plant aimed to serve 550,000 people in five surrounding cities, while the Ifraz would serve 600,000 in Erbil. In 2010, after the two projects were complete and under Iraqi control, SIGIR visited both to evaluate their effects.

SIGIR evaluators met with local and national Iraqi government officials and commissioned a public opinion poll to obtain the local Iraqis' views.

A remarkable contrast emerged. Both contracts were executed well, but the operations and maintenance of the Nassiriya plant was much worse than at Ifraz. The former plant had begun to suffer breakdowns shortly after its transfer to Iraqi control. But the Kurdish water authorities expanded Ifraz, which was perhaps the most successful of all large infrastructure projects accomplished in Iraq.

The Nassiriya plant produced water at 61% of capacity (a number that fell to 20% during frequent electricity shortages); 67% of the people serviced by the plant said they were dissatisfied with the service; and 95% were dissatisfied with the water quality.

The Ifraz plant functioned at nearly 100% of capacity; 88% of the people serviced by the plant were satisfied with water availability; and 85% were satisfied with the water quality.

The Department of State later determined these goals to be unrealistic because there was no baseline data on Iraq's water and sanitation infrastructure. Moreover, the country lacked a metering system to measure results.[215] State changed its water-sector metrics from the percentage of Iraqis with access to water and sanitation to the estimated number of Iraqi people who would benefit from water and sanitation projects. The new end-state goal was to provide an additional 8.4 million people with access to potable water and an additional 5.3 million with access to sewerage services.[216] The water sector's plans suffered a severe setback because of funding reductions implemented in the 2004–2005 reprogrammings. By mid-2005, the IRRF 2 allocation to the sector was half the original number ($2.15 billion, down from $4.33 billion).[217] The U.S. government now planned to use $1.5 billion to fund projects to increase potable water access, while using the remainder to build sewerage systems, improve irrigation, and repair the 149-mile Sweetwater Canal.[218] Between February 2003 and September 2012, the U.S. government obligated $2.78 billion and expended $2.71 billion to rehabilitate and improve Iraq's water and sanitation sector. More than 60% of the obligations supported projects to produce and distribute potable water.[219] The IRRF funded three-quarters of the projects. The emphasis on large infrastructure at the beginning of the program resulted in the obligation of 90% of the funding by September 2006.[220] Water projects included some of the costliest U.S.-funded reconstruction efforts in the entire program, including the Nassiriya and Ifraz Water Treatment Plants and the Falluja Waste Water Treatment System, with a combined U.S. cost of $545 million.[221] See Table 5.3 for a list of major U.S.-funded water and sanitation projects.

SIGIR PA-07-105
Danger and Waste at the Mosul Dam

The Mosul Dam, completed in 1984, lies on the Tigris River in northern Iraq. The soils beneath the dam are subject to erosion. Their movement created potentially threatening cavities beneath the dam's structural support. Reports in the Iraqi press said the deficiencies at the dam presented a potential danger. Since the 1980s, the Iraqi Ministry of Water Resources implemented remediation measures at the dam, including a continuous grouting program to fill sub-surface cavities. In 2005, the U.S. government partnered with the GOI to initiate improvements, executing 21 contracts worth a combined $27 million to mitigate the dam's deficiencies. SIGIR inspectors visited the dam in 2007, finding that the project was poorly designed and inadequately executed. Equally troubling, the team found no dedicated monitor for the project. The inspection concluded that approximately $19.4 million worth of equipment and materials for implementing improvements to the grouting operations was not being used. To its credit, the U.S. Mission responded quickly by following up on these problems, adding new investment and oversight to help remedy the issues SIGIR uncovered.

Table 5.3. Major U.S.-funded Water and Sanitation Projects
$ Millions

Project Name	Province	Contractor Name	Contract Award Date	Completion Date		Fund	U.S. Cost
				Original	Actual		
Nassiriya Water Supply	Thi-Qar	Fluor/AMEC, LLC	4/21/2004	12/13/2007	9/11/2007	IRRF 2	259.9
Erbil - Ifraz Water Project	Erbil	Fluor/AMEC, LLC	4/21/2004	10/1/2005	7/20/2006	IRRF 2	185.3
Falluja Waste Water Treatment Plant	Anbar	Fluor/AMEC, LLC; Various	6/26/2004	1/1/2006	5/2/2011	IRRF 2, ESF, CERP	99.8
Nassiriya Drainage Pump Station	Thi-Qar	Washington International Black & Veatch	11/14/2004	12/31/2006	2/28/2007	IRRF 2	73.9
Sadr City R3 Water Treatment Plant	Baghdad	Bechtel, Washington International, Inc./ Black & Veatch	1/5/2004	10/31/2005	12/31/2008	IRRF 2	65.8
Rural Water Supply Project Implementation	Multiple	Bechtel National, Inc.	6/13/2004	11/1/2005	9/15/2006	IRRF 2	62.0
Basrah Sewer Project	Basrah	Fluor/AMEC, LLC	6/15/2004	4/7/2006	10/30/2006	IRRF 2	50.5
Balad Rooz Water Treatment Plant	Diyala	Fluor/AMEC, LLC	4/30/2004	10/1/2005	5/31/2006	IRRF 2	40.0
Eastern Euphrates Drain	Muthanna	Ministry of Water Resources	8/29/2006	1/29/2009	12/31/2010	IRRF 2	38.4

SIGIR Audit 12-007, PA-08-144 to 148

Fallujah Waste Water Treatment System: A Case Study in Wartime Contracting

U.S.-completed Components:
U.S.-funded Expandable "Backbone" System to be completed at a cost of **$108 million***

- Wastewater Treatment Plant (WWTP)
- 3 pump stations
- 4 trunk lines
- 9,116 house connections

*Includes $8.0 million in DFI funding.

GOI Components:
Portion of the original project completed by the GOI for approximately **$87 million**

- 3 pump stations
- 3 trunk lines
- 25,259 house connections

U.S.-funded sewer networks and 9,116 house connections for 3 collection areas

GOI-funded sewer networks and 25,259 house connections for 5 collection areas

Highway 10 was the only road from Baghdad to the job site. Contractors traversed a gauntlet of sniper-fire positions and roadblocks through terrorist strongholds. At the height of insurgent activity, the U.S. military required all dump trucks to be emptied and reloaded at checkpoints to search for IEDs.

Opened in May 2011, the WWTP ran initially on generator power but is now connected to the Anbar essential services electrical line, which provides 20 hours of power per day. State awarded a $1 million operations and maintenance grant in September to train plant operators on the use of purification chemicals.

	2004 Initial estimate	2011 Snapshot	% Change from 2004	2014 Estimated Completion	% Change from 2004
Cost	$35 M	$108 M	209%	$195 M	457%
Months to Completion	18	86	389%	114	533%
Residents Served	100,000 (estimated)	38,400 (50,390 target)	62%	220,000 (estimated)	120%
Contracts/Grants	1	42	4,200%	42+ GOI	>4,200%

Before: Sewage in the streets in 2004

After: Completed WWTP in 2011

The Fallujah Waste Water Treatment System was meant to rid Fallujah's city streets of raw sewage, alleviate contamination of potable water sources, and reduce instances of illness and death linked to poor sanitation. The project was undertaken in 2004 when the city was wracked with violence. Limited planning, a minimal understanding of site conditions, an unskilled workforce, and no clear idea about how much the system would cost burdened the project. Violence became so prevalent that trenches and pipes laid by U.S. contractors were regularly blown up. Several times, the U.S. military had to stop construction until security conditions improved.

Other adversities include:
- On-site progress assessment is could not be performed.
- The original task order required Fluor/AMEC to complete the system in 18 months, but because of security delays, construction did not begin until early 2005.
- The shift of $2.2 billion out of the water sector occurred just as more money was needed for the project.
- The choice of a more complicated plan: design and the lack of reliable power from the grid caused delays and increased costs.
- The mid-2005 shift from large design-build contracts to smaller contracts carried out by Iraqi contractors caused delays.

In March 2010, the State Department reported it had achieved its 2006 water and sanitation targets, saying that U.S.-funded water projects generated almost a quarter of the potable water produced in Iraq each day, servicing 8.7 million people; U.S.-funded sanitation projects processed 1.2 million cubic meters of wastewater per day, servicing 5.3 million people.[222] But State pointed out that the lack of water metering in Iraq made it difficult to assess how much water was reaching the intended users.[223] After the United States turned over the large water projects to Iraqi control, reconstruction officials discovered that, in many cases, the Iraqis were not operating these projects properly. Shortfalls included equipment theft, badly trained staff, poor operations and maintenance practices, and inadequate supplies of electricity and treatment chemicals.[224] In response, the U.S. government set aside $116 million in ESF funding in 2006 to create a program to "assist the Iraqi people in the proper operation and maintenance of 40-plus selected U.S.- government-supported water and wastewater facilities." This Water Sector Supply Program provided facility assessments, technical assistance, spare parts, and repair services.[225] In March 2011, the United Nations reported that, while Iraq had the second-highest amount of available water per capita in the Middle East, its water quality was poor, violating Iraq National Standards and World Health Organization guidelines.[226] In a separate survey conducted that same year, about two-thirds of the households said they relied on the public water supply as their main source for drinking water, with a quarter of them noting that they had access to potable water less than two hours per day and just 38% rating drinking water as "good" or "very good."[227]

Oil and Gas

Iraq has the world's third-largest proven reserves of crude oil, estimated in 2010 at just over 143 billion barrels.[228] Recent discoveries indicate that the number may be much higher. Iraq's ability to extract these reserves varied significantly over time (see Figure 5.5). After peaking at 3.5 million barrels per day in 1979, the country's crude oil production plummeted to 1.0 MBPD in 1981, rebounded to 2.9 MBPD in 1989, but then hit a low of 0.3 MBPD in 1991 following the 1991 Gulf War. Lingering damage from that conflict along with international sanctions kept oil production low through 1996. Output recovered thereafter, though erratically. During the two-month period before the March 2003 invasion, oil production jumped to just over 2.5 MBPD.[229] Iraq's extraordinary petroleum riches led to the pre-war presumption that revenues from their sale would finance the country's reconstruction. To ensure this, U.S. planners deemed a rapid post-invasion restoration of the oil sector as critical to achieving the Coalition's strategic goals.[230]

SIGIR SA-05-001 Al-Fatah Pipe Dream

During the 2003 invasion, Coalition forces bombed al-Fatah Bridge in north-central Iraq, severing the 15 oil and gas pipelines it carried across the Tigris River. This damage cut off oil flows to the Bajii refinery, Iraq's largest. Repairing the pipelines was crucial to the recovery of Iraq's oil sector.

Originally estimated at $5 million, the al-Fatah project planned to repair the bridge and the pipelines.

> But the CPA and the Ministry of Oil decided instead to use horizontal directional drilling to re-route the pipelines under the river, which increased the estimated project costs to $28 million.
>
>
>
> Coalition bombing damaged al-Fatah Bridge in 2003.
>
> An initial study of the geological conditions beneath the river produced a recommendation against drilling because of the sandy soil. But horizontal drilling work pressed ahead anyway, with tens of millions of dollars wasted on churning sand, as attempt after attempt to drill failed to make headway. The $75.7 million in DFI funds allocated to the project was spent accomplishing just 28% of the project's scope. Ultimately, the drilling plan was abandoned, with the bridge and its pipelines repaired under a new $29.7 million IRRF-funded contract that the U.S. government awarded to Parsons Iraq Joint Venture. Because of the nature of the original contract, the government was unable to recover any of the money wasted on this project.

In February 2003, the Department of the Army developed a program to restore Iraq's oil infrastructure so that it could reach pre-war production and export levels: 2.5 MBPD and 2.1 MBPD, respectively.[231] On March 8, 2003, USACE awarded Kellogg Brown & Root a non-competitive contract with a $7 billion ceiling to restore and operate Iraq's oil infrastructure. It was the largest reconstruction contract for Iraq's rebuilding and the largest known sole-source contract in U.S. history.[232] After the invasion, USACE surveyed Iraq's oil infrastructure, estimating that combat operations and the looting that followed caused $1.4 billion in damage: $457 million from military action and $943 million from post-war depredations. Moreover, years of neglect during the Saddam era had left major pieces of the infrastructure in need of urgent maintenance. Repairing the oil system to a level that could support the CPA's production and export goals would require at least $1.7 billion.[233]

In July 2003, the Iraqi Ministry of Oil and the CPA initiated a plan that anticipated executing 226 projects costing $1.14 billion. Task Force Restore Iraqi Oil worked to restore the damaged oil infrastructure and revive Iraq's oil production and export capacity.[234]

The task force's efforts helped the CPA meet initial production goals by September 2003. But by mid-2004, production and export levels dropped to below pre-war levels, due to a combination of focused insurgent attacks on oil pipelines, failing infrastructure, and a general deterioration of the security situation. Between December 2004 and May 2005, production flat-lined at about 2.1 MBPD, with exports hovering between 1.4 MBPD and 1.6 MBPD.

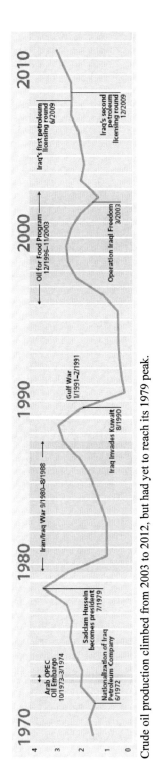

Crude oil production climbed from 2003 to 2012, but had yet to reach its 1979 peak.

Figure 5.5. Crude Oil Production, 1970–2012; Million Barrels per Day.

These declines occurred notwithstanding that through June 2005 the U.S. government had obligated nearly $1.2 billion to restore and sustain Iraq's crude oil production and export levels.[235]

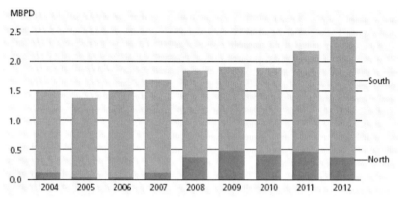

Since 2004, most crude oil exports came from the large southern fields.

Figure 5.6. Crude Oil Exports, North vs. South, 2004–2012.

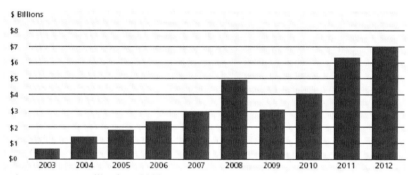

Oil receipts have grown steadily since 2009.

Figure 5.7. Oil Receipts, Monthly Average by Year, 2003–2012.

Between 2003 and 2007, more than 400 attacks hit Iraq's pipelines, refineries, and workers. Corruption troubled the oil sector as well, including the smuggling or diversion of refined products, which contributed to decreased exports.[236] In early 2007, Iraq suffered a post-2003 production low, but levels began to rise later that year, as the Coalition strategy to repress attacks on oil facilities took effect. By July 2007, output stood at 2.1 MBPD. Exports resumed growth too, reaching 1.98 MBPD by November 2007.[237] The Infrastructure Security Program's Pipeline Exclusion Zone, a project designed to secure pipeline corridors, helped reduce attacks. It protected the crucial pipelines linking Iraq's northern oil fields to the Turkish port at Ceyhan.[238] The U.S. government obligated and expended $1.76 billion for projects to restore, build, and protect facilities in Iraq's oil and gas sector and to provide technical training for Ministry of Oil employees. All of the U.S. funding came from the IRRF, with the majority of obligations occurring during the first two years of the reconstruction program.[239] See Table 5.4 for a list of major U.S.-funded projects. By late 2012, Iraq's oil exports topped 2.62 MBPD, a rise of nearly 45% from early 2009, and averaged about 2.42 MBPD for the year (see Figure 5.6).[240] The rise in exports, coupled with oil price increases, generated large increases in Iraq's national income, with oil receipts more than doubling from 2009 to 2012 (see Figure 5.7).[241]

Table 5.4. Major U.S.-funded Oil and Gas Projects
$ Millions

| Project Name | Province | Contractor Name | Contract Award Date | Completion Date | | Fund | U.S. Cost |
				Original	Actual		
Restore Natural Gas Liquid and Liquefied Petroleum Gas Plants	Basrah	Kellogg Brown and Root	5/2/2004	12/31/2005	5/29/2007	IRRF 1	146.7
Well Logging	Basrah	Parsons Iraq Joint Venture	10/27/2005	6/1/2006	9/25/2006	IRRF 2	88.1
Restore Gas and Oil Separation Plants	Basrah	Kellogg Brown and Root	5/2/2004	4/1/2006	12/31/2006	IRRF 1	84.5
Project West Qurna 8	Basrah	Kellogg Brown and Root	5/2/2004	NA	NA	IRRF 1	82.3
Al Fatah and Kirkuk Pipeline Crossings	Tameem	Parsons Iraq Joint Venture	11/19/2004	NA	4/1/2006	IRRF 2	65.7
Al-Basrah Oil Terminal	Basrah	Parsons Iraq Joint Venture	3/11/2005	12/31/2006	7/27/2007	IRRF 2	64.0
Qarmat Ali Pressure Maintenance and Pipeline Replacement	Basrah	Parsons Iraq Joint Venture	4/7/2005	1/1/2006	NA	IRRF 2	31.2

In 2009, the Ministry of Oil launched the first of four bidding rounds for rights to develop the country's petroleum reserves, which the ministry had revised upward from 115 billion to 143 billion barrels in late 2010. By the completion of the fourth round in mid-2012, the GOI had entered into contracts with international oil companies for the development of 17 fields: 13 for crude oil development and 4 for natural gas.[242]

Despite gains in production and exports, an array of problems still burdened Iraq's oil and gas sector. For example, pipeline bottlenecks limited export volume, and the new single-point mooring systems supporting off-shore exports sometimes operated at just 50% of capacity. At the end of 2012, Iraq needed more pipelines and storage facilities to realize its vast potential.[243] Tensions between the GOI in Baghdad and leaders of the Kurdistan Regional Government also limited oil exports, with KRG leaders reducing the flow of the Region's oil into the northern pipeline to Ceyhan in 2012 because of disputes over reimbursement payments from Baghdad. These tensions dimmed prospects for parliamentary agreement on

Transportation and Communications

During the 1970s and 1980s, the Iraqi government invested heavily in the country's transportation infrastructure. Iraq had two international and three domestic airports, six cargo ports, more than 40,000 kilometers of roads, and almost 2,500 kilometers of rail lines. The 1991 Gulf War damaged much of this infrastructure. Saddam's neglect, international sanctions, the 2003 invasion, and post-war looting further devastated the system.[245]

United Nations sanctions prevented Iraqi Airways from resuming commercial airline service between 1991 and 2000. Iraq had only minimal aviation capacity up to 2003. When the Coalition invaded, no Iraqi airport could support commercial air operations because the country lacked avionics support systems.[246] Iraq's ports also suffered. Submerged wreckage and poor dredging made the import and export of goods by sea very challenging.[247]

The country's communications systems were equally debilitated after 1990. By 2003, Iraq had just 833,000 landline connections and 80,000 mobile phone subscribers, supporting a population of 27 million. The invasion aggravated matters, destroying 12 of Baghdad's 38 telephone exchanges along with all of Iraq's international switching and satellite-earth stations. Post-war looting inflicted further damage, causing telephone access to become virtually nonexistent.[248] The United Nations and the World Bank estimated in 2003 that the transportation and communications sector required $3.38 billion of investment.[249] The CPA planned to rehabilitate and restore strategic transportation and telecommunications sectors to pre-war levels and introduce advanced technologies. Specifically, it called for re-opening Iraqi airspace and airports, repairing the broken telephone networks, and developing new mobile phone services.[250] As of September 2012, the U.S. government had obligated $1.31 billion and expended $1.25 billion on projects to repair and improve Iraq's transportation and communication capabilities. Almost 70% of the funds came from the two IRRF appropriations. More than one-half of the obligations occurred by July 2005 and more than 90% by September 2007. No new obligations occurred after July 2011.[251] Table 5.5 lists major projects in the transportation and telecommunications sector.

Table 5.5. Major U.S.-funded Transportation and Communications Projects
$ Millions

| Project Name | Province | Contractor Name | Contract Award Date | Completion Date | | Fund | U.S. Cost |
				Original	Actual		
Advanced First Responder Network	Multiple	Lucent Technologies, Inc.	9/26/2004	6/30/2005	1/15/2006	IRRF 1 & 2, ISFF	198.0
Digital Microwave Radio Communications Network	Multiple	Volpe Center, Mafeks International, LLC	2/20/2006	9/2009	9/2011	IRRF 2, ESF	48.0

Project Name	Province	Contractor Name	Contract Award Date	Completion Date Original	Completion Date Actual	Fund	U.S. Cost
Consolidated Fiber Network	Multiple	Bechtel National, Inc.	1/5/2004	3/31/2006	6/30/2006	IRRF 2	47.0
Al-Mamoon Exchange and Communications Center	Baghdad	Alfa Consult, The Kufan Group	7/31/2005	2/13/2007	6/30/2011	IRRF 2	32.4
Telecom Subscriber Service	Multiple	Bechtel National, Inc.	2/7/2003	3/13/2004	3/13/2004	IRRF 1	32.3
Airport Administration	Multiple	Skylink Air and Logistical Support	3/21/2003	1/31/2005	1/31/2005	IRRF 2	27.2
Communications Based Train Control System	Multiple	Volpe Center, Mafeks International, LLC	3/31/2005	9/30/2010	3/2011	IRRF 2	17.3
Umm Qasr Dredging Phase 2	Basrah	Bechtel National, Inc.	2/7/2003	10/31/2005	10/22/2003	IRRF 1	15.9
New Radar for Basrah International Airport	Basrah	CDM/CAPE	9/27/2006	11/30/2008	2/1/2009	IRRF 2	15.0

Approximately $350 million in CERP funds were spent on transportation projects, mostly for road construction.

SIGIR PA-06-057
Baghdad Railway Station: A Train Station on Time

The Baghdad Railway Station, the center for all rail service in Iraq, contains the offices for the Ministry of Transportation and the Iraq Republic Railway. Iraq monitors, controls, and coordinates all national train movements from this station. According to a 2004 estimate by the Iraq Reconstruction Management Office, Iraq's economy was losing $17.5 million per week because of the country's inability to transport goods by rail.

> The U.S. government spent $6 million to renovate the Baghdad Railway Station. The project worked.
>
> A SIGIR Inspection team visited the station in May 2006, concluding that the project's results were consistent with the contract's objectives. The Iraq Republic Railway now had work spaces that offered a much safer and healthier environment for its employees and visitors, and the station's structures and utility systems had been modernized to sufficiently support the railway's services and operations.
>
>
>
> The United States spent $6 million modernizing the Baghdad Railway Station. (USACE photo).

Transportation

More than $853 million (65%) of the major U.S. reconstruction funds obligated in this sector supported transportation projects to rehabilitate and improve Iraq's railways, roads, airports, and ports. The five largest transportation projects, all funded with the IRRF and costing $94 million, improved Iraq's airport operations and railway communications, and reopened the Port of Umm Qasr.[252] The U.S. government used CERP funding for thousands of transportation-related projects, including several multimillion-dollar undertakings, such as the $5.4 million effort to provide solar street lighting for the city of Falluja and $4.2 million project to construct the Baghdad International Airport Caravan Hotel.[253]

Civil Aviation

In August 2003, Iraq's airspace re-opened. But, by October 2003, Iraq's two international airports were only handling Coalition and non-commercial charter flights. Early U.S. government-funded aviation projects focused on rehabilitating runways and terminals, providing power generation, and improving avionics and radars. In August 2004, Iraqi Airways flights between Amman, Jordan, and Baghdad began.[254]

By January 2012, all of Iraq's civil aviation assets, including six airports and six aviation towers previously operated by the U.S. government, were under GOI control.[255] More than 20 airlines provided service to Iraq throughout 2012. Of note, in April of that year, the Iraq Civil Aviation Authority announced the resumption of commercial air service between Iraq and Kuwait for the first time since 1990.[256]

A retired Federal Aviation Administration controller contracted by the ICAA advises an Iraqi air traffic controller at Baghdad International Airport. (U.S. Air Force photo).

Railroads

The U.S. government spent about $200 million to provide railroad equipment and rehabilitate more than 200 railway stations across Iraq.[257] In 2009, efforts to improve Iraq's railway system resulted in the first successful rail trip from the western Syrian seaport of Tartous to Umm Qasr port via Baghdad.[258]

The most significant work in this sector entailed two major undertakings, the $17.3 million Communications-Based Train Control and the $48 million Digital Microwave Radio Communications Network, which together significantly upgraded Iraq's antiquated system of dispatching, controlling, and tracking trains. Both projects were completed in 2011, providing the country with a state-of-the-art train control system allowing dispatchers to manage rail movements across the country via data and voice methods.[259]

Roads and Bridges

Reconstruction managers obligated nearly 40% of all transportation funding to improve Iraq's systems of roads and bridges. The CERP and the IRRF supported more than 1,500 projects to repair and repave village roads and bridges throughout Iraq. While there were several multimillion-dollar projects, the vast majority of the individual transportation projects were relatively inexpensive (less than $200,000).[260]

Ports

The United States obligated more than $130 million on projects to dredge and upgrade the Port of Umm Qasr, Iraq's only deepwater port. Three of the projects, valued at more than $43 million, removed more than one million cubic meters of silt and debris from the port, opening Umm Qasr for regular commercial traffic.[261]

Communications

The United States obligated more than $350 million on projects to rehabilitate and upgrade Iraq's communications networks.[262] The three largest projects consumed the majority of this funding.

- The **Advanced First Responder Network** improved public safety by increasing the communications capabilities between the Ministry of Interior's first responders and Iraqi citizens. The project provided infrastructure and equipment, including more than 30,000 first-responder radios. By the time the Iraqis took control of the system in June 2006, the U.S. government had expended $198 million on it.[263]
- USAID managed the $47.0 million project to build a **Consolidated Fiber Network**, which improved Iraq's voice transmission network. The project, completed in June 2006, employed 1,000 Iraqis. However, a USAID audit found insufficient documentation to verify that the project met the end-user and employment goals.[264]
- The $32.4 million **al-Mamoon Exchange and Communications Center** was designed to serve as the telecommunications hub for the Ministry of Communications. The seven-story office building included state-of-the-art equipment to improve radio transmissions, cellular and landline telephone communications, and high-speed Internet service in Baghdad. Originally awarded in 2006, this project encountered contracting problems and sabotage during construction, delaying its completion until June 2011 and increasing its originally planned cost by more than 60%.[265]

The $18.3 million al-Mamoon Exchange and Communications Center in Baghdad was turned over to the GOI on June 30, 2011, almost five years after its originally forecasted completion date. (USACE photo).

Of the more than 300 CERP-funded communications projects, the five most expensive collectively cost $6.9 million. These projects rehabilitated Baghdad International Airport's communications building, constructed radio towers, and provided satellite service for mobile phones.[266]

By November 2004, the number of landline customers served in Iraq exceeded the pre-war level of 833,000, and, by the following month, the number of mobile phone subscribers surpassed landline customers.[267] As of mid-2005, nearly 1 million new landlines had been installed and more than 2.4 million new mobile telephone subscriptions initiated.[268] By mid-2011, Iraq's mobile phone users topped 23 million (see Figure 5.8).[269] Despite these improvements, Iraq's telecommunications sector remained one of the least developed in the Middle East.[270]

SIGIR Audit 07-002
Responding to First Responders: Emergency Action Leads to Success

In March 2004, USACE awarded a contract for an Advanced First Responder Network. By the time this $214 million project was completed, in May 2006, the government had spent $192 million in U.S. funds.

SIGIR audited the AFRN project in July 2006, identifying significant deficiencies: the project failed to produce a reliable nationwide first-responder communication system, and the network's command and control system did not provide an effective means for dispatching and directing first responders. A follow-up audit in April 2007 found that the contractor had remedied the deficiencies. The operational effectiveness of the AFRN system had greatly improved, as demonstrated by its increasing use by Iraqi citizens.

There was more wrong with the AFRN project than just poor performance. On September 21, 2012, the Department of Justice announced that, as a result of a whistleblower suit, the contractor had agreed to pay the United States $4.2 million to settle False Claims Act allegations alleging that, between January and July 2005, it had submitted misleading testing certifications to the Army in connection with the design, construction, and modernization of the AFRN.

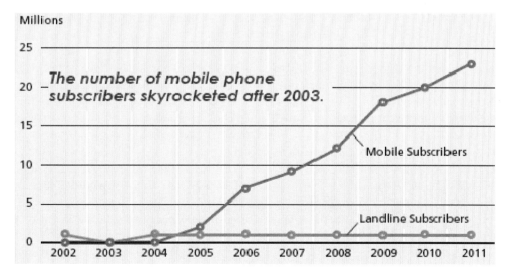

Figure 5.8. Landline and Mobile Phone Subscribers, 2002–2011.

Security and Rule of Law

The CPA designated security as a core area of emphasis. It listed the following priorities as necessary for progress:[271]

- developing and training Iraq's security forces
- developing national security and civilian oversight mechanisms
- ensuring border security
- building the justice system and improving the penal system
- ensuring that Iraq is free of weapons of mass destruction

As the security situation worsened in 2003, the United States allocated an initial $3.24 billion from the IRRF 2 for "security and law enforcement" and an additional $1.32 billion for justice and related programs.[272] Because of contracting delays, the CPA could not access these IRRF 2 funds until the late spring of 2004, after Iraq's meager security forces had failed in their first major venture into the field.[273]

The security challenges associated with post-war rehabilitation went far beyond the wave of looting that immediately followed Saddam's fall. They were seeded by long-standing sectarian and ethnic differences, the democratic ascent of Iraq's majority Shia population, and a Sunni-fomented insurgency. Sunni-Shia divisions erupted into violence after the 2003 invasion, gravely complicating the rebuilding of Iraq's security apparatus and impeding implementation of the rule of law.[274]

Aggravating matters, the Arab-Kurd ethnic divide widened over the course of the program, as the three northern Kurdish provinces formed a semiautonomous regional government, maintained independent security forces, and pursued an expansive agenda regarding claims over hydrocarbon resources and territory. See Figure 5.9 for the boundaries still in dispute between the Government of Iraq and the Kurdistan Regional Government.[275]

Over the first half of 2004, Iraq destabilized by the week, with security incidents averaging 75 per day.[276] When sovereignty transferred to the Interim Iraqi Government in June 2004, Iraq was far from secure. Moreover, just 6% of its police forces had adequate training, and the Army was weak. Rising violence threatened the state.[277] The U.S. government responded by establishing the Multi-National Security Transition Command-Iraq and reprogramming roughly $3 billion in IRRF 2 allocations from the water, electricity, and other large infrastructure sectors to increase funding for security, ruleof-law, and related programs.[278]

In May 2005, the Congress appropriated an initial tranche of $5.39 billion to the new Iraq Security Forces Fund for MNSTC-I's use. The ISFF bolstered the training and equipping of Iraq's Ministry of Defense and Interior forces.[279] Creating the new fund was crucial because, from mid-2004 through mid-2005, lethal security incidents became commonplace, averaging more than 90 per day.[280] They continued to rise through 2006, peaking in 2007 at 185 per day (see Figure 5.9).

The task of establishing Iraqi forces capable of providing internal security and protecting the country faced extraordinary challenges in 2006 and early 2007, when Iraq slipped into a state of virtual civil war (see Figure 5.9).

The United States provided funding and other support to help the Ministries of Finance and Foreign Affairs recover from the devastating bombings of their buildings on August 19, 2009. (ATF photo).

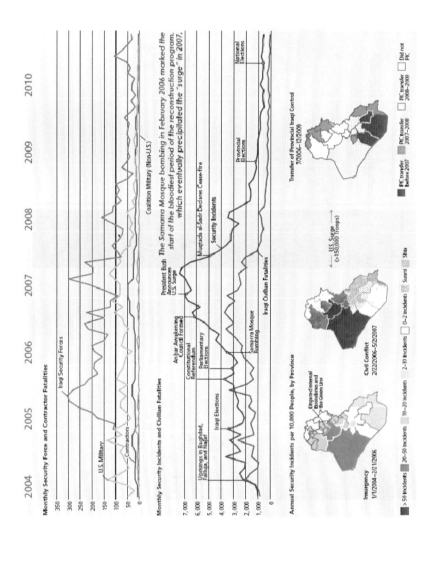

Figure 5.9. Security Incidents, Fatalities, and Transfer of Security Control in Iraq, 1/2004–12/2010.

In response, U.S. investment in the sector massively increased, helping security program managers develop an ISF that could support the U.S. counterinsurgency strategy in 2007 (see Figure 5.10). The "surge" of more than 25,000 U.S. troops into the country complemented increases in the pace of ISF training, a renewed tactical rebuilding emphasis, and the creation of the Sons of Iraq program. Funded with Commander's Emergency Response Program money, the SOI effort paid for 100,000 mostly Sunni men to work with the Coalition rather than fight it. While investments in the SOI and in Iraq's military and police forces paid off, support for anticorruption and other rule-of-law efforts—so crucial to the long-term stabilization of Iraq—proved less robust and thus less successful.[281]

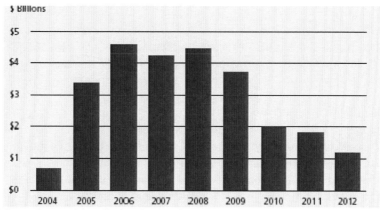

The United States invested heavily in ISF development during 2005–2008 to enable Iraq to assume security control in 2009.

Figure 5.10. Security and Rule of Law: Expenditures, by Year, 2004–2012.

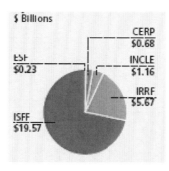

Figure 5.11. Security and Rule of Law: Cumulative Obligations, by Fund, as of 9/30/2012.

By early 2008, levels of violence had significantly diminished.[282] The improved security stemmed from several factors, including the surge in troops, the deployment of competent ISF personnel, the success of the SOI program,[283] and an August 2007 cease-fire declared by Muqtada al-Sadr, who controlled the violent Mahdi Army, a Shia militia .[284] These improvements permitted U.S. military authorities to resume the transfer of regional security responsibilities to Iraqi control.[285]

Despite substantial surge-driven salutary developments in the security sector, Iraq was still a dangerous place in early 2009.[286] Thus, the ISF continued to receive substantial training and equipping from the United States over the next four years. This investment paid off. By 2012, the number of daily security incidents amounted to a tiny fraction of 2007 levels. But targeted attacks on security personnel, assassinations of government and tribal leaders, and occasional mass-casualty bombings continued to inflict terror.[287]

The ethnic divide between Kurdish and Arab populations worsened in 2011 and 2012 as the KRG pressed claims to exploit hydrocarbon resources in disputed areas. In Kirkuk, the Kurds looked ready to fight in the spring of 2011, deploying *Peshmerga* militia to advance its claims. Baghdad pushed back, sending armed troops to the city; but, with U.S. intervention, conflict was averted.[288]

Establishing a secure and safe environment in Iraq and enforcing the rule of law proved to be daunting, lengthy, and expensive tasks, consuming about half of the funds the United States poured into the reconstruction effort. From 2003 to 2012, the United States obligated $27.30 billion and expended $26.16 billion in this reconstruction area. Almost 72% of all obligations came from the ISFF (see Figure 5.11).[289]

The United States obligated almost 80% of security and rule-of-law funding by January 2009 (see Figure 5.12). Nearly 70% of these funds had been expended by that time, averaging $3.48 billion per year. The money chiefly went to rebuild security infrastructure, train and equip the ISF, and field them in the counterinsurgency fight. After 2008, U.S. expenditures fell to an average of $2.20 billion per year, with spending focused on large equipment purchases, specialized training programs, and sustainment initiatives designed to support the maturing ISF.[290]

Almost 93% of all U.S. outlays for security and rule-of-law programs went to rebuilding the Iraq's military and police forces, border guards, and facilities protections units. The remaining $1.83 billion went to justice and corrections programs to rebuild Iraq's courts and prisons and to provide infrastructure security (see Figure 5.13).[291]

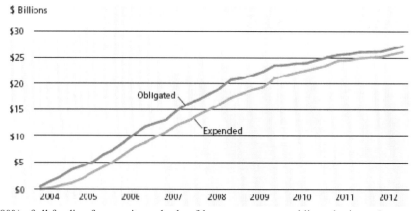

Almost 80% of all funding for security and rule-of-law programs was obligated prior to January 2009.

Figure 5.12. Security and Rule of Law: Cumulative Obligations and Expenditures, FY 2004–FY 2012.

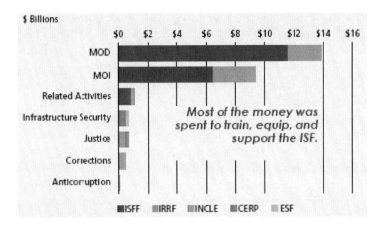

Figure 5.13. Security and Rule of Law: Expenditures, by Sector, FY 2004–FY 2012.

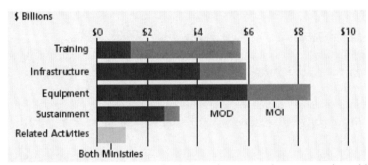

More than one-third of ISF expenditures funded equipment and transportation, with most of it supporting the MOD.

Figure 5.14. Expenditures To Rebuild the ISF, by Subactivity, FY 2004–FY 2012.

Rebuilding the ISF

As of September 2012, the United States had obligated $25.26 billion and expended $24.33 billion on training, equipping, and sustaining the ISF and providing infrastructure for the MOD and MOI. More than 57% of those expenditures went to MOD activities, while the MOI received 38%. Expenditures on "related activities," benefiting both the MOD and MOI, accounted for just over 4%. More than one-third of the expenditures funded equipment and transportation for the ISF, while 24% was spent on infrastructure, 23% on training, and 13% on sustainment activities (see Figure 5.14).[292]

After disbanding the Iraqi Army in 2003, the CPA sought to establish modest police forces using Iraqi funding from the Development Fund for Iraq and limited U.S. funding from IRRF 1.[293] It authorized new programs like the CERP and Commander's Humanitarian Relief and Reconstruction Program to help U.S. commanders respond to the urgent humanitarian relief and reconstruction requirements of local populations.[294]

The Iraqi military and police forces expanded rapidly from 2004 to 2006, adapting to the counterinsurgency mission. Their training accounted for more than 40% of U.S.-funded security expenditures during this period. Importantly, these programs supported ISF counterinsurgency training, with graduates moving out to field operations under the control of the Multi-National Corps-Iraq.[295]

Parts of the growing force structure constituted a conflation of previously autonomous militias, many of them sectarian-based and sometimes attendant to an immediate commander's interests rather than the security institution itself.[296] These strains became most prevalent within the MOI. Tribal and community leaders frequently vetted police recruits, a process rife with politicization and patronage.[297] On the other hand, the Multi-National Security Transition Command-Iraq effectively oversaw the recruiting of trainees for the Iraqi Army, creating a diverse force not tied to a particular area, sect, ethnicity, or tribal group.[298]

Equipment became a priority from mid-2006 through the end of 2007 as the tempo of counterinsurgency operations increased. The United States spent $2.03 billion on equipment during this span, amounting to about one-fourth of the equipment purchases made throughout the entire program. But meeting the ISF's requirements became problematic when loose accountability undercut equipment provision.[299] Moreover, the GOI commonly reported that it did not have enough of the necessary equipment to manage Iraq's challenging security environment.[300]

As the "surge" ramped up in 2007, the ISF began to meet broad Coalition targets on training and equipping,[301] with many IA units becoming capable of operating independently and controlling their own areas of responsibility.[302] ISF force strength grew through aggressive recruiting, including an initiative by the Prime Minister to overfill counterinsurgency units and increase the number of IA battalions.[303]

The ISF reportedly had a trained and equipped strength of more than 560,000 in December 2008, as transition of security authority to the GOI approached (see Figure 5.15). The Defense Department reported that 175 (of 179) MOD battalions were "conducting operations," as were 57 of 64 National Police units assessed.[304] But all were still dependent on the Coalition for intelligence, logistics, and sustainment.[305]

The security sector program managers emphasized infrastructure spending as well, which totaled almost $5.9 billion. Most of the spending ($4.2 billion) occurred during 2004–2008, when bases, forts, police stations, and training facilities were built or rehabilitated to support the expanding ISF. Building up the security infrastructure became haphazard during violent periods, which inevitably slowed completion rates.[306]

After 2009, the U.S. government focused expenditures on equipping, training, and sustaining the MOD as it transitioned from a force with an internally focused mission to one capable of providing defense against external threats.[307] The broad range of equipment purchases in 2009–2010, totaling $2.29 billion, focused on acquiring artillery, armor, and heavy wheeled equipment to support the this evolution. Similarly, the $1.83 billion expended during this period on training reflected an increased operational tempo for police forces under the MOI's aegis.[308]

By late 2011, Iraq reported that its combined security strength amounted to more than 930,000 trained security forces, 70% of which belonged to the MOI (see Table 5.6).

MOD Support

As of September 2012, the U.S. government expended approximately $13.90 billion to equip and train personnel, construct critical infrastructure, and provide sustainment and logistics support for Iraq's Ministry of Defense.[309]

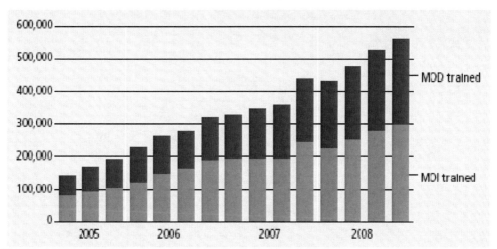

To complement the U.S. surge, a recruiting push resulted in a 71% increase in total ISF personnel from the beginning of 2007 through 2008.

Figure 5.15. Iraqi Security Forces, 2005–2008.

MOD Equipment and Transportation

Early in the program, equipment and transportation purchases embraced a wide range of items necessary to meet ISF force-generation requirements.[310] These included outfitting infantry, intelligence, artillery, armored, and bomb-disposal units. After 2009, half of all MOD-directed expenditures purchased equipment.[311]

The GOI also procured equipment through the FMS program and made direct purchases outside of the program.

The Defense Security Cooperation Agency administered these procurements—predominantly for the Ministry of Defense—which included the purchase of heavy mechanized equipment and artillery, training and cargo aircraft, and marine assets (such as patrol boats), together with related training and sustainment contracts. One of the most important cases delivered 140 M1A1 tanks by August 2012 at a cost of $810 million. Two others bought 36 F-16 fighter aircraft, with base development and pilot and maintenance personnel training well underway in 2012.[312]

In an unusual innovation, the FMS program in Iraq used U.S. funds (from the Iraq Security Forces Fund) for procurements, calling them "pseudo-FMS" cases. From 2005 through 2012, these pseudo-FMS cases purchased aircraft, naval vessels, police vehicles, tanks, and armored personnel carriers.

Peak expenditures, amounting to almost $800 million, occurred in the fourth quarter of FY 2009, purchasing helicopters, vehicles, weapons, and spare parts through these cases.[313]

Through September 2012, the FMS program in Iraq provided 496 separate cases valued at $12.79 billion—237 FMS cases funded by the GOI for about $9.44 billion and 259 pseudo-FMS cases funded by the United States through the ISFF for about $3.35 billion. An additional 74 cases, with an estimated value of $10.23 billion and all funded by the GOI, were in various stages of request and approval at the end of FY 2012 (see Figure 5.16).[314]

Table 5.6. Iraqi Security Forces, as of 12/31/2011

Service			Assigned Personnel
Ministry of Defense	Iraqi Army		200,000
	Training and Support		68,000
	Air Force		5,053
	Navy		3,650
	Army Air Corps		2,400
	Total MOD		279,103
Ministry of Interior	Iraqi Police		325,000
	Training and Support		89,800
	Facilities Protection Service		95,000
	Department of Border Enforcement		60,000
	Iraqi Federal Police		45,000
	Oil Police		35,000
	Total MOI		649,800
Counter-Terrorism Force			4,200
Total			933,103

SIGIR Audits 06-032 and 09-014
Logistics and Sustainment:
Breaking "Use It Till It Breaks"

In 2006, the Commander of the Multi-National Force-Iraq cited logistics and sustainment as the keys to the Iraqi Security Forces assuming the lead in provincial security.

A 2006 SIGIR review of ISF preparations to assume logistics operations found significant challenges, including incomplete planning for transitioning from U.S. to GOI management and operations.

With weak ministerial capacity at both the MOD and MOI, the United States had to develop the ministries' logistics and sustainment capabilities. This effort—part of the formidable challenge of changing Iraq's "use it till it breaks" culture—entailed awarding an enormous Global Maintenance and Supply Services contract.

In examining the contract's ISFF task orders that supported the Iraqi Army, SIGIR found that three of them, totaling $628.2 million, had been modified 161 times, which added $420 million to the contract's cost. SIGIR also found that:

- Documentation did not support contractor costs.
- Financial data on purchases did not reconcile.
- The MOD refused to accept responsibility for maintenance and supply operations, causing Multi-National Security Transition Command-Iraq to extend the period of contractor performance at U.S. expense.

Although the task orders provided significant logistics support to the Iraqi Army, the effort fell well short of achieving the goal of training Iraqi Army personnel to perform maintenance functions and operate a supply system. "Use it till it breaks" lives on.

The Depot Distribution Central Operation storage facilities at Camp Taji was completed in November 2010. (USACE photo).

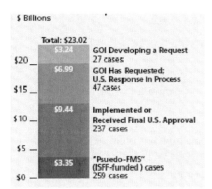

At least 74 GOI-funded cases, valued at more than $10.2 billion, awaited processing or approval at the end of 2012.

Figure 5.16. Current and Prospective FMS Cases, as of 9/30/2012.

MOD Infrastructure

The United States initially met the infrastructure needs of the MOD through large outlays of the IRRF, with more than $1 billion expended to renovate or construct military bases. ISFF expenditures on infrastructure through the end of FY 2008 amounted to an additional $2.2 billion. But spending fell sharply thereafter when the Congress prohibited the use of ISFF money for new infrastructure projects. As of September 2012, the United States had expended a combined total of nearly $4.05 billion to renovate, expand, and construct MOD bases.[315] See Table 5.7 for selected projects.

USF-I instructors train Iraqi Army soldiers to maneuver MIAI tanks purchased by the Ministry of Defense through the U.S.-administered FMS program. (U.S. Army photo).

The renovated Iraqi Ministry of Defense headquarters in Baghdad.

MOD Training

Military program managers spent a total of $1.32 billion to train MOD forces, with more than $850 million of that amount expended by the end of 2008. The build-up of personnel boosted MOD's cumulative force to more than 200,000.[316] But, as with the police, the number of troops reporting for duty fell continually fell below desired levels, with AWOL rates exceeding 3% per month.[317] As MOD forces rapidly expanded, senior non-commissioned officer and commissioned officer positions became difficult to fill, with vacancy rates of 30% or more persisting into 2008.[318] By the end of that year, thanks to a new program to recruit and train officers and NCOs from the Saddam era, almost 100,000 more senior personnel (85% of whom were NCOs) were brought into the Iraqi Army.[319] As the January 2009 transfer of security authority approached, the United States embedded 183 Military Transition Teams at all levels of the Iraqi military to assist units in achieving full capability.[320] After 2009, ISF training comprised a stable, albeit smaller, portion of overall U.S. expenditures. Blanket training orders funded by the ISFF (administered as pseudo-FMS cases) for Iraq's Army, Navy, and Air Force complemented a wide range of GOI-funded training activities procured through the FMS program.[321]

MOD Sustainment

From 2005 through 2008, the United States expended nearly $1.4 billion to sustain the MOD. These expenses included operations and maintenance services, contractor-delivered logistics support, and life support. The MOD did not have a logistics and sustainment capability when it assumed full security authority in 2009, and an additonal $1.2 billion in U.S. expenditures, spent from 2009 to 2012, closed that gap. To ameliorate its logistical problems, the GOI procured sustainment contracts from U.S. providers.[322]

MOD Weaknesses

While significantly more advanced than the MOI at the time of the U.S. troop departure, Iraq's MOD lacked critical capabilities in logistics, intelligence, and operational sustainment. Weaknesses in counterterrorism and intelligence capabilities at the tactical, operational, and cross-ministry levels impeded collaboration and information sharing throughout the national security framework.[323] At the end of 2012, Iraq had no fixed-wing combat-air capability to defend its airspace and only a small fleet of littoral patrol vessels to guard its coastline and the vital infrastructure that supports oil exports.

Table 5.7. Major U.S.-funded Security Construction Projects
$ Millions

Project Name	Province	Contractor Name	Contract Award Date	Completion Date			Fund	U.S. Cost
				Original	Actual			
Taji National Maintenance Depot Project	Baghdad	AECOM Government Services	12/31/2007	12/31/2009	12/31/2009		ISFF	220.0
Baghdad Police Academy	Baghdad	Parsons Delaware, Inc., Laguna Construction, Others	5/6/2004	1/1/2005	Various		IRRF 2, ISFF	137.6
Tallil Military Base	Thi-Qar	Weston Solutions, Inc.	4/14/2004	3/31/2005	1/29/2006		ISFF	119.5
Camp India Facilities at Falluja	Anbar	Environmental Chemical Corporation	11/7/2004	5/1/2005	3/31/2008		IRRF 2	83.4
Military Base at Kirkuk	Tameem	Environmental Chemical Corporation	4/15/2004	1/15/2005	3/15/2006		IRRF 2	73.6
Al-Rasheed Brigade Base	Baghdad	Tetra Tech Inc	12/17/2004	11/21/2005	7/2006		IRRF 2	64.0
Renovate Base at Habbaniyah	Anbar	Environmental Chemical Corporation	7/23/2005	8/1/2005	4/30/2007		IRRF 2	63.5
Renovate An Numaniyah Military Base, Phase 1B	Wassit	Environmental Chemical Corporation	4/22/2004	1/15/2005	6/30/2005		ISFF	57.4
Federal Police Sustainment Brigade	Baghdad	Areebel Engineering & Logistics	9/27/2008	10/19/2010	Ongoing		ISFF	47.7
Renovate Ministry of Defense Headquarters	Baghdad	Laguna Construction Co.	3/26/2004	4/30/2005	5/31/2005		IRRF 2	31.5

MOI Support

The United States expended $9.35 billion to train, staff, and equip Iraq's police forces.[324] The CPA and then State, through its Bureau of International Narcotics and Law Enforcement Affairs, initially managed support for the MOI.

With the stand-up of MNSTC-I in late 2004, Defense Department military organizations in Iraq assumed responsibility for the program from State, assigning INL to oversee contracts for the police-advisor portion the program.

When U.S. troops withdrew in 2011, responsibility for the program transitioned back to INL, which runs the continuing effort through the Police Development Program.[325]

Iraqi soldiers conduct operations as part of a live-fire exercise under USF-I supervision in northern Iraq on February 24, 2011. (USF-I photo).

SIGIR Audit 11-004
Iraq Special Operations Force: Special Results but Spurious Control

As the security situation in Iraq deteriorated, the Secretary of Defense directed the formation of a new Iraqi counterterrorism capability, the Iraq Special Operations Force. Army Rangers and Navy SEALS took on the training mission, funded in part with $237 million in U.S. rebuilding money.

In a review of the program, SIGIR auditors determined that the ISOF could conduct independent operations and maintain equipment and facilities. The program succeeded; the ISOF played important roles during the "Surge," providing a force of more than 4,100 expertly capable soldiers deployed throughout Iraq.

One flaw uncovered in SIGIR's review: USF-I did not account separately for funds used to equip and provide infrastructure for ISOF training, so the total costs of the program remained unknown.

The ultimate success of the ISOF is in the hands of the GOI, with the most troubling development being the move of ISOF control from the MOD to the Office of the Prime Minister.

Iraqi Special Forces commandos in Basrah prepare an assault after being dropped off by Iraqi Army helicopters during a joint military exercise in April 2011. (USF-I photo).

MOI Equipment, Infrastructure, and Sustainment

The United States obligated $2.03 billion for MOI equipment. By the time Iraq assumed responsibility for security in 2009, the United States had expended most of the sector's funding. About $1.0 billion purchased uniforms and personal body armor, and $500 million bought M117 Armored Security Vehicles and support.[326] The MOI received obligations of $1.43 billion in infrastructure support, which supported the construction of training centers, police stations, and border forts, some of which SIGIR inspected and reported on. Selected projects are included in Table 5.7. Obligations to cover life support and other sustainment costs for the MOI totaled $660 million.[327]

MOI Training

The United States obligated $5.61 billion and expended $5.44 billion on MOI training.[328] Unlike the MOD, which completely rebuilt its force structure, the MOI's force-base came from the prior regime. But the situation was chaotic in the summer of 2003. Only small numbers of police reported regularly for duty, and under-funded training plans, aggravated by the CPA's use of threats to try to get police to return to duty, produced few results.[329] Some security personnel, like the Facilities Protection Service, appeared to be little more than a mask for various sectarian and militia elements within ministries.[330] In May 2004, NSPD 36 assigned the mission of organizing, training, and equipping Iraq's security forces (including the police) to the U.S. Central Command, which established MNSTC-I to oversee the mission. INL awarded a large multiyear police-training contract in early 2004 to provide police-training advisors for the U.S. program. Although other U.S. agencies and other nations provided additional advisory support, the contract engaged the largest contingent of trainers. State managed the contract for the advisors, providing logistical support, even after Defense took over MOI training in mid-2004. SIGIR auditors determined that INL lacked sufficient personnel to adequately oversee the contract, concluding that $2.5 billion was vulnerable to waste and fraud.[331] MNSTC-I assumed police-training duties in June 2004. The already-operational Civilian Police Assistance Training Team became a subordinate command to MNSTC-I. Additional U.S. military units provided police training at the local level. The Iraq Training and Advisory Mission subsumed MNSTC-I and its subordinate units.[332] In 2006, Iraqi instructors assumed responsibility for providing most of the academic training for the MOI. MNSTC-I continued to advise and assist at the police training centers, with police training teams supporting police stations. The GOI assumed responsibility for all academic training and most of the advanced training courses by December 2008, with U.S. military and police advisors continuing to provide advice and quality control.[333] The number of recruits usually exceeded the capacity of the police-training program, which put a constant strain on the training cycle. The "recruit-to-train" mode prioritized basic training over training for senior personnel in a rush to get police into the field during the insurgency.[334] Expansion of the Baghdad Police College, which received $96.5 million in IRRF and ISFF funds, increased police training rates in early 2008, reducing bottlenecks.[335]

Police forces under the MOI's aegis in 2008 totaled approximately 400,000.[336] Facilities Protection Service personnel were formally integrated into the MOI over time, but they served directly under the ministries whose facilities they were assigned to protect. The core police forces—the Iraqi Police, the National Police, and the Department of Border Enforcement—usually incorporated militias that had agreed to be "integrated."[337] "Ghost employees" (those who received paychecks but did not work) and attrition were significant problems among their ranks.[338]

Many police elements within the MOI suffered from corruption and sectarianism, but these afflictions particularly affected the National Police. The NP received priority training and equipping from MNSTC-I, but its force structure had been pieced together from Saddam-era commando units and Shia militias.[339] Accused of frequent human-rights abuses,[340] the NP underwent extensive "re-bluing" (retraining and sifting out) during 2006–2008.[341]

In 2010, when the State Department began planning to take over police training, the actual capabilities of the Iraqi police were still unknown. A SIGIR review of the program in October 2010 determined that no formal assessments of capabilities had ever been made, as was required. State's original plans for the Police Development Program envisioned an ambitious $2.09 billion effort.[342] In response to SIGIR audits, the findings of an INL review, and the desires of the MOI, State significantly reduced the scope of the PDP, implementing a new program (called PDP 2) in 2012. PDP 2 focuses on, among other things, antiterrorism and organized crime, forensic evidence analysis, information technology, and border security.[343]

MOI Weaknesses

In September 2012, some MOI police forces failed to meet minimum operational standards. Only the Federal Police and the Oil Police were assessed as operationally capable. The Iraqi Police, Department of Border Enforcement, and Port of Entry services demonstrated improving technical skills, but MOI security forces generally suffered from funding gaps, weak command and control, and a poor logistics system.[344]

SIGIR observed a riot-response exercise during a visit to an Iraqi police training center in April 2010.

SIGIR Audits 11-003, 12-006, and 12-020
Audits Save Dollars: Downsizing the Police Development Program

In 2009, U.S. officials began planning the transfer of responsibilities for managing the support to Iraq's police forces from the Department of Defense to the Department of State. As originally conceived, State's Police Development Program was to be a five-year, multibillion-dollar effort—the largest single State Department program worldwide—involving 350 police advisors at three hub locations across Iraq. In an October 2010 audit report, SIGIR expressed concerns about a variety of planning shortfalls, including the failure to execute a comprehensive assessment of the police forces' capabilities.

A follow-up audit found that only 12% of program funds would be used to pay for advising, mentoring, and developing Iraqi police, with the other 88% funding security and life support. Moreover, the Senior Deputy Minister of Interior told SIGIR that he had serious doubts about the efficacy of the PDP. He said that Iraq did not need it as it was then conceived.

In 2012, State downsized the program to 35 police advisors, one-tenth the original number. This substantially reduced program costs, but not before at least $206 million was spent on facilities that would never be used for their intended purpose.

INL spent more than $100 million renovating facilities at former Forward Operating Base Shield, which was to be the main PDP basing area, before terminating construction, removing all advisors from the site, and turning the property over to the GOI.

SIGIR conducted project surveys of 21 border forts located along the Iraq-Iran border.

SIGIR Audit 11-010
Sons of Iraq: Work, Don't Fight

Insurgent attacks in 2006 spiked, particularly in western Iraq. While Sunni tribes supported the growth of al-Qaeda in Iraq—the chief catalyst of renewed violence—attacks began to hit local citizens, particularly in Anbar province. This caused some Sunni leaders to seek cooperation with Coalition forces in what came to be called the "Anbar Awakening." DoD credited these leaders with helping to improve security in tribal areas.

To advance the Awakening, Multi-National Corps-Iraq began to award CERP contracts in June 2007 chiefly to employ Sunnis. The leaders agreed to keep their people off the battlefield in exchange for CERP-funded jobs providing security for buildings, checkpoints, and neighborhoods.

This effort, known as the "Sons of Iraq" program, entailed approximately 780 separate agreements calling for the stationing of almost 100,000 in 9 provinces across Iraq.

The sheer number of agreements and personnel involved made this the largest CERP program in Iraq. SIGIR noted in its review of the SOI program that the contracting process, which spent $370 million in CERP funds, was far from transparent.

Financial controls were weak, program managers could not tell whether SOI members received their U.S.-funded salaries, and Defense was unable to provide any evaluations of the program's outcomes.

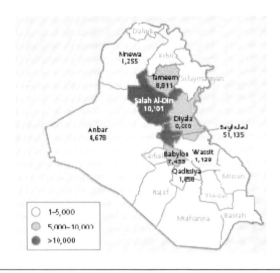

Infrastructure Security

Obligations for infrastructure security activities totaled almost $670 million, with 55% ($370 million) supporting the CERP-funded Sons of Iraq program.[345]

Throughout the SOI effort, which began in June 2007, the Multi-National Corps-Iraq awarded contracts to sheiks and other local leaders to provide security at checkpoints, buildings, neighborhoods, and other key locations.

The program aimed to convert former insurgents and passive supporters into participants in the U.S. counterinsurgency effort, thereby reducing overall levels of violence.[346]

The ESF-funded Infrastructure Security Protection program addressed facilities protection.

Three U.S. entities coordinated the effort—the Iraq Transition Assistance Office, U.S. Army Corps of Engineers, and Energy Fusion Cell.

Initiated in 2006, the program sought to reduce the incidents of insurgent damage to the oil pipeline system, electrical distribution system, and other important infrastructure throughout Iraq.[347]

Rule-of-law Programs

As of September 2012, the United States had obligated at least $1.37 billion and expended $1.20 billion for rule-of-law programs in Iraq. The majority of rule-of law funding (57%) was spent on justice programs, predominantly to expand the capacity of Iraq's courts.

Training for the Iraqi Corrections Service and funding for prison construction accounted for 38% of spending, while 5% was expended on anticorruption programs. The IRRF provided support for more than 57% of all rule-of-law activities early in the reconstruction program (see Figure 5.17).[348]

Pre-war planning efforts placed considerable emphasis on establishing the rule of law in Iraq. In 2002, working groups specifically addressed the needs of rule-of-law institutions and the fight against institutionalized corruption that infected the government.[349]

As the CPA stood up, it incorporated rule-of-law and anticorruption edicts into the process for Iraq's growth as an open and democratic society.[350] But these goals never received the funding to realize the necessary organizational capacity.[351]

Subsequent U.S. programs assigned individual agencies with responsibilities for various aspects of the rule-of-law programs, but none had charge of coordinating the disparate efforts.[352]

Beginning in 2003, judges became targets of frequent assassination attempts, with 49 judges murdered by 2012.[353] Iraq continues to struggle to protect its judges from terrorist activity, and their security personnel still do not carry firearms because the MOI has yet to grant them weapon permits. The court system contends with human rights issues, including reported acts of torture and retaliatory prosecutions by police and military authorities. Judges have expressed frustration over a lack of legal tools available to confront abuses by security forces.[354]

Justice Programs

Immediately after the fall of Saddam, legal and law-enforcement experts from the United States and other Coalition countries assessed the status of the Iraqi judicial system, finding it in a state of chaos.[355]

Table 5.8. Major U.S.-funded Judicial and Corrections Construction Projects $ Millions

Project Name	Province	Contractor Name	Contract Award Date	Completion Date		Fund	U.S. Cost
				Original	Actual		
Nassiriya Prison	Thi-Qar	Parsons Delaware, Inc., al-Bare'a Engineering, al-Basheer Company	5/11/2004	11/2/2005	3/29/2010	IRRF 2, INCLE	68.1
Khan Bani Sa'ad Prison	Diyala	Parsons Delaware, Inc., al-Bare'a Engineering Co	5/11/2004	3/31/2006	5/29/2007	IRRF 2	38.3
Chamchamal Correctional Facility	Sulaymaniyah	Chroo Group, Ltd.	11/1/2007	1/23/2009	3/18/2009	ESF	28.7
Iraqi Special Tribunal Court	Baghdad	Parsons Delaware, Inc.	8/19/2004	4/27/2005	4/15/2005	IRRF 2	19.3
Fort Suse Prison	Sulaymaniyah	Daban Company	9/10/2007	8/18/2009	3/8/2010	INCLE	13.4
Anbar Rule of Law Complex	Anbar	ALMCO Limited	4/25/2008	5/15/2009	6/15/2009	IRRF 2	12.8
Rusafa Courthouse & Witness Security	Baghdad	Tama Company	8/20/2006	4/28/2008	8/28/2008	IRRF 2	12.5
New Basrah Courthouse	Basrah	Al-Dayer United Co.	6/9/2006	3/1/2008	9/25/2008	IRRF 2	11.0
Central Court, Karkh	Baghdad	Al-Juthoor Contracting Co.	4/27/2005	8/14/2006	8/12/2007	IRRF 2	10.4
Judicial Education & Development Institute	Baghdad	Al-Barih General Contracting	9/13/2008	6/5/2009	9/25/2010	INCLE	10.0

> **SIGIR Audits 06-021, 07-007, 08-008, 08-016, and 08-023**
> **Anticorruption Drumbeat, but Downbeat Results**
>
> Corruption daunted Iraq in the Saddam era, and it continued to dog the country after his fall. A 2006 SIGIR audit urged reforms to programs to help Iraq fight its corruption problem, warning that other reconstruction priorities had diluted efforts to reduce GOI graft. But one year later, SIGIR found corruption getting worse. The Embassy eventually recognized the need to design and implement a comprehensive, integrated anticorruption strategy and began to advance such in 2008.
>
> Two subsequent SIGIR reports found encouraging signs of progress, including the appointment of a senior official as the Coordinator for Anticorruption Initiatives at the Embassy. However, the effort lacked metrics and baseline data for assessing the program's impact on reducing corruption.
>
> Further, State failed to move aggressively to secure the necessary funding to support a large and effective anticorruption program.

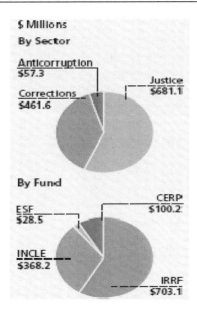

Figure 5.17. Expenditures for Rule-of-law Activities from Major Funds, as of 9/30/2012.

Iraq's court system received the largest portion of rule-of-law funding, with nearly $771.8 million obligated as of September 2012, for construction and non-construction projects. Of the $681.1 million expended, the IRRF funded more than half.[356]

IRRF expenditures supported the construction and upgrade of court facilities, as well as the building of witness protection sites across the country. Most rule-of-law money obligated from 2003 to 2005 funded infrastructure projects under a design-build contract awarded to Parsons Delaware; but the United States terminated that contract after court-related projects suffered significant deficiencies and cost overruns. The largest construction project was the $21.5 million Anbar Judicial Complex completed in June 2009. The United States contributed

$12.8 million from the IRRF to the project, which a SIGIR inspection found to be successful.[357] Table 5.8 includes major U.S.-funded judicial facilities.

Soft reconstruction projects included training by the U.S. Marshals Service, witness protection, court-staff training, and computer instruction, as well as instruction in technical investigative methods and the development of standard operating procedures for security search techniques.

The IRRF funded several capacity-development programs through the Justice Integration Project, Major Crimes Task Force, and the Public International Law and Policy Group.

Important equipment purchases included armored cars and vehicles for judges and witnesses, security equipment, and furniture for courthouses and judicial complexes.[358]

INCLE and ESF funds supported these rule-of-law programs:[359]

- **Judicial outreach**—From 2003 to 2012, INL funded DoJ's Office of Overseas Prosecutorial Development, Assistance, and Training with about $24 million to deploy criminal prosecutors to Iraq as Resident Legal Advisors to assist and mentor officials in the Higher Judicial Council and the Central Criminal Court of Iraq.
- **Judicial development**—INL provided about $81 million for training on forensic evidence and training for judicial investigators, the Regime Crimes Liaison Office, improved access to justice and treatment of juveniles in detention, review of the Iraqi Criminal Penal Code, and efforts to enhance judicial independence.
- **Court administration**—INL spent about $33 million to increase the effectiveness of the administration of the Iraqi court system.
- **Judicial security**—INL provided $60 million for judicial security, including mentorship and technical support by the U.S. Marshals Service.

Corrections

USACE spent at least $165 million to build prisons. The first two major projects—construction of the Khan Bani Sa'ad and Nassiriya correctional facilities—were awarded to Parsons Delaware in May 2004. USACE eventually terminated both for default after a combined expenditure of $62 million. Parsons failed to make sufficient progress on the projects, to adhere to the construction schedule, and to control costs.[360]

Another contractor completed the Nassiriya prison in 2010, spending an additional $37 million. But the Khan Bani Sa'ad facility remains unfinished, even after the expenditure of an additional $7.2 million, resulting in a waste of almost $40 million. The third-most expensive prison-construction project—the $28.7 million Chamchamal Correctional Facility—finished on schedule in 2009 (but without a permanent power source).[361]

Table 5.8 includes major U.S.-funded prison construction projects. According to the International Criminal Investigative Training Assistance Program, U.S. projects added more than 6,000 beds to the Iraqi prison system.[362]

Rampant overcrowding burdened the Iraqi prison system. U.S. officials cited the inability of the GOI to process detainees as the primary reason; it often took months to check whether a detainee had an outstanding warrant. Moreover, the Ministry of Justice, which administers Iraq's corrections officers, controlled 22 prisons, while the MOI ran more than 1,200 small jails. Thus, the ministry with the necessary skills (the MOJ) lacked the required facilities to manage the many incarcerations associated with its cases.[363]

INL provided more than $125 million for ICITAP activities to reconstitute the Iraqi Corrections Service. ICITAP managed corrections training and assistance programs through the end of 2011. In January 2012, it began a $1.6 million Pre-trial Detentions Program, but the Iraqi government soon decided to forbid non-Iraqis from assessing its pretrial detention facilities. Thus, INL ended the program in June 2012.[364]

Anticorruption

Corruption was the rule in Iraq under Saddam Hussein. It continued into the chaotic conditions of the early post-conflict years, draining resources from GOI programs. In 2006, Prime Minister alMaliki referred to corruption as "a second insurgency."[365]

Since 2003, the GOI's income from crude oil sales rapidly increased as did the magnitude of graft. Between 2004 and 2007, corruption's costs were estimated at $18 billion. In a 2005 review, Iraq's Board of Supreme Audit concluded $1.3 billion had been lost due to corruption in a series of MOD contracts.[366]

A 2012 BSA audit concluded that, of the roughly $1 billion transferred out of Iraq each week via currency auctions conducted by the Central Bank of Iraq, up to $800 million was laundered money transferred illegally under false pretenses. Calculated cumulatively over the course of a year, this presents the possibility that up to $40 billion was leaving the country annually because of corruption.[367]

Early on, U.S. reconstruction authorities identified corruption as an important issue that threatened the goal of establishing an environment of trust and confidence within the Iraqi government. But they devoted relatively modest resources to combat the problem.[368]

The $29 million Chamchamal Correctional Facility was completed in March 2009.

The CPA Administrator authorized a budget of $35 million to implement the comprehensive reform of Iraq's anticorruption system. A total of $20 million of this came from the Development Fund for Iraq, with $15 million from IRRF 2. The varying initiatives called for drafting new legislation and the anchoring of anticorruption power in these three specific institutions:[369]

- **The Commission on Public Integrity.** Established in January 2004, the CPI ostensibly was to be the primary agent in the fight against corruption. The CPA charged it to investigate allegations against GOI officials and, if warranted, forwards them to the Central Criminal Court of Iraq for prosecution.[370]

  The CPI enjoyed a productive start. In its first 18 months, it filed 541 cases against GOI officials, including 42 against ministers or other high-ranking individuals. But the backlash was swift and severe. The GOI shielded many of the accused from prosecution by the use of a Saddam-era law, and, when cases did go to trial, the accused frequently were acquitted. The CCC-I's conviction rate during 2004–2007 was only 8%. To worse effect, 31 CPI employees were assassinated from 2004 to 2007. In August 2007, the CPI Commissioner fled to the United States, where he received political asylum. Efforts thereafter to revive investigative activity proved mostly unsuccessful, and the CPI (now known as the Commission of Integrity) is currently a marginally effective force.[371]

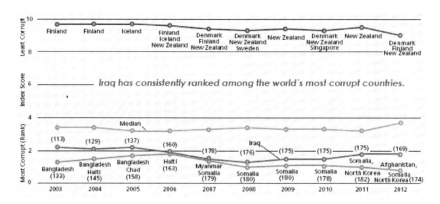

Figure 5.18. Transparency International's Corruption Perceptions Index, Iraq vs. Other Countries, 2003–2012.

- **Inspectors General.** Thirteen days after establishing the CPI, CPA Administrator Bremer signed an order creating a novel system of inspectors general in Iraq. Most were placed within GOI ministries for five-year terms with the power to audit ministry records and activities, conduct administrative investigations, and pursue allegations of fraud, waste, and abuse. The IGs were to report specific findings to their ministers and issue annual reports.[372]

  The system faced challenges from the start. Although the 2004 order creating the IGs noted they could only be effective if provided adequate resources, few were forthcoming. On the day before the CPA's closure, Ambassador Bremer provided $11 million to fund the new system. In 2005, the DoD OIG Investigations and Evaluations Directorate trained and advised IGs in the Ministries of Defense and Interior, continuing that work at least through 2008. And in 2007, the Department of State appointed a consultant to the IGs, who was responsible for training, mentoring, and advising the other ministries; but the position had no budget. SIGIR also provided IG training.[373]

Aside from inadequate funding, the IGs suffered an image problem that reduced their effectiveness. Created by the United States and inserted into a GOI that had no understanding of their mission, the IGs came to be seen as obstructers and even spies for the "U.S. occupiers." The GOI decided in early 2012 to eliminate some IGs at smaller ministries, and the Joint Anticorruption Council, a body responsible to the Council of Ministers, declared that all remaining IGs would periodically face an evaluation board comprising representatives from the Office of the Prime Minister, CoM, COI, and BSA.[374] The system's future is very much in doubt.

- **Board of Supreme Audit.** In April 2004, the CPA issued an order to reconstitute the BSA, an agency first established during the British administration of Iraq in the 1920s. U.S. funding for the agency was limited. But the BSA prospered chiefly because it is well led and is recognized as the oldest and most authoritative anticorruption institution in the country. The BSA's role is similar to that of the Government Accountability Office in the United States. It is the GOI auditing agency with oversight of all public contracts.[375]

As of September 2012, the United States had obligated $67.7 million for U.S. anticorruption efforts in Iraq, just under half funded by the INCLE ($31.8 million) with the remainder coming from the IRRF ($36.0 million). Despite this support for the fight against corruption, apparently little changed between 2003 and 2012.[376] As depicted in Figure 5.18, Iraq has been consistently perceived as being among the most corrupt countries in the world.

Governance

For almost three decades prior to the 2003 invasion, Iraq suffered under a highly centralized government dominated by Saddam Hussein's repressive rule.[377] Presidential "elections" carried out by Saddam's dictatorial regime reflected its culture of corruption, with outcomes never in question. In 2002, for example, Saddam was reelected with 100% of the vote.[378]

In 2003, prewar planners anticipated a rapid transfer of power to a new Iraqi government after Saddam's removal, with a hoped-for minimal disruption in government services. This calculation proved off the mark. Postwar looting and the exodus of government bureaucrats from public service—both voluntary and involuntary—caused a complete collapse in governance capacities. The country's broken system required a virtually complete reconstruction, literally and figuratively.[379]

The CPA established these goals for developing governance in Iraq:[380]

- a constitution drafted and approved by Iraqis
- institutions and processes to conduct free and fair elections
- measures to improve the effectiveness of elected officials and strengthening local government systems
- effective and fair justice systems
- respect for the rule of law and human rights
- creation of a vibrant civil society

Although the CPA laid the predicate for the eventual accomplishment of much of this, it realized little of it during its 14-month tenure.[381]

Through September 2012, the U.S. government obligated $8.32 billion and expended $7.48 billion to provide humanitarian relief, support democratic institutions, build government capacity, and grow public services in Iraq.[382]

Early funding focused on programs and projects to restore public services, promote democracy, and build civil society. By early 2007, the U.S. government had obligated nearly half of the money for governance programs, including more than $1.7 billion to improve Iraq's public services (see Figure 5.19). At the same time, the U.S. strategy shifted toward capacity development. Funding for governance came from three sources—the IRRF, ESF, and CERP (see Figure 5.20). Responsible for about 44% of this reconstruction area's total obligations and expenditures, USAID served as the principal U.S. agency leading governance reforms in Iraq.[383]

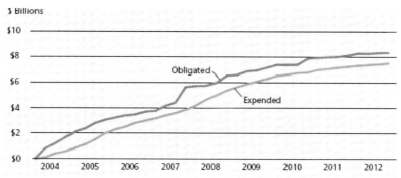

Half of the expenditures occurred by the end of 2007.

Figure 5.19. Governance: Cumulative Obligations and Expenditures, FY 2004–FY 2012.

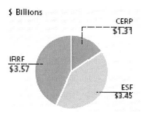

Figure 5.20. Governance: Cumulative Obligations, by Fund, as of 9/30/2012.

Democracy and Civil Society

As of September 2012, the U.S. government had obligated $1.91 billion and expended $1.82 billion to strengthen democratic governance and civil society in Iraq.[384] More than half of the funding came from the IRRF, with the remainder from the ESF.[385] USAID was responsible for more than $1.6 billion (84%) of the total obligations.[386]

Constitution and Elections

In November 2003, the CPA announced it would pass sovereignty to an interim Iraqi government by the end of June 2004. Among others, two important actions took place before that event:[387]

- an interim constitution (called the Transitional Administrative Law) was approved
- local caucuses elected leaders for the Iraqi Transitional National Assembly

The Transitional Administrative Law, signed on March 8, 2004, required the Transitional National Assembly, eventually elected on January 30, 2005, to draft a new constitution by August 15, 2005, and put it to a referendum on October 15, 2005.[388]

The U.S. government shaped the development of the new Iraqi constitution and implemented countless projects to support elections in Iraq through USAID's Elections and Political Process Strengthening program. Initially funded by $156 million from the IRRF, three organizations implemented the program: the National Democratic Institute, the International Republican Institute, and the International Foundation for Electoral Systems.[389]

State's Bureau of Democracy, Human Rights, and Labor awarded 12 grants, collectively worth nearly $250 million, to two USAID implementing partners (IRI and NDI) to promote democracy-building activities in Iraq. The grants supported efforts such as political training, women's political participation, and election assistance.[390]

The Constitutional Drafting Committee began work on drafting a permanent Iraqi constitution in late June 2005. The United Nations Assistance Mission in Iraq oversaw the process, with Iraqis accomplishing the actual drafting in what became a very politically charged atmosphere.[391]

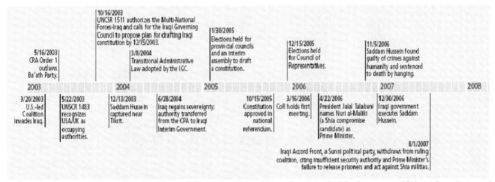

In the first seven years after the downfall of Saddam Hussein, Iraq held six successful major electoral events.

Figure 5.21. Governance Timeline.

NDI and IRI contributed as well through a $20.5 million program that provided international constitutional experts who shared their expertise, facilitated public input, and provided administrative support. The drafting committee ostensibly completed its work by August 15, but changes to the document continued right up to the eve of its approval in October.[392]

A woman in Kirkuk shows that she just voted in the October 15, 2005, referendum on the new constitution. (USAID photo).

Influential Sunni Arab political groups and others, including the Shia Grand Ayatollah Ali al-Sistani, criticized the process as well as the document's substance. Notwithstanding resistance, especially from Sunnis, Iraqis approved the constitution in a relatively peaceful referendum on October 15, 2005. Notably, the new law of the land accorded the Kurdistan Region substantial autonomy, but left these critical issues for later resolution:[393]

- clarification of the relationships between and among the local, provincial, and federal governments, especially regarding the governance authority of local councils[394]
- the distribution of territory and mineral interests in Kirkuk and surrounding areas[395]

Political imbroglios aside, the peaceable execution of multiple democratic elections in Iraq is a reconstruction success story. USAID provided substantial support to the Independent High Electoral Commission's administration of six electoral events: the referendum on the draft constitution, two parliamentary elections, two provincial elections, and the election of the KRG President (see Figure 5.21).[396]

Financial support came primarily from USAID's Electoral Technical Assistance Program, which provided about $103 million .[397] The program included administrative guidance, professional mentoring, and technical training for the IHEC.[398]

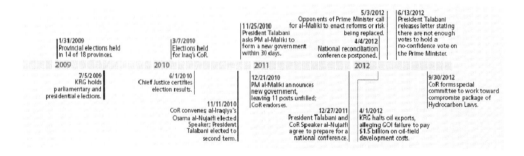

Election support is expensive. In preparation for the January 2010 parliamentary election, USAID expended $42 million in developing information and communication systems to tally election results and update voter registration records.[399] In September 2011, USAID extended its agreement with IHEC to continue the Electoral Training Assistance Program through 2014.[400]

In March 2012, USAID's Inspector General conducted a review of the Electoral Technical Assistance Program, finding it impossible to measure the effects of program's activities. For example, USAID failed to use a performance management plan to define elections assistance delivery and measure what it achieved. UNAMI also provided significant support to IHEC, and thus, in the absence of a performance management plan, USAID's Inspector General could not determine which organization achieved which results.[401]

Similarly, a SIGIR audit found that DRL could not measure the impact of the grants it awarded for democracy-building activities, concluding that only 41% of grant funds were spent on direct program activities, with the remaining spent on security and overhead costs.[402]

Community Development

The United States implemented a series of programs aimed at fostering what the CPA called a "vibrant civil society." One of the largest was USAID's three-phase, $740 million Community Action Program, which lasted from May 2003 to September 2012.[403] The program fostered civic development, improved government responsiveness to local needs, and assisted civilian war victims.[404] In late 2012, USAID announced a successor to the CAP program, a three-year, $75 million initiative called Broadening Participation through Civil Society. This program focuses on strengthening Iraq's continuing growth as a parliamentary democracy by encouraging greater citizen-participation in Iraq's social and political development.[405]

It is difficult to measure accurately the effects of the USAID programs established to encourage the spread of democratic principles in Iraq. These efforts trained tens of thousands of civil servants on improving government responsiveness and sought to open the eyes of countless citizens to the benefits of living in a free democracy. But no meaningful metrics were established to assess the results of these activities. Perhaps the problem lies in the nature of the program itself: how do you empirically capture the effects of civics training on the ability of a person to be a better citizen?[406]

Capacity Development

From May 2003 through September 2012, the U.S. government obligated $2.45 billion and expended $2.27 billion to increase Iraq's capacity for governance through targeted capacity-development programs and projects executed at the national, regional, and local levels. The ESF served as the primary funding source for these efforts, contributing more than three-fourths of the money.[407]

Nearly one-fourth of all funding for capacity development (about $550 million) was obligated in the fourth quarter of 2007. Total obligations had been relatively flat during the preceding year, but, in May 2007, the Congress required that the GOI demonstrate satisfactory progress toward 18 benchmarks before releasing any new ESF funding. In July 2007, the President signed a waiver to this requirement for $642.5 million, which was then

164   Special Inspector General for Iraq Reconstruction

released for new obligations.[408] This coincided with the mid-2007 surge of civilian personnel deployed to stem sectarian violence by focusing on neighborhood reconstruction (through the PRT program).[409]

National Programs

Two programs established in 2006 focused on national capacity development in Iraq: the Department of State's $45 million Ministerial Capacity Development program and USAID's $339.4 million National Capacity Development program, or *Tatweer* (Arabic for "development").[410]

The MCD effort focused on strengthening the central government by increasing ministry effectiveness and improving GOI budget execution.[411] Despite these efforts, budget execution remained a persistent problem. For example, while the GOI executed the majority of its operational budget in 2010, the rate of execution for capital budgets remained low, with 13 ministries spending less than half their capital budgets and three ministries with expenditure rates below 20%.[412]

Tatweer sought to create a national training center to develop the Iraqi Civil Service. USAID abandoned this goal after U.S. officials determined that the GOI lacked the capacity to manage it. *Tatweer* then shifted focus to training 76,000 GOI personnel on the basic skills of administrative governance. In 2008, the program's emphasis moved to a "train the trainers" approach, seeking to inculcate a culture of professionalism and continual education within the GOI's public sector. According to a USAID-sponsored evaluation of *Tatweer,* "soft impacts"—such as organizational culture changes, the embrace of modern techniques, and systemic improvements— were not achieved because top-level managers in ministries failed to implement reforms.[413]

In June 2011, USAID created a four-year, $156.7 million Administrative Reform Project, called *Tarabot*, or "linkages" in Arabic, as a follow-on to *Tatweer. Tarabot* sought to strengthen federal, provincial, and local governments' capacities to manage public-policy decision making and government resources.[414]

Local and Provincial Programs

USAID's single-largest development initiative in Iraq was the Local Governance Program. Begun in April 2003 and lasting through June 2011, this $807 million effort aimed to improve the management and administration of local, municipal, and provincial governments.[415]

The LGP executed projects in communications, conflict resolution, leadership skills, and political analysis, among other things. [416] Evaluations executed toward the end of the effort raised concerns about the program's longer-term effects because of the failure by Iraq's central government to devolve power to the provincial and local governments. To remedy this weakness, in late 2011, USAID began a five-year, $117 million Governance Strengthening Project to follow upon the work of the LGP, but aimed chiefly at bolstering the decentralization of power in Iraq.[417]

The Provincial Reconstruction Team program was perhaps the most innovative and, where it worked, the most integrated capacity-building initiative in Iraq. Among other things, PRTs helped local and provincial government officials identify rebuilding needs and then tried to meet some of them with available resources. The PRTs supported capacity-building efforts targeted at city and provincial governments to improve their ability to deliver essential services to the citizenry. Further, they worked with Iraqi Provincial Reconstruction Development Councils, which were groups of local officials and community leaders in the 15 southern provinces empowered to make decisions about local reconstruction priorities. The PRDCs served as a training ground in program and project management for local government officials. They were supposed to ensure the sustainment of U.S.-funded projects—a calling that produced mixed results.[418]

As of September 2012, the United States had obligated about $618 million and expended about $590 million for PRDC projects that supported programs in the water and sanitation, electricity, education, and other reconstruction sectors.[419]

The two largest PRDC projects were the Erbil Emergency Hospital (nearly $13 million) in northern Iraq and the Missan Surgical Hospital (more than $16 million) in southern Iraq. The Erbil Emergency Hospital was completed in less than two years—fast by reconstruction program standards.[420] But the Missan Surgical Hospital, a project started in September 2007 with a required completion date of September 2009, remained unfinished as of October 2012. As of September 2012, the State Department still managed $42.7 million in PRDC projects.[421]

The PRTs chiefly used money from the State Department's Quick Response Fund to help provincial governments accomplish short-term projects. State created the QRF in August 2007 to provide a flexible means for supporting short-term, high-impact projects.[422] It modeled the program on the CERP, hoping that it would prove a "flexible tool to quickly execute programs that will improve the local community." State shared program implementation with USAID.[423]

PRTs provided QRF funds through grants, microgrants, direct procurements, and micropurchase agreements to and with local government officials and community-based groups, such as nonprofit organizations, business and professional associations, charities, and educational institutions. SIGIR audits of the QRF found serious recordkeeping deficiencies with State's project management processes, including indications of potential fraud, but USAID's implementation met standards.[424] As of September 2012, the ESF had funded $287 million in QRF projects.[425]

Public Services

After the 2003 invasion, the Iraqi government had difficulty providing basic public services to its citizens.[426] Schools and hospitals were destroyed, damaged, or closed because they lacked essential supplies; uncollected trash piled up in the streets; sewage spewed in many places.[427]

As of September 2012, United States had obligated $3.06 billion and expended $2.55 billion to help the GOI rebuild its capacity to provide public services. More than three-quarters of the funding came from the IRRF and CERP, with the ESF providing the balance. At just over $1 billion, health care received the largest portion of the funding (33%), followed by civic cleanup and infrastructure repair at $977 million (32%), education at $789 million (26%), and public safety at $296 million (10%). More than one-third of the total obligations occurred by mid-2005.[428]

> **SIGIR Audit 06-026 and PA-08-160**
> **Basrah Children's Hospital: Still Patiently Waiting, Patients Still Waiting**
>
> The largest individual healthcare construction project was the Basrah Children's Hospital, which USAID awarded to Bechtel in 2004 for $50 million. The project would eventually cost $165 million. The hospital was envisioned as a 94-bed, "state-of-the-art" pediatric oncology hospital that would serve southern Iraq.
>
>
>
> U.S. soldiers look over the grounds of the Basrah Children's Hospital under construction in May 2009. (U.S. Army photo).
>
> During the planning stages, USAID and Project HOPE signed a memorandum of understanding, providing that the U.S government would be responsible for construction of the hospital, while Project HOPE would be responsible for installing advanced medical equipment and training medical staff.
>
> Work moved slowly. Deteriorating security, bad site conditions, and poor contractor performance pushed up costs and pushed out the completion date. By 2008, the contractor had been terminated, and new funding poured in. Construction was completed in 2010, and the hospital opened for limited treatment in October of that year. But in late 2012, USACE still had several ongoing ESF-funded projects for equipment procurement, installation, and training.

Health

In the 1970s, Iraq had one of the better healthcare systems in the Middle East, with access available to 97% of urban and 79% of rural populations. Over the next 30 years, a combination of wars, sanctions, and reckless neglect by Saddam's regime caused the Iraqi health system to fall into a grave state of dysfunction.[429] In 2003, USAID described Iraq's health care as very poor, reaching only part of the population, and "particularly weak" with respect to maternal and child care and health information systems.[430]

USAID's broad goal for postwar Iraq was to ensure that all Iraqis received basic health care. To accomplish this, it set milestones with expected dates of completion, though they tended, in retrospect, to be a bit optimistic. For example, USAID planned on basic health services to be available to 25% of the entire population and 50% of mothers and children within 60 days of the invasion.[431] The CPA's plans superseded USAID's. They included restoring basic health services to 95%–100% of prewar levels by October 2003 and enhancing primary care, prevention, and wellness services by January 2004.[432]

From May 2003 to September 2012, the U.S. government obligated about $1 billion and expended $934 million for health projects, both construction and non-construction.[433] Brick-and-mortar projects included the construction or rehabilitation of hospitals and clinics throughout Iraq. The $362 million Primary Healthcare Center (PHC) program, the single-largest IRRF-funded activity within the health sector, aimed to build 150 clinics. A SIGIR review found the program gravely deficient in execution.[434] Table 5.9 lists of some of the largest healthcare construction projects (including projects funded under the PRDC program discussed in the Capacity Development subsection above).

U.S.-funded non-construction projects provided medical supplies and equipment for newly constructed or rehabilitated hospitals and clinics and training for medical personnel. USACE funded two projects worth more than $53 million to supply medical equipment to the PHCs, including x-ray machines and dental chairs; but this equipment was largely never used, as revealed in SIGIR reporting.[435] From late 2009 through 2010, USAID's $5 million Health Promotion Program in Iraq helped the Ministry of Health design implement, and evaluate programs to improve public awareness of health issues, such as malnutrition.[436] In 2011, USAID started the four-year, $72.9 million Primary Health Care Project in Iraq, seeking to strengthen the delivery of primary healthcare services across the country.[437] State and USAID reported that U.S.-funded projects resulted in the vaccination of millions of children against measles, mumps, and rubella. In addition, by 2011, the national infant-mortality rate had decreased by 68% since 2003.[438]

Civic Cleanup and Infrastructure Repairs

Military commanders used CERP funds to promote quick-impact, high-visibility projects aimed at reducing the high level of unemployment among young, non-skilled Iraqis and improving local perceptions of the Coalition. As of September 2012, the military had obligated $317.8 million and expended $291.6 million on civic cleanup and infrastructure repair projects throughout Iraq.

Of the obligated amount, $204.1 million (64%) funded cleanup projects, while $113.6 million (36%) supported infrastructure repairs.[439] In May 2006, as the security situation deteriorated, USAID collaborated with the U.S. military to establish a program to complement counterinsurgency operations in strategic cities. USAID initially used $30 million in IRRF funding for this "focused stabilization" effort.[440] Soon $619 million in ESF funding followed, and this effort evolved into what became the four-year Community Stabilization Program.

The program supported the U.S. military's efforts to roll back the insurgency by creating initiatives that reduced incentives for violence by at-risk youth.[441]

SIGIR PA-09-178 Safe at Home in Erbil: A Perfect Project

The $3.7 million Erbil Orphanage and Senior Citizen Assisted Living Center project involved the demolition of an existing orphanage, which people in Erbil said was "like a prison," and the construction of a new first-of-its-kind complex to provide a safe and clean living environment for 345 destitute orphans and 60 senior citizens.

The contractor engaged local officials and incorporated their suggestions into the facility's design, which included ramps, motion-activated automatic doors, and other features to accommodate children and seniors with physical limitations.

The contractor also included, at his own expense, a geotechnical study of the soil to determine the allowable soil-bearing capacity. USACE provided diligent on-site quality-assurance support, including identifying and reporting construction deficiencies and following up with the contractor to ensure corrective actions had been taken.

SIGIR visited the facility in July 2009, five months after it had been turned over to the KRG, and found it fully functioning and in immaculate condition. The contractor's quality of work—including spiral staircases, decorative ceramic tiles, and floor-to-ceiling glass exterior wall—was the best SIGIR ever observed in Iraq.

The KRG's Ministry of Social Affairs contributed to the success of this project by providing commercial-grade furniture for the living areas and appliances for the kitchen. The facility's exterior included a children's playground and swimming pool. The contractor, ministry, and USACE personnel agreed that the safe security environment significantly contributed to the overall success of this project.

The quality of work at the U.S.-funded project in Erbil was the best SIGIR ever observed.

Table 5.9. Major U.S.-funded Healthcare Construction Projects
$ Millions

Project Name	Province	Contractor Name	Contract Award Date	Completion Date Original	Completion Date Actual	Fund	U.S. Cost
Primary Health Care Centers	Multiple	Parsons Delaware, Inc., Others	3/25/2004	12/26/2005	10/1/2008	IRRF 2	361.5
Basrah Children's Hospital	Basrah	Bechtel National, Inc.	8/3/2004	12/31/2005	10/21/2010	IRRF 2	103.9
Missan Surgical Hospital	Missan	Eastern Deffaf Al-Nahraen	9/20/2007	5/19/2009	N/A	ESF	16.0
Erbil Emergency Hospital	Erbil	Tigris Engineering Consultancy Electric	7/28/2008	12/4/2009	5/31/2010	ESF	12.9
Ba'quba General Hospital	Diyala	Liqaa al-Mustakbal Co.	11/24/2007	12/2/2008	12/26/2010	ESF	8.0

This "non-lethal counterinsurgency program" sought to stem the accelerating violence in Iraq by generating employment, rehabilitating infrastructure, and stimulating local businesses.[442] According to USAID, the CSP operated in 17 "insurgency-affected" cities, directly employed more than 47,000 individuals on a long-term basis, provided vocational training to more than 41,000, helped place more than 9,900 vocational training graduates into apprenticeship programs, approved a total of $77.4 million in grants to more than 10,250 business owners, and enrolled nearly 339,000 Iraqi youth in soccer, arts, and life-skills programs.[443]

SIGIR Audit 09-015, PA-06-042–046, PA-08-133, PA-08-134, PA-08-157, PA-08-158
Primary Healthcare Centers: If You Build It (or Not), We Will Pay You

The CPA awarded a $243 million task order in 2004 to construct and equip 150 primary healthcare centers across Iraq by December 2005. In March 2006, citing little progress, the US. government terminated the task order "for convenience" and reduced the number of PHCs to 142. SIGIR reviewed the PHC program, concluding that $186 million had been spent with only six PHCs accepted by USACE as complete.

After contract termination, USACE was responsible for assessing the condition of the partially constructed PHCs, estimating costs and completion dates, and awarding firm-fixed-price contracts to Iraqi contractors to complete them. These additional contracts added $57 million to the PHC program. In September 2006, USACE predicted half of the PHCs would be completed by the end of 2006 and the remainder by early 2007. Actual completion dates slipped significantly. Nine PHCs were not completed due to security, including one partially constructed PHC that was bombed twice within two months.

Poor performance by follow-on contractors, along with weak U.S. government program oversight, led to the contractors' termination, a drop in the number of PHCs to be delivered to 133, and a $102 million increase in costs. Tens of millions more were spent, but SIGIR's reviews indicated that the construction, installation of equipment, and necessary training were not adequately completed for a significant number of PHCs. Operational and sustainability issues persisted, which required an additional $16.5 million to correct deficiencies at 17 PHCs long after program closure.

SIGIR inspects a poorly constructed block wall, one of many deficiencies that SIGIR identified at PHCs throughout the country.

170   Special Inspector General for Iraq Reconstruction

Two reviews of the CSP revealed mixed results. The USAID Inspector General was unable to establish a causal relationship between CSP initiatives and a reduction in violence in the strategic cities where it operated. In addition, the USAID OIG could not substantiate CSP's claims regarding employment generated by the program. More disturbingly, the inspector general found evidence that potentially millions of dollars in CSP funds had been diverted to insurgents.[444]

Education

Until the 1980s, Iraq's education system was among the best in the Middle East, producing high literacy rates. But Saddam's despotism, a debilitating war, and consequent restrictive sanctions sunk the system. By 2003, school attendance had dropped significantly, with literacy among girls at 45% and 80% of the 30,000 primary schools in poor condition. A UN and World Bank report said restoring the Iraqi education system to 1980s levels would take $4.8 billion.[445]

Iraq's "greatest challenges in education are related to improving the curriculum, materials and supplies, and quality of teaching," said USAID's *Vision for Post-Conflict Iraq*. Following upon this, the CPA established goals to revise textbooks and rehabilitate 1,000 schools by October 2003, initiate curriculum reform, and ensure the availability of school supplies by January 2004.[446]

USAID awarded the largest IRRF-funded education project, a $48.3 million contract to provide supply kits to primary school children and teachers throughout Iraq.[447] The project reportedly procured and delivered more than 500,000 school kits to Iraqi school children in over 2,200 schools by December 2005.[448] Additional USAID contracts rehabilitated schools across the country; by early 2006, USAID had supported the construction or rehabilitation of 2,943 schools.[449]

From 2004 through 2010, USF-I reported the completion of 3,493 CERP-funded projects in the education sector.[450] CERP-funded school projects, primarily costing less than $500,000, supported such things as refurbishments, installing new air conditioning units, and restoring utilities.[451]

By September 2010, USACE reported that it had completed more than 1,100 education projects.[452] The largest project was the $5.4 million Baghdad Academy of Health and Science, which provided a new training facility for healthcare providers.[453]

U.S. government assistance in the education sector transitioned in 2009 from construction and rehabilitation to capacity development.[454] State and USAID funded workshops to train Iraqi professionals in the field of student advising and career development, provided books, equipment, and distance-learning technology, and expanded the Fulbright Visiting Scholar Program for Iraq.[455]

By 2011, Iraq's primary school enrollment had increased 27% since 2002, more than 33,000 teachers had been trained, and 8.6 million new textbooks had been purchased to modernize the curriculum.[456]

As of September 2012, the U.S. government had obligated $788.9 million and expended $379.4 million to rebuild Iraq's school infrastructure and curriculum. Of this amount, the CERP accounted for more than three-fourths of the expenditures, with the remainder coming from the IRRF.[457]

Despite this notable investment, the Education Committee of Iraq's Council of Representatives estimated in 2011 that 5 million Iraqis were illiterate. The Minister of

Education called this "appalling" and attributed it to overcrowding of classrooms and the poor quality of teachers.[458] At the end of September 2012, USAID launched a new five-year $89.1 million Primary Education Strengthening Project, called *Ajyal* (Arabic for "generations"), with the goal of strengthening the GOI's ability to deliver quality primary education through improved teacher skills.[459]

Humanitarian Relief

Prewar planning efforts centered on avoiding humanitarian disasters and prioritizing food relief in case of shortages following military operations. With decades of relevant experience, USAID was tapped to develop programs to prevent or minimize acts of reprisal and maximize high-visibility projects that could earn the goodwill of the Iraqi people.[460]

Though the 2003 invasion did not produce the expected humanitarian crises, the ensuing chaos brought by criminal conduct and the insurgency did cause the destruction of numerous facilities and the displacement of as many as 2 million Iraqis.[461]

In 2003, USAID established an IRRF-funded program to help Iraqi civilians injured by Coalition Forces. Carried out as part of USAID's Community Action Program, this program (later renamed the Marla Ruzicka Iraqi War Victims Fund in May 2005) provided wheelchairs and prosthetics to those with disabilities and rehabilitated local schools and hospitals.[462] By September 2012, the fund had expended nearly $30 million, which USAID reported had assisted millions of Iraqi civilians. Marla Fund activities generated goodwill from local communities; however, USAID warned that Iraq may be ill-prepared to sustain these activities once U.S. funding ceased.[463]

As of September 2012, the U.S. government had obligated $893.8 million and expended $840.8 million from three major U.S. reconstruction funding sources—the IRRF, CERP, and ESF—on projects and programs to support humanitarian relief. The IRRF provided $608.9 million for this sector, while the CERP contributed $189.9 million, and the ESF provided $95 million.[464]

However, these three major funds accounted for less than one-third of the total U.S. obligations for humanitarian relief. About $2.15 billion came from the Migration and Refugee Assistance, Emergency Refugee & Migration Assistance, International Disaster Assistance, and P.L. 480 funds (see Figure 5.22).[465]

The State Department's Bureau of Population, Refugees, and Migration developed humanitarian programs for Iraq utilizing its international and non-governmental partners to assist the needs of displaced Iraqis and facilitate their return and reintegration to Iraq.[466] As of September 2012, PRM had obligated $1.6 billion to support Iraqi refugees and internally displaced persons. Since 2006, more than 936,000 IDPs and refugees had returned to their place of origin.[467]

USAID's Office of Foreign Disaster Assistance contributed more than $450 million toward humanitarian assistance programs in Iraq. Of this amount, OFDA expended $261 million to distribute essential emergency relief supplies, provide emergency shelter, improve access to water and sanitation services, and support livelihood and economic recovery opportunities.[468] USAID obligated and expended $395 million in funding from the "Food for Peace" program, combating hunger and malnutrition through the donation of U.S. agricultural commodities.[469]

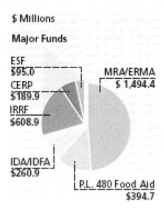

Figure 5.22. Humanitarian Relief Obligations, by Fund Type, as of 9/30/2012.

Economy

From 1991 to 1999, Iraq's annual gross domestic product averaged under $20 billion—roughly one-quarter of the 1990 peak level of nearly $75 billion. Crude oil production, which had reached a record 3.5 million barrels per day in July 1990, was about 1 MBPD below that level on the eve of the 2003 invasion. Iraq's banks, isolated by sanctions for a decade, no longer functioned as traditional lending institutions and had become cash troughs for Saddam and his cronies. More than half of all working-age Iraqis were either unemployed or underemployed.[470]

The events of March and April 2003 aggravated these conditions. When post-invasion looting ended, just two of the 170 Rafidain Bank branches remained open for business, the Central Bank vault had been largely cleaned out, and most of Iraq's 190-odd state-owned enterprises, the heart of the country's non-oil industrial sector that provided employment and income for 12% of Iraq's workforce, had shut down. Iraq's economy was on its knees.[471]

The CPA set a broad initial goal for rebuilding Iraq's non-oil economy: create conditions for growth.[472] But the CPA faced a significant structural obstacle: Iraq had a long-standing command economy, driven by an entirely state-owned oil and gas sector. Converting this centrally controlled system into one anchored by free and open markets was too ambitious for the CPA's time-limited missions. Instead, it sought to "set the Iraqi economy on the path for sustained growth and establish strong momentum toward an open economy."[473]

The CPA set these three initial tasks to put free-market foundations in place:[474]

- **Build financial market structures**—This included legislation to reform the Central Bank of Iraq as an independent body, arming it with powers to oversee the nation's commercial banking system and conduct monetary policy free from political interference. Market reform included national budget reform, the issuing of new bank notes, and a restructuring of the commercial banking system.
- **Promote private business**—This entailed streamlining bureaucratic codes and regulations, reducing restrictions on capital investment, and generating credit programs to provide small and medium-sized enterprises access to capital.

- **Determine the future of the state-owned enterprises**—This required conducting a limited privatization or leasing of competitive SOEs, then assessing the potential for selling the remaining large ones to private-sector buyers.

The CPA pursued several other policy initiatives to reform the economy, including plans to phase out a program that provided a basket of subsidized food items for every Iraqi, to build a new social safety net, and to design a national trust fund fed by a percentage of the country's oil revenues that would flow to Iraqi nationals—either directly as cash payments or indirectly via government programs. A planned trade stimulus initiative would end tariffs, create trade credits, and liberalize Iraq's transportation and telecom sectors consistent with World Trade Organization conditions.[475]

The United Nations and the World Bank estimated that Iraq's SOEs would require $356 million in technical assistance and capacity-building support from 2004 through 2007 to become viable entities. They further concluded $81 million in technical assistance and capital investments would be required to restore the financial sector, while $340 million would be required to boost Iraq's overall investment climate.[476]

The country's long-neglected agricultural sector, which employed 20% of the country's workforce but contributed only 8% of the GDP, would need more than $2 billion to upgrade irrigation systems and another $1 billion for fertilizers, seed, and other farm-level inputs.[477]

From 2003 through September 2012, the United States obligated $1.82 billion to revive the country's non-oil economy—less than 4% of the $49.37 billion in total obligations from the five major reconstruction funds. Just over half of this amount came from the IRRF, slightly less than a third came from the ESF, and the remaining 14% came from the CERP (see Figure 5.23). The United States divided the funds between supporting the goals of improving economic governance and fostering private-sector development. The United States obligated half of the $1.82 billion by the end of 2005, with more than 90% obligated by the end of 2010 (see Figure 5.24).[478]

Private-sector Development

Financial Sector

In the late spring and summer of 2003, the CPA moved to reform Iraq's banking sector. It suspended Saddam-era banking laws that had given the Ministry of Finance the exclusive right to authorize loans to government ministries. The Central Bank of Iraq was re-established as an independent body and given control over monetary and credit policy. It also took over responsibilities for supervising commercial banks.[479]

With Iraq's banking system effectively incapable of issuing commercial credit, the CPA established a new bank—the Trade Bank of Iraq—authorizing an initial capitalization of $100 million to finance business dealings, including imports and exports.[480]

In its first seven years, the TBI issued letters of credit valued at more than $45 billion. It financed important infrastructure projects and led banking sector modernization efforts.[481] Although the TBI was considered a success story, in June 2011, Prime Minister al-Maliki accused TBI chairman Hussein al-Uzri of "financial violations" and announced an investigation into the bank's actions. Al-Uzri fled the country, and al-Maliki replaced him with an executive from the state-owned Rafidain Bank, Hamida al-Jaf.[482]

Several U.S. reconstruction programs subsequently were implemented to strengthen the CPA's reforms. For example, the five-year $53 million, ESF-funded Financial Development Program, which USAID began in July 2010, drew on the knowledge of experts from the CBI, private-sector banks, and university business schools to strengthen private-sector bank capacity, improve the quality and availability of finance and business education, and establish new institutions such as a credit bureau, a bank training institute, and a retail payments system.[483]

Under the leadership of former United Nations economist Sinan al-Shabibi, the CBI's monetary policies created the stability required for economic growth.[484]

The CBI failed, however, to implement effective oversight policies to control the commercial banking sector. GOI anticorruption officials believed that banking industry involvement in money laundering had become widespread.

A 2012 audit conducted by the Board of Supreme Audit confirmed this, estimating that as much as 80% of all money transferred out of Iraq involved money-laundered funds.[485]

The findings triggered a warrant for Governor al-Shabibi's arrest while he was out of the country.

He had yet to return by early 2013. Meanwhile, the CBI's independence diminished following apparently successful efforts to transfer control over the CBI from the Council of Representatives to the Council of Ministers.[486]

Transforming Iraq's antiquated state-dominated banking sector proved difficult. As of mid-2012, Iraq's private banks continued to account for less than 15% of Iraq's banking activity.

A 2011 survey conducted by USAID indicated that only 1.4% of all Iraqis had accounts in private banks. Private banks also remained cautious, preferring to hoard cash rather than issue new loans.[487] For a comparison cash-to-deposit ratios of Iraq private banks and their international counterparts, see Table 5.10.

The two large state-owned Rasheed and Rafidain banks remained the country's largest financial institutions; both resisted U.S.-led efforts to restructure and reform.

As a result, they continued to work inefficiently and carry large debt loads that prevented them from being a significant lending source.[488]

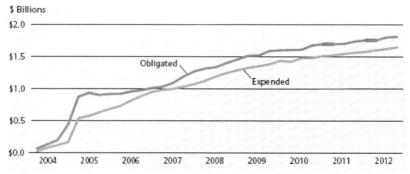

Half of the funds to rebuild Iraq's non-oil economy were obligated by the end of 2005.

Figure 5.24. Economy: Cumulative Obligations and Expenditures, FY 2004–FY 2012.

Table 5.10. International and Iraqi Bank Comparison of Cash-to-deposit Ratios, 2009

Private Bank	Cash/Deposits
Standard Chartered	6.2%
JPMorgan Chase	2.7%
Arab Bank, PLC	23.2%
Average of 21 Iraqi Private Banks	84.8%

The Trade Bank of Iraq led efforts to modernize the banking sector.

State-owned Enterprise Reform

During the decade of sanctions before the 2003 war, Iraq's State-owned Enterprises met a broad range of industrial and consumer needs for a people cut off from the world around it. Moreover, they employed hundreds of thousands of workers. But damage from the 2003 invasion and the looting that followed left most SOEs idle.[489]

The United States authorized $100 million in FY 2007 and FY 2008 to revitalize Iraq's SOEs. This money went to the Task Force for Business and Stability Operations, established by the Defense Department in June 2006 to help revitalize Iraq's economy. Between FY 2007 and FY 2010, a total of $174 million in Iraq Freedom Fund money was appropriated for the TFBSO. The group reported that, as of December 31, 2010, one month prior to its dissolution, TFBSO had obligated less than half ($85.7 million) of these funds and expended just $65.1 million for reindustrialization projects.[490]

In early 2012, U.S. Mission Iraq provided a $1 million grant to support a project that would value the assets of SOEs as an early step toward possible privatization.[491] As of September 2012, a small number of SOEs had become viable thanks to the input of foreign capital, but they remained the exception. Most SOEs survived only because of substantial GOI subsidies that in 2012 amounted to around 3% of GDP. They functioned much as a welfare program, distributing paychecks to the estimated 600,000 Iraqis on SOE payrolls, many of whom perform no actual work.[492]

Promoting Private Business

The U.S. reconstruction effort supported the growth of Iraq's nascent private business sector in several specific areas, providing:[493]

- direct assistance to would-be entrepreneurs in the form of microgrants, business development services, and training
- targeted reform of an administrative environment that under three decades of Saddam's control had made it deliberately difficult for businesses to function
- support to revive the banking sector as an efficient provider of capital to fuel the growth of private business
- promotion of free trade, including an initiative to prepare Iraq for entry into the WTO (Figure 5.25 shows factors in Iraq affecting international trade.)

The $140.2 million USAID Private Sector Development Program named *Izdihar*, or "prosperity" in Arabic, ran from 2004 to 2008, supporting the growth of micro, small, and medium enterprises by providing entrepreneurs with operational and capital grants in addition to training and other technical assistance. This program aimed to create a more market-friendly environment for privatesector-led economic growth.[494]

Izdihar was followed in 2008 by USAID's Provincial Economic Growth Program called *Tijara*, or "trade" in Arabic, a $192.5 million effort with similar goals. Both programs included job creation as an important objective, with a component of *Tijara* assistance directed toward developing capacity within small-business development centers to address youth unemployment.[495]

Izdihar and *Tijara* produced a national network of 12 microfinance institutions that provided access to affordable capital, especially for those unable to meet the stringent requirements for commercial bank loans. Collectively under the *Tijara* program, USAID reported these institutions dispensed nearly 350,000 loans ranging from $500 to $25,000 for business start-ups. The smaller *Izdihar* program issued more than $17 million in loans and grants and established Iraq's first microfinance institutions.[496]

A USAID evaluation of *Tijara* praised the program's efforts to assist small-business development, singling out projects directed at youth development as especially effective. However, it concluded that results on a second program goal—to integrate Iraq "into the global economy"—were "less positive." Factors contributing to poor outcomes, included sclerotic customs procedures and a lack of interest on the part of the GOI's Ministry of Trade.[497]

Programs to reduce the level of bureaucracy and promote trade had marginal results. The World Bank's 2013 global ranking of 185 countries according to their ease of doing business placed Iraq 165th overall (see Figure 5.26). It was 177th in ease of starting a business. Iraq's placement constituted the second and third worst rankings respectively among all Middle East and North Africa nations. Efforts to promote free trade produced similarly poor results, with Iraq finishing last among Arab World nations in six separate categories, according to the World Bank study *Doing Business in the Arab World 2012*.[498]

USAID's Tijara program provided microfinance loans to help small shop owners expand business. (USAID photo).

Agriculture

The first U.S. reconstruction contract to boost Iraq's farming sector supported a three-year $101 million Agricultural Reconstruction and Development Program. USAID awarded it in October 2003 to identify where resources should be used and to build capacity in the sector.[499]

A five-year follow-on agribusiness program, providing nearly $180 million and known as *Inma*, or "growth" in Arabic, began in mid-2007 and ended in late 2012. Its program goals included boosting productivity to enable Iraq to become more food self-sufficient and lowering production and marketing costs. During 2006–2008, more than $37 million in CERP money was spent on agricultural renewal programs, including projects to revive Iraq's date palm trees, formerly renowned for producing the world's most prized dates.[500]

Efforts to expand and upgrade Iraq's irrigation system yielded modest results. By late 2012, about 30% of Iraq's wheat-growing areas remained without irrigation, a reality that required the GOI to import about 3 million tons of wheat to meet demand in 2012. Much of the acreage under irrigation depended on age-old techniques and obsolete equipment.[501]

USAID claimed *Inma* programs led to $142 million in commodity sales and created nearly 15,000 jobs. But, as the agency launched an $80 million follow-on program in the fall of 2012, it noted the sector continued to labor under significant inefficiencies, a result of outdated, inefficient, or inappropriate policies. For example, without protective tariffs, domestic farm producers continued to be swamped by cheaper and higher-quality imports, a development that weakened the agricultural sector. As a result, in 2012, 80% of Iraq's food needs were met by imports.[502]

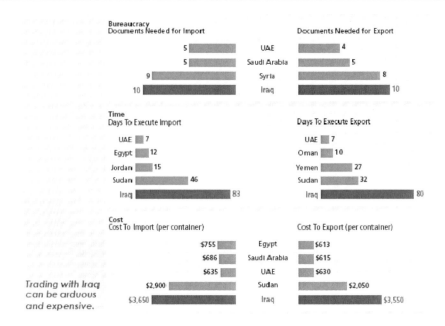

Figure 5.26. World Bank "Ease of Doing Business" Rankings, Iraq vs. Selected Countries, 2006–2013.

A May 2010 USAID evaluation concluded *Inma* fell short of its full potential due to several shortcomings, including an overly complex, top-down management structure and an overly academic approach to activities that were developed in a "self-reflective vacuum" rather than in response to needs on the ground.[503]

A melon grower loads his crop onto a truck for transport to market following the 2011 harvest. (USAID photo).

Economic Governance

Institutional and Regulatory Reform

The United States obligated $285.6 million in IRRF and ESF funds to support USAID's Economic Governance program. Just under $77 million was obligated for the first phase, which began in July 2003, aiming to stimulate Iraq's long-dormant international trade, boost employment, and generate a broad-based prosperity.[504] The CPA approved 38 specific projects under the program but an audit carried out by the USAID OIG near the end of the first year found the program had been slowed by security problems and a "unique" management structure. Among those dampened projects was an ambitious effort to introduce a sophisticated budget control system into the Ministry of Finance.[505] The $222.2 million Economic Governance II program ran from September 2004 to September 2009, promoting an open, modern, mixed-market economy by improving economic governance and encouraging private sector growth. It targeted seven specific areas, including tax, fiscal, commercial law and institutional reform.[506] Economic Governance II embraced 398 specific projects. A USAID OIG audit found the agency's failure to establish an effective system to monitor the projects weakened overall program management.[507]

CERP-funded Projects

Between early 2004 and 2010, the U.S. government expended nearly $110 million from the Commander's Emergency Response Program on more than 5,700 projects related to the improvement of Iraq's economy. The expenditure amounted to a small fraction of CERP's $3.73 billion expenditures, and only a handful of the projects exceeded $1 million. The majority of them were under $10,000, with some budgeted at only a few hundred dollars.[508]

Among the largest projects, $2.9 million was disbursed in April 2008 for construction of a large farmer's market located on a major highway in central Iraq. Construction of the market, initially estimated to take two months, required 18 months to complete. More typical was a $2,500 microgrant issued for a carpentry shop.[509]

Iraq's Economy in 2012

Iraq enjoyed a strong economic performance in 2012 because of its prospering oil sector. The country's GDP grew at 10.2%, nearly double the average among the Middle East and North Africa nations. With core inflation at just over 5% and interest rates at 6% for the third straight year, important fundamentals were in place for further growth. For 2013, the IMF projected Iraq's GDP would grow at a rate of 14.7%, one of the world's highest.[510]

Iraq's economy in 2012 was dominated by the oil sector. About 98% of the country's foreign exchange earnings come directly from the sale of crude oil.

Because the oil sector provides only 1% of the country's jobs, unemployment—estimated to be well above the official rate of 15%–18%—is a significant problem.[511]

The precise impact of the $1.8 billion the United States spent to revive the non-oil sectors of Iraq's economy is difficult to assess because there was little follow-up documentation available to measure its effectiveness. More than nine years after the start of the reconstruction program, Iraq is still far from having a vibrant, market-based private sector.

A March 2011 IMF review of Iraq's economy projected Iraq's non-oil economy would produce just over 1.6% of the country's exports in 2012.[512] Fundamental structural impediments—vis-à-vis an entirely state-owned oil sector afflicted by corruption—make it unlikely that Iraq's non-oil economy will see much near-term expansion. Corruption and debt payments reduced the amount of GOI capital budgets available to support initiatives to broaden the economy beyond oil.

More than two decades after Saddam Hussein ordered Iraqi forces to invade neighboring Kuwait in August 1990, the GOI continued to pay compensation equivalent to 5% of its oil revenues to those who suffered personal or property loss as a result of the military action. According to the United Nations Compensation Commission, the GOI had paid almost $40 billion in claims as of January 2013.

A total of $12.34 billion in approved claims still remained to be paid, mainly to Kuwait petroleum industry entities.[513] Figure 5.27 shows the status of Iraq's payment of the UN-mandated international claim.

SIGIR Audits 08-001 and 08-007
The Iraq Financial Management System: Transparency Intercepted

The CPA concluded in 2003 that the GOI's financial management system provided limited insight into ministerial budgets. This left them vulnerable to fraud, waste, and the misappropriation of funds.

It resolved to develop a high-tech electronic solution—the Iraq Financial Management Information System—and enlisted USAID to manage the project. USAID awarded a contract to develop and implement the IFMIS, with a September 2005 completion date.

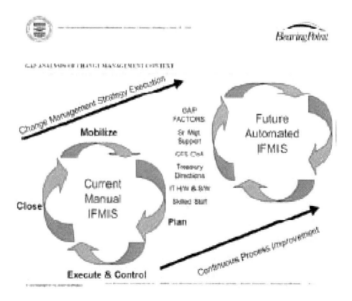

The contractor's May 2005 change-management strategy for transitioning from a manual to an automated FMS.

> Development of the IFMIS was driven by U.S. reconstruction policy decisions, CPA guidance, and contractor work plans, without any attempt to identify ministry requirements. The GOI resisted using a program it never approved and sensed was being forced upon it.
>
> In May 2007, the project was disrupted when one of the contractor's consultants and four security guards were kidnapped from the Ministry of Finance.
>
> The four guards were subsequently killed; the consultant was held hostage until December 2009. One month after the kidnapping, the Embassy suspended the IFMIS program because of security issues and a lack of GOI support.
>
> In 2012, after the expenditure of $32.6 million, the IFMIS remained incomplete and unused. SIGIR learned in early 2012 that another firm was working with the Ministry of Finance to develop a new prototype system that would use much of the IFMIS data.

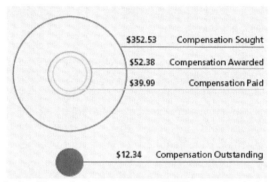

By October 2012, Iraq had paid nearly three-quarters of U.N.- mandated claims related to Saddam's 1990 invasion of Kuwait.

Figure 5.27. Status of Processing and Payment of International Claims Against Iraq, as of 1/2013.

PATHWAYS TOWARD REFORM

The Department of State, Department of Defense, and U.S. Agency for International Development share responsibilities for responding to stabilization and reconstruction operations. None of the three, however, clearly has charge of planning, executing, or overseeing them. Duties are diffused among the three agencies. Processes for SRO management remain opaque or undefined.

In Iraq, no U.S. government office possessed sufficient authority to lead the reconstruction program. The U.S. approach amounted to an *adhocracy,* which failed to coalesce into a coherent whole. Some lessons learned were applied along the way, but those were temporary fixes.

The Iraq reconstruction program's improvised nature, its constant personnel turnover, and its shifting management regimes forced U.S. strategy to change speed and course continually, wasting resources along the way and exposing taxpayer dollars to fraud and abuse. Management and funding gaps caused hundreds of projects to fall short of promised results, leaving a legacy of bitter dissatisfaction among many Iraqis.

As the difficulties in carrying out reconstruction operations in Iraq became apparent, the United States implemented a variety of strategies to remedy weaknesses, but a permanent solution never emerged. The current fix, embodied by the Department of State's Bureau of Conflict and Stabilization Operations, has limited resources and a conflict-prevention focus. It probably will not bring about the kind of large-scale interagency integration for SROs required for future success.

No reform effort to date has optimized the government's ability to manage SROs. As things stand, the U.S. government is not much better prepared for the next stabilization operation than it was in 2003. True, there are many more hands experienced in the field, but no structure exists to integrate them. Contingency contracting has undergone reform, but not in a comprehensive fashion. Various agencies have preparations in place, but no locus exists for integrative SRO planning. The Congress created the Global Security Contingency Fund, a good "interagency" idea, but one that remains untested. No integrated data system exists for tracking rebuilding projects. The list of current shortfalls, cumulatively imposing a strategic national security weakness, goes on.

Despite this grim litany, there is a path that could lead to the effective applications of Iraq's lessons. A wise approach to SRO reform would aim at producing a unified system that plans and executes operations integratively, averts significant waste, increases the likelihood of tactical success, and better protects U.S. national security interests. Such a reform would concentrate the SRO mission into a single structure, pulling the scattered pieces of the current inchoate system under a single roof.

That structure, which could be called the U.S. Office for Contingency Operations, would have a clear mandate and sufficient capacity to command and carry out stabilization and reconstruction operations. Importantly, this organization would be held accountable for results. See Appendix A for a draft USOCO bill.

The Coalition Provisional Authority had neither the time nor the resources to plan effectively for what quickly became the largest rebuilding program in history, one much larger than originally envisioned. The United States anticipated spending about $2 billion on reconstruction, with Iraq shouldering the remaining costs. But, by the end of 2003, planned U.S. expenditures had increased about ninefold and, by the end of 2012, expenditures were more than 25 times higher than originally anticipated.

Many of the challenges faced by the CPA were beyond its control, most notably the collapse in security. Nevertheless, a well-developed contingency rebuilding plan, implemented by an already-established interagency management office, could have brought a more robust capacity to bear on the many problems that erupted in Iraq in 2003– 2004 and thereafter.

Moreover, such an entity would have been better prepared to make timely and effective adjustments as events unfolded.

If USOCO had existed at the outset of the Iraq program, the United States might have avoided wasting billions of taxpayer dollars. Furthermore, the unity of effort that USOCO presumably could have applied would have ensured better effect from the massive outlays in Iraq. Ultimately, the Office of Reconstruction and Humanitarian Assistance, the CPA, and the entire adhocracy became necessary because no established structure existed in 2003 to manage SROs. That void still largely exists.

Falluja had become a lawless, chaotic place by mid-2004, with insurgents in complete control of the city, yet in June of that year the CPA awarded a $28.6 million task order calling for the completion of a new sewerage network by February 2006. (USACE photo).

Responding to Deficiencies

When faced with problems in Iraq's reconstruction, the Congress acted to ameliorate them by taking incremental steps that provided guidance on specific issues. For example, the Congress required the following:

- creation of a database of information on the integrity of persons awarded contracts[514]
- linking contract award fees to outcomes[515]
- ensuring that asset-transfer agreements, with commitments to maintain U.S.-funded infrastructure, be implemented before certain funds are used[516]
- making funds for civilian assistance available in a manner that uses Iraqi entities[517]
- an end to "contracting with the enemy" in Iraq or Afghanistan (including at the subcontractor level)[518]
- ensuring that Defense, State, and USAID have the capability to collect and report data on contract support for overseas contingency operations[519]
- that Defense, State, and USAID contracts discourage subcontracting more than 70% of the total cost of work performed[520] (or excessive "tiering" of subcontractors)[521]
- that Defense, State, and USAID assess and plan to mitigate operational and political risks associated with contractor performance of critical functions[522]
- designation of a "lead Inspector General" in SROs to oversee and report on them[523]
- that Defense, State, and USAID have suspension and debarment officials who are independent of their respective agencies' acquisition offices[524]
- that Defense, State, and USAID assess whether the host country wanted proposed capital projects (and could sustain them) before obligating funds for them[525]

Two Steps Forward and One Step Back: State's Coordinator for Reconstruction and Stabilization

In July 2004, the Administration began implementing reforms addressing evident SRO-management problems. Pursuant to a National Security Council decision, the Secretary of State created the Office of the Coordinator for Reconstruction and Stabilization within State.[526]

In December 2004, the Congress authorized S/CRS to monitor unstable situations worldwide, catalogue U.S. government nonmilitary SRO resources and capabilities, determine appropriate civilian efforts to respond, coordinate the development of interagency contingency plans, and train civilians to perform stabilization and reconstruction activities.[527]

S/CRS was supposed to solve the "who's in charge" question regarding SROs. It did not.

From the outset, the organization struggled to find its footing. First, it failed to receive the funding necessary to succeed. Then it found itself marginalized within State's turf-conscious bureaucracy.

Moreover, S/ CRS concentrated on an arguably peripheral task—putting together a corps of civilian responders—rather than engaging in Iraq.

In 2012, the Bureau of Conflict and Stabilization Operations supplanted and absorbed S/CRS, as prescribed by the State Department's December 2010 Quadrennial Diplomacy and Development Review.[528]

Notwithstanding its difficult history, S/CRS- cum-CSO comprises a valuable set of resources; however, its current direction and resourcing means that it is not the comprehensive solution to resolving SRO planning and execution problems.

CERP in Iraq: Congress as the Program Office

The multibillion-dollar Commander's Emergency Response Program began modestly in July 2003, expanded greatly in 2005, and served as a significant reconstruction funding source through 2010. SIGIR uncovered weaknesses along the way.

The Congress responded to these weaknesses, taking a series of steps over the years to rein in the program. For example, in 2008 the Committees on Appropriations directed Defense to "establish minimum guidelines for commanders to follow in monitoring project status and performance indicators to assess the impact of CERP projects," and to improve reporting on the CERP.[532]

It further imposed a limit of $2 million on the amount of U.S. CERP funds that could be contributed to any project in Iraq. The Congress required the Secretary or the Deputy Secretary of Defense to certify that any project funded from CERP at a level of $1 million or more addressed the urgent humanitarian relief and reconstruction requirements of the Iraqi people.[533]

In the Conference Report on the National Defense Authorization Act for Fiscal Year 2010, the Congress directed the Secretary of Defense to review the CERP and assess "the process for generating and justifying [the] CERP budget; the existing management and oversight of CERP funds and contracts ... and coordination with the host government on CERP projects, including procedures for ensuring the sustainment" of CERP projects.[53]

A CERP-funded project in Iraq renovated the electrical distribution grid in the northeast Baghdad neighborhood known as Muhalla 312 at a cost of $11.7 million.

Revolution at the Pentagon: Defense Directive 3000.05

In November 2005, the Secretary of Defense issued Defense Directive 3000.05, *Military Support for Stability, Security, Transition, and Reconstruction Operations,* committing the military to developing and expanding its stabilization capabilities.[529] This fundamentally transformed the Pentagon's approach to post-conflict operations, adding stabilization operations to the Army's existing duties to execute offensive and defensive operations.

The directive stated that stability operations are a "core U.S. military mission" that should be given priority comparable to combat operations.[530] In 2009, Defense reissued Directive 3000.05 as an instruction to make permanent the military's responsibility to be ready to support civilian agencies in stability operations.[531]

Despite repeatedly recognizing the centrality of a "civilian lead" for SROs, Defense made limited progress in integrating the relevant civilian agencies into its approach. It generally conceives of SRO work as an aspect of counterinsurgency operations. The civilian agencies see post-conflict contingencies as predominantly relief and reconstruction endeavors. Creating USOCO could provide a platform for the development of an integrated interagency understanding, a cultural rapprochement, and a common terminology applicable to future SROs.

The original contract for construction of Nassiriya Prison was terminated for default after the U.S. government spent $31 million. The project was eventually completed, more than four years later than originally planned, after the expenditure of an additional $37 million.

Reaching for More Reform: NSPD 44

In December 2005, President Bush issued National Security Presidential Directive 44, *Management of Interagency Efforts Concerning Reconstruction and Stabilization,* stating that "reconstruction and stabilization are more closely tied to foreign policy leadership and diplomacy than to military operations."[535] Through this order, the President sought to set in motion a process for improving the coordination, planning, and implementation of U.S. government stabilization and reconstruction missions. Although a sensible response to observed organizational weaknesses, the President's directive foundered on the shoals of competing interagency interests. For example, NSPD 44 charged the Secretary of State with leading the development of a strong stability and reconstruction response mechanism and ordered State and Defense to "integrate stabilization and reconstruction contingency plans with military contingency plans when relevant and appropriate."[536] This did not happen. State's S/CRS played no role in Iraq (and it only intermittently deployed small numbers of personnel to Afghanistan).[537] Despite the White House's reform impetus, State and Defense failed to integrate civilian SRO systems with military capabilities. State's role in managing the reconstruction of Iraq ebbed and flowed in cycles driven by the personalities involved, with State frequently on the losing end of arguments, notwithstanding the President's directive.

Authority Is Not Action: RSCMA and Dual Key Approaches

The 2009 National Defense Authorization Act enacted the Reconstruction and Stabilization Civilian Management Act of 2008.[538] Elaborating on S/CRS's original mandate, the RSCMA assigned chief responsibility for planning and managing the civilian response to overseas contingencies to State through S/CRS. Though RSCMA provided S/CRS ample authority, the Administration did not implement very many of its provisions. For example, it failed to nominate a coordinator for Senate confirmation, indicating an apparent lack of confidence in and commitment to S/CRS's capacities or future.

In a notable effort to promote "jointness," Secretary of Defense Robert Gates sent a memorandum to Secretary of State Hillary Clinton in 2009 suggesting "a new model of shared responsibility and pooled resources for cross-cutting security challenges." The proposal envisioned a pooled-funding mechanism, requiring joint approval by Defense and State for support of SRO efforts in security, capacity development, stabilization, and conflict prevention.[539] The "Global Security Contingency Fund," adopted in the National Defense Authorization Act for Fiscal Year 2012, sought to realize this vision. As of January 2013, while Nigeria, Philippines, Bangladesh, Libya, Hungary, Romania, and Slovakia had been designated as possible recipients of assistance, programs to employ the fund were still being developed.

Reform but Not Integration: State's Quadrennial Diplomacy and Development Review

In its inaugural Quadrennial Diplomacy and Development Review, State proposed several new structural reforms to improve SRO management. Along with creating CSO, the QDDR's recommendations included:[540]

- expanding joint civil-military training programs for senior State personnel
- evaluating success in interagency assignments when making promotions into State's senior ranks[541]

The Review called upon CSO to expand the Civilian Response Corps[542] and to "enhance" the Civilian Reserve Corps.[543] It charged CSO with coordinating State's efforts in conflict prevention, managing the rapid deployment of civilian responders, and serving as State's institutional locus for developing SRO policy and operational capacities.[544] It left opaque CSO's relations with other agencies, including USAID, noting that the bureau would be "working closely with [USAID] senior leadership."[545] CSO became operational in April 2012, led by a highly qualified assistant secretary, Rick Barton, who possessed the broad mandate of acting as the Secretary of State's senior adviser on "conflict and instability."[546] In September 2012, CSO reported that it had "obligated $30 million of programming to top-priority countries, expanded the contracting capabilities of the U.S. government in places facing crisis, and provided fresh talent and customized initiatives to embassies in need."[547] It expended 80% of its effort in four areas: Syria, the northern tier of Central America, Kenya, and Burma. The balance was spread among more than 15 other countries, including Afghanistan, El Salvador, Libya, Somalia, and South Sudan.[548] Notwithstanding its merits, the CSO solution is incomplete. Establishing it was a step toward better coordination, but the new bureau provides little impetus toward true interagency integration on SROs. While CSO advances State's thinking and practice about SRO management within the Department, it does not ultimately resolve existing interagency disconnects. "Stovepiping" continues.

A Plausible Solution

In recent years, the United States pursued an SRO management strategy dubbed "whole of government." This simultaneously elliptical and glib term has yet to generate an operational structure that is either comprehensive or coherent. Whole-of-government's core flaw is that everyone is partly in charge, ensuring that no one is fully in charge. In 2007, the Interagency Management System became the chief coordinative mechanism for addressing SRO issues on a whole-ofgovernment basis. A National Security Council committee chaired by the director of S/CRS, the IMS ostensibly provided guidance on issues bubbling up from the Iraq and Afghanistan SROs. But, in truth, it had limited effect on the actual execution of operations in either theater and is now nonoperational.

Advantages of an Integrated SRO Management Office
Creating USOCO would knock down stovepipes. Further, it would allow Defense, State, and USAID to focus on their core competencies while working closely with USOCO on the post-conflict reconstruction mission. See Appendix A for a draft USOCO bill. USOCO would provide these immediate benefits:

- Planning and managing SROs would move from being an additional duty at several departments (State, Defense, USAID, Treasury, and Justice) to the primary duty of one agency (USOCO).
- Providing an institutional home for the management of SROs would ensure that lessons learned from Iraq become lessons applied to future operations.
- The civilian-led office would mitigate the perception that U.S. assistance programs have become militarized.
- The proposed structure would eliminate redundancies and save taxpayer dollars.

Institutional Changes That USOCO Would Quickly Implement

USOCO would provide the integrated nexus for developing SRO solutions by taking these actions:

- Draft doctrine. USOCO would develop clear-cut SRO doctrine, with the National Security Council defining requirements and identifying implementing mechanisms.
- Integrate planning. USOCO would bring together all relevant agencies to develop integrated contingency plans for SROs.
- Rationalize budgeting. The National Security Council and Office of Management and Budget would work with USOCO to develop realistic budget requirements for potential contingencies.
- Incentivize personnel. Existing federal personnel regulations would be adjusted to provide stronger incentives that rewarded civilian employees for accepting temporary deployments in support of SROs.
- Consolidate training. Existing SRO training initiatives would be consolidated into an interagency training center with a joint curriculum modeled on the U.S. Army Training and Doctrine Command's Interagency Fellowship Program.
- Reform contracting. USOCO would implement new contingency contracting procedures and prescribe a new "Contingency Federal Acquisition Regulation" for use across SROs by all agencies, which would improve contract management in theater and ensure a more accountable program.
- Coordinate with contractors. USOCO would provide contractors with a single point of contact, simplifying reporting responsibilities and improving coordination.
- Anticipate international involvement. USOCO would develop curricula, programs, and systems that anticipate international participation in future contingency operations.
- Integrate information technology. USOCO would develop a single interoperable IT system capable of tracking all relief and reconstruction projects in theater.
- Ensure oversight. USOCO's structure would include an independent Special Inspector General for Overseas Contingency Operations who would provide effective oversight through audits and investigations of all funds used during the SRO.

From a fiscal perspective, USOCO makes sense. The cost of running the office would be easily covered by the waste averted through improved SRO planning.[549] As the Commission on Wartime Contracting in Iraq and Afghanistan reported, unacceptable waste continues in Afghanistan because operational responsibilities for executing stabilization operations remain diffused across too many agencies.[550] Consolidating existing systems under one roof would induce unity of effort and produce significant savings.

To ensure operational agility and low overhead, USOCO would scale its size according to the needs of the mission at hand. When no SRO is ongoing, USOCO's permanent staff would engage in formulating plans and conducting exercises to prepare for future activities. The truth, however, is that the United States has been engaged in some form of SRO almost every year since 1980. Given that history, USOCO should expect no fallow time.

A Solution on the Table: The Elements of an Effective SRO Reform Bill

SROs do not fit easily into any of the "3 Ds": defense, diplomacy, and development. They are executed during unsettled periods, occurring between the termination of full-blown conflict and the implementation of long-term development. Thus, legislation creating USOCO must define SROs precisely. Stabilization and reconstruction operations could usefully be described in law as providing a combination of security, reconstruction, relief, and development services provided to unstable fragile or failing states (see Appendix A).

Clarifying USOCO's Operational Space

The best institutional analogue to USOCO is the Federal Emergency Management Agency. Statutorily, USOCO's operational engagement could roughly mirror the approach defined under the Stafford Act, which governs FEMA. USOCO's enabling statute could draw from the Stafford Act's paradigm by tying its operational authority—and the availability of emergency funds—to a Presidential declaration.[551] In the event of an SRO, the President would issue a declaration specifying the SRO's commencement, activating USOCO's access to SRO funds, and outlining the SRO's geographical and operational parameters. During the life of the operation, the USOCO Director's relationship with the Ambassador would be similar to the kind of relationship the USAID Administrator has with the Ambassador. USOCO programs and projects would harmonize with the State Department's foreign policy and development goals. USOCO staff would embed within the combatant command overseeing the affected theater to ensure close coordination with military units on SRO activities. When the need for reconstruction support to an overseas contingency operation no longer exists, the President would issue a declaration terminating the SRO. USOCO would then transfer remaining programs and projects to the appropriate entity, presumably the host nation or State/USAID.

Defining USOCO Leadership and Reporting Requirements

The President would appoint the USOCO Director, who would have Under Secretary rank with the authority to convene meetings with the Assistant Secretaries of State and Defense. The Director would operate under the general supervision of the Secretary of State *and* the Secretary of Defense. This dual-reporting scheme, though rare in government, reflects SIGIR's reporting scheme, which worked effectively in the oversight of Iraq's reconstruction. Both Departments have a major role in SROs; thus, both should have a major say in their planning and execution. Additionally, the Director would report to the National Security Advisor so that USOCO's engagement is woven into the policy decision-making process. The office would have robust reporting responsibilities to the Congress. Within 30 days after the end of each fiscal-year quarter, the director would submit to the appropriate committees of the Congress a comprehensive report summarizing USOCO's activities and expenditures for that quarter. Each quarterly report would include a detailed statement of all obligations, expenditures, and revenues associated with any ongoing stabilization and reconstruction operations.

Consolidating SRO Structures under USOCO

Current SRO lines of responsibility, accountability, and oversight are poorly defined. To remedy this predicament, USOCO's enabling legislation would consolidate certain aspects of existing agency offices responsible for discrete SRO components. The long-term benefits of developing an integrated SRO management office decidedly outweigh any near-term restructuring costs, which would be partially offset through consolidation.

Institutionalizing Oversight: Special Inspector General for Overseas Contingency Operations

An independent inspector general office would be an integral part of this reform. A new inspector general within USOCO would have the authority to oversee all accounts, spending, and activities related to an SRO regardless of the implementing agency. This would ensure the uninterrupted supervision of U.S. expenditures made during stabilization and reconstruction operations, not merely those made by USOCO. The Commission on Wartime Contracting in Iraq and Afghanistan recommended the creation of just such a permanent inspector general for contingency operations with broad authority extending beyond SRO activities.[552]

Other Statutory Powers

USOCO's enabling act should empower its director to take the following actions:

- Issue contingency acquisition regulations for use in stabilization and reconstruction emergencies.
- Prepare information and financial management systems for use in SROs.
- Establish an interagency training, preparation, and evaluation framework for all personnel supporting SROs.
- Establish a Stabilization and Reconstruction Reserve Fund that USOCO would administer during a presidentially declared SRO.

Arguing for USOCO

Key stakeholders in the U.S. interagency community generally agree on the need for robust SRO reform, but dispute continues as to the shape such reform should take. State is pressing ahead with the CSO solution, but its mandate does not indicate that it will be operating aggressively on an interagency level to plan and execute SROs. Others argue for creating an independent USAID and giving it the full SRO mission. Some support a quasi-independent SRO management entity. In discussions with SIGIR, Ambassador Ryan Crocker and former National Security Advisor Lieutenant General Brent Scowcroft endorsed the idea of an independent SRO office like USOCO. So did Senator John McCain, former Congressman Bill Delahunt, and former Under Secretary of Defense (Comptroller) Dov Zakheim. Dr. Zakheim's views carry special weight because he also served on the Commission on Wartime Contracting in Iraq and Afghanistan. Ambassador James Dobbins expressed support for creating a USOCOlike entity, but believes it could best operate within USAID. Former CENTCOM commander General Anthony Zinni likes the concept, but advocates embedding it within Defense as a combatant-command analogue. Housing a new SRO office within State, USAID, or Defense, however, leaves unresolved the stovepiping and agency-bias issues. With the Iraq experience fresh in mind, circumstances are ripe for bold reform. Implementing USOCO could be the means by which the hard lessons from Iraq are turned into best practices for future SROs. Consolidating existing resources and structures under USOCO would achieve money-saving management efficiencies that would avert waste and produce real financial savings. Moreover, integrating the planning, management, and execution of SROs would ensure that the next time the United States undertakes such an operation, those deployed to execute the mission will have the mandate, expertise, and resources to succeed. The bottom line is that creating USOCO would dramatically improve the bottom line of our SRO balance sheet, significantly increase the likelihood of success in future SROs, better protect U.S. national security interests abroad, and strengthen the stewardship of scarce taxpayer dollars in the next stabilization and reconstruction operation. The need for such reform is great: that next operation may soon be upon us.

FINAL LESSONS

The foregoing litany of data, interviews, analyses, and history provides a substantial and sound basis from which to derive lessons about the Iraq reconstruction program. The Iraqis, the recipients of the United States' extraordinary reconstruction largesse, largely lament the lost potential that the massive amounts of U.S. aid promised. U.S. senior leaders firmly grasp the shortfalls faced in Iraq, absorbing them as lessons learned and recognizing the need for improving the U.S. approach to stabilization and reconstruction operations. Congressional members acknowledged missed opportunities for more oversight but expressed approval of varying innovations elicited during the effort and anticipate reifying reform proposals that could strengthen future operations. This final report from SIGIR, standing as it does upon our prior work and girded by the insightful interviews in Chapter 2, provides a solid foundation on which to base seven final lessons learned from Iraq.

1. Create an Integrated Civilian-Military Office to Plan, Execute, and Be Accountable for Contingency Rebuilding Activities during Stabilization and Reconstruction Operations

This lesson suggests a solution to a problem recognized by virtually everyone possessing at least a passing familiarity with the Iraq program: the current system for managing SROs is inadequate. SIGIR previously proposed the creation of the U.S. Office for Contingency Operations, whose mission would be the one set forth by this lesson. That proposal is reiterated here because no sustainable alternative has yet evolved from the agencies. Among others, Senator John McCain, former Representative Bill Delahunt, and Dr. Dov Zakheim, the former Defense Comptroller and Commission on Wartime Contracting member, believe creating such an office would strengthen the protection of U.S. national security interests. Ambassador Ryan Crocker does as well. Importantly, USOCO would provide clarity about who is responsible for planning and executing rebuilding activities, truly resolving the dual systemic weaknesses of the Iraq program: the lack of unity of command and poor unity of effort. Ambassador Christopher Hill noted that the "bureaucratic clash" of agency cultures weakened the rebuilding program. Ambitious though this proposal may be, the Congress could make it happen. Stabilization and reconstruction operations will recur, and the current system for their execution is inchoate, at best. The United States is not sufficiently structured or prepared for the next SRO. As former Representative Delahunt said, creating USOCO or something like it would establish a firm planning locus to ensure that it is. Chairman Buck

McKeon soberly observed that, in Iraq, "we won the war, but we have not won the peace." This is a cri de coeur for reforming the U.S. approach to SROs.

President Barack Obama, Vice President Joe Biden, Deputy Defense Secretary Ashton B. Carter, Chairman of the Joint Chiefs of Staff General Martin E. Dempsey, and Army General Lloyd J. Austin III attend December 20, 2011, ceremony commemorating the return of U.S. troops from Iraq. (DoD photo).

U.S. soldiers guide tactical vehicles out of Iraq on December 6, 2011, for redeployment back to the U.S. Third Army. (U.S. Army photo).

2. Begin Rebuilding Only after Establishing Sufficient Security, and Focus First on Small Programs and Projects

Grasping this lesson requires defining what "establishing sufficient security" means. It is not an absolute. Rather, the injunction anticipates that reconstruction decisions will be made along a spectrum of possible security conditions. The bottom line in making rebuilding choices is: the more unstable the situation, the smaller the project should be. As Deputy Secretary of State William Burns said, advancing an ambitious rebuilding agenda amid insecure conditions is unwise, but in Iraq, enormous projects pressed forward despite an ever-more-aggravated security environment—a costly mistake, as General Raymond Odierno observed. Limited projects executed in less than perfectly stable conditions can have a counterinsurgency effect. But they must be sized to the situation and wisely targeted to meet local needs. The best CERP projects in Iraq, as General Lloyd Austin acknowledged, followed these guidelines. Finally, poor security conditions commonly signal a weak rule-of-law system. The United States underinvested in strengthening Iraq's capacity to enforce the rule of law, and this contributed to breakdowns that permitted corruption to metastasize within the Government of Iraq. Iraq's top oversight official, Dr. Abdul Basit Turki al-Sae'ed, believes that corruption in Iraq has "become an institution unto itself." Indeed, "corruption today is worse than ever," said Baqir al-Zubeidi, a member of the Council of Representatives and former Minister of Finance and Interior.

3. Ensure Full Host-Country Engagement in Program and Project Selection, Securing Commitments to Share Costs (Possibly through Loans) and Agreements to Sustain Completed Projects after Their Transfer

In 2003, the Coalition Provisional Authority did engage with Iraqis about reconstruction choices. But the common chorus coming from virtually all Iraqi leaders interviewed for this report complains that consultations by the CPA and its successors were inadequate, causing the construction of projects that Iraq did not need or want. Ambassador James Jeffrey noted this concern, stating that "there was never an impression that the Iraqis were included in any decision process" about programs and projects. Ambassador Crocker also said that the United States frequently failed to secure "genuine" Iraqi buy-in. An important caveat: it may be difficult to distinguish a want from a need during an SRO. Notwithstanding that truth, the Iraq experience demands a concrete rule: defer to and fully engage with the host nation's authorities when selecting programs and projects. As USAID Mission Director Christopher Crowley said, you must define what is needed for sustainability at the program's start. The program's history foists forward two other rules on this score: do not build above a country's capacity, and secure commitments to share costs and sustain projects. USAID Administrator Rajiv Shah highlighted the benefits that cost sharing eventually produced in Iraq, which included greater buy-in and improved sustainment. In an era of severe domestic economic constraint, sharing SRO costs where possible is not just a good idea, it is a requirement.

4. Establish Uniform Contracting, Personnel, and Information Management Systems That All SRO Participants Use

Interagency conflicts pervaded the Iraq program. In Senator Claire McCaskill's vivid metaphor, these conflicts sometimes amounted to a "circular firing squad." Good coordination was the exception, usually achieved by the serendipitous convergence of complementary personalities from different agencies. Serendipity, however, is not a strategy; systematic planning is. As suggested by Lieutenant General Thomas Bostick, who was present at the beginning and the end of the rebuilding program, creating a uniform set of contingency contracting regulations would lend coherence and bring efficiency to SRO contracting. In Iraq, each agency used its own amended version of the Federal Acquisition Regulation, leading to a wide and waste-inducing divergence of practice. Similarly, asynchronous personnel assignments created interagency friction as reconstruction team members from participating agencies arrived and departed on vastly varying deployment schedules. Finally, SIGIR's oversight was made especially difficult by the fact that no single database contained all of the programs and projects accomplished in Iraq. The Iraq Reconstruction Management System, designed to capture this data, was used by some agencies but not by others. SIGIR found IRMS to contain only a portion of the projects ostensibly accomplished. The fact is we do not know all of what we built. If created, USOCO would ensure integrated planning on contracting, personnel, and information management systems, among other things.

5. Require Robust Oversight of SRO Activities from the Operation's Inception

As Senator Susan Collins said, SIGIR was created in late 2003 because the Congress was not receiving the oversight it needed from departmental inspectors general. Eventually, SIGIR had over 50 investigators, auditors, and inspectors on the ground in country, and they produced work at a very high rate under quite dangerous conditions. Representative Peter Welch acknowledged the need for this robust presence, noting that without it, the Congress would have been unaware of the challenges the rebuilding program faced. Further, General David Petraeus said that "the Iraq experience proved the value of oversight." And General Austin said SIGIR provided the "necessary help" that was needed to track the increased appropriations for Iraq's reconstruction. The key structural aspects that helped make SIGIR successful were its strong multijurisdictional mandate, exceptional employment provisions, powerful audit and investigative powers, and sufficient resources.

The owner of a feed mill in Sayafiyah accepts a microgrant from members of the Baghdad embedded Provincial Reconstruction Team. (U.S. Army photo).

6. Preserve and Refine Programs Developed in Iraq, Like the Commander's Emergency Response Program and the Provincial Reconstruction Team Program, That Produced Successes When Used Judiciously

As General Petraeus said, there were a number of notable successes in the Iraq program. Interior Ministers al-Zubeidi and al-Bolani complimented the crucial contributions provided by the Multi-National Security Transition Command-Iraq. General Odierno identified the training of the Iraqi Security Forces and the CERP as "good investments, successes when compared with some of the other programs." Indeed, CERP and the PRT program both achieved significant progress when wisely managed. Lieutenant General Robert Caslen stated that the PRTs are "something we have to continue. That is one of the huge takeaways from this experience." The agencies and the Congress should study these and other programs that worked in Iraq with an eye toward preserving their best aspects for use in future SROs.

7. Plan in Advance, Plan Comprehensively and in an Integrated Fashion, and Have Backup Plans Ready to Go

As Secretary of Defense Leon Panetta noted, the Iraq program's early phases revealed "a lack of thought" with regard to planning. This was perhaps symptomatic of the significant shift in strategy that occurred in April 2003, when the program apparently, though not yet expressly, moved from a "liberate and leave" approach to one of "occupy and rebuild." Rather than effecting a rapid transfer of sovereignty, as in Afghanistan, Iraq saw the creation of the Coalition Provisional Authority, whose mandate reached, with United Nations' sanction, to the complete governance of the country and whose reconstruction program grew to a level several orders of magnitude larger than the one approved by the President at the March 10, 2003, National Security Council principals' meeting. Swamped by systemic and security problems, the CPA never achieved the capacity to reach many of its goals. The rebuilding program then devolved into a series of perennial re-evaluations and reprogrammings that drove "off-budget" supplemental requests. In retrospect, the Iraq reconstruction experience looks like nine one-year programs rather than a nine-year program. There are reasons: the volatile security situation, the constant rotation of U.S. personnel, the quandaries of war-zone contracting, and the ebb and flow of sectarianism in Iraq, among others. But, as General Petraeus observed, developing a comprehensive understanding of the society, culture, governance, and institutions of the host country is crucial to an SRO's success. This fits with what Deputy Secretary of State Thomas Nides said when listing his biggest lessons from Iraq: you must "plan more strategically (in five-year, not one-year, increments)." And as Kurdish Minister Qubad Talabani said of the Iraq program, there "was usually a Plan A but never a Plan B." All useful and instructive—but how and where to do the necessary planning with regard to future SROs remains an open question.

AFTERWORD

The Congress created SIGIR as a temporary organization to oversee and report on Iraq's reconstruction. Its mission was without precedent in U.S. history. I have had the rare and very great pleasure of leading this modest federal agency from its inception. We have accomplished much during our tenure, including:

- 35 Quarterly Reports to the U.S. Congress
- 220 audits, with over $1.61 billion in financial benefits
- 170 inspections

196 Special Inspector General for Iraq Reconstruction

- 82 convictions, with over $191 million in financial results
- 9 lessons-learned reports
- 3 special reports and 1 evaluation
- 35 congressional testimonies
- 34 IG trips to Iraq

Hundreds of thousands served in Iraq carrying out an ambitious and challenging program to secure and rebuild that country, and hundreds served with SIGIR to oversee and report on those efforts. Ours was a special calling executed in accord with the core values I set for the organization: professionalism, productivity, and perseverance.

I thank President Bush and Secretaries Rumsfeld and Powell for their faith in selecting and appointing me to lead this mission. I thank President Obama and Secretaries Rice, Gates, Clinton, and Panetta for their support of SIGIR over the years. I thank Generals Sanchez, Casey, Petraeus, Odierno, and Austin, as well as Ambassadors Bremer, Negroponte, Khalilzad, Crocker, Hill, Jeffrey, and Beecroft for their interest in and patience with our work. I thank our reporting committees in the Congress for sustainment and follow-through.

I thank all of those who faithfully served alongside me at SIGIR as we carried out our ever-challenging but ever-rewarding mission: oversight under fire. I am especially grateful for the long hours and hard work put in by my writing and production staff, led by Executive Editor Bill Maly, his Deputy Karen Burchard, and Christine BathZachery, Leland Bettis, Michael Diakiwsky, Bradley Larson, Tyler Marshall, Kevin O'Connor, Claudia Smith, Bonnie Stephens, and Gwendolyn Toops. *Learning From Iraq* succeeds because of their collective commitment to excellence. I also thank my SIGIR leadership team for its many contributions to this final report: Deputy Inspector General Glenn Furbish, Chief of Staff Paul Cooksey, Assistant Inspector General for Audits Jim Shafer, Assistant Inspector General for Investigations Dan Willkens, Assistant Inspector General for Congressional Affairs Hillel Weinberg, Assistant Inspector General for Management and Administration Christopher Williams, General Counsel Michael Mobbs, Director of Operations Karl Tool, Executive Assistant Dena Nevarez, and Special Assistant to the Inspector General Sahar Salem. Finally, and most of all, I thank my wife, Adriana, and my children for much love.

APPENDIX A: A BILL TO ESTABLISH THE UNITED STATES OFFICE FOR CONTINGENCY OPERATIONS, AND FOR OTHER PURPOSES

Be it enacted by the Senate and House of Representatives of the United States of America in Congress assembled,

SECTION 1. SHORT TITLE; TABLE OF CONTENTS.
(a) SHORT TITLE.—This Act may be cited as the "Stabilization and Reconstruction Integration Act of 2013".
(b) TABLE OF CONTENTS.—The table of contents is as follows:
Sec. 1. Short title; table of contents.
Sec. 2. Definitions.
Sec. 3. Findings and purposes.

Sec. 4. Construction; severability.

Sec. 5. Effective date.

TITLE I—UNITED STATES OFFICE FOR CONTINGENCY OPERATIONS: ESTABLISHMENT, FUNCTIONS, AND PERSONNEL

Sec. 101. Establishment of the United States Office for Contingency Operations.

Sec. 102. Responsibilities of the Director, Deputy Director, Inspector General, and other offices.

Sec. 103 Personnel system.

TITLE II—PREPARING AND EXECUTING STABILITY AND RECONSTRUCTION OPERATIONS

Sec. 201. Sole control.

Sec. 202. Relation to Department of State and United States Agency for International Development.

Sec. 203. Relation to Department of Defense combatant commands performing military missions.

Sec. 204. Stabilization Federal Acquisition Regulation.

Sec. 205. Stabilization and Reconstruction Fund.

TITLE III—RESPONSIBILITIES OF THE INSPECTOR GENERAL

Sec. 301. Inspector General.

TITLE IV—RESPONSIBILITIES OF OTHER AGENCIES

Sec. 401. Responsibilities of other agencies for monitoring and evaluation requirements.

Sec. 402. Transition of stabilization and reconstruction operations. Sec. 403. Sense of Congress.

TITLE V—AUTHORIZATION OF APPROPRIATIONS Sec. 501. Authorization of appropriations.

SEC. 2. DEFINITIONS.

In this Act, the following definitions apply:

(1) **APPROPRIATE CONGRESSIONAL COMMITTEES.—**

The term "appropriate congressional committees"means—

(A) the Committees on Appropriations, Armed Services, Foreign Affairs, and Oversight and Government Reform of the House of Representatives; and the Committees on Appropriations, Armed Services, Foreign Relations, and Homeland Security and Governmental Affairs of the Senate.

(2) **DIRECTOR.**—The term "Director"means the Director of the United States Office for Contingency Operations.

(3) **FUNCTIONS.**—The term "functions"includes authorities, powers, rights, privileges, immunities, programs, projects, activities, duties, and responsibilities.

(4) **IMMINENT STABILIZATION AND RECONSTRUCTION OPERATION.—** The term "imminent stabilization and reconstruction operation"is a condition in a foreign country which the Director believes may require in the immediate future a response from the United States and with respect to which preparation for a stabilization and reconstruction operation is necessary.

(5) **INTELLIGENCE COMMUNITY.**—The term "intelligence community"has the meaning given that term in section 3(4) of the National Security Act of 1947 (50 U.S.C. 401a(4)).

(6) OFFICE.—The term "Office"means the United States Office for Contingency Operations.

(7) PERSONNEL.—The term "personnel"means officers and employees of an Executive agency, except that the term does not include members of the Armed Forces.

(8) POTENTIAL STABILIZATION AND RECONSTRUCTION OPERATION.— The term "potential stabilization and reconstruction operation"is a possible condition in a foreign country which in the determination of the Director may require in the immediate future a response from the United States and with respect to which preparation for a stabilization and reconstruction operation is advisable.

(9) STABILIZATION AND RECONSTRUCTION EMERGENCY.—The term 'stabilization and reconstruction emergency" is a stabilization and reconstruction operation which is the subject of a Presidential declaration pursuant to section 103.

STABILIZATION AND RECONSTRUCTION OPERATION.—The term 'stabilization and reconstruction operation"—

(A) means a circumstance in which a combination of security, reconstruction, relief, and development services, including assistance for the development of military and security forces and the provision of infrastructure and essential services (including services that might be provided under the authority of chapter 4 of part II of the Foreign Assistance Act of 1961 (22 U.S.C. 2346 et seq.; relating to the Economic Support Fund)), should, in the national interest of the United States, be provided on the territory of an unstable foreign country;

(B) does not include a circumstance in which such services should be provided primarily due to a natural disaster (other than a natural disaster of cataclysmic proportions); and

(C) does not include intelligence activities.

(11) **COVERED CONTRACT.**—The term 'covered contract' means a contract entered into by any department or agency, with any public or private sector entity, in any geographic area with regard to a stabilization or reconstruction operation or where the Inspector General of the United States Office for Contingency Operations is exercising its special audit or investigative authority for the performance of any of the following:

(A) To build or rebuild physical infrastructure of such area.

(B) To establish or reestablish a political or governmental institution of such area.

(C) To provide products or services to the local population of the area.

(12) **UNITED STATES.**—The term "United States", when used in a geographic sense, means any State of the United States, the District of Columbia, the Commonwealth of Puerto Rico, the Virgin Islands, Guam, American Samoa, the Commonwealth of the Northern Mariana Islands, any possession of the United States, and any waters within the jurisdiction of the United States.

SEC. 3. FINDINGS AND PURPOSES.

(a) FINDINGS.—Congress finds the following:

(1) Responsibilities for overseas stability and reconstruction operations are divided among several agencies. As a result, lines of responsibility and accountability are not well-defined.

Despite the establishment of the Office of the Coordinator for Reconstruction and Stabilization within the Department of State, the reaffirmation of the Coordinator's mandate by the National Security Presidential Directive 44, its codification with title XVI of the Duncan Hunter National Defense Authorization Act for Fiscal Year 2009, the issuance of the Department of Defense Directive 3000.05, and the creation of the Bureau of Conflict and

Stabilization by the Department of State, serious imbalances and insufficient interagency coordination remain.

The United States Government has not effectively or efficiently managed stabilization and reconstruction operations during recent decades.

Based on recent history, the United States will likely continue to find its involvement necessary in stabilization and reconstruction operations in foreign countries in the wake of violence or cataclysmic disaster.

The United States has not adequately applied the lessons of its recent experiences in stabilization and reconstruction operations, and despite efforts to improve its performance is not yet organized institutionally to respond appropriately to the need to perform stabilization and reconstruction operations in foreign countries. The failure to learn the lessons of past stabilization and reconstruction operations will lead to further inefficiencies, resulting in greater human and financial costs.

(b) PURPOSES.—The purposes of this Act are to—

(1) protect the national security interests of the United States by providing an effective means to plan for and execute stabilization and reconstruction operations in foreign countries;

(2) provide for unity of command, and thus achieve unity of effort, in the planning and execution of stabilization and reconstruction operations;

(4) provide accountability for resources dedicated to stabilization and reconstruction operations;

(4) maximize the efficient use of resources, which would lead to budget savings, eliminated redundancy in functions, and improvement in the management of stabilization and reconstruction operations; and

(5) establish an entity to plan for stabilization and reconstruction operations across the relevant agencies, including the Department of Defense, Department of State, and United States Agency for International Development, and, when directed by the President, coordinate and execute such operations, eventually returning responsibility for such operations to other agencies of the United States Government as the situation becomes normalized.

SEC. 4. CONSTRUCTION; SEVERABILITY.

Any provision of this Act held to be invalid or unenforceable by its terms, or as applied to any person or circumstance, shall be construed so as to give it the maximum effect permitted by law, unless such holding shall be one of utter invalidity or unenforceability, in which event such provision shall be deemed severable from this Act and shall not affect the remainder thereof, or the application of such provision to other persons not similarly situated or to other, dissimilar circumstances.

SEC. 5. EFFECTIVE DATE.

This Act shall take effect on the date that is 60 days after the date of the enactment of this Act.

TITLE I—UNITED STATES OFFICE FOR CONTINGENCY OPERATIONS: ESTABLISHMENT, FUNCTIONS, AND PERSONNEL

SEC. 101. ESTABLISHMENT OF THE UNITED STATES OFFICE FOR CONTINGENCY OPERATIONS.

There is established as an independent entity the United States Office for Contingency Operations, which shall report to the Department of State and the Department of Defense.

SEC. 102. RESPONSIBILITIES OF THE DIRECTOR, DEPUTY DIRECTOR, INSPECTOR GENERAL, AND OTHER OFFICES.

(a) DIRECTOR.—

(1) IN GENERAL.—The Office shall be headed by a Director, who shall be—

(A) appointed by the President, by and with the advice and consent of the Senate; and

(B) compensated at the rate of basic pay for level II of the Executive Schedule under section 5313 of title 5, United States Code.

(2) SUPERVISION.—

(A) IN GENERAL.—The Director shall report directly to, and be under the general supervision of, the Secretary of State and the Secretary of Defense. Such supervision may not be delegated.

(B) INFORMATION SHARING.—The Director shall report to the National Security Advisor keeping the Advisor fully and continually informed of the activities of the Office.

(3) FUNCTIONS.—The functions of the Director shall include the following:

(A) Monitoring, in coordination with relevant offices and bureaus of the Department of Defense, the Department of State, and the United States Agency for International Development, political and economic instability worldwide in order to anticipate the need for mobilizing United States and international assistance for the stabilization and reconstruction of a country or region that is at risk of, in, or in transition from, conflict or civil strife.

(B) Assessing the various types of stabilization and reconstruction crises that could occur and cataloging and monitoring the military and non-military resources, capabilities, and functions of agencies that are available to address such crises.

(C) Pre-intervention assessment and planning and post-intervention evaluation of strategies to achieve US interests and objectives through such activities as demobilization, disarmament, capacity building, rebuilding of civil society, policing and security sector reform, and monitoring and strengthening respect for human rights that commonly arise in stabilization and reconstruction crises.

Developing, in coordination with all relevant agencies, stabilization plans and procedures to mobilize and deploy civilian and military personnel to conduct stabilization and reconstruction operations.

(D) Coordinating with counterparts in foreign governments and international and nongovernmental organizations on stabilization and reconstruction operations to improve effectiveness and avoid duplication.

(E) Aiding the President, as the President may request, in preparing such rules and regulations as the President prescribes, for the planning, coordination, and execution of stabilization and reconstruction operations.

(F) Advising the Secretary of State and the Secretary of Defense, as the Secretary of State or the Secretary of Defense may request, on any matters pertaining to the planning, coordination, and execution of stabilization and reconstruction operations.

(G) Planning and conducting, in cooperation with the Secretary of State, the Administrator of the United States Agency for International Development, the Secretary of Defense, and commanders of unified combatant commands or specified combatant commands, a series of exercises to test and evaluate doctrine relating to stabilization and reconstruction operations and procedures to be used in such operations.

(H) Executing, administering, and enforcing laws, rules, and regulations relating to the preparation, coordination, and execution of stabilization and reconstruction operations.

(I) Administering such funds as may be appropriated or otherwise made available for the preparation, coordination and execution of stabilization and reconstruction operations.

(J) Planning for the use of contractors who will be involved in stabilization and reconstruction operations.

(K) Prescribing standards and policies for project and financial reporting for all agencies involved in stabilization and reconstruction operations under the direction of the Office to ensure that all activities undertaken by such agencies are appropriately tracked and accounted for.

Establishing an interagency training, preparation, and evaluation framework for all personnel deployed, or who may be deployed, in support of stabilization and reconstruction operations.

Such training and preparation shall be developed and administered in partnership with such universities, colleges, or other institutions (whether public, private, or governmental) as the Director may determine and which agree to participate.

(4) RESPONSIBILITIES OF DIRECTOR FOR ASSESSMENT, MONITORING AND EVALUATION REQUIREMENTS.—

(A) Assessment.—The Director shall draw upon all sources of information and intelligence within the government to develop a common understanding of the causes of the conflict and the salient impediments to stabilization as a guide to subsequent planning.

(B) Monitoring.—The Director shall establish, in coordination with the agencies involved in the SRO, measures for determining whether the programs and activities they are implementing are achieving US objectives.

The Director shall have the authority to direct up to 5% of the amount of program expenditures for assessment, monitoring and evaluation purposes.

(C) EVALUATIONS.—The Director shall plan and conduct evaluations of the impact of stabilization and reconstruction operations carried out by the Office.

(D) REPORTS.—

(i) IN GENERAL.—Not later than 30 days after the end of each fiscal-year quarter, the Director shall submit to the appropriate congressional committees a report summarizing all stabilization and reconstruction operations that are taking place under the supervision of the Director during the period of each such quarter and, to the extent possible, the period from the end of each such quarter to the time of the submission of each such report.

Each such report shall include, for the period covered by each such report, a detailed statement of all obligations, expenditures, and revenues associated with such stabilization and reconstruction operations, including the following:

(I) Obligations and expenditures of appropriated funds.

(II) A project-by-project and program-by-program accounting of the costs incurred to date for the stabilization and reconstruction operation that are taking place, together with the estimate of any department or agency that is undertaking a project in or for the stabilization and reconstruction of such country, as applicable, of the costs to complete each project and each program.

(III) Revenues attributable to or consisting of funds provided by foreign countries or international organizations, and any obligations or expenditures of such revenues.

(IV) Revenues attributable to or consisting of foreign assets seized or frozen, and any obligations or expenditures of such revenues.

(V) An analysis on the impact of stabilization and reconstruction operations overseen by the Office, including an analysis of civil-military coordination with respect to the Office.

(ii) FORM.—Each report under this subsection may include a classified annex if the Director determines such is appropriate.

(iii) RULE OF CONSTRUCTION.—Nothing in this paragraph shall be construed to authorize the public disclosure of information that is specifically prohibited from disclosure by any other provision of law, specifically required by Executive order to be protected from disclosure in the interest of national defense or national security or in the conduct of foreign affairs, or a part of an ongoing criminal investigation.

(b) DEPUTY DIRECTOR.—

(1) IN GENERAL.—There shall be within the Office a Deputy Director, who shall be—

(A) appointed by the President; and compensated at the rate of basic pay for level III of the Executive Schedule under section 5314 of title 5, United States Code.

(2) FUNCTIONS.—The Deputy Director shall perform such functions as the Director may from time to time prescribe, and shall act as Director during the absence or disability of the Director or in the event of a vacancy in the Office of the Director.

(d) FUNCTIONS OF THE PRESIDENT.—

(1) DECLARATION.—The President may, if the President finds that the circumstances and national security interests of the United States so require, declare that a stabilization and reconstruction emergency exists and shall determine the geographic extent and the date of the commencement of such emergency. The President may amend the declaration as circumstances warrant.

(2) TERMINATION.—If the President determines that a stabilization and reconstruction emergency declared under paragraph (1) is or will no longer be in existence, the President may terminate, immediately or prospectively, a prior declaration that such an emergency exists.

(3) PUBLICATION IN FEDERAL REGISTER.—Declarations under this subsection shall be published in the Federal Register.

(e) AUTHORITIES OF OFFICE FOLLOWING PRESIDENTIAL DECLARATION.—If the President declares a stabilization and reconstruction emergency pursuant to subsection (d), the President may delegate to the Director the authority to coordinate all Federal efforts with respect to such stabilization and reconstruction emergency, including the authority to direct any Federal agency to support such efforts, with or without reimbursement.

SEC. 104. PERSONNEL SYSTEM.

(a) PERSONNEL.—

(1) IN GENERAL.—The Director may select, appoint, and employ such personnel as may be necessary for carrying out the duties of the Office, subject to the provisions of title 5, United States Code, governing appointments in the excepted service, and the provisions of chapter 51 and subchapter III of chapter 53 of such title, relating to classification and General Schedule pay rates, and may exercise the authorities of subsections (b) through (i) of section 3161 of title 5, United States Code (to the same extent and in the same manner as those authorities may be exercised by an organization described in subsection (a) of such section). In exercising the employment authorities under subsection (b) of such section 3161, paragraph (2) of such subsection (relating to periods of appointments) shall not apply.

(2) SUBDIVISIONS OF OFFICE; DELEGATION OF FUNCTIONS.—The Director may establish bureaus, offices, divisions, and other units within the Office.

The Director may from time to time make provision for the performance of any function of the Director by any officer or employee, or office, division, or other unit of the Office.

(3) REEMPLOYMENT AUTHORITIES.—The provisions of section 9902(g) of title 5, United States Code, shall apply with respect to the Office.

For purposes of the preceding sentence, such provisions shall be applied—

(A) by substituting "the United States Office for Contingency Operations"for "the Department of Defense"each place it appears;

(B) by substituting "the Stabilization and Reconstruction Operations Interagency Enhancement Act of 2011"for "the National Defense Authorization Act for Fiscal Year 2004 (Public Law 108–136)"in paragraph (2)(A) thereof; and

(C) by substituting "the Director of the United States Office for Contingency Operations"for "the Secretary"in paragraph (4) thereof.

(b) INTERIM OFFICERS.—

(1) IN GENERAL.—The President may authorize any persons who, immediately prior to the effective date of this Act, held positions in the Executive Branch of the Government, to act as Director, Deputy Director, Associate Director, and Inspector General of the Office until such positions are for the first time filled in accordance with the provisions of this Act .

(2) COMPENSATION.—The President may authorize any such person described in paragraph (1) to receive the compensation attached to the Office in respect of which such person so serves, in lieu of other compensation from the United States.

(c) CONTRACTING SERVICES.—

(1) IN GENERAL.—The Director may obtain services of experts and consultants as authorized by section 3109 of title 5, United States Code.

(2) ASSISTANCE.—To the extent and in such amounts as may be provided in advance by appropriations Acts, the Inspector General may enter into contracts and other arrangements for audits, studies, analyses, and other services with public agencies and with private persons, and make such payments as may be necessary to carry out the duties of the Inspector General.

(d) INCENTIVIZING EXPERTISE IN PERSONNEL TASKED FOR STABILIZATION AND RECONSTRUCTION OPERATIONS.—

(1) STUDY.—The Director shall commission a study to measure the effectiveness of personnel in stabilization and reconstruction operations.

The study shall seek to identify the most appropriate qualifications for personnel and incentive strategies for agencies to effectively recruit and deploy employees to support stabilization and reconstruction operations.

(2) The Office shall apply preferences promoting the employment of veterans and the use of veteran-owned businesses.

(3) SENSE OF CONGRESS.—It is the sense of Congress that, in the selection and appointment of any individual for a position both within the Office and other agencies in support of stabilization and reconstruction operations, due consideration should be given to such individual's expertise in such operations and interagency experience and qualifications.

TITLE II—PREPARING AND EXECUTING STABILITY AND RECONSTRUCTION OPERATIONS

SEC. 201. SOLE CONTROL.

The Director shall have primary management responsibilities over relief and reconstruction activities conducted during a stabilization and reconstruction emergency declared by the President.

SEC. 202. RELATION TO DEPARTMENT OF STATE AND UNITED STATES AGENCY FOR INTERNATIONAL DEVELOPMENT.

(a) COORDINATION.—

(1) IN GENERAL.—The Director shall, to the greatest degree practicable, coordinate with the Secretary of State and the Administrator of the U.S. Agency for International Development regarding the Office's plans for relief and reconstruction activities conducted during stabilization and reconstruction operations. The Director shall give the greatest possible weight to the views of the Secretary and the Administrator on matters within their jurisdiction. During a declaration under section 103 of a stabilization and reconstruction emergency, the Director shall work closely with the Secretary and the Administrator in planning, executing, and transitioning operations relevant to their respective jurisdictions.

(2) IN-COUNTRY.—During a stabilization and reconstruction emergency, the Director shall work closely with the Chief of Mission, or with the most senior Department of State or Agency for International Development officials responsible for the country in which such emergency exists, to ensure that the actions of the Office and all the agencies involved support the attainment of US interests and objectives and do not conflict with the foreign or development policies of the United States.

(b) DETAILING.—The heads of the various departments and agencies of the United States Government (other than the Secretary of Defense) shall provide for the detail on a reimbursable or nonreimbursable basis of such civilian personnel as may be agreed between such heads and the Director for the purposes of carrying out this Act. The heads of such departments and agencies shall provide for appropriate recognition and career progress for individuals who are so detailed upon their return from such details.

SEC. 203. RELATION TO DEPARTMENT OF DEFENSE COMBATANT COMMANDS PERFORMING MILITARY MISSIONS.

(a) COORDINATION WITH SECRETARY OF DEFENSE AND COMBATANT COMMANDS.—To the greatest degree practicable, the Director shall coordinate with the Secretary of Defense and commanders of unified and specified combatant commands established under section 161 of title 10, United States Code, regarding the relief and reconstruction plans of the Office for stabilization and reconstruction operations.

(b) STAFF COORDINATION.—The Director shall detail personnel of the Office to serve on the staff of a combatant command to assist in planning when a military operation will involve likely Armed Forces interaction with non-combatant populations, so that plans for a stabilization and reconstruction operation related to a military operation—

(1) complement the work of military planners; and

(2) as provided in subsection (c), ease interaction between civilian direct-hire employees and contractors in support of the stabilization and reconstruction operation and the Armed Forces.

(c) LIMITATIONS.—

(1) DIRECTOR.—The authority of the Director shall not extend to small-scale programs (other than economic development programs of more than a de minimis amount) designated by the Secretary of Defense as necessary to promote a safe operating environment for the Armed Forces or other friendly forces.

MILITARY ORDER.—Nothing in this Act shall be construed as permitting the Director or any of the personnel of the Office (other than a member of the Armed Forces assigned to the Office under subsection (e)) to issue a military order.

(d) SUPPORT.—

(1) ASSISTANCE REQUIRED.—The commanders of combatant commands shall provide assistance, to the greatest degree practicable, to the Director and the personnel of the Office as they carry out their responsibilities.

(2) PERSONNEL.—The Secretary of Defense shall provide for the detail or assignment, on a reimbursable or nonreimbursable basis, to the staff of the Office of such Department of Defense personnel between the Secretary and the Director as necessary to carry out the duties of the Office.

SEC. 204. STABILIZATION FEDERAL ACQUISITION REGULATION.

(a) REQUIREMENT TO PRESCRIBE STABILIZATION FEDERAL ACQUISITION REGULATION.—

The Director, in consultation with the Director of the Office of Management and Budget, shall prescribe a Stabilization Federal Acquisition Regulation.

The Regulation shall apply, under such circumstances as the Director prescribes, in lieu of the Federal Acquisition Regulation with respect to contracts intended for use in or with respect to stabilization and reconstruction emergencies or in imminent or potential stabilization and reconstruction operations.

(b) PREFERENCE TO CERTAIN CONTRACTS.—It is the sense of Congress that the Stabilization Federal Acquisition Regulation required by subsection (a) should include provisions requiring an agency to give a preference to contracts that appropriately, efficiently, and sustainably implement programs and projects undertaken in support of a stabilization and reconstruction operation.

DEADLINE.—The Director shall prescribe the Stabilization Federal Acquisition Regulation required by subsection (a) by the date occurring one year after the date of the enactment of this Act.

If the Director does not prescribe the Regulation by that date, the Director shall submit to Congress a statement explaining why the deadline was not met.

SEC. 205. STABILIZATION AND RECONSTRUCTION FUND.

(a) IN GENERAL.—There is established in the Treasury of the United States a fund, to be known as the "Stabilization and Reconstruction Emergency Reserve Fund,"to be administered by the Director at the direction of the President and with the consent of the Secretary of State and the Secretary of Defense for the following purposes with respect to a stabilization and reconstruction operation.

(b) CONGRESSIONAL NOTIFICATION.—

(1) PRESIDENTIAL DIRECTION.—At the time the President directs the Director to carry out or support an activity described in subsection (a), the President shall transmit to appropriate congressional committees a written notification of such direction.

(2) ACTIVITIES IN A COUNTRY.—Not less than 15 days before carrying out or supporting an activity described in subsection (a), the Director shall submit to the appropriate congressional committees information related to the budget, implementation timeline (including milestones), and transition strategy with respect to such activity and the stabilization or reconstruction operation at issue.

(c) AUTHORIZATION OF APPROPRIATIONS.—There is authorized to the appropriated to the fund established under subsection (a) such sums as may be necessary to carry out the purposes specified in such subsection. Such sums—

(1) shall be available until expended;

(2) shall not be made available for obligation or expenditure until the President declares a stabilization and reconstruction emergency pursuant to section 103; and

(3) shall be in addition to any other funds made available for such purposes.

SEC. 206. SENSE OF CONGRESS.

It is the sense of Congress that, to the extent possible, the Director and staff should partner with the country in which a stabilization and reconstruction operation is taking place, other foreign government partners, international organizations, and local nongovernmental organizations throughout the planning, implementation, and particularly during the transition stages of such operations to facilitate long term capacity building and sustainability of initiatives.

TITLE III—RESPONSIBILITIES OF THE INSPECTOR GENERAL
SEC. 301. INSPECTOR GENERAL.

(a) IN GENERAL.—There shall be within the Office an Office of the Inspector General, the head of which shall be the Inspector General of the United States Office for Contingency Operations (in this Act referred to as the "Inspector General"), who shall be appointed as provided in section 3(a) of the Inspector General Act of 1978 (5 U.S.C. App.).

(b) TECHNICAL AMENDMENTS AND ADDITIONAL AUTHORITIES.—The Inspector General Act of 1978 (5 U.S.C. App.) is amended—

(1) in section 12—

(A) in paragraph (1), by inserting ", or the United States Office for Contingency Operations"after "the Director of the Federal Housing Finance Agency"; and

(B) in paragraph (2), by inserting "the United States Office for Contingency Operations,'after "the Federal Housing Finance

(2) in section 8J, by striking "8E or 8F"and inserting "8E, 8F, or 8M";

(3) by inserting after section 8L the following new section:

'SEC. 8M. SPECIAL PROVISIONS CONCERNING THE INSPECTOR GENERAL OF THE UNITED STATES OFFICE FOR CONTINGENCY OPERATIONS.

"(a) SPECIAL AUDIT AND INVESTIGATIVE AUTHORITY.— "(1) IN GENERAL.—When directed by the President, or otherwise provided by law, and in addition to the other duties and responsibilities specified in this Act, the Inspector General of the United States Office for Contingency Operations—shall, with regard to the reconstruction and stabilization operations under the supervision of the Director have audit and investigative authority over all accounts, spending, programs, projects, and activities undertaken with respect to such reconstruction and stabilization operations of agencies of the United States Government without regard to the agency carrying out such operations.

"(3) ADMINISTRATIVE OPERATIONS.—In any case in which the Inspector General of the United States Office for Contingency Operations is exercising or preparing to exercise special audit and investigative authority under this subsection, the head of any department or agency undertaking or preparing to undertake the activities described in paragraph (2) shall provide such Inspector General with appropriate and adequate office space within the offices of such department or agency or at appropriate locations of that department or agency overseas, together with such equipment, office supplies, and communications facilities and services as may be necessary for the operation of such offices, and shall provide necessary maintenance services for such offices and the equipment and facilities located therein.

"(b) ADDITIONAL DUTIES.—

"(1) IN GENERAL.—It shall be the duty of the Inspector General of the United States Office for Contingency Operations to conduct, supervise, and coordinate audits and investigations of the treatment, handling, and expenditure of amounts appropriated or otherwise made available for activities to be carried out by or under the direction or supervision of the Director of the United States Office for Contingency Operations, or for activities subject to the special audit and investigative authority of such Inspector General under subsection (a), and of the programs, operations, and contracts carried out utilizing such funds, including—

(A) the oversight and accounting of the obligation and expenditure of such funds;

(B) the monitoring and review of activities funded by such funds;

(C) the monitoring and review of contracts funded by such funds; the monitoring and review of the transfer of such funds and associated information between and among departments, agencies, and entities of the United States, and private and nongovernmental entities; and

"(E) the maintenance of records on the use of such funds to facilitate future audits and investigations of the use of such funds.

'"(2) SYSTEMS, PROCEDURES, AND CONTROLS.—The Inspector General of the United States Office for Contingency Operations shall establish, maintain, and oversee such systems, procedures, and controls as such Inspector General considers appropriate to discharge the duty under paragraph (1).

"(c) PERSONNEL AUTHORITY.—

(1) IN GENERAL.—The Inspector General of the United States Office for Contingency Operations may select, appoint, and employ such officers and employees as may be necessary for carrying out the functions, powers, and duties of the Office, subject to the provisions of title 5, United States Code, governing appointments in the excepted service, and the provisions of chapter 51 and subchapter III of chapter 53 of such title, relating to classification and General Schedule pay rates.

(2) EMPLOYMENT AUTHORITY.—The Inspector General of the United States Office for Contingency Operations may exercise the authorities of subsections (b) through (i) of section 3161 of title 5, United States Code (without regard to subsection (a) of that section).

In exercising the employment authorities under subsection (b) of section 3161 of title 5, United States Code, as provided under paragraph

(1) of this subsection, paragraph

(2) of such subsection (b) (relating to periods of appointments) shall not apply.

(3) EXEMPTION.—Section 6(a)(7) shall not apply with respect to the Inspector General of the United States Office for Contingency Operations.

REPORTS UNDER SECTION 5 OF THIS ACT.—

In addition to reports otherwise required to be submitted under this subsection, the Inspector General of the United States Office for Contingency Operations— may issue periodic reports of a similar nature to the quarterly reports submitted under paragraph (1) with respect to activities subject to the special audit and investigative authority of such Inspector General under subsection (a)

"(6) FORM OF SUBMISSION.—Each report under this subsection may include a classified annex if the Inspector General of the United States Office for Contingency Operations considers it necessary.

"(7) DISCLOSURE OF CERTAIN INFORMATION.— Nothing in this subsection shall be construed to authorize the public disclosure of information that is—

"(A) specifically prohibited from disclosure by any other provision of law; specifically required by Executive order to be protected from disclosure in the interest of national defense or national security or in the conduct of foreign affairs; or a part of an ongoing criminal investigation.

TITLE IV—RESPONSIBILITIES OF OTHER AGENCIES
SEC. 401. RESPONSIBILITIES OF OTHER AGENCIES FOR MONITORING AND EVALUATION REQUIREMENTS.

The head of any agency under the authority of the Director in support of a stabilization and reconstruction operation pursuant to section 103 shall submit to the Director—

(1) on-going evaluations of the impact of agency activities on the stabilization and reconstruction operation , using the measures developed by the Director in consultation with the agencies involved, including an assessment of interagency coordination in support of such operation;

(2) any information the Director requests, including reports, evaluations, analyses, or assessments, to permit the Director to satisfy the quarterly reporting requirement under section 103(a) (4); and

(3) an identification, within each such agency, of all current and former employees skilled in crisis response, including employees employed by contract, and information regarding each such agency's authority mechanisms to reassign or reemploy such skilled personnel and mobilize rapidly associated resources in response to such operation.

TITLE V—AUTHORIZATION OF APPROPRIATIONS
SEC. 501. AUTHORIZATION OF APPROPRIATIONS.

There are authorized to be appropriated such sums as may be necessary to carry out this Act for each of fiscal years 2011 through 2016.

Any amounts appropriated to carry out this Act shall remain available until expended.

APPENDIX B: TABLES

Table B.1. Department of State Programs

Bureau of International Narcotics and Law Enforcement Affairs (INL)	Since 2003, INL has operated programs to train and equip Iraq's police, including reestablishing a police academy in Baghdad and funding international police trainers through the Department of Justice (DoJ). INL's rule-of-law programs have built capacity in the Iraqi judiciary, provided rule-of-law advisors, and funded initiatives such as the Iraqi Justice Integration Project, Major Crimes Task Force, and courthouse security upgrades. INL's Anti-Corruption Coordination Office (ACCO) has coordinated many of these efforts, including funding of initiatives by UNDP and UNODC to help Iraq implement a national anticorruption strategy that will help it to comply with its commitments under the *United Nations Convention Against Corruption* (ratified in 2008), to train IGs, assist COI with financial investigations, and work with the Kurdistan Regional Government on budget execution. More than $21 million in ACCO programs remained ongoing as of September 30, 2012, including funding for DoJ's Overseas Prosecutorial Development Assistance and Training (OPDAT) anti-money-laundering program. Since September 2010, INL has funded the Financial Crimes Training Program, implemented by the Department of the Treasury's Office of Technical Assistance (OTA), with $1.9 million of the INCLE. The program (expected to run through October 2013) funds an OTA resident advisor, who provides training assistance to enhance the COI's capacity to prevent, detect, investigate, and prosecute government corruption and related serious financial crimes. The two-year, $1.5 million, ESF-funded English as a Second Language Project (*Tumooh*) was implemented by UNDP through September 2013. INL also supported the Iraqi Corrections Service with training programs and other initiatives, including funding $16.8 million for the DoJ's International Criminal Investigative Training Assistance Program (ICITAP), which ended in September 2012 and transitioned its work to UNODC.
Bureau of Population, Refugees, and Migration (PRM)	Most programs supported internally displaced persons (IDPs) inside Iraq and refugees living in Syria, Turkey, Jordan, Lebanon, and Egypt. PRM assisted Iraqi refugees and Special Immigrant Visa (SIV) holders who elected to receive refugee benefits to resettle in the United States. Humanitarian initiatives have addressed agriculture and food security, economic recovery and market systems, water and sanitation, and hygiene. PRM worked in coordination with USAID's OFDA. As of September 30, 2012, more than 73,000 refugees had resettled in the United States through the U.S. Refugee Admissions Program since FY 2007.
Bureau of Democracy, Human Rights, and Labor (DRL)	DRL administered foreign assistance programs intended to support Iraqi governance, human rights, and civil society under the strategic goal of governing justly and democratically. They were aimed at providing greater public accountability and freedom of expression, as well as religious freedom. DRL grant projects supported war widows, strengthened human rights prosecution, supported women's political and economic empowerment, assessed knowledge and attitudes regarding gender-based violence, and supported freedom of the press and members of the lesbian, gay, bisexual, and transgender community.
Bureau of Political-Military Affairs	The bureau served as the principal link between DoS and DoD to facilitate U.S./Coalition military operations with a mission to use diplomacy and military power to foster a stable and secure international environment receptive to American values and interests. Funded by DoS's NADR account, the Bureau's Office of Weapons Removal and Abatement has managed the Conventional Weapons Destruction (CWD) program in Iraq since 2003, working on clearance and safe disposal of landmines, unexploded ordnance, and excess conventional weapons and munitions. As of September 30, 2012, approximately $22 million in NADR-funded contracts were ongoing, employing 609 program personnel (98% Iraqi) and 177 security contractors.
Office of Export Control Cooperation	The office assisted the GOI in developing trade control systems; helped to ensure those systems met existing international standards; and built capacity to detect, interdict, investigate, and prosecute illicit trade in weapons of mass destruction and conventional arms. During FY 2009–FY 2012, the $4 million Export Controls and Related Border Security (EXBS) program worked with GOI to deploy TRACKER software system to improve ability to control exports of sensitive items.

Table B.2. Other Civilian Agency Programs

Department of Justice (DoJ)	The Office of the Justice Attaché coordinated a number of anticorruption, rule-of-law, and corrections programs via the OPDAT program, the FBI Legal Attaché, and the ICITAP program. DoJ supported the Iraqi Corrections Service from 2003 through 2011 to build 30 prisons that house 20,000 inmates and employ more than 12,000 staff. DoJ's Major Crimes Task Force (MCTF) addressed complex crimes and terrorist activity. The International Contract Corruption Task Force; Bureau of Alcohol, Tobacco, Firearms, and Explosives; U.S. Marshals; Regime Crimes Liaison Office; and Drug Enforcement Agency each played supporting roles.
Department of Homeland Security (DHS	The DHS Attaché coordinated services to assess operations and security for borders and ports of entry (land, sea, and air) and provided infrastructure protection, terrorist financing investigations, and naturalization services to U.S. military members. Immigration and Customs Enforcement officials advised and mentored primarily Iraq's Federal Information and Investigations Agency and Customs Police on the issues of human trafficking, narcotics smuggling, and financial crimes. Customs and Border Protection (CBP) provided non-intrusive inspections equipment to GOI customs inspectors. The U.S. Coast Guard (USCG) worked with the GOI to improve port security and with the Department of Transportation (DoT) Attaché to bring the Port of Umm Qasr into compliance with the International Ship and Port Facility Security Code. The U.S. Citizenship and Immigration Service has interviewed Iraqi refugee applicants who have worked for the U.S. government, U.S. military, or a U.S.-affiliated media or non-governmental organization to determine whether they qualify for consideration for resettlement in the United States.
Department of the Treasury	The U.S. Treasury's Office of Technical Assistance (OTA) conducted activities to develop modern financial, budgetary, banking, and taxation policies and provide limited assistance to Iraq's Commission on Integrity. OTA's Economic Crimes Team shifted from working with the Central Bank of Iraq on anti-money-laundering activities to support the COI with case management and modern financial analysis. The Revenue Team worked on a series of reforms to broaden Iraq's tax base and formulate filing requirements and penalties for non-compliance. The Banking Team assisted the GOI with restructuring state-owned banks and automating data systems. The Budget Team worked with Iraq's Ministry of Finance and other GOI entities on budget planning and execution. These other Treasury offices also supported work in Iraq: the Office of International Affairs, Office of the Comptroller of the Currency, Financial Management Service, Internal Revenue Service, and Office of the General Counsel.
Department of Transportation (DoT)	The Office of Transportation Attaché at U.S. Embassy-Baghdad worked with the GOI—in particular, the Ministry of Transportation—on reforming and modernizing its transportation regulations and infrastructure to bring them into line with international norms, thereby improving Iraqi access to global markets. Staff included the Senior Aviation Advisor and Maritime/Ports Advisor. DoT supported delivery of the $17.3 million U.S.-funded Computer Based Train Control System and training and certification of Iraq's air-traffic controllers.
Department of Commerce	Commerce once had a staff of six in Baghdad, but one was killed, and several of the Iraqi employees resigned because they were threatened. Commerce has worked to assist U.S. businesses to gain entry to and succeed in the Iraqi market. Commerce compiled due diligence reports for U.S. firms on potential Iraqi partners and worked with small and medium enterprises based in the United States to assess their suitability for the Iraqi market and assist them to obtain the information and licensing. Commerce facilitated advocacy cases to gain contracts for firms when it served the U.S. national interest.
Department of Agriculture (USDA	The Office of Agricultural Affairs (OAA) at U.S. Embassy-Baghdad performed outreach to farmers through the PRT program from 2009 to 2011, then transitioned to engagement with senior officials at the Ministry of Agriculture to offer policy advice and assist in resolving issues that arose after implementation of new import regulations. The USDA has sponsored training under the Cochran and Borlaug Fellowship programs, and OAA has supported veterinary medicine initiatives.
Department of Health and Human Services	Although one of the five agencies authorized apportionments of the IRRF, the department did not receive any. The department's $1 million SAMHSA mental health and substance-abuse prevention program for Iraq provided outreach services in 2011 and 2012.
Export-Import Bank (Ex-Im)	Since commencement of work in Iraq in July 2010, the Ex-Im Bank provided more than $45.1 million in loans, guarantees, or insurance policies for at least four U.S. companies providing services in Iraq.
Overseas Private Investment Corporation (OPIC)	OPIC facilitated U.S. private investment in Iraq by offering political risk insurance, investment guarantees, and direct loans. It focused on stimulating economic development in Iraq by sponsoring lending facilities (such as the Iraq Middle Market Development Foundation, funded by $330,000) that have provided loans to credit-worthy businesses and Iraqi private-sector institutions, and providing Iraqi limited liability corporations funding to support small-and-medium-enterprise and microfinance portfolios in Iraq.
U.S. Institute of Peace (USIP)	USIP undertook peacekeeping efforts in Iraq with $10 million provided by the IRRF 2. DRL provided funding for USIP's work to support formation of the Iraqi Constitution and address women's issues.

Table B.3. U.S. Appropriated Funds
$ Millions

Major Funds	P.L. 108-7, P.L. 108-11 (FY 2003)	P.L. 108-106, 108-287 (FY 2004)	P.L. 109-13 (FY 2005)	P.L. 109-102, 109-148, 109-234 (FY 2006)	P.L. 109-289, 110-5, 110-28 (FY 2007)	P.L. 110-92, 110-116, 110-137, 110-149, 110-161, 110-252 (FY 2008)	P.L. 110-252, 111-32 (FY 2009)	P.L. 111-117, 111-118, 111-212 (FY 2010)	P.L. 112-10 (FY 2011)	P.L. 112-74 (FY 2012)	Total Appropriated	Obligated	Expended	Expired
Iraq Relief and Reconstruc-tion Fund (IRRF 1 and IRRF 2)	2,475	18,389									20,864	20,343	20,076	504
Iraq Security Forces Fund (ISFF)			5,490	3,007	5,542	3,000	1,000	1,000	1,155		20,194	19,569	18,762	625
Economic Support Fund (ESF)				1,469	1,554	562	542	383	326	299	5,134	4,578	4,199	260
Commander's Emergency Response Program (CERP)		140	718	708	750	767	747	245	44		4,119	3,728	3,728	391
International Narcotics Control and Law Enforcement (INCLE)				91	170	85	20	702	115	130	1,313	1,155	989	
Subtotal	2,475	18,529	6,208	5,276	8,016	4,414	2,309	2,330	1,639	429	51,624	49,373	47,754	1,781
Other Assistance Programs														

| Major Funds | P.L. 108-7, P.L. 108-11 | P.L. 108-106, P.L. 108-287 | P.L. 109-13 | P.L. 109-102, P.L. 109-148, P.L. 109-234 | P.L. 109-289, P.L. 110-5, P.L. 110-28 | P.L. 110-92, P.L. 110-116, P.L. 110-137, P.L. 110-149, P.L. 110-161, P.L. 110-252 | P.L. 110-252, P.L. 111-32 | P.L. 111-117, P.L. 111-118, P.L. 111-212 | P.L. 112-10 | P.L. 112-74 | | | | |
	FY 2003	FY 2004	FY 2005	FY 2006	FY 2007	FY 2008	FY 2009	FY 2010	FY 2011	FY 2012	Total Appropriated	Obligated	Expended	Expired
Migration and Refugee Assistance (MRA) and Emergency Refugee & Migration Assistance (ERMA)	40				78	278	260	316	280	249	1,501	1,494	1,339	
Foreign Military Financing (FMF)										850	850			
Natural Resources Risk Remediation Fund (NRRRF)	801										801	801	801	
Iraq Freedom Fund (Other Reconstruction Activities)	700										700	680	654	
P.L. 480 Food Aid (Title II and Non-Title II)	368		3			24					395	395	395	

Major Funds	P.L. 108-7, P.L. 108-11	P.L. 108-106, P.L. 108-287	P.L. 109-13	P.L. 109-102, P.L. 109-148, P.L. 109-234	P.L. 109-289, P.L. 110-5, P.L. 110-28	P.L. 110-92, P.L. 110-116, P.L. 110-137, P.L. 110-149, P.L. 110-161, P.L. 110-252	P.L. 110-252, P.L. 111-32	P.L. 111-117, P.L. 111-118, P.L. 111-212	P.L. 112-10	P.L. 112-74				
	FY 2003	FY 2004	FY 2005	FY 2006	FY 2007	FY 2008	FY 2009	FY 2010	FY 2011	FY 2012	Total Appropriated	Obligated	Expended	Expired
International Disaster Assistance (IDA) and International Disaster and Famine Assistance (IDFA)	24		7		45	85	51	42	17		272	261	261	
Democracy Fund (DF) and Human Rights & Democracy Fund (HRDF)					190	75	1				266	266	262	
U.S. Contributions to International Organizations (CIO)						38	30	33	33	44	179			
Iraq Freedom Fund (TFBSO)					50	50	74				174	86	65	
Nonproliferation, Anti-terrorism, Demining, and Related Programs (NADR)					19	16	36	30	30	32	163	62	62	
Department of Justice (DoJ)	37		6	11	23	26	8	9	10	4	133	121	119	

Table B.3. (Continued)

Major Funds	P.L. 108-7, P.L. 108-11 (FY 2003)	P.L. 108-106, P.L. 108-287 (FY 2004)	P.L. 109-13 (FY 2005)	P.L. 109-102, P.L. 109-148, P.L. 109-234 (FY 2006)	P.L. 109-289, P.L. 110-5, P.L. 110-28 (FY 2007)	P.L. 110-92, P.L. 110-116, P.L. 110-137, P.L. 110-149, P.L. 110-161, P.L. 110-252 (FY 2008)	P.L. 110-252, P.L. 111-32 (FY 2009)	P.L. 111-117, P.L. 111-118, P.L. 111-212 (FY 2010)	P.L. 112-10 (FY 2011)	P.L. 112-74 (FY 2012)	Total Appropriated	Obligated	Expended	Expired
Child Survival and Health Programs Fund (CSH)	90										90	90	90	
Education and Cultural Exchange Programs				7	5	7	7	7	8	5	46			
Overseas Humanitarian, Disaster and Civic Aid (OHDACA)	9	15	3								27	27	10	
International Affairs Technical Assistance				13	3						16	16	14	
International Military Education and Training (IMET)					1	2	2	2	2	2	11	9	6	
U.S. Marshals Service			1	3	2	2	1				9	9	9	
Alhurra-Iraq Broadcasting		5									5	5	5	
Subtotal	2,069	21	20	34	416	602	468	440	380	1,187	5,638	4,323	4,093	

Major Funds	P.L. 108-7, P.L. 108-11	P.L. 108-106, P.L. 108-287	P.L. 109-13	P.L. 109-102, P.L. 109-148, P.L. 109-234	P.L. 109-289, P.L. 110-5, P.L. 110-28	P.L. 110-92, P.L. 110-116, P.L. 110-137, P.L. 110-149, P.L. 110-161, P.L. 110-252	P.L. 110-252, P.L. 111-32	P.L. 111-117, P.L. 111-118, P.L. 111-212	P.L. 112-10	P.L. 112-74	Total Appropriated	Obligated	Expended	Expired
	FY 2003	FY 2004	FY 2005	FY 2006	FY 2007	FY 2008	FY 2009	FY 2010	FY 2011	FY 2012				
Reconstruction-Related Operating Expenses														
Coalition Provisional Authority (CPA)		908									908	832	799	
Project and Contracting Office (PCO)				200	630						830			
Office of Security Cooperation-Iraq (OSC-I)										524	524			
USAID Operating Expenses (USAID OE)	21	38	24	79	37	41	48	52	51	54	446	320	286	
DoD OSC-I Support									129		129			
Iraq Freedom Fund (PRT Administra-tive Costs)					100						100			
Subtotal	21	946	24	279	767	41	48	52	180	578	2,937	1,152	1,085	
Reconstruction Oversight														

Major Funds	P.L. 108-7, P.L. 108-11 / FY 2003	P.L. 108-106, P.L. 108-287 / FY 2004	P.L. 109-13 / FY 2005	P.L. 109-102, P.L. 109-148, P.L. 109-234 / FY 2006	P.L. 109-289, P.L. 110-5, P.L. 110-28 / FY 2007	P.L. 110-92, P.L. 110-116, P.L. 110-137, P.L. 110-149, P.L. 110-161, P.L. 110-252 / FY 2008	P.L. 110-252, P.L. 111-32 / FY 2009	P.L. 111-117, P.L. 111-118, P.L. 111-212 / FY 2010	P.L. 112-10 / FY 2011	P.L. 112-74 / FY 2012	Total Appropriated	Obligated	Expended	Expired
Special Inspector General for Iraq Reconstruc-tion (SIGIR)		75		24	35	3	44	23	22	20	245	229	222	
Defense Contract Audit Agency (DCAA)				16	14	14	13	24	30		111	111	111	
DoS Office of the Inspector General (DoS OIG)				1	3	4	6	7	5	9	35			
USAID Office of the Inspector General (USAID OIG)	4	2	3		3	7	4	7			29			
DoD Office of the Inspector General (DoD OIG)				5		21					26			
Subtotal	4	77	3	46	55	48	67	61	57	29	445	340	333	
Total	4,569	19,573	6,255	5,634	9,255	5,104	2,892	2,883	2,256	2,223	60,644	55,187	53,265	1,781

Table B.4. ISFF: Requests, Justifications, Appropriations, and Earmarks, FY 2005–FY 2011
$ Billions

Request	Administration's Budget Justification	Appropriation	Congressional Earmarks and Restrictions
FY 2005 Supplemental $5.70	Provide assistance to the ISF to enable independent counterinsurgency operations and a secure environment; build institutional logistics and training capacity; help field and increase capabilities of security and support forces; improve equipment, sustainment, and command and control; and provide Quick Response Funding	P.L. 109-13 $5.49 Expired 9/30/2006	Provides $5.70, of which $0.21 is transferred to the Army O&M account to reimburse for costs incurred to train and equip the ISF; provides broad transfer authority to other accounts or agencies to fulfill purpose and provide for contributions to ISFF from other governments and international organizations (both requiring notification and continuing into future FYs)
FY 2006 Supplemental $3.70	Continue current train-and-equip program, build operational units' capabilities and readiness, and develop institutional logistics and administrative functions	P.L. 109-234 $3.01 Expired 9/30/2007	Conference agreement notes that it would not have been possible for the full request to be fully obligated and expended in the remaining months of FY 2006 and that "the reduction is taken without prejudice"; conference report urges DoD and Administration to seek support for the ISF from regional countries
FY 2007 Regular $1.70	Joint regular and supplemental appropriations request to build and sustain ISF institutional capability and generate a professional and capable ISF; reorient ISF to quell sectarian violence; provide MOD logistics capabilities, combat support units, mobility/force protection, and equipment; provide MOI with embedded U.S. advisors	P.L. 109-289 $1.70 Expired 9/30/2008	Conference report directs DoD to provide comprehensive financial plans for the ISF
FY 2007 Supplemental $3.80		P.L. 110-28 $3.84 Expired 9/30/2008	Includes funding to disarm, demobilize, and reintegrate militias; requires OMB to submit cost-to-complete reports on a project-by-project basis and an estimated total cost to train and equip the ISF
FY 2008 Regular $2.00	Continue ministerial development and advisory functions to enhance Iraqi air and naval capabilities; develop IED defeat capabilities; standardize weapons and vehicle fleets; support logistics development, primarily at Taji	P.L. 110-161 $1.50 Expired 9/30/2009	Includes standard appropriation language for ISFF
FY 2008 Supplemental $1.00	Includes additional FY 2008 appropriation to support adding 100,000 ISF personnel "required for Iraq to concurrently secure its borders and conduct COIN operations," as well as to hold areas recently cleared as U.S. forces increasingly assume an overwatch mission	P.L. 110-252 $1.50 Expired 9/30/2009	Prohibits ISFF to be "utilized for the provision of salaries, wages, or bonuses to personnel of the Iraqi Security Forces"
FY 2009 Bridge $2.00	Enable the GOI to improve its ability to manage Iraqi security institutions and increase the operational independence of the ISF; support ministerial development, logistics and sustainment capacity, equipment replenishment, and equipment for enabler units	P.L. 110-252 $0.00 Expired 9/30/2009	Appropriates $1.00, which is later rescinded by P.L. 111-32; FY 2009 bridge funding is under a separate heading of the same name as the FY 2008 supplemental funding; (the FY 2009 NDAA prohibits ISFF spending on new infrastructure)

Table B.4. (Continued)

Request	Administration's Budget Justification	Appropriation	Congressional Earmarks and Restrictions
FY 2009 Supplemental $0.00	Request to extend the period of obligation for FY 2009 bridge funding through 9/30/2010 (no new funding)	P.L. 111-32 $1.00 Expired 9/30/2010	Rescinds $1.00 in FY 2009 bridge funding and appropriates the same amount to remain available until 9/30/2010; does not include authority to transfer ISFF to other accounts or agencies; provided in FY 2005–FY 2008; sets limits on "investment unit cost" of purchased items
FY 2010 Supplemental $1.00	Strengthen the ISF "to fulfill their vital role" and ensure "no degradation in progress;" focus on MOD sustainment, including transfer of U.S. equipment, modernization of mechanized division, improved asset management, and aircraft sustainment; support MOI training and advisory activities	P.L. 111-212 $1.00 Expired 9/30/2011	Includes standard appropriation language for ISFF (without authority to transfer funds to other accounts or agencies); conference report directs DoD to submit monthly commitment, obligation, and expenditure data to the congressional committees no later than 30 days after each month
FY 2011 Regular $2.00	Achieve "minimum essential capability" prior to U.S. withdrawal; focus on remaining MOD equipment requirements, including divisional-level ISR and signal capabilities and full organizational communications and armored transport; continued training of defense forces and equipping and sustaining the police	P.L. 112-10 $1.16 Expired 9/30/2012	If funds are used for the purchase of any item or service for Iraqi Security Forces, the funds may not cover more than 80% of the cost of the item or service; obligations cannot exceed $1.00 until the GOI adequately builds the logistics and maintenance capacity of the ISF, develops the institutional capacity to manage such forces independently, and develops a culture of sustainment for equipment provided by the United States or acquired with United States assistance.

Table B.5. ESF: Requests, Justifications, Appropriations, and Earmarks, FY 2006–FY 2012
$ Millions

Request	Administration's Budget Justification	Appropriation	Congressional Earmarks and Restrictions
FY 2006 Regular $360	Develop economic governance programs and new training; enhance employment centers; continue work in legal, fiscal, institutional, and regulatory frameworks for private sector; continue agriculture and water resources programs.	P.L. 109-102 $60 Expired 9/30/2007	Not less than $56 shall be made available for democracy, governance and rule-of-law programs in Iraq; Conference Report provided $28 for IRI and $28 for NDI; $5 to be transferred to the IRRF to support the Marla Ruzicka Iraqi War Victims Fund.
FY 2006 Supplemental $1,489	$675 for PRTs to improve local government capacity, enhance security, and promote development; $287 to secure infrastructure; $355 to sustain U.S.-funded projects; $125 to increase MOF and CBI capacity, transparency, and accountability; $37 for RCLO; $10 for democracy promotion.	P.L. 109-234 $1,409 Expired 9/30/2007	$50 for CAP (of which $5 to be transferred to the Marla Fund); $50 to promote democracy, rule of law, and reconciliation (including $10 for IRI, $10 for NDI, and $10 for the International Foundation for Electoral Systems). $1,485 was appropriated; P.L.110-161 later rescinded $76.

Request	Administration's Budget Justification	Appropriation	Congressional Earmarks and Restrictions
FY 2007 Supplemental $2,072	Reform key sectors of the economy, including agriculture; increase commercial lending and microfinance; provide business development services; help ministries execute budgets; support GOI in improving economic governance; engage political parties, civil society organizations, and national political institutions; support independent media, national reconciliation, and women's and human rights.	P.L. 110-28 $1,554 Expired 9/30/2008	Funds conditional on certification that Iraq was meeting benchmarks, including legislation related to de-Ba'athification, hydrocarbons, and semi-autonomous regions, as well as a constitutional review, reduced sectarian violence, improved ISF, and implementation of the Baghdad Security Plan; Conference Report allocations include: PRTs ($620), CSP ($354), CAP ($95, of which $5 was for the Marla Fund), LGP ($90), and the COM fund ($57).
FY 2008 Regular $298	Stabilize strategic Iraqi cities through rehabilitation of community infrastructure, job training and vocational education, youth programs, and microloans; improve local and provincial governance through PRT projects directed, while continuing governance reforms at the national level.	P.L. 110-92, P.L. 110-137, P.L. 110-149 $123 Expired 12/31/2007	Series of Continuing Appropriations extends FY 2007 budget authority through 11/16/2007 (P.L. 110-92), 12/14/2007 (P.L. 110-137), and ultimately 12/31/2007 (P.L. 110-149).
		P.L. 110-161 $15 Expired 9/30/2008	Provides $10 through the Middle East Partnership Initiative to rescue scholars in Iraq and $5 to the Marla Fund.
FY 2008 Supplemental $797	Support PRTs; secure infrastructure; generate employment and finance business; improve Iraqi ability to sustain projects and execute budgets; fund democracy and governance programs ahead of elections and Kirkuk referendum; reform GOI economic policies; establish business capital fund.	P.L. 110-252 $424 Expired 9/30/2009	Makes funds for most programs conditional on GOI dollar-for-dollar matching; prohibits funds for prison construction; makes PRT funding conditional on submission of a DoS report detailing plans to wind down and close out PRTs, anticipated costs for PRT programming and security, and anticipated placement and costs for future consulates.
FY 2009 Regular $300	Train local leaders in good governance, project implementation, and conflict resolution; build ministry capacity in financial management, budgeting, and procurement; support political parties and CoR functions; foster civil society and independent media; promote macroeconomic reforms, agriculture, and microfinance.	P.L. 110-252 $103 Expired 9/30/2009	FY 2009 regular appropriations—referred to as bridge funding—become available on 10/1/2008.
FY 2009 Supplemental $449	Support elections, civil society, independent media, and political institutions ($112); fund LGP ($55) and CAP ($35) to strengthen local governments; support ministerial capacity development ($60), Marla Fund ($3.5), and Iraqi widows ($5); promote policy, legal, and regulatory reforms ($50); fund PEG ($27.5) to support business development; support agriculture ($43).	P.L. 111-32 $439 Expired 9/30/2010	Funds conditional on GOI matching; Conference Report allocations included allocations to CAP ($50), Democracy and Civil Society ($118), Iraq Cultural Antiquities ($2), Marla Fund ($10), the COM's discretionary fund ($15), and Widows' Assistance ($5); conferees directed greater clarification of democracy and governance programs and expressed concern for women and minorities.

Table B.5. (Continued)

Request	Administration's Budget Justification	Appropriation	Congressional Earmarks and Restrictions
FY 2010 Regular $416	Support ministerial capacity (Tatweer) and local government capacity (PRTs and CAP); foster civil society and independent media; reintegrate Iraqi refugees and IDPs; provide anticorruption and election support; promote sustainable, diversified economic growth; pursue economic, legal, and regulatory reforms; build the capacity of economic institutions.	P.L. 111-117 $383 Expired 9/30/2011	Conference Report allocations included: Democracy and Civil Society ($126), CSP ($50), MCD ($50), Iraqi Minorities ($10), and Marla Fund ($5); conferees expressed belief that the GOI should fund future ministerial capacity development and directed DoS and USAID to consult with the Congress on the process for assessing the benefits versus security costs of work in Iraq.
FY 2011 Regular $383	Promote conflict mitigation (QRF); assist in legislative drafting, budget analysis and execution, and constituent relations; support community groups in promoting stability, providing assistance, and generating employment; provide technical assistance to the health care, education, and social services sectors; support agriculture, microcredit, and public financial management; promote sound macroeconomic and monetary policies.	P.L. 112-10 $326 Expired 9/30/2012	The full-year continuing appropriation for Foreign Operations was made late in the fiscal year and was not accompanied by a committee report; according to DoS, the FY 2011 allocation was the same as its FY 2012 request: $326; DoS submitted a spend plan to the Congress on 7/5/2011.
FY 2012 Regular $326	Institutionalize electoral systems that meet international standards; improve professionalism, outreach, and responsiveness of political parties, CoR, and provincial councils; clarify role of federal government; increase capacity and effectiveness of civil society, media, and anticorruption institutions; pursue community conflict prevention and reconciliation; improve rule of law and promote human rights; provide technical assistance to health and education sectors; support the Marla Fund; promote economic growth and job creation.	P.L. 112-74 $299 Expires 9/30/2013	Funds conditional on GOI matching; as Iraqi oil revenue increases, the Conference Report assumes development and security costs currently funded by the Department of State and USAID will shift toward Iraqi responsibility; recommends, at the determination of the Chief of Mission, $10 for stabilization programs in Iraq; funds shall not be used for cultural programs or for costs usually associated with Department of State operations.

Table B.6. INCLE: Requests, Justifications, Appropriations, and Earmarks, FY 2006–FY 2012
$ Millions

Request	Administration's Budget Justification	Appropriation	Congressional Earmarks and Restrictions
FY 2006 Regular $26.47	Provide bilateral technical assistance to the MOI and MOJ; assign up to five senior advisors to advise on police, border enforcement, prosecutors, courts, and prisons; provide advanced and specialized training programs; maintain logistics and transportation support	P.L. 109-102 $0.00	Conference report provides $99.7 for "other programs," with the expectation that DoS will give programs in Iraq the highest priority with either FY 2006 INCLE funds or prior year unobligated funds; INL reported no appropriations received.
FY 2006 Supplemental $107.70	$100 for construction and renovation of correctional facilities; $7.7 for the protection of Iraqi judges	P.L. 109-234 $91.40 Expired 9/30/2008	

Request	Administration's Budget Justification	Appropriation	Congressional Earmarks and Restrictions
FY 2007 Regular $254.60	Strengthen human rights enforcement; promote integration of police, courts and prisons; develop anticorruption laws; develop legal assistance centers; provide courthouse security enhancements and protection for Iraqi judges; fund corrections advisors and INL administration and oversight costs	P.L. 110-5 $20.05 Expired 9/30/2009	
FY 2007 Supplemental $200.00	Promote judicial security by protecting judges, witnesses, court staff, and facilities; train and mentor judges, prosecutors, and judicial investigators; integrate various components of the judicial system; support anticorruption efforts; construct additional jail/prison beds	P.L. 110-28 $150.00 Expired 9/30/2008	Funds cannot be used for prison construction.
FY 2008 Regular $75.80	Support programs in development of the criminal justice system, public integrity, justice and rule of law; provide administrative oversight	P.L. 110-161 $0.00	House Appropriations Committee recommends no funding for Iraq; no funding ultimately provided.
FY 2008 Supplemental $159.00	Expand judicial and court security, judicial capacity, justice integration, and anticorruption assistance to the provinces; continue to expand detention facilities	P.L. 110-252 $85.00 Expired 9/30/2009	Funds cannot be used for prison construction.
FY 2009 Regular $75.00	Provide training, advice, and support to the courts/judiciary and Iraqi Corrections Service; maintain administrative oversight	P.L. 111-8 $0.00	Senate Appropriations Committee recommends $25; no funding ultimately provided.
FY 2009 Supplemental $20.00	$9 for judicial training, security, and court administration; $5 for subject matter experts to work on police transition planning; $3 for rule of law advisors; $3 for program support and oversight	P.L. 111-32 $20.00 Expired 9/30/2010	Funds are subject to a form of GOI "matching."
FY 2010 Regular $52.00	Provide training, advising, and support to the courts/judiciary and corrections; address problems of corruption and illegal drugs; engage Iraqi law enforcement development and reform efforts; provide administrative oversight	P.L. 111-117 $52.00 Expired 9/30/2011	Funds may not be used for new construction.
FY 2010 Supplemental $517.40	Fund start-up costs for the police program, including base camp and aviation facility upgrades, security infrastructure, and aircraft procurement	P.L. 111-212 $650.00 Expired 9/30/2012	$450 for one-time start up costs and limited operational costs of the Iraqi police program; $200 for implementation, management, security, communications, and other expenses related to the Iraqi police program.
FY 2011 Regular $314.56	Hire police advisors and managers, contract personnel, and staff to develop and implement the police program; provide advanced training, capacity building, and standardized procedures for the judiciary; continue the deployment of rule-of-law advisors	P.L. 112-10 $114.56 Expired 9/30/2012	
FY 2012 Regular $1,000.00	Support the Police Development Program, including approximately 190 advisors and an instructor development program, training at regional and national Iraqi academies, capacity-building work in the justice sector by addressing judicial and courthouse security, administrative processes, and investigative practices; funds will also pay for Embassy-provided security and life support, aviation, and other transportation operations and maintenance, and personnel recruitment and training.	P.L. 112-74 $129.60 Expires 9/30/2013	

ACRONYMS

Acronym	Definition
ABO	U.S. Army Budget Office
ACC	Army Contract Command
ACCO	Anti-Corruption Coordination Office (INL)
AFCEE	Air Force Center for Engineering and the Environment (formerly the Air Force Center for Environmental Excellence)
AFRN	Advanced First Responder Network
Ajyal	Arabic for "generations" (Education Strengthening Project, USAID)
AQI	al-Qaeda in Iraq
ARDI	Agriculture Reconstruction and Development Program for Iraq
BBG	Broadcasting Board of Governors
BSA	Board of Supreme Audit
C-JTSCC	CENTCOM Joint Theater Support Contracting Command
CAFTT	Coalition Air Force Transition Team
CAP	Community Action Program
CBI	Central Bank of Iraq
CBP	Customs and Border Protection
CCC-I	Central Criminal Court of Iraq
CEFMS	Corps of Engineers Financial Management System
CENTCOM	U.S. Central Command
CENTCOM OIG	U.S. Central Command Office of Inspector General
CERP	Commander's Emergency Response Program
CIGIE	Council of Inspectors General for Integrity and Efficiency
CIO	Contributions to International Organizations
CJTF-7	Combined Joint Task Force 7
CMATT	Coalition Military Assistance Training Team
COI	Commission of Integrity (previously known as Commission on Public Integrity)
COIN	counterinsurgency
COM	Chief of Mission
CoM	Council of Ministers
CoR	Council of Representatives
CPA	Coalition Provisional Authority
CPA-IG	Coalition Provisional Authority Inspector General
CPATT	Civilian Police Assistance Training Team
CPI	Commission on Public Integrity
CRS	Congressional Research Service
CSH	Child Survival and Health Programs Fund
CSO	Bureau for Conflict and Stabilization Operations (State)
CSP	Community Stabilization Program
CWC	Commission on Wartime Contracting in Iraq and Afghanistan
CWD	Conventional Weapons Destruction program
DART	Disaster Assistance Response Team
DCAA	U.S. Defense Contract Audit Agency
DCC-W	Defense Contracting Command-Washington
DCMA	Defense Contract Management Agency
Defense	Department of Defense
DF	Democracy Fund
DFAS	Defense Finance and Accounting Service

Acronym	Definition
DFI	Development Fund for Iraq
DoD	Department of Defense
DoD OIG	Department of Defense Office of Inspector General
DoJ	Department of Justice
DoL	Department of Labor
DoS	Department of State
DoT	Department of Transportation
DRL	Bureau of Democracy, Human Rights, and Labor (State)
DSCA	Defense Security Cooperation Agency
ECA	Education and Cultural Exchange programs (State)
EIA	Energy Information Agency
ERMA	Emergency Refugee & Migration Assistance fund
ESF	Economic Support Fund
EXBS	Export Controls and Related Border Security
Ex-Im	Export-Import Bank
FAR	Federal Acquisition Regulation
FEMA	Federal Emergency Management Agency
FMF	Foreign Military Financing
FMR	Financial Management Regulation
FMS	Foreign Military Sales
FY	fiscal year
GAO	Government Accountability Office
GDP	gross domestic product
GOI	Government of Iraq
GRD	Gulf Region Division (also Gulf Region District)
H.R.	House Resolution
HCA	Head of Contracting Activity
HJC	Higher Judicial Council
HRDF	Human Rights and Democracy Fund
HSAD	Arabic for "harvest" (Harmonized Support for Agricultural Research in the Dry Areas, USAID)
IA	Iraqi Army
IAO	Iraq Area Office (USACE Middle East District)
ICAA	Iraq Civil Aviation Authority
ICITAP	International Criminal Investigative Training Assistance Program
IDA	International Disaster Assistance
IDFA	International Disaster and Famine Assistance
IDIQ	indefinite-delivery indefinite-quantity
IDP	internally displaced person
IED	improvised explosice device
IFC	International Finance Corporation
IFF	Iraq Freedom Fund
IFMIS	Iraq Financial Management Information System
IG	inspector general
IGC	Iraqi Governing Council
IHEC	Independent High Electoral Commission
IMET	International Military Education and Training
IMF	International Monetary Fund
IMS	Interagency Management System
INCLE	International Narcotics Control and Law Enforcement account (INL)

(Continued)

Acronym	Definition
INL	Bureau of International Narcotics and Law Enforcement Affairs (State)
Inma	Arabic for "growth" (Agribusiness Program, USAID)
IRI	International Republican Institute
IRMO	Iraq Reconstruction Management Office
IRMS	Iraq Reconstruction Management System
IRRF	Iraq Relief and Reconstruction Fund
ISAM	Iraq Security Assistance Mission
ISF	Iraqi Security Forces
ISFF	Iraq Security Forces Fund
ISOF	Iraq Special Operations Force
ISP	Infrastructure Security Protection Program
ISPO	Iraq Strategic Partnership Office
ITAM	Iraq Training and Advisory Mission
ITAO	Iraq Transition Assistance Office
ITAO/ESD	Iraq Transition Assistance Office/Electric Services Division
Izdihar	Arabic for "prosperity" (Private Sector Development Program, USAID)
JCC-I	Joint Contracting Command-Iraq
JCC-I/A	Joint Contracting Command-Iraq/Afghanistan
KBR	Kellogg Brown & Root
KRG	Kurdistan Regional Government
LGP	Local Governance Program
LPG	liquefied petroleum gas
MAAWS	Money as a Weapon System
MBPD	million barrels per day
MCD	Ministerial Capacity Development
MCTF	Major Crimes Task Force
MIM	Ministry of Industry and Minerals
MNC-I	Multi-National Corps-Iraq
MNF-I	Multi-National Force-Iraq
MNSTC-I	Multi-National Security Transition Command-Iraq
MOD	Ministry of Defense
MOE	Ministry of Electricity
MOF	Ministry of Finance
MOI	Ministry of Interior
MOJ	Ministry of Justice
MoPDC	Ministry of Planning and Development Cooperation
MRA	Migration and Refugee Assistance fund
MW	megawatt
NADR	Nonproliferation, Anti-terrorism, Demining, and Related Programs
NATO	North Atlantic Treaty Organization
NCO	non-commissioned officer
NDAA	National Defense Authorization Act
NDI	National Democratic Institute
NEA-I	Bureau of Near Eastern Affairs-Iraq (State)
NGO	non-governmental organization
NP	National Police
NRRRF	Natural Resources Risk Remediation Fund
NSPD	National Security Presidential Directive

Acronym	Definition
OAA	Office of Agricultural Affairs
O&M	operations and maintenance
OFDA	Office of Foreign Disaster Assistance
OHDACA	Overseas Humanitarian, Disaster and Civic Aid
OMB	Office of Management and Budget
OPA	Office of Provincial Affairs (U.S. Embassy-Baghdad)
OPDAT	Office of Overseas Prosecutorial Development and Assistance Training (DoJ)
OPEC	Organization of the Petroleum Exporting Countries
OPIC	Overseas Private Investment Corporation
ORHA	Office of Reconstruction and Humanitarian Assistance
OSC-I	Office of Security Cooperation-Iraq
OTA	Office of Technical Assistance (Treasury)
OUSD(AT&L)	Office of the Under Secretary of Defense (Aquisitions, Technology & Logistics)
OUSD(C)	Office of the Under Secretary of Defense (Comptroller)
P.L.	public law
PCIE	President's Council for Integrity and Efficiency
PCO	Project and Contracting Office
PDP	Police Development Program
PEZ	pipeline exclusion zone
PHC	primary healthcare center
PIC	Provincial Iraqi Control
PM	Bureau of Political-Military Affairs (State)
PMO	Program Management Office
PRDC	Provincial Reconstruction Development Council
PRM	Bureau of Population, Refugees and Migration (State)
PRT	provincial reconstruction team
PSC	private security contractor
PUK	Patriotic Union of Kurdistan
QDDR	Quadrennial Diplomacy and Development Review (State)
QRF	Quick Response Fund
RAMCC	Regional Air Movement Control Center
RCLO	Regime Crimes Liaison Office
RIE	Restore Iraqi Electricity (USACE task force)
RISE	Revitalization of Iraqi Schools and Stabilization of Education (USAID)
RSCMA	Reconstruction and Stabilization Civilian Management Act
S.	Senate bill
S/CRS	Department of State Office of the Coordinator for Reconstruction and Stabilization
SIGIR	Special Inspector General for Iraq Reconstruction
SIGPRO	SIGIR Prosectutorial Initiative
SIV	Special Immigrant Visa
SOE	state-owned enterprise
SOI	Sons of Iraq
SPOT	Synchronized Pre-Deployment and Operational Tracker
SRO	stabilization and reconstruction operation
State	Department of State
TAL	Transitional Administrative Law
Tarabot	Arabic for "linkages" (Administrative Reform Project, USAID)
Tatweer	Arabic for "development" (National Capacity Development Program, USAID)
TBI	Trade Bank of Iraq
TFBSO	Task Force for Business and Stability Operations

(Continued)

Acronym	Definition
Tijara	Arabic for "trade" (Provincial Economic Growth Program, USAID)
TNA	Transitional National Assembly
Treasury	Department of the Treasury
Tumooh	Arabic for "ambition" (English as a Second Language Project, State)
UN	United Nations
UNAMI	United Nations Assistance Misison in Iraq
UNCC	United Nations Claims Commission
UNCTAD	United Nations Conference on Trade and Development
UNDP	United Nations Development Programme
UNHCR	United Nations High Commisioner for Refugees
UNICEF	United Nations Children's Fund
UNODC	United Nations Office on Drugs and Crime
UNSCR	United Nations Security Council Resolution
USA	U.S. Army
USACE	U.S. Army Corps of Engineers
USAID	U.S. Agency for International Development
USAID OIG	U.S. Agency for International Development Office of Inspector General
U.S.C.	U.S. Code
USCG	United States Coast Guard
USDA	U.S. Department of Agriculture
USF-I	U.S. Forces-Iraq
USG	U.S. government
USIP	U.S. Institute of Peace
USMC	United States Marine Corps
USOCO	U.S. Office for Contingency Operations
USTDA	U.S. Trade and Development Agency
WERC	Worldwide Environmental Restoration and Construction (AFCEE contract)
WHO	World Health Organization
WTO	World Trade Organization
WWTP	wastewater treatment plant

End Notes

[1] GOI, CoR, "Federal Budget Law for the Fiscal Year 2012," Articles 1, 2, 36, 2/23/2012, and "Federal Public Budget Law for the Fiscal Year 2011," Article 2, 2/23/2011; GOI, MOF, information provided to SIGIR, 6/27/2011; "GOI Budget" (as approved by TNA and written into law December 2005); GOI, Presidency of the Iraqi Interim National Assembly, "The State General Budget for 2005," 2005; GOI, MoPDC, "Indicators of the Investment Budget for Year 2010," Table 17, 2011; GOI, "Budget Revenues and Expenses 2003, July–December," 2003; SIGIR, *Quarterly and Semiannual Reports to the United States Congress*, 3/30/2004–4/30/2011; U.S. Treasury, responses to SIGIR data calls, 1/4/2008 and 4/9/2009.

[2] SIGIR, *Quarterly and Semiannual Reports to the United States Congress*, 3/30/2004–10/30/2012; CEFMS, *ISFF Funds Execution Reports*, 10/1/2007 and 1/8/2008; DFAS, responses to SIGIR data calls, 1/9/2008–4/10/2009; DoD, Secretary of the Army Updates, 8/31/2007 and 9/30/2007; DoS, response to SIGIR data call, 4/5/2007, and *Section 2207 Reports*, 10/2004–10/2008; GRD, Program Review Board, 3/3/2007, and responses to SIGIR data calls, 4/5/2008–7/18/2009; INL, responses to SIGIR data calls, 1/4/2008–10/16/2012; IRMO, *Weekly Status Reports*, 4/17/2007 and 6/26/2007; IRMS, *ESF Cost to Complete Reports*, 7/5/2007–1/5/2009, and *USF-I CERP Category Report*, 9/20/2010; ITAO, *Essential Indicators Reports*, 10/2/2007–5/14/2009, and responses to SIGIR data calls, 10/10/2007–3/29/2009; NEA-I, responses to SIGIR data calls, 1/6/2010–

10/2/2012; OMB, *Section 2207 Reports*, 1/2004–7/2004; OSD, responses to SIGIR data calls, 7/9/2008–10/2/2012; DoD, *Secretary of the Army Finance Reports,* 12/31/2006–7/8/2007; U.S. Treasury, responses to SIGIR data calls, 4/6/2007– 4/2/2009; U.S. Embassy-Baghdad, responses to SIGIR data calls, 7/6/2009–10/1/2012; USACE, responses to SIGIR data calls, 4/7/2007–10/1/2012; USAID, *Activities Report*, 7/12/2007, and responses to SIGIR data calls, 4/6/2007–4/2/2012; USTDA, responses to SIGIR data calls, 10/1/2007–4/2/2009.

[3] Congressional Research Service, CRS Report for Congress, "Iraq: Paris Club Debt Relief," 1/19/2005, p. 1.

[4] Congressional Research Service, CRS Report for Congress, "Iraq: Paris Club Debt Relief," 1/19/2005, pp. 1–5.

[5] SIGIR Audit 11-010, "Sons of Iraq Program: Results Are Uncertain and Financial Controls Were Weak," 1/28/2011, p. 2.

[6] SIGIR, *Iraq Reconstruction: Lessons in Contracting and Procurement*, 7/2006, p. 35, and *Quarterly Reports to the United States Congress*, 10/30/2011, p. 35, and 10/30/2012, p. 16.

[7] Secretary of Defense Rumsfeld, cited in SIGIR, *Hard Lessons: The Iraq Reconstruction Experience*, 2/2009, p. 326.

[8] For sources of funding data and authority, see endnote 2.

[9] SIGIR, *Quarterly and Semiannual Report to the United States Congress*, 7/30/2010, p. 2.

[10] SIGIR, *Iraq Reconstruction: Lessons in Program and Project Management*, 3/2007, p. 8.

[11] SIGIR, *Hard Lessons: The Iraq Reconstruction Experience*, 2/2009, pp. 33–34.

[12] SIGIR, *Hard Lessons: The Iraq Reconstruction Experience*, 2/2009, pp. 42–44.

[13] SIGIR, *Hard Lessons: The Iraq Reconstruction Experience*, 2/2009, pp. 26, 49, *Iraq Reconstruction: Lessons in Contracting and Procurement*, 7/2006, pp. 20–21, and *Iraq Reconstruction: Lessons in Program and Project Management*, 3/2007, pp. 24–25.

[14] SIGIR, *Hard Lessons: The Iraq Reconstruction Experience*, 2/2009, pp. 26, 49, *Iraq Reconstruction:Lessons in Contracting and Procurement*, 7/2006, pp. 20–21, *Iraq Reconstruction: Lessons in Program and Project Management*, 3/2007, pp. 24–25, and Audit 11- 007, "Iraq Relief and Reconstruction Fund 1: Report on Apportionments, Expenditures, and Canceled Funds," 1/25/2011, summary.

[15] SIGIR, *Iraq Reconstruction: Lessons in Program and Project Management*, 3/2007, pp. 24–25, *Hard Lessons: The Iraq Reconstruction Experience*, 2/2009, p. 26, and *Iraq Reconstruction: Lessons in Contracting and Procurement*, 7/2006, p. 29.

[16] SIGIR, *Iraq Reconstruction: Lessons in Contracting and Procurement*, 7/2006, p. 29.

[17] SIGIR, *Hard Lessons: The Iraq Reconstruction Experience*, 2/2009, p. 63–64.

[18] SIGIR, *Iraq Reconstruction: Lessons in Contracting and Procurement*, 7/2006, p. 27, and Audit 11-007, "Iraq Relief and Reconstruction Fund 1: Report on Apportionments, Expenditures, and Canceled Funds," 1/25/2011, p. 4.

[19] SIGIR, *Iraq Reconstruction: Lessons in Program and Project Management*, 3/2007, p. 9.

[20] SIGIR, *Hard Lessons: The Iraq Reconstruction Experience*, 2/2009, pp. 64, 69, 73–77.

[21] SIGIR, *Hard Lessons: The Iraq Reconstruction Experience*, 2/2009, pp. 64, 69, 73–77.

[22] SIGIR, *Iraq Reconstruction: Lessons in Contracting and Procurement*, 7/2006, p. 21.

[23] SIGIR, *Hard Lessons: The Iraq Reconstruction Experience*, 2/2009, pp. 82–83, and *Iraq Reconstruction: Lessons in Human Capital Management*, 1/2006, pp. 8–12. See also Section 3161 in U.S. Code, Title 5, "Employment and Compensation of Employees," which allows hiring for temporary services under such circumstances.

[24] SIGIR, *Hard Lessons: The Iraq Reconstruction Experience*, 2/2009, pp. 100–101, 326.

[25] SIGIR, *Hard Lessons: The Iraq Reconstruction Experience*, 2/2009, pp. 100–101, 326, and *Iraq Reconstruction: Lessons in Contracting and Procurement*, 7/2006, pp. 65–66. USAID received $3 billion of the IRRF 2—one-third of what it requested. Most funding went to Bechtel II for a second Infrastructure Rehabilitation and Reconstruction Program. USAID also issued five democracy-building grants to support elections and five cooperative agreements under the CAP. OTI got more funding under IRRF 2 than IRRF 1 as demands for democracy and civic-involvement programs increased.

[26] SIGIR, *Hard Lessons: The Iraq Reconstruction Experience*, 2/2009, pp. 327–328, and *Iraq Reconstruction: Lessons in Contracting and Procurement*, 7/2006, pp. 46–49. Reconstruction plans that had just been developed on a two-year timetable now had to shift, and the rush began to prepare Iraq's government to stand on its own in seven months.

[27] SIGIR, *Iraq Reconstruction: Lessons in Program and Project Management*, 3/2007, p. 52.

[28] SIGIR, *Hard Lessons: The Iraq Reconstruction Experience*, 2/2009, p. 108.

[29] SIGIR, *Iraq Reconstruction: Lessons in Contracting and Procurement*, 7/2006, pp. 48–49.

[30] SIGIR, *Iraq Reconstruction: Lessons in Contracting and Procurement*, 7/2006, pp. 63–64.

[31] SIGIR Audit 04-013, "CPA's Contracting Processes Leading Up to and Including Contract Award," 7/27/2004, p. i.

[32] SIGIR, *Iraq Reconstruction: Lessons in Program and Project Management*, 3/2007, pp. 81–82, and *Hard Lessons: The Iraq Reconstruction Experience*, 2/2009, p. 165.

[33] SIGIR, *Iraq Reconstruction: Lessons in Program and Project Management*, 3/2007, p. 82.

[34] SIGIR, *Hard Lessons: The Iraq Reconstruction Experience*, 2/2009, pp. 157, 166.

[35] SIGIR, *Iraq Reconstruction: Lessons in Contracting and Procurement*, 7/2006, pp. 42, 46, and *Hard Lessons: The Iraq Reconstruction Experience*, 2/2009, p. 167.

[36] SIGIR Testimony 05-003, "Statement of Stuart W. Bowen, Jr., before the United States House of Representatives Committee on National Security, Emerging Threats, and International Relations," 10/18/2005, and Audit 05-029, "Challenges Faced in Carrying Out Iraq Relief and Reconstruction Fund Activities," p. iii.

[37] P.L. 109-13. For the sources of funding data, see endnote 2.

[38] SIGIR, *Hard Lessons: The Iraq Reconstruction Experience*, 2/2009, pp. 176–177, 231.

[39] SIGIR Audit 05-028, "GRD-PCO Management of the Transfer of IRRF-funded Assets to the Iraqi Government," 1/24/2006, Audit 06-006, "Multi-National Security Transition Command-Iraq Management of the Transfer of Iraq Relief and Reconstruction Fund Projects to the Iraqi Government," 4/29/2006, Audit 06-007, "U.S. Agency for International Development Management of the Transfer of Iraq Relief and Reconstruction Fund Projects to the Iraqi Government," 4/29/2006, and Audit 06-010, "Review of the Multi-National Security Transition Command-Iraq Reconciliation of the Iraqi Armed Forces Seized Assets Fund," 4/28/2006.

[40] SIGIR, *Hard Lessons: The Iraq Reconstruction Experience*, 2/2009, p. 330.

[41] SIGIR Audit 05-022, "Managing Sustainment for Iraq Relief and Reconstruction Fund Programs," 10/24/2005.

[42] SIGIR, *Hard Lessons: The Iraq Reconstruction Experience*, 2/2009, p. 330.

[43] SIGIR Audit 07-014, "Status of the Provincial Reconstruction Team Program Expansion in Iraq," 7/25/2007, p. 1, and *Hard Lessons: The Iraq Reconstruction Experience*, 2/2009, pp. 240–241.

[44] SIGIR, *Hard Lessons: The Iraq Reconstruction Experience*, 2/2009, p. 241.

[45] SIGIR Audit 09-013, "Provincial Reconstruction Teams' Performance Measurement Process Has Improved," 1/28/2009, p. 2, and *Quarterly and Semiannual Reports to the United States Congress*, 7/30/2009–1/30/2012.

[46] UN Security Council, press release, "Iraq's Political Transition Increasingly Threatened by Inter-Sectarian Violence, Special Representative Tells Security Council," 3/15/2006.

[47] SIGIR, *Hard Lessons: The Iraq Reconstruction Experience*, 2/2009, pp. 295–296, 299, 306.

[48] SIGIR, *Quarterly and Semiannual Report to the United States Congress*, 1/30/2011, p. 66; Babak Rahimi, "The Future of Moqtada al-Sadr's New Jaysh al-Mahdi," USMA Combating Terrorism Center, 1/15/2009.

[49] SIGIR, *Quarterly and Semiannual Report to the United States Congress*, 7/30/2010, p. 2.

[50] SIGIR Audit 07-015, "Review of the Effectiveness of the Provincial Reconstruction Team Program in Iraq," 10/18/2007.

[51] SIGIR, Hard Lessons: The Iraq Reconstruction Experience, 2/2009, pp. 330–331.

[52] SIGIR, Quarterly and Semiannual Report to the United States Congress, 7/30/2008, p. 2.

[53] SIGIR, Quarterly and Semiannual Report to the United States Congress, 7/30/2008, p. 4.

[54] SIGIR Testimony 07-017T, "Statement of Stuart W. Bowen, Jr., before the Subcommittee on State, Foreign Operations, and Related Programs, House Committee on Appropriations," 10/30/2007, p. 5.

[55] SIGIR, Quarterly Report to the United States Congress, 10/30/2008, pp. 36–38.

[56] SIGIR, Quarterly Report to the United States Congress, 10/30/2008, p. 5.

[57] SIGIR, Quarterly Report to the United States Congress, 4/30/2009, p. 6.

[58] SIGIR, Quarterly and Semiannual Report to the United States Congress, 1/30/2010, p. 31.

[59] SIGIR, Quarterly and Semiannual Reports to the United States Congress, 7/30/2009, pp. 54–62, and 10/30/2009, pp. 36–39.

[60] SIGIR, Quarterly and Semiannual Reports to the United States Congress, 7/30/2009, pp. 54–62, 10/30/2009, pp. 36–39, and 1/30/2010, pp. 31–33.

[61] SIGIR, Quarterly and Semiannual Reports to the United States Congress, 1/30/2010, p. 33, and 4/30/2010, p. 60. USACE had 75 military personnel and 290 contractor personnel working among its two districts.

[62] SIGIR, Quarterly and Semiannual Reports to the United States Congress, 10/30/2009, pp. 35–36, and 7/30/2010, pp. 41–44.

[63] SIGIR, Quarterly Report to the United States Congress, 10/30/2010, p. 4.

[64] SIGIR, Quarterly Report to the United States Congress, 10/30/2011, p. 6.

[65] SIGIR, Quarterly Report to the United States Congress, 10/30/2012, p. 18.

[66] SIGIR, Quarterly and Semiannual Report to the United States Congress, 1/30/2012, pp. 37, 47–48.

[67] SIGIR Audit 13-001, "Sustaining the Progress Achieved by U.S. Rule of Law Programs in Iraq Remains Questionable," 10/25/2012.

[68] SIGIR Audit 13-001, "Sustaining the Progress Achieved by U.S. Rule of Law Programs in Iraq Remains Questionable," 10/4/2012, Audit 12- 020, "Iraq Police Development Program: Lack of Iraqi Support and Security Problems Raise Questions about the Continued Viability of the Program," 7/30/2012, and Quarterly Report to the United States Congress, 10/30/2012, p. 32.

[69] SIGIR, Quarterly and Semiannual Reports to the United States Congress, 4/30/2011–10/30/2012. USAID's implementing contractor staffs were not always reported in SPOT data received by SIGIR. In one quarter, for example, SIGIR received direct reporting from USAID that indicated the SPOT system did not account for approximately 1,700 contractor staff.

[70] SIGIR, Quarterly Report to the United States Congress, 10/30/2012, pp. 2, 4.

[71] For the sources of funding data, see endnote 2.

[72] For the sources of funding data, see endnote 2.

[73] For the sources of funding data, see endnote 2.

[74] SIGIR, Quarterly and Semiannual Reports to the United States Congress, 1/30/2010, p. 33, and 10/30/2012, pp. 55–58, and Audit 13-003, "Development Fund for Iraq: U.S. Army Corps of Engineers Has Missing Receiving Reports and Open Task Orders," 10/26/2012; IRMS, Global Benchmark, 9/3/2012.

[75] SIGIR, Quarterly Report to the United States Congress, 10/30/2012, pp. 55–58; USACE, information provided to SIGIR Audits, 11/20/2012.

[76] For the sources of funding data, see endnote 2.

[77] SIGIR Audit 07-008, "Fact Sheet on the Roles and Responsibilities of U.S. Government Organizations Conducting IRRF-funded Reconstruction Activities," 7/26/2007.

[78] SIGIR Audit 07-008, "Fact Sheet on the Roles and Responsibilities of U.S. Government Organizations Conducting IRRF-funded Reconstruction Activities," 7/26/2007.

[79] SIGIR Audit 07-008, "Fact Sheet on the Roles and Responsibilities of U.S. Government Organizations Conducting IRRF-funded Reconstruction Activities," 7/26/2007, and Quarterly and Semiannual Report to the United States Congress, 1/30/2010, p. 24.

[80] OSC-I, response to SIGIR data call, 10/3/2012.

[81] OSC-I, response to SIGIR data call, 10/2/2012.

[82] SIGIR, Iraq Reconstruction: Lessons in Contracting and Procurement, 7/2006, p. 29, and Quarterly Report to the United States Congress, 10/30/2012, p. 48.

[83] SIGIR Audit 11-007, "Iraq Relief and Reconstruction Fund 1: Report on Apportionments, Expenditures, and Canceled Funds," 1/25/2011; USAID, Bureau for the Middle East, Office of Iraq and Arabian Peninsula Affairs, information provided to SIGIR Audits, 10/23/2012.

[84] SIGIR, Quarterly Report to the United States Congress, 10/30/2012, p. 38.

[85] NEA-I, responses to SIGIR data calls, 9/28/2011, 9/25/2012, 10/1/2012, and 10/2/2012; USACE, response to SIGIR data call, 10/1/2012; U.S. Embassy-Baghdad, responses to SIGIR data calls, 10/5/2011, 1/4/2012, 4/3/2012, 7/3/2012, and 10/1/2012.

[86] SIGIR, Quarterly Report to the United States Congress, 10/30/2009, pp. 40–41, and Special Report No. 2, "The Human Toll of Reconstruction or Stabilization during Iraqi Freedom," 7/2012.

[87] SIGIR, Quarterly and Semiannual Report to the United States Congress, 7/30/2009, pp. 46–47.

[88] SIGIR, Quarterly and Semiannual Report to the States Congress, 7/30/2009, pp. 46–47.

[89] SIGIR, Quarterly Report to the United States Congress, 10/30/2009, p. 40.

[90] DoD, OUSD(AT&L), SPOT Program Support, responses to SIGIR data calls, 4/2011–10/2012. USAID's implementing contractor staffs were not always reported in SPOT data received by SIGIR. In one quarter, for example, SIGIR received direct reporting from USAID that indicated the SPOT system did not account for approximately 1,700 contractor staff.

[91] See, for example, SIGIR Audit 07-016, "Interim Review of DynCorp International, LLC, Spending under Its Contract for the Iraqi Police Training Program," and SIGIR's Iraq Reconstruction: Lessons in Contracting and Procurement.

[92] SIGIR, Iraq Reconstruction: Lessons in Contracting and Procurement, 7/2006, p. 54.

[93] SIGIR, Iraq Reconstruction: Lessons in Contracting and Procurement, 7/2006, p. 109, and Audit 07-008, "Fact Sheet on the Roles and Responsibilities of U.S. Government Organizations Conducting IRRF-funded Reconstruction Activities," 7/26/2007.

[94] SIGIR, Iraq Reconstruction: Lessons in Contracting and Procurement, 7/2006, pp. 57–62.

[95] SIGIR, Iraq Reconstruction: Lessons in Program and Project Management, 3/2007, pp. 53–55.

96 SIGIR Audit 04-004, "Task Orders Awarded by the Air Force Center for Environmental Excellence in Support of the Coalition Provisional Authority," 7/28/2004, p. 5. AFCEE was called the Air Force Center for Environmental Excellence during the tenure of the PMO.

97 SIGIR, Iraq Reconstruction: Lessons in Contracting and Procurement, 7/2006, p. 66. For more on contract management and the costs incurred on Phase I and II contracts, including lessons learned, see SIGIR Audit 07-009, "Review of Bechtel's Spending under Its Phase II Iraq Reconstruction Contract."

98 SIGIR, Iraq Reconstruction: Lessons in Contracting and Procurement, 7/2006, pp. 56, 63. Indefinite delivery, indefinite quantity (IDIQ) contracts "provide for an indefinite quantity, within stated maximum and minimum limits, of specific supplies or services" to be furnished within an unspecified time period. Under these contracts, task orders are issued on either a cost-reimbursement (e.g., cost-plus) or fixed- price basis. Under fixed-price task orders, "payment is made to the contractor on the basis of preestablished prices." Under cost-reimbursement task orders, the U.S. government reimburses the contractor for all allowable, allocable, and reasonable contract costs. Cost-reimbursement contracts are typically used in risky situations when the U.S. government is unable to provide sufficient information for offerors to accurately determine a competitive price.

99 SIGIR Audit 07-009, "Review of Bechtel's Spending under Its Phase II Iraq Reconstruction Contract," 7/24/2007, and Audit 08-010, "Outcome, Cost, and Oversight of Iraq Reconstruction Contract W914NS-04-D-0006," 1/28/2008.

100 SIGIR, Iraq Reconstruction: Lessons in Contracting and Procurement, 7/2006, p. 62.

101 SIGIR Audit 06-028, "Review of Administrative Task orders for Iraq Reconstruction Contracts," 10/23/2006, Audit 07-009, "Review of Bechtel's Spending under Its Phase II Iraq Reconstruction Contract," 7/24/2007, Audit 08-010, "Outcome, Cost, and Oversight of Iraq Reconstruction Contract W914NS-04-D-0006," 1/28/2008, and *Iraq Reconstruction: Lessons in Contracting and Procurement*, 7/2006.

102 SIGIR Audit 13-006, "Government Agencies Cannot Fully Identify Projects Financed with Iraq Relief and Reconstruction Funds," 3/2013.

103 P.L. 108-11; P.L. 108-106; P.L. 108-287; P.L. 109-13; P.L. 109-102; P.L. 109-148; P.L. 109-34; P.L. 109-289; P.L. 110-28; P.L. 110-92; P.L. 110- 116; P.L. 110-137; P.L. 110-149; P.L. 110-61; P.L. 110-252; P.L. 111-32; P.L. 111-117; P.L. 111-118; P.L. 111-212; P.L. 112-10, P.L. 112-74; ABO, response to SIGIR data call, 1/18/2012; BBG, response to SIGIR data call, 3/7/2011; DCAA, response to SIGIR data call, 10/4/2011; DoJ, Justice Management Division, response to SIGIR data call, 10/9/2012; DoS, PM, response to SIGIR data call, 7/6/2011; DoS, "Congressional Budget Justification: Foreign Assistance," Summary Tables, FY 2009–FY 2011; DoS, "Executive Budget Summary Function 150 & Other International Programs, Fiscal Year 2013," p. 173; DRL, response to SIGIR data call, 7/9/2012; ECA, response to SIGIR data call, 4/14/2010; OMB, response to SIGIR data call, 6/21/2010; INL, response to SIGIR data call, 10/16/2012; USAID, "U.S. Overseas Loans and Grants [Greenbook]," 2008; U.S. Treasury, OTA, "Office of Technical Assistance Overview," 12/30/2005; TFBSO, response to SIGIR data call, 1/4/2011; SIGIR Audit 11-007, "Iraq Relief and Reconstruction Fund 1: Report on Apportionments, Expenditures, and Cancelled Funds," 12/28/2010; USAID, responses to SIGIR data calls, 1/12/2009, 4/8/2009, 10/2/2012, and 10/15/2012; U.S. Embassy-Baghdad, responses to SIGIR data calls, 10/3/2009, 10/5/2011, 1/4/2012, 4/3/2012, 7/3/2012, and 10/1/2012; NEA-I, responses to SIGIR data calls, 10/4/2010, 10/6/2010, 4/15/2011, 9/28/2011, 9/20/2012, 9/27/2012, 9/25/2012, 10/1/2012, 10/2/2012, and 10/10/2012; OUSD(C), "United States Department of Defense Fiscal Year 2012 Budget Request," Overview, 2/2012, p. 66, and responses to SIGIR data calls, 10/14/2010 and 10/2/2012; USACE, responses to SIGIR data calls, 10/6/2008 and 10/1/2012.

104 GOI, Former Minister of Housing, Finance, and Interior Baqir Jabr al-Zubeidi, meeting with SIGIR, 9/19/2012, and Former Minister of Interior Jawad al-Bolani, meeting with SIGIR, 9/19/2012.

105 P.L. 108-106; P.L. 108-11; P.L. 109-102; P.L. 109- 13; P.L. 109-234; P.L. 109-289; P.L. 110-137; P.L. 110-149; P.L. 110-161; P.L. 110-252; P.L. 110-28; P.L. 110-5; P.L. 110-92; P.L. 111-117; P.L. 111-212; P.L. 111-32; P.L. 111-8; P.L. 112-10; P.L. 112-74.

106 P.L. 108-11; P.L. 108-106; P.L. 108-287; P.L. 109-13; P.L. 109-102; P.L. 109-148; P.L. 109-34; P.L. 109-289; P.L. 110-28; P.L. 110-92; P.L. 110- 116; P.L. 110-137; P.L. 110-149; P.L. 110-61; P.L. 110-252; P.L. 111-32; P.L. 111-117; P.L. 111-118; P.L. 111-212; P.L. 112-10, P.L. 112-74; ABO, response to SIGIR data call, 1/18/2012; BBG, response to SIGIR data call, 3/7/2011; DCAA, response to SIGIR data call, 10/4/2011; DoJ, Justice Management Division, response to SIGIR data call, 10/9/2012; DoS, PM, response to SIGIR data call, 7/6/2011; DoS, "Congressional Budget Justification: Foreign Assistance," Summary Tables, FY 2009–FY 2011; DoS, "Executive Budget Summary Function 150 & Other International Programs, Fiscal Year 2013," p. 173; DRL, response to SIGIR data call, 7/9/2012; ECA, response to SIGIR data call, 4/14/2010; OMB,

response to SIGIR data call, 6/21/2010; INL, response to SIGIR data call, 10/16/2012; USAID, "U.S. Overseas Loans and Grants [Greenbook]," 2008; U.S. Treasury, OTA, "Office of Technical Assistance Overview," 12/30/2005; TFBSO, response to SIGIR data call, 1/4/2011; SIGIR Audit 11-007, "Iraq Relief and Reconstruction Fund 1: Report on Apportionments, Expenditures, and Cancelled Funds," 12/28/2010; USAID, responses to SIGIR data calls, 1/12/2009, 4/8/2009, 10/2/2012, and 10/15/2012; U.S. Embassy-Baghdad, responses to SIGIR data calls, 10/3/2009, 10/5/2011, 1/4/2012, 4/3/2012, 7/3/2012, and 10/1/2012; NEA-I, responses to SIGIR data calls, 10/4/2010, 10/6/2010, 4/15/2011, 9/28/2011, 9/20/2012, 9/27/2012, 9/25/2012, 10/1/2012, 10/2/2012, and 10/10/2012; OUSD(C), "United States Department of Defense Fiscal Year 2012 Budget Request," Overview, 2/2012, p. 66, and responses to SIGIR data calls, 10/14/2010 and 10/2/2012; USACE, responses to SIGIR data calls, 10/6/2008 and 10/1/2012.

[107] P.L. 108-7; P.L. 108-11; P.L. 108-106; P.L. 108-287; P.L. 109-13; P.L. 109-102; P.L. 109-148; P.L. 109-34; P.L. 109-289; P.L. 110-28; P.L. 110-92; P.L. 110-116; P.L. 110-137; P.L. 110-149; P.L. 110-161; P.L. 110-252; P.L. 111-32; P.L. 111-117; P.L. 111-118; P.L. 111-212; P.L. 112-10, P.L. 112-74; ABO, response to SIGIR data call, 1/18/2012; BBG, response to SIGIR data call, 3/7/2011; DCAA, response to SIGIR data call, 10/4/2011; DoJ, Justice Management Division, response to SIGIR data call, 10/9/2012; PM, response to SIGIR data call, 7/6/2011; DoS, "Congressional Budget Justification: Foreign Assistance," Summary Tables, FY 2009–FY 2011; DoS, "Executive Budget Summary Function 150 & Other International Programs, Fiscal Year 2013," p. 173; DRL, response to SIGIR data call, 7/9/2012; ECA, response to SIGIR data call, 4/14/2010; OMB, response to SIGIR data call, 6/21/2010; INL, response to SIGIR data call, 10/16/2012; USAID, "U.S. Overseas Loans and Grants [Greenbook]," 2008; U.S. Treasury, OTA, "Office of Technical Assistance Overview," 12/30/2005; TFBSO, response to SIGIR data call, 1/4/2011; SIGIR Audit 11-007, "Iraq Relief and Reconstruction Fund 1: Report on Apportionments, Expenditures, and Cancelled Funds," 12/28/2010; USAID, responses to SIGIR data calls, 1/12/2009, 4/8/2009, 10/2/2012, and 10/15/2012; U.S. Embassy-Baghdad, responses to SIGIR data calls, 10/3/2009, 10/5/2011, 1/4/2012, 4/3/2012, 7/3/2012, and 10/1/2012; NEA-I, responses to SIGIR data calls, 10/4/2012, 10/6/2010, 4/15/2011, 9/28/2011, 9/20/2012, 9/27/2012, 9/25/2012, 10/1/2012, 10/2/2012, and 10/10/2012; OUSD(C), "United States Department of Defense Fiscal Year 2012 Budget Request," Overview, 2/2012, p. 6-6; OUSD(C), responses to SIGIR data calls, 10/14/2010 and 10/2/2012; USACE, responses to SIGIR data calls, 10/6/2008 and 10/1/2012; GOI, CoR, "Federal Budget Law for the Fiscal Year 2012," Articles 1, 2, and 36, 2/23/2012, and "Federal Public Budget Law for the Fiscal Year 2011," Article 2, 2/23/2011; GOI, MOF, information provided to SIGIR, 6/27/2011; "GOI Budget" (as approved by TNA and written into law December 2005); GOI, Presidency of the Iraqi Interim National Assembly, "The State General Budget for 2005," 2005; GOI, MoPDC, "Indicators of the Investment Budget for Year 2010," Table 17, 2011; GOI, "Budget Revenues and Expenses 2003, July–December," 2003; SIGIR, *Quarterly and Semiannual Reports to the United States Congress*, 3/30/2004–4/30/2011; U.S. Treasury, responses to SIGIR data calls, 1/4/2008 and 4/9/2009. NEA-I, responses to SIGIR data calls, 4/5/2011, 4/7/2011, and 7/12/2011; World Bank, "World Bank Operations in Iraq," 12/31/2011; Embassy of Japan in Iraq, press release, "Provision of Yen Loan to Iraq," 5/29/2012.

[108] INL, response to SIGIR data call, 10/16/2012; ABO, response to SIGIR data call, 1/18/2012; CENTCOM OIG, information provided to SIGIR audits, 1/14/2013; NEA-I, responses to SIGIR data calls, 9/28/2011, 9/20/2012, 9/25/2012, 10/1/2012, and 10/2/2012; USACE, response to SIGIR data call, 10/1/2012; U.S. Embassy-Baghdad, responses to SIGIR data calls, 10/5/2011, 1/4/2012, 4/3/2012, 7/3/2012, 10/1/2012; SIGIR Audit 11-007, "Iraq Relief and Reconstruction Fund 1: Report on Apportionments, Expenditures, and Cancelled Funds," 12/28/2010; OUSD(C), response to SIGIR data call, 10/2/2012; P.L. 108-106; P.L. 108- 11; P.L. 109-102; P.L. 109-13; P.L. 109-234; P.L. 109-289; P.L. 110-137; P.L. 110-149; P.L. 110-161; P.L. 110-252; P.L. 110-28; P.L. 110-5; P.L. 110-92; P.L. 111-117; P.L. 111-212; P.L. 111-32; P.L. 111-8; P.L. 112-10; P.L. 112-74.

[109] SIGIR, *Iraq Reconstruction: Lessons in Contracting and Procurement*, 7/2006, p. 27, and Audit 11-007, "Iraq Relief and Reconstruction Fund 1: Report on Apportionments, Expenditures, and Cancelled Funds," 1/25/2011, p. 4.

[110] CPA, info memo, Chief of Staff to CPA Staff, "President's Supplemental–CPA Program Management Office," unclassified, 9/9/2003.

[111] SIGIR, *Hard Lessons: The Iraq Reconstruction Experience*, 2/2009, p. 103.

[112] SIGIR, *Hard Lessons: The Iraq Reconstruction Experience*, 2/2009, p. 105, and *Iraq Reconstruction: Lessons in Contracting and Procurement*, 7/2006, p. 25. In June 2003, the Assistant Secretary of the Army-ATL established a contracting cell in Iraq, called the Head of Contracting Activity (HCA), to execute contracting

for the IRRF 2. For a discussion of the challenges of contracting the IRRF, see SIGIR's *Iraq Reconstruction: Lessons in Contracting and Procurement*.

[113] NEA-I, response to SIGIR data call, 9/20/2012; SIGIR Audit 11-007, "Iraq Relief and Reconstruction Fund 1: Report on Apportionments, Expenditures, and Cancelled Funds," 12/28/2010, and *Quarterly and Semiannual Reports to the United States Congress*, 3/30/2004–10/30/2012.

[114] P.L. 108-106.

[115] SIGIR, *Quarterly Report to the United States Congress*, 4/30/2006, p. 5.

[116] Conference Report 109-494, to accompany H.R. 4939, 6/8/2006, p. 99.

[117] P.L. 109-13; P.L. 109-234; P.L. 109-289; P.L. 110- 28; P.L. 110-161; P.L. 110-252; P.L. 111-32; P.L. 111-212; P.L. 112-10.

[118] P.L. 108-11; P.L. 108-106; P.L. 108-287; P.L. 109-13; P.L. 109-102; P.L. 109-148; P.L. 109-34; P.L. 109-289; P.L. 110-28; P.L. 110-92; P.L. 110- 116; P.L. 110-137; P.L. 110-149; P.L. 110-61; P.L. 110-252; P.L. 111-32; P.L. 111-117; P.L. 111-118; P.L. 111-212; P.L. 112-10, P.L. 112-74; ABO, response to SIGIR data call, 1/18/2012; BBG, response to SIGIR data call, 3/7/2011; DCAA, response to SIGIR data call, 10/4/2011; DoJ, Justice Management Division, response to SIGIR data call, 10/9/2012; DoS, PM, response to SIGIR data call, 7/6/2011; DoS, "Congressional Budget Justification: Foreign Assistance," Summary Tables, FY 2009–FY 2011; DoS, "Executive Budget Summary Function 150 & Other International Programs, Fiscal Year 2013," p. 173; DRL, response to SIGIR data call, 7/9/2012; ECA, response to SIGIR data call, 4/14/2010; OMB, response to SIGIR data call, 6/21/2010; INL, response to SIGIR data call, 10/16/2012; USAID, "U.S. Overseas Loans and Grants [Greenbook]," 2008; U.S. Treasury, OTA, "Office of Technical Assistance Overview," 12/30/2005; TFBSO, response to SIGIR data call, 1/4/2011; SIGIR Audit 11-007, "Iraq Relief and Reconstruction Fund 1: Report on Apportionments, Expenditures, and Cancelled Funds," 12/28/2010; USAID, responses to SIGIR data calls, 1/12/2009, 4/8/2009, 10/2/2012, and 10/15/2012; U.S. Embassy-Baghdad, responses to SIGIR data calls, 10/3/2009, 10/5/2011, 1/4/2012, 4/3/2012, 7/3/2012, and 10/1/2012; NEA-I, responses to SIGIR data calls, 10/4/2010, 10/6/2010, 4/15/2011, 9/28/2011, 9/20/2012, 9/27/2012, 9/25/2012, 10/1/2012, 10/2/2012, and 10/10/2012; OUSD(C), "United States Department of Defense Fiscal Year 2012 Budget Request," Overview, 2/2012, p. 66, and responses to SIGIR data calls, 10/14/2010 and 10/2/2012; USACE, responses to SIGIR data calls, 10/6/2008 and 10/1/2012.

[119] MNSTC-I, former Deputy J5, SIGIR interview, 7/24/2008; OMB, "FY 2005 Emergency Supplemental Request," 2/14/2005, pp. 25–26.

[120] The total for regular appropriations includes FY 2009 "bridge" funding, which was forward-funded in the FY 2008 supplemental appropriations. DoD, "FY 2005 Supplemental Request for Operation Iraqi Freedom (OIF), Operation Enduring Freedom (OEF), and Operation Unified Assistance," 2/2005, pp. 78-79; DoD, "FY 2006 Supplemental Request for Operation Iraqi Freedom (OIF) and Operation Enduring Freedom (OEF)," 2/2006, pp. 60–61; DoD, "Amendment to FY 2007 Emergency Supplemental Request for the Global War on Terror," 3/2007, p. 5; DoD, "FY 2007 Emergency Supplemental Request for the Global War on Terror," 2/2007, pp. 38–49; DoD, "FY 2008 Global War on Terror Request," 2/2007, pp. 34-40; DoD, "FY 2008 Global War on Terror Amendment, Department of Defense," 10/2007, pp. 26–27; DoD, "FY 2009 Global War on Terror Bridge Request," 5/2008, pp. 15–16; DoD, "FY 2009 Supplemental Request," 4/2009, pp. 41–43; DoD, "FY 2011 Budget Request Overview," 2/2010, pp. 6-8–6-9; P.L. 109-13; P.L. 109-234; P.L. 109-252; P.L. 109-289; P.L. 110-28; P.L. 110- 161; P.L. 111-32; P.L. 111-212; P.L. 112-10.

[121] OUSD(C), response to SIGIR data call, 10/2/2012; SIGIR, *Quarterly and Semiannual Reports to the United States Congress*, 3/30/2004– 10/30/2012.

[122] OUSD(C), response to SIGIR data call, 10/2/2012; SIGIR, *Quarterly and Semiannual Reports to the United States Congress*, 3/30/2004– 10/30/2012.

[123] OUSD(C), response to SIGIR data call, 10/2/2012; P.L. 109-13; P.L. 109-234; P.L. 109- 252; P.L. 109-289; P.L. 110-28; P.L. 110-161; P.L. 111-32; P.L. 111-212; P.L. 112-10.

[124] OUSD(C), response to SIGIR data call, 10/2/2012; SIGIR, *Quarterly and Semiannual Reports to the United States Congress*, 3/30/2004– 10/30/2012.

[125] OUSD(C), response to SIGIR data call, 10/2/2012; SIGIR, *Quarterly and Semiannual Reports to the United States Congress*, 3/30/2004– 10/30/2012.

[126] P.L. 112-10; SIGIR Audit 12-016, "Interim Report on Spend Plans for Fiscal Years 2011–2012 Iraq Security Forces Fund," 4/2012; OSC-I, response to SIGIR data call, 4/2/2012. The Congress originally appropriated $1.50 billion to the ISFF in FY 2011 against the Administration's request of $2.00 billion, but DoD later requested and received Congressional approval to reprogram $345 million of the ISFF to meet DoD needs in Afghanistan and other mission areas, thus reducing FY 2011 ISFF budget authority to $1.145 billion.

[127] SIGIR Audit 12-018, "Status of Fiscal Years 2011–2012 Iraq Security Forces Fund," 7/27/2012, p. 3.

[128] P.L. 109-102; P.L. 109-234; P.L. 110-28; P.L. 110- 92; P.L. 110-137; P.L. 110-149; P.L. 110-161; P.L. 110-252; P.L. 111-32; P.L. 111-117; P.L. 112-10; P.L. 112-74.

[129] NEA-I, responses to SIGIR data calls, 9/28/2011, 9/25/2012, 10/1/2012, and 10/2/2012; USACE, response to SIGIR data call, 10/1/2012; U.S. Embassy-Baghdad, responses to SIGIR data calls, 10/5/2011, 1/4/2012, 4/3/2012, 7/3/2012, and 10/1/2012; SIGIR, *Quarterly and Semiannual Reports to the United States Congress*, 3/30/2004–10/30/2012.

[130] P.L. 109-102; House Report 109-265, to accompany H.R. 3057, 11/2/2005, p. 86; P.L. 109-234; House Report 109-494, to accompany H.R. 4939, 6/8/2006, pp. 95–96; P.L. 110-28; House Report 110-107, to accompany H.R. 1591, 4/24/2007, pp. 202–204; P.L. 110-92; P.L.110-137; P.L. 110-149; P.L.110-161; House Appropriations Committee, "Consolidated Appropriations Act, 2008, Committee Print: Division J—Department of State, Foreign Operations, and Related Programs Act, 2008," 1/30/2008, pp. 2177–2178, 2208; P.L. 110-252; Senate Explanatory Statement, to accompany H.R. 2642, 6/26/2008; P.L. 111-32; Conference Report 111-151, to accompany H.R. 2346, 6/12/2009, pp. 127–129; P.L. 111-117; Conference Report 111-366, to accompany H.R. 3288, 12/8/2009, pp. 1466, 1470; DoS, "Foreign Operations Congressional Budget Justification, FY 2006," p. 448; House Document 109-90, "Request for FY 2006 Budget Amendments," 2/28/2006, p. 26; DoS, "Foreign Operations Congressional Budget Justification, FY 2008," pp. 48, 128–129, 138, 490; DoS and USAID, "Supplemental Appropriations Justification, FY 2008," p. 38; DoS, "Foreign Operations Congressional Budget Justification, FY 2009," pp. 543–544; DoS and USAID, "Supplemental Justification, FY 2009," pp. 40–43; DoS, "Foreign Operations Congressional Budget Justification, Annex: Regional Perspectives, FY 2010," pp. 421–426; DoS, "Foreign Operations Congressional Budget Justification, Annex: Regional Perspectives, FY 2011," pp. 471–477; DoS, "Foreign Operations Congressional Budget Justification, Annex: Regional Perspectives, FY 2012," pp. 522–528; USAID, "USAID Awards Community Stabilization Program in Iraq," 8/11/2006.

[131] In the fourth quarter of FY 2008, the rate of obligation exceeded $6.2 million per day on average and dropped to approximately $2.2 million per day on average in the fourth quarters of FY 2009 and FY 2010. The average obligation rate for the first three fiscal year quarters of FY 2006–FY 2011 was $1.2 million per day.

[132] NEA-I, responses to SIGIR data calls, 9/28/2011, 9/25/2012, 10/1/2012, and 10/2/2012; U.S. Embassy-Baghdad, responses to SIGIR data calls, 10/5/2011, 1/4/2012, 4/3/2012, 7/3/2012, and 10/1/2012; USACE, response to SIGIR data call, 10/1/2012.

[133] NEA-I, responses to SIGIR data calls, 9/28/2011, 9/25/2012, 10/1/2012, and 10/2/2012; U.S. Embassy-Baghdad, responses to SIGIR data calls, 10/5/2011, 1/4/2012, 4/3/2012, 7/3/2012, and 10/1/2012; USACE, response to SIGIR data call, 10/1/2012; SIGIR, *Quarterly and Semiannual Reports to the United States Congress*, 4/30/2007–4/30/2011.

[134] SIGIR Audit 05-014, "Management of Commander's Emergency Response Program for Fiscal Year 2004," 10/13/2005, p. 2.

[135] P.L. 108-106.

[136] ABO, response to SIGIR data call, 1/18/2012; CENTCOM OIG, information provided to SIGIR Audits, 1/14/2013.

[137] SIGIR, *Quarterly and Semiannual Report to the United States Congress*, 1/30/2011, Insert, and Audit 11-021, "Management of the Iraq Commander's Emergency Response Program Needs to Be Improved (Interim Report)," 7/29/2011, pp. 1–2.

[138] ABO, response to SIGIR data call, 1/18/2012; CENTCOM OIG, information provided to SIGIR Audits, 1/14/2013.

[139] ABO, responses to SIGIR data call, 7/14/2011 and 7/15/2011; P.L. 112-10.

[140] ABO, response to SIGIR data call, 1/18/2012; CENTCOM OIG, information provided to SIGIR Audits, 1/14/2013.

[141] ABO, response to SIGIR data call, 1/18/2012; CENTCOM OIG, information provided to SIGIR Audits, 1/14/2013.

[142] ABO, response to SIGIR data call, 1/18/2012; CENTCOM OIG, information provided to SIGIR audits, 1/14/2013; SIGIR, *Quarterly and Semiannual Reports to the United States Congress*, 3/30/2004–10/30/2012.

[143] SIGIR, *Quarterly and Semiannual Report to the United States Congress*, 1/30/2011, Insert.

[144] GOI officials, SIGIR interviews, 9/2012–11/2012.

[145] SIGIR, *Quarterly and Semiannual Report to the United States Congress*, 1/30/2011, Insert.

[146] ABO, responses to SIGIR data calls, 10/4/2010, 10/8/2010, 12/6/2010, 12/22/2010, 4/5/2011, 4/18/2011, 7/5/2011, 7/14/2011, 10/18/2011, and 1/18/2012; USF-I, response to SIGIR data call, 1/3/2012.

234 Special Inspector General for Iraq Reconstruction

[147] P.L. 112-36, Section 117; U.S. House of Representatives, 112th Congress, H.R. 2219, "Making Appropriations for the Department of Defense for the Fiscal Year Ending September 30, 2012, and for Other Purposes," 7/8/2011, Sec. 9005; House Report 112-110 to accompany H.R. 2219, 6/16/2011, p. 298.

[148] ABO, response to SIGIR data call, 1/18/2012; CENTCOM OIG, information provided to SIGIR Audits, 1/14/2013.

[149] SIGIR, *Quarterly Report to the United States Congress*, 10/30/2011, p. 27.

[150] P.L. 109-102; P.L.109-234; P.L.110-5; P.L.110-28; P.L.110-161; P.L.110-252; P.L.111-8; P.L.111-32; P.L.111-117; P.L.111-212; P.L.112-10; P.L.112-74.

[151] INL, response to SIGIR data call, 10/16/2012.

[152] INL, response to SIGIR data call, 4/2/2012.

[153] INL, response to SIGIR data call, 10/1/2012.

[154] INL, response to SIGIR data call, 10/16/2012.

[155] U.S. Embassy-Baghdad, response to SIGIR data call, 10/1/2012.

[156] PRM, response to SIGIR data call, 10/1/2012.

[157] P.L. 108-11; P.L. 108-106; P.L. 108-287; P.L. 109-13; P.L. 109-102; P.L. 109-148; P.L. 109-34; P.L. 109-289; P.L. 110-28; P.L. 110-92; P.L. 110- 116; P.L. 110-137; P.L. 110-149; P.L. 110-61; P.L. 110-252; P.L. 111-32; P.L. 111-117; P.L. 111-118; P.L. 111-212; P.L. 112-10, P.L. 112-74; ABO, response to SIGIR data call, 1/18/2012; BBG, response to SIGIR data call, 3/7/2011; DCAA, response to SIGIR data call, 10/4/2011; DoJ, Justice Management Division, response to SIGIR data call, 10/9/2012; DoS, PM, response to SIGIR data call, 7/6/2011; DoS, "Congressional Budget Justification: Foreign Assistance," Summary Tables, FY 2009–FY 2011; DoS, "Executive Budget Summary Function 150 & Other International Programs, Fiscal Year 2013," p. 173; DRL, response to SIGIR data call, 7/9/2012; ECA, response to SIGIR data call, 4/14/2010; OMB, response to SIGIR data call, 6/21/2010; INL, response to SIGIR data call, 10/16/2012; USAID, "U.S. Overseas Loans and Grants [Greenbook]," 2008; U.S. Treasury, OTA, "Office of Technical Assistance Overview," 12/30/2005; TFBSO, response to SIGIR data call, 1/4/2011; SIGIR Audit 11-007, "Iraq Relief and Reconstruction Fund 1: Report on Apportionments, Expenditures, and Cancelled Funds," 12/28/2010; USAID, responses to SIGIR data calls, 1/12/2009, 4/8/2009, 10/2/2012, and 10/15/2012; U.S. Embassy-Baghdad, responses to SIGIR data calls, 10/3/2009, 10/5/2011, 1/4/2012, 4/3/2012, 7/3/2012, and 10/1/2012; NEA-I, responses to SIGIR data calls, 10/4/2012, 10/6/2010, 4/15/2011, 9/28/2011, 9/20/2012, 9/27/2012, 9/25/2012, 10/1/2012, 10/2/2012, and 10/10/2012; OUSD(C), "United States Department of Defense Fiscal Year 2012 Budget Request," Overview, 2/2012, p. 66, and responses to SIGIR data calls, 10/14/2010 and 10/2/2012; USACE, responses to SIGIR data calls, 10/6/2008 and 10/1/2012.

[158] OSC-I, response to SIGIR data call, 10/2/2012.

[159] P.L. 108-11; P.L. 108-106; P.L. 108-287; P.L. 109-13; P.L. 109-102; P.L. 109-148; P.L. 109-34; P.L. 109-289; P.L. 110-28; P.L. 110-92; P.L. 110- 116; P.L. 110-137; P.L. 110-149; P.L. 110-61; P.L. 110-252; P.L. 111-32; P.L. 111-117; P.L. 111-118; P.L. 111-212; P.L. 112-10, P.L. 112-74; ABO, response to SIGIR data call, 1/18/2012; BBG, response to SIGIR data call, 3/7/2011; DCAA, response to SIGIR data call, 10/4/2011; DoJ, Justice Management Division, response to SIGIR data call, 10/9/2012; DoS, PM, response to SIGIR data call, 7/6/2011; DoS, "Congressional Budget Justification: Foreign Assistance," Summary Tables, FY 2009–FY 2011; DoS, "Executive Budget Summary Function 150 & Other International Programs, Fiscal Year 2013," p. 173; DRL, response to SIGIR data call, 7/9/2012; ECA, response to SIGIR data call, 4/14/2010; OMB, response to SIGIR data call, 6/21/2010; INL, response to SIGIR data call, 10/16/2012; USAID, "U.S. Overseas Loans and Grants [Greenbook]," 2008; U.S. Treasury, OTA, "Office of Technical Assistance Overview," 12/30/2005; TFBSO, response to SIGIR data call, 1/4/2011; SIGIR Audit 11-007, "Iraq Relief and Reconstruction Fund 1: Report on Apportionments, Expenditures, and Cancelled Funds," 12/28/2010; USAID, responses to SIGIR data calls, 1/12/2009, 4/8/2009, 10/2/2012, and 10/15/2012; U.S. Embassy-Baghdad, responses to SIGIR data calls, 10/3/2009, 10/5/2011, 1/4/2012, 4/3/2012, 7/3/2012, and 10/1/2012; NEA-I, responses to SIGIR data calls, 10/4/2012, 10/6/2010, 4/15/2011, 9/28/2011, 9/20/2012, 9/27/2012, 9/25/2012, 10/1/2012, 10/2/2012, and 10/10/2012; OUSD(C), "United States Department of Defense Fiscal Year 2012 Budget Request," Overview, 2/2012, p. 66, and responses to SIGIR data calls, 10/14/2010 and 10/2/2012; USACE, responses to SIGIR data calls, 10/6/2008 and 10/1/2012.

[160] This $246 million includes FY 2013 funding and does not match the SIGIR total listed in the "U.S. Appropriated Funds" table, which only accounts for funds through FY 2012.

[161] P.L. 108-11; P.L. 108-106; P.L. 108-287; P.L. 109-13; P.L. 109-102; P.L. 109-148; P.L. 109-34; P.L. 109-289; P.L. 110-28; P.L. 110-92; P.L. 110- 116; P.L. 110-137; P.L. 110-149; P.L. 110-61; P.L. 110-252; P.L. 111-32; P.L. 111-117; P.L. 111-118; P.L. 111-212; P.L. 112-10, P.L. 112-74; ABO, response to SIGIR data call,

1/18/2012; BBG, response to SIGIR data call, 3/7/2011; DCAA, response to SIGIR data call, 10/4/2011; DoJ, Justice Management Division, response to SIGIR data call, 10/9/2012; DoS, PM, response to SIGIR data call, 7/6/2011; DoS, "Congressional Budget Justification: Foreign Assistance," Summary Tables, FY 2009–FY 2011; DoS, "Executive Budget Summary Function 150 & Other International Programs, Fiscal Year 2013," p. 173; DRL, response to SIGIR data call, 7/9/2012; ECA, response to SIGIR data call, 4/14/2010; OMB, response to SIGIR data call, 6/21/2010; INL, response to SIGIR data call, 10/16/2012; USAID, "U.S. Overseas Loans and Grants [Greenbook]," 2008; U.S. Treasury, OTA, "Office of Technical Assistance Overview," 12/30/2005; TFBSO, response to SIGIR data call, 1/4/2011; SIGIR Audit 11-007, "Iraq Relief and Reconstruction Fund 1: Report on Apportionments, Expenditures, and Cancelled Funds," 12/28/2010; USAID, responses to SIGIR data calls, 1/12/2009, 4/8/2009, 10/2/2012, and 10/15/2012; U.S. Embassy-Baghdad, responses to SIGIR data calls, 10/3/2009, 10/5/2011, 1/4/2012, 4/3/2012, 7/3/2012, and 10/1/2012; NEA-I, responses to SIGIR data calls, 10/4/2012, 10/6/2010, 4/15/2011, 9/28/2011, 9/20/2012, 9/27/2012, 9/25/2012, 10/1/2012, 10/2/2012, and 10/10/2012; OUSD(C), "United States Department of Defense Fiscal Year 2012 Budget Request," Overview, 2/2012, p. 66, and responses to SIGIR data calls, 10/14/2010 and 10/2/2012; USACE, responses to SIGIR data calls, 10/6/2008 and 10/1/2012.

[162] SIGIR, *Hard Lessons: The Iraq Reconstruction Experience*, 2/2009, pp. 3–45.

[163] SIGIR, *Hard Lessons: The Iraq Reconstruction Experience*, 2/2009, pp. 8–12.

[164] SIGIR, *Hard Lessons: The Iraq Reconstruction Experience*, 2/2009, pp. 8–12.

[165] SIGIR, *Hard Lessons: The Iraq Reconstruction Experience*, 2/2009, pp. 19, 33–34.

[166] SIGIR, *Hard Lessons: The Iraq Reconstruction Experience*, 2/2009, p. 42.

[167] P.L. 108-11.

[168] SIGIR, *Hard Lessons: The Iraq Reconstruction Experience*, 2/2009, pp. 63–64.

[169] President George W. Bush, request for 2004 supplemental appropriations for ongoing military and intelligence operations in Iraq, Afghanistan, and elsewhere, 9/17/2003.

[170] SIGIR, *Hard Lessons: The Iraq Reconstruction Experience*, 2/2009, p. 103.

[171] SIGIR, *Hard Lessons: The Iraq Reconstruction Experience*, 2/2009, p. 55.

[172] SIGIR, *Hard Lessons: The Iraq Reconstruction Experience*, 2/2009, pp. 59–60, 86, 90.

[173] SIGIR, *Hard Lessons: The Iraq Reconstruction Experience*, 2/2009, pp. 73–74.

[174] SIGIR, *Hard Lessons: The Iraq Reconstruction Experience*, 2/2009, pp. 75–77.

[175] SIGIR, *Hard Lessons: The Iraq Reconstruction Experience*, 2/2009, pp. 70.

[176] SIGIR, *Hard Lessons: The Iraq Reconstruction Experience*, 2/2009, pp. 20–24.

[177] ORHA, *A Unified Mission Plan for Post-Hostilities Iraq*, draft, 4/2003.

[178] CPA, *Achieving the Vision: Taking Forward the CPA Strategic Plan for Iraq*, 7/23/2003, and *Achieving the Vision to Restore Full Sovereignty to the Iraqi People*, working document as of 10/1/2003.

[179] P.L. 108-106.

[180] UN/World Bank, "Joint Iraq Needs Assessment," 10/2003, pp. vi, 4.

[181] SIGIR, *Hard Lessons: The Iraq Reconstruction Experience*, 2/2009, p. 94.

[182] CPA, *Achieving the Vision: Taking Forward the CPA Strategic Plan for Iraq*, 7/23/2003.

[183] SIGIR, *Iraq Reconstruction: Lessons in Inspections of U.S.-funded Stabilization and Reconstruction Projects*, 12/2011, p. 1.

[184] SIGIR Audit 11-007, "Iraq Relief and Reconstruction Fund 1: Report on Apportionments, Expenditures, and Cancelled Funds," pp. 4, 13–14. **Note:** The $1.1 billion in USAID expenditures does not include any of the $202 million in costs that USAID incurred prior to enactment of P.L. 108-11 and for which it was reimbursed with IRRF 1 funds.

[185] For sources of funding data, see endnote 2.

[186] SIGIR, *Hard Lessons: The Iraq Reconstruction Experience*, 2/2009, pp. 179–192.

[187] GAO Report No. 05-872, "Rebuilding Iraq: U.S. Water and Sanitation Efforts Need Improved Measures for Assessing Impact and Sustained Resources for Maintaining Facilities," 9/2005; SIGIR Evaluation EV-10-002, "Review of Major U.S. Government Infrastructure Projects in Iraq: Nassiriya and Ifraz Water Treatment Plants," 10/28/2010.

[188] EIA, International Energy Annual 2006; UN/ World Bank, "Joint Iraq Needs Assessment," 10/2003, p. 28.

[189] SIGIR, *Hard Lessons: The Iraq Reconstruction Experience*, 2/2009, p. 65; EIA, *International Energy Annual 2006*; GOI, MOE data; UN/ World Bank, "Joint Iraq Needs Assessment," 10/2003, p. 28.

[190] GAO Report No. 04-902R, "Rebuilding Iraq: Resource, Security, Governance, Essential Services, and Oversight Issues," 6/2004, pp. 4, 85.

236   Special Inspector General for Iraq Reconstruction

[191] CPA, Office of Policy, Planning, and Analysis "Post-Conflict Planning in Iraq" 12/29/2006, pp. 46–47, and *Achieving the Vision: Taking Forward the CPA Strategic Plan for Iraq*, 7/23/2003.

[192] SIGIR, *Hard Lessons: The Iraq Reconstruction Experience*, 2/2009, pp. 149–150.

[193] SIGIR, *Hard Lessons: The Iraq Reconstruction Experience*, 2/2009, pp. 149–151; ITAO/ ESD, *Electric Daily Performance Reports*, 6/1/2006–6/30/2011; DoS, *Iraq Status Reports*, 10/25/2006, slide 11, and 5/9/2007, slide 11.

[194] SIGIR, *Hard Lessons: The Iraq Reconstruction Experience*, 2/2009, pp. 114, 151.

[195] Bechtel Corporation, press release, "USAID Awards Bechtel National Iraq Infrastructure II Contract," 1/6/2004.

[196] For sources of funding data, see endnote 2.

[197] SIGIR Audit 07-009, "Review of Bechtel's Spending under Its Phase II Iraq Reconstruction Contract," 7/24/2007, p. 52.

[198] USACE, information provided to SIGIR Audits, 11/20/2012.

[199] SIGIR, *Hard Lessons: The Iraq Reconstruction Experience*, 2/2009, p. 146, and *Quarterly Report to the United States Congress*, 4/30/2009, p. 71.

[200] SIGIR, *Quarterly Report to the United States Congress*, 4/30/2009, p. 71; ITAO/ESD, *Electric Daily Performance Reports*, 6/1/2006–6/30/2011.

[201] ITAO/ESD, *Electric Daily Performance Reports*, 6/1/2006–6/30/2011; DoS, *Iraq Status Reports*, 10/25/2006, slide 11, and 5/9/2007, slide 11; U.S. Embassy-Baghdad, responses to SIGIR data calls, 1/22/2012, 4/13/2012, 7/3/2012, and 10/1/2012; GOI, NMC, "Status of the Ministry of Electricity," selected reports, 9/1/2012–9/30/2012.

[202] U.S. Embassy-Baghdad, responses to SIGIR data calls, 1/22/2012, 4/13/2012, 7/3/2012, and 10/1/2012; GOI, NMC, "Status of the Ministry of Electricity," selected reports, 9/1/2012– 9/30/2012; SIGIR, *Quarterly and Semiannual Report to the United States Congress*, 1/30/2012, p. 74.

[203] SIGIR, *Quarterly and Semiannual Reports to the United States Congress*, 10/30/2009, pp. 62–63, 4/30/2011, p. 116, 7/30/2011, p. 97, and 10/30/2012, p. 69.

[204] ITAO/ESD, *Electric Daily Performance Reports*, 6/1/2006–6/30/2011; U.S. Embassy-Baghdad, responses to SIGIR data calls, 1/22/2012, 4/13/2012, 7/3/2012, and 10/1/2012; GOI, NMC, "Status of the Ministry of Electricity," selected reports, 9/1/2012–9/30/2012; SIGIR, *Quarterly and Semiannual Reports to the United States Congress*, 7/30/2010, p. 72, and 10/30/2012, p. 69.

[205] ITAO/ESD, *Electric Daily Performance Reports*, 6/1/2006–6/30/2011; DoS, *Iraq Status Reports*, 10/25/2006, slide 11, and 5/9/2007, slide 11; U.S. Embassy-Baghdad, responses to SIGIR data calls, 1/22/2012, 4/13/2012, 7/3/2012, and 10/1/2012; GOI, NMC, "Status of the Ministry of Electricity," selected reports, 9/1/2012–9/30/2012.

[206] SIGIR, *Quarterly Report to the United States Congress*, 10/30/2010, pp. 101–102.

[207] SIGIR, *Quarterly and Semiannual Reports to the United States Congress*, 10/30/2009, pp. 64–65, and 1/30/2012, p. 74.

[208] SIGIR, *Quarterly and Semiannual Report to the United States Congress*, 7/30/2010, pp. 11, 73.

[209] SIGIR, *Quarterly Report to the United States Congress*, 10/30/2012, pp. 69–70.

[210] UNICEF, "Iraq Watching Briefs: Water and Environmental Sanitation," 7/2003, pp. 2, 7–8.

[211] UNICEF, "Iraq Watching Briefs: Water and Environmental Sanitation," 7/2003, Executive Summary.

[212] SIGIR, *Quarterly and Semiannual Report to the United States Congress*, 1/30/2006, p. 31.

[213] SIGIR, *Hard Lessons: The Iraq Reconstruction Experience*, 2/2009, p. 187.

[214] CPA, "CPA Strategic Plan—Essential Services, Endstate," 4/23/2004, p. 20.

[215] GAO Report No. 05-872, "Rebuilding Iraq: U.S. Water and Sanitation Efforts Need Improved Measures for Assessing Impact and Sustained Resources for Maintaining Facilities," 9/2005, pp. 13-14.

[216] SIGIR, *Quarterly and Semiannual Report to the United States Congress*, 1/30/2007, pp. 54–55.

[217] SIGIR, *Hard Lessons: The Iraq Reconstruction Experience*, 2/2009, p. 170.

[218] SIGIR, *Hard Lessons: The Iraq Reconstruction Experience*, 2/2009, p. 187.

[219] IRMS, *USF-I CERP Category Report*, 9/20/2012; NEA-I, response to SIGIR data call, 9/20/2012; USACE, response to SIGIR data call, 10/1/2012. For funding sources, see endnote 2.

[220] For funding sources, see endnote 2.

[221] SIGIR EV-10-002, "Review of Major U.S. Government Infrastructure Projects in Iraq: Nassiriya and Ifraz Water Treatment Plants," 10/2010, p. 1 and Audit 12-007, "Falluja Waste Water Treatment System: A Case Study in Wartime Contracting," 10/30/2011, p. 1.

[222] SIGIR, *Quarterly Report to the United States Congress*, 4/30/2010, pp. 70–71.

223 GAO Report 05-872, "Rebuilding Iraq: U.S. Water and Sanitation Efforts Need Improved Measures for Assessing Impact and Sustained Resources for Maintaining Facilities," 9/2005, p. 14.

224 GAO Report 05-872, "Rebuilding Iraq: U.S. Water and Sanitation Efforts Need Improved Measures for Assessing Impact and Sustained Resources for Maintaining Facilities," 9/2005, p. 25.

225 SIGIR, *Quarterly Report to the United States Congress*, 10/30/2006, p. 49; DoS, *Section 2207 Report*, Appendix III, Economic Support Fund (ESF), 1/2008, pp. III-1, III-8–III-9.

226 UN, Inter-Agency Information and Analysis Unit, "Water in Iraq Factsheet," 3/2011.

227 SIGIR, *Quarterly and Semiannual Report to the United States Congress*, 1/30/2012, p. 76.

228 SIGIR, *Quarterly Report to the United States Congress*, 10/30/2010, p. 90.

229 SIGIR, *Hard Lessons: The Iraq Reconstruction Experience*, 2/2009, p. 136; EIA, "World Crude Oil Production, 1960-2008," www.eia.doe.gov, accessed 12/30/2009, and *International Energy Statistics, Iraq*, www.eia.gov/cfapps/ipdbproject/ iedindex3.cfm?tid= 50&pid=53&aid=1&cid= r5,&syid=2002&eyid=2003&freq=M&unit= TBPD, accessed 1/18/2013; GOI, Ministry of Oil, "Domestic Consumption," www.oil.gov. iq, accessed 1/4/2013; GAO Report GAO-07- 677, "Rebuilding Iraq: Integrated Strategic Plan Needed to Help Restore Iraq's Oil and Electricity Sectors," 5/2007, p. 8.

230 SIGIR, *Hard Lessons: The Iraq Reconstruction Experience*, 2/2009, p. 28.

231 SIGIR, *Iraq Reconstruction: Lessons in Program and Project Management*, 3/2007, p. 29.

232 SIGIR, *Hard Lessons: The Iraq Reconstruction Experience*, 2/2009, p. 29.

233 SIGIR, *Hard Lessons: The Iraq Reconstruction Experience*, 2/2009, p. 95.

234 SIGIR PA-06-080, "Al Basrah Oil Terminal, Basrah, Iraq," 4/26/2007, p. 6, and *Hard Lessons: The Iraq Reconstruction Experience*, 2/2009, pp. 139–140.

235 GAO Report GAO-05-876, "Rebuilding Iraq: Status of Funding and Reconstruction Efforts," pp. 15–16. For sources of funding data, see endnote 2.

236 SIGIR PA-08-137, "Kirkuk to Baiji Pipeline Exclusion Zone–Phase 3, Kirkuk, Iraq," 7/24/2008, p. 3.

237 NEA-I, responses to SIGIR data calls, 6/4/2010, 7/6/2010, 1/11/2011, 4/5/2011, 7/7/2011, 10/17/2011, and 1/6/2012; GOI, Ministry of Oil, "Crude Oil Exports," www.oil.gov.iq, accessed 1/4/2013.

238 SIGIR PA-08-137, "Kirkuk to Baiji Pipeline Exclusion Zone–Phase 3, Kirkuk, Iraq," 7/24/2008, pp. 22–23.

239 For sources of funding data, see endnote 2.

240 GOI, Ministry of Oil, "Crude Oil Exports," www.oil.gov.iq, accessed 1/4/2013, and "Iraqi Oil Exports for September Elevate to 2.6 Million Barrels per Day," 10/13/2012, www. oil.gov.iq/moo/feeds.php?lang=en&page_ name=new&id=491, accessed 10/13/2012; NEA-I, responses to SIGIR data calls, 6/4/2010, 7/6/2010, 1/11/2011, 4/5/2011, 7/7/2011, 10/17/2011, and 1/6/2012.

241 U.S. Treasury, responses to SIGIR data calls, 4/10/2009, 2/25/2010, 4/12/2011, 1/10/2012, and 10/16/2012.

242 SIGIR, *Quarterly and Semiannual Reports to the United States Congress*, 10/30/2010, p. 90, 4/30/2012, p. 88, and 7/30/2012, p. 95.

243 SIGIR, *Quarterly and Semiannual Report to the United States Congress*, 1/30/2012, pp. 86–87; Ambassador James Jeffrey, information provided to SIGIR, 10/23/2012.

244 SIGIR, *Quarterly Report to the United States Congress*, 10/30/2012, pp. 60, 83.

245 UN/World Bank, "Joint Iraq Needs Assessment," 10/2003, p. 23; SIGIR, *Quarterly Report to the United States Congress*, 4/30/2006, p. 38, and PA-06-057, "Baghdad Railway Station Rehabilitation, Baghdad, Iraq," 7/25/2006, p. 4.

246 SIGIR, *Quarterly Report to the United States Congress*, 10/30/2009, p. 70; UN/World Bank, "Joint Iraq Needs Assessment," 10/2003, p. 24.

247 DoS, *Section 2207 Report*, 1/5/2004, p. 74.

248 UN/World Bank, "Joint Iraq Needs Assessment," 10/2003, p. 26; SIGIR, *Hard Lessons: The Iraq Reconstruction Experience*, 2/2009, p. 65.

249 SIGIR, *Quarterly Report to the United States Congress*, 4/30/2006, p. 38.

250 CPA, *Achieving the Vision: Taking Forward the CPA Strategic Plan for Iraq*, 7/18/2003, pp. 15–16, 18.

251 For funding sources, see endnote 2.

252 USACE, response to SIGIR data call, 10/1/2012; NEA-I, response to SIGIR data call, 9/20/2012; IRMS, *USF-I CERP Category Report*, 9/20/2010, and *Global Benchmark*, 9/3/2010; OSD, response to SIGIR data call, 4/10/2009.

253 USACE, information provided to SIGIR Audits, 11/20/2012; IRMS, *USF-I CERP Category Report*, 9/20/2010.

254 DoS, *Section 2207 Report*, 10/14/2003, p. 7; CPA, "An Historic Review of CPA Accomplishments 2003–2004," p. 37.

238   Special Inspector General for Iraq Reconstruction

[255] SIGIR, *Quarterly and Semiannual Reports to the United States Congress*, 10/30/2011, p. 84, and 1/30/2012, pp. 90–91.

[256] SIGIR, *Quarterly Report to the United States Congress*, 4/30/2012, p. 90.

[257] IRMS, *Global Benchmark*, 9/3/2010; NEA-I, response to SIGIR data call, 9/20/2012.

[258] DoS, "Civil Capacity Development in Iraq," 7/2011, p. 10.

[259] SIGIR, *Quarterly and Semiannual Report to the United States Congress*, 1/30/2012, p. 91; IRMS, *Global Benchmark*, 9/3/2012; DoS, "Civil Capacity Development in Iraq," 7/2011, p. 10.

[260] IRMS, *Global Benchmark*, 9/3/2010.

[261] USAID, "Bechtel, USAID, and the Iraq Infrastructure Reconstruction Program: Accomplishments and Challenges," p. 4; IRMS, *Global Benchmark*, 9/3/2010.

[262] IRMS, *USF-I CERP Category Report*, 9/20/2010; USACE, response to SIGIR data call, 10/1/2012; OSD, response to SIGIR data call, 4/10/2009; NEA-I, response to SIGIR data call, 9/20/2012.

[263] SIGIR, Audit 07-002, "Status of the Advanced First Responder Network," 4/25/2007, pp. 1, 2, 4.

[264] SIGIR, *Quarterly and Semiannual Report to the United States Congress*, 7/30/2007, pp. 108–109, and Audit 07-009, "Review of Bechtel's Spending Under Its Phase II Iraq Reconstruction Contract," 7/24/2007, p. 61.

[265] SIGIR, *Quarterly and Semiannual Reports to the United States Congress*, 4/30/2010, p. 75, and 7/30/2011, p. 101.

[266] USACE, information provided to SIGIR Audits, 11/20/2012.

[267] SIGIR, *Quarterly Report to the United States Congress*, 4/30/2005, p. 83.

[268] SIGIR, *Quarterly Report to the United States Congress*, 10/30/2010, p. 22.

[269] SIGIR, *Quarterly and Semiannual Report to the United States Congress*, 1/30/2012, p. 90.

[270] SIGIR, *Quarterly Report to the United States Congress*, 10/30/2012, p. 85.

[271] CPA, *Achieving the Vision to Restore Full Sovereignty to the Iraqi People*, working document as of 10/1/2003.

[272] SIGIR, *Hard Lessons: The Iraq Reconstruction Experience*, 2/2009, p. 104.

[273] SIGIR, *Hard Lessons: The Iraq Reconstruction Experience*, 2/2009, pp. 133–135. Many elements of the New Iraqi Army proved unwilling or unable to fight when Sunni insurgents and Shia militia separately attacked Coalition and Iraqi troops at cities across the country in April 2004. High rates of desertion, mutiny under fire, and collapsing units were exacerbated when "trained" ISF joined those attacking Coalition troops and their former security force colleagues.

[274] SIGIR, *Quarterly Report to the United States Congress*, 10/30/2012, pp. 60–61, 74.

[275] SIGIR, *Hard Lessons: The Iraq Reconstruction Experience*, 2/2009, pp. 4, 5, 13, 73–74, 131, 133, 189, 205–206, 254. The "Green Line" on the first map in the figure denotes the boundary beyond which Iraqi forces retreated during the Gulf War in 1991.

[276] SIGIR, *Quarterly and Semiannual Reports to the United States Congress*, 4/30/2008, p. 95, and 1/30/2011, p. 66.

[277] SIGIR, *Hard Lessons: The Iraq Reconstruction Experience*, 2/2009, p. 135.

[278] SIGIR, *Hard Lessons: The Iraq Reconstruction Experience*, 2/2009, p. 170.

[279] SIGIR, *Hard Lessons: The Iraq Reconstruction Experience*, 2/2009, p. 199.

[280] DoD, *Measuring Stability and Security in Iraq*, 2/2006–9/2009; DoL, responses to SIGIR data calls, 11/25/2009, 1/5/2010, 4/12/2010, 7/7/2010, and 1/14/2011; Brookings Institution, *Iraq Index*, 12/30/2010, pp. 12, 14; SIGIR, *Quarterly and Semiannual Reports to the United States Congress*, 4/30/2009, 10/30/2009, and 1/30/2010; GOI, response to SIGIR data call, 12/21/2009; USF-I, response to SIGIR data call, 1/4/2011.

[281] SIGIR Audit 11-010, "Sons of Iraq Program: Results Are Uncertain and Financial Controls Were Weak," 1/28/2011.

[282] SIGIR, *Quarterly Report to the United States Congress*, 4/30/2008, p. 95.

[283] SIGIR, *Quarterly Report to the United States Congress*, 4/30/2008, p. 95.

[284] The Mahdi Army, a militia created by Shiite cleric Muqtada al-Sadr, had filled the security vacuum left by the disbanded Iraqi Army and police. Between 2004 and 2007, the Mahdi Army repeatedly attacked Coalition and ISF as well as rival Shia militia. A ceasefire declared by al-Sadr from August 2007 is credited with reducing violence against the ISF. In March 2008 the IA launched successful operations against Mahdi Army forces in Sadr City and in Basrah.

[285] National Security Council, "National Strategy for Victory in Iraq," 11/2005, p. 2.

[286] SIGIR, *Quarterly Report to the United States Congress*, 4/30/2008, p. 7.

[287] SIGIR Special Report No. 2, "The Human Toll of Reconstruction or Stabilization Operations during Operation Iraqi Freedom," 7/2012, p. 6.

[288] SIGIR, *Quarterly Report to the United States Congress*, 10/30/2012, pp. 60–61, 74.

289 DoS, response to SIGIR data call, 4/5/2007; INL, response to SIGIR data call, 10/16/2012; IRMS, *USF-I CERP Category Report*, 9/20/2010; NEA-I, responses to SIGIR data call, 9/20/2012 and 9/25/2012; OSD, response to SIGIR data call, 10/2/2012; USACE, response to SIGIR data call, 10/1/2012.

290 For the sources of funding data, see endnote 2.

291 DoS, response to SIGIR data call, 4/5/2007; INL, response to SIGIR data call, 10/16/2012; IRMS, *USF-I CERP Category Report*, 9/20/2010; NEA-I, responses to SIGIR data call, 9/20/2012 and 9/25/2012; OSD, response to SIGIR data call, 10/2/2012; USACE, response to SIGIR data call, 10/1/2012.

292 NEA-I, response to SIGIR data call, 9/20/2012; OSD, response to SIGIR data call, 10/2/2012; INL, response to SIGIR data call, 10/16/2012; IRMS, *USF-I CERP Category Report*, 9/20/2010.

293 SIGIR, *Hard Lessons: The Iraq Reconstruction Experience*, 2/2009, pp. 79–81.

294 SIGIR, *Hard Lessons: The Iraq Reconstruction Experience*, 2/2009, p. 81

295 *Experience*, 2/2009, p. 197; NEA-I, response to SIGIR data call, 9/20/2012; OSD, response to SIGIR data call, 10/2/2012.

296 USIP, "Iraq's Interior Ministry: The Key to Police Reform," 9/2009.

297 SIGIR, *Hard Lessons: The Iraq Reconstruction Experience*, 2/2009, p. 201.

298 SIGIR, *Hard Lessons: The Iraq Reconstruction Experience*, 2/2009, p. 201.

299 SIGIR, *Hard Lessons: The Iraq Reconstruction Experience*, 2/2009, pp. 198, 200–201. In response to a SIGIR audit, MNSTC-I implemented a tracking system for equipment provided to the ISF, but was apparently unable to consistently collect physical records on equipment that was issued.

300 GOI, Prime Minister, meeting with SIGIR, 9/16/2012; OSC-I Chief, meeting with SIGIR, 9/21/2012.

301 DoS, *Section 2207 Report*, 1/2007, "Selected Metrics," p. 10.

302 DoS, *Section 2207 Report*, 7/2006, p. I-3.

303 DoS, *Section 2207 Report*, 1/2007, p. I-2.

304 DoD, *Measuring Stability and Security in Iraq*, 3/2009, p. 34.

305 SIGIR, *Quarterly Report to the United States Congress*, 1/30/2009, pp. 43–47.

306 SIGIR, *Hard Lessons: The Iraq Reconstruction Experience*, 2/2009, p. 130; SIGIR, *Quarterly Report to the United States Congress*, 4/30/2006, p. 21.

307 SIGIR, *Quarterly Report to the United States Congress*, 10/30/2010 p. 74.

308 DSCA, response to SIGIR data call, 10/3/2012.

309 NEA-I, response to SIGIR data call, 9/20/2012; OSD, response to SIGIR data call, 10/2/2012.

310 DoS, *Section 2207 Report*, 10/2005, p. I-13.

311 DSCA, response to SIGIR data call, 10/3/2012.

312 DSCA, response to SIGIR data call, 10/3/2012.

313 DSCA, response to SIGIR data call, 10/3/2012.

314 OSC-I, response to SIGIR data call, 10/3/2012.

315 P.L. 110-252; NEA-I, response to SIGIR data call, 9/20/2012; OSD, response to SIGIR data call, 10/2/2012.

316 SIGIR, *Quarterly Report to the United States Congress*, 4/30/2008, p. 97.

317 SIGIR, *Quarterly Report to the United States Congress*, 4/30/2008, p. 99.

318 SIGIR, *Quarterly Report to the United States Congress*, 4/30/2008, p. 99.

319 SIGIR, *Quarterly Report to the United States Congress*, 1/30/2009, p. 49.

320 DoD, *Measuring Stability and Security in Iraq*, 9/2008, p. 51.

321 DSCA, response to SIGIR data call, 10/3/2012.

322 DSCA, response to SIGIR data call, 10/3/2012.

323 DoS, Remarks of James F. Jeffrey, U.S. Ambassador to Iraq before the Senate Foreign Relations Committee, "Iraq: The Challenging Transition to a Civilian Mission," 2/1/2011.

324 OSD, response to SIGIR data call, 10/2/2012; NEA-I, response to SIGIR data call, 9/20/2012; INL, response to SIGIR data call, 10/16/2012.

325 SIGIR Audit 06-029, "Review of DynCorp International, LLC, Contract Number S LMAQM-04-C-0030, Task Order 0338, for the Iraqi Police Training Program Support," 1/30/2007, and *Quarterly Report to the United States Congress*, 10/30/2011, pp. 2–3.

326 For the sources of funding data, see endnote 2.

327 NEA-I, response to SIGIR data call, 9/20/2012; OSD, response to SIGIR data call, 10/2/2012.

328 INL, response to SIGIR data call, 10/16/2012; NEA-I, response to SIGIR data call, 9/20/2012; OSD, response to SIGIR data call, 10/2/2012.

329 SIGIR, *Hard Lessons: The Iraq Reconstruction Experience*, 2/2009, pp. 126–127.

330 SIGIR, *Hard Lessons: The Iraq Reconstruction Experience*, 2/2009, p. 127.

240 Special Inspector General for Iraq Reconstruction

[331] SIGIR Audit 11-008, "Interim Report: Action Needed To Address Missing Iraq Transaction Data," 1/28/2011, p. 2. From 2005 to 2007, SIGIR found inadequate INL staffing and contract oversight of the DynCorp contract, prompting INL to completely reconcile invoicing and reconceived its invoicing process. In 2010, SIGIR found that the $2.5 billion obligated under the DynCorp contract was vulnerable to waste and fraud. Further, SIGIR concluded that State's in-country contracting officers had failed to perform adequate invoice reviews, and they did not ensure costs were allowable and supported, that property was controlled, that leases protected U.S. interests, and that the government received services in accord with the contract.

[332] Defense also provided U.S. military personnel, life support, and security that benefit the program at costs that are significant but that are not readily available. See SIGIR, Audit 11-003, "Iraqi Security Forces: Police Training Program Developed Sizeable Force, but Capabilities Are Unknown," 10/25/2010.

[333] SIGIR, *Quarterly Report to the United States Congress*, 4/30/2008, p. 100.

[334] SIGIR, *Quarterly Report to the United States Congress*, 4/30/2008, p. 100.

[335] SIGIR, *Quarterly Report to the United States Congress*, 4/30/2008 p. 100. However, SIGIR Project Assessments found serious weaknesses in contractor oversight of construction. For more details, see SIGIR PA-08-154 to 156, "Report on Plumbing Repairs at the Baghdad Police College, Baghdad, Iraq," 1/22/2009, and PA-06-78.2 & 79.2, "Baghdad Police College," 1/29/2007.

[336] SIGIR, *Quarterly Reports to the United States Congress*, 4/30/2007, p. 60, and 4/30/2008, p. 97.

[337] SIGIR, *Hard Lessons: The Iraq Reconstruction Experience*, 2/2009, p. 201.

[338] SIGIR, *Quarterly Reports to the United States Congress*, 1/30/2007, p. 86, and 4/30/2008, pp. 98–99, and Audit 08-15, "Interim Analysis of Iraqi Security Force Information Provided by the Department of Defense Report, *Measuring Stability and Security in Iraq*," 5/25/2008.

[339] SIGIR, *Hard Lessons: The Iraq Reconstructio Experience*, 2/2009, p. 201.

[340] SIGIR, *Hard Lessons: The Iraq Reconstruction Experience*, 2/2009, p. 202.

[341] SIGIR, *Quarterly and Semiannual Reports to the United States Congress*, 1/30/2007, pp. 86–87, 4/30/2008, p. 100, and 7/30/2008, p. 86.

[342] SIGIR Audit 12-020, "Iraq Police Development Program: Lack of Iraqi Support and Security Problems Raise Questions about the Continued Viability of the Program," 7/30/2012.

[343] SIGIR, *Quarterly and Semiannual Reports to the United States Congress*, 7/30/2012, p. 36, and 10/30/2012, pp. 32–33.

[344] SIGIR, *Quarterly Report to the United States Congress*, 10/30/2010, p. 77.

[345] IRMS, *Global Benchmark*, 9/3/2012; USACE, response to SIGIR data call, 10/1/2012.

[346] SIGIR Audit 11-010, "Sons of Iraq Program: Results Are Uncertain and Financial Controls Were Weak," 1/28/2011.

[347] SIGIR PA-08-137, "Kirkuk to Baiji Pipeline Exclusion Zone–Phase 3, Kirkuk, Iraq," 7/24/2008. Through this program, U.S. personnel developed the concept of a Pipeline Exclusion Zone to secure pipeline corridors against attacks, which were slowing the flow of oil through Iraq's pipeline to Ceyhan, Turkey. The idea worked. In the first 11 months after the start of the Kirkuk-to-Baiji PEZ in July 2007, northern crude oil exports increased by 91.3 million barrels, or $8.13 billion. ISP personnel credited the PEZ as the single-largest contributing factor to the dramatic rise in these exports. It was almost three years before the first attacks on the PEZ-protected pipelines were reported.

[348] For sources of funding data, see endnote 2.

[349] SIGIR, *Hard Lessons: The Iraq Reconstruction Experience*, 2/2009, pp. 6–7.

[350] SIGIR, *Hard Lessons: The Iraq Reconstruction Experience*, 2/2009, p. 96.

[351] SIGIR, *Hard Lessons: The Iraq Reconstruction Experience*, 2/2009, p. 159.

[352] SIGIR, *Hard Lessons: The Iraq Reconstruction Experience*, 2/2009, p. 206.

[353] SIGIR, *Quarterly Report to the United States Congress*, 7/30/2012, p. 87.

[354] SIGIR, *Quarterly Report to the United States Congress*, 10/30/2012, p. 77.

[355] SIGIR, Audit 13-001, "Sustaining the Progress Achieved by U.S. Rule of Law Programs in Iraq Remains Questionable," 10/25/2012.

[356] DoS, response to SIGIR data call, 4/5/2007; INL, response to SIGIR data call, 10/16/2012; IRMS, *USF-I CERP Category Report*, 9/20/2010; NEA-I, responses to SIGIR data call, 9/20/2012 and 9/25/2012.

[357] SIGIR, Audit 08-019 "Outcome, Cost, and Oversight of the Security and Justice Contract with Parsons Delaware, Inc.," 7/28/2008, p. iv, and PA-08-152, "Anbar Rule of Law/Judicial Complex, Ramadi, Iraq," pp. i–iii, 4.

[358] DoS, *Section 2207 Report*, 4/2005, pp. I-27–I-29, 7/2005, Appendix I, pp. 16–20, 25–27, 7/2006, pp. I-19–I-20, I-30–I-31, and 4/2007, pp. I-17–I-19.

[359] SIGIR Audit 13-001, "Sustaining the Progress Achieved by U.S. Rule of Law Programs in Iraq Remains Questionable," 10/25/2012.

[360] SIGIR Audit 08-019, "Outcome, Cost, and Oversight of the Security and Justice Contract with Parsons Delaware, Inc.," 7/28/2008; USACE, information provided to SIGIR Audits, 11/20/2012.

[361] SIGIR Audit 08-019, "Outcome, Cost, and Oversight of the Security and Justice Contract with Parsons Delaware, Inc.," 7/28/2008, and *Quarterly Report to the United States Congress*, 4/30/2009, p. 61; USACE, information provided to SIGIR Audits, 11/20/2012.

[362] SIGIR Audit 13-001, "Sustaining the Progress Achieved by U.S. Rule of Law Programs in Iraq Remains Questionable," 10/25/2012, p. 21.

[363] SIGIR, *Quarterly Report to the United States Congress*, 10/30/2010, pp. 16–17.

[364] IGIR Audit 13-001, "Sustaining the Progress Achieved by U.S. Rule of Law Programs in Iraq Remains Questionable," 10/25/2012.

[365] SIGIR, *Hard Lessons: The Iraq Reconstruction Experience*, 2/2009, pp. 210–211.

[366] SIGIR, *Hard Lessons: The Iraq Reconstruction Experience*, 2/2009, p. 213, and *Quarterly and Semiannual Report to the United States Congress*, 1/30/2012, p. 97.

[367] SIGIR, *Quarterly Report to the United States Congress*, 10/30/2012, p. 3.

[368] SIGIR Audit, 06-021, "Joint Survey of the U.S. Embassy-Iraq's Anticorruption Program, 7/28/2006, p. i, and *Hard Lessons: The Iraq Reconstruction Experience*, 2/2009, p. 207.

[369] SIGIR, *Hard Lessons: The Iraq Reconstruction Experience*, 2/2009, pp. 211–212.

[370] SIGIR, *Hard Lessons: The Iraq Reconstruction Experience*, 2/2009, p. 212.

[371] SIGIR, *Hard Lessons: The Iraq Reconstruction Experience*, 2/2009, pp. 212–214.

[372] SIGIR, *Hard Lessons: The Iraq Reconstruction Experience*, 2/2009, p. 214.

[373] SIGIR, *Hard Lessons: The Iraq Reconstruction Experience*, 2/2009, p. 215.

[374] SIGIR, *Hard Lessons: The Iraq Reconstruction Experience*, 2/2009, p. 214; GOI, MIM IG, interview with SIGIR, 6/3/2012.

[375] SIGIR, *Hard Lessons: The Iraq Reconstruction Experience*, 2/2009, pp. 211, 215.

[376] INL, response to SIGIR data call, 10/16/2012; NEA-I, response to SIGIR data call, 9/20/2012.

[377] SIGIR, *Hard Lessons: The Iraq Reconstruction Experience*, 2/2009, p. 115.

[378] USAID, "Evaluation of USAID/Iraq's Assistance to the Independent High Electoral Commission," 7/5/2010, p. 5.

[379] SIGIR, *Hard Lessons: The Iraq Reconstruction Experience*, 2/2009, pp. 60, 115.

[380] CPA, "Achieving the Vision," 7/23/2003, pp. 4–5.

[381] SIGIR, *Hard Lessons: The Iraq Reconstruction Experience*, 2/2009, p. 159.

[382] For funding sources, see endnote 2.

[383] USAID, Bureau for the Middle East, Office of Iraq and Arabian Peninsula Affairs, information provided to SIGIR Audits, 9/30/2012. For sources of funding data, see endnote 2.

[384] For funding sources, see endnote 2.

[385] NEA-I, responses to SIGIR data call, 9/20/2012, 9/25/2012, and 10/2/2012.

[386] SIGIR Audit 09-001, "Opportunities to Enhance U.S. Democracy-Building Strategy for Iraq," 10/22/2008, p. 1.

[387] SIGIR, *Hard Lessons: The Iraq Reconstruction Experience*, 2/2009, p. 121.

[388] SIGIR, *Hard Lessons: The Iraq Reconstruction Experience*, 2/2009, pp. 121, 154.

[389] SIGIR, *Hard Lessons: The Iraq Reconstruction Experience*, 2/2009, p. 206; USAID, "Monitoring and Evaluation Performance Program, Phase II, Final Report for Political Process Assistance Review," 12/13/2005, p. 2.

[390] SIGIR Audit 10-012, "Department of State Grant Management: Limited Oversight of Costs and Impact of International Republican Institute and National Democratic Institute Democracy Grants," 1/26/2010, pp. 1–2, 24.

[391] UNAMI, "UNAMI Focus, Voice of the Mission, Mid-year Issue," 7/2006, p. 2, United States Institute of Peace, Special Report 155, "Iraq's Constitutional Process II, An Opportunity Lost," 11/2005, pp. 2, 6, 8; DoS OIG ISP-IQO-06-01, "Inspection of Rule of Law Programs, Embassy Baghdad," 10/2005, p. 10; International Business & Technical Consultants, Inc., "Monitoring and Evaluation Performance Program, Phase II (MEPP II): Final Report for Political Process Assistance Review," 12/13/2005.

[392] SIGIR, *Quarterly Reports to the United States Congress*, 4/30/2010, p. 4, and 10/30/2011, pp. 89, 92, and *Hard Lessons: The Iraq Reconstruction Experience*, 2/2009, p. 119; USIP, "Iraq's Constitutional Process II, An Opportunity Lost," Special Report 155, 11/2005, p. 8.

393 SIGIR, *Quarterly Reports to the United States Congress*, 4/30/2010, p. 4, and 10/30/2011, p. 89, and *Hard Lessons: The Iraq Reconstruction Experience*, 2/2009, p. 119; USIP, "Iraq's Constitutional Process II, An Opportunity Lost," Special Report 155, 11/2005, p. 8.

394 SIGIR, *Quarterly and Semiannual Report to the United States Congress*, 1/30/2008, p. 5.

395 SIGIR, *Quarterly and Semiannual Report to the United States Congress*, 1/30/2008, p. 5.

396 SIGIR, *Quarterly Report to the United States Congress*, 4/30/2012, p. 47; USAID OIG Audit E-267-12-003-P, "Audit of USAID/Iraq's Electoral Technical Assistance Program," 3/22/2012, p. 27.

397 USAID OIG Audit E-267-12-003-P, "Audit of USAID/Iraq's Electoral Technical Assistance Program," 3/22/2012, p. 1.

398 USAID, "Evaluation of USAID/Iraq's Assistance to the Independent High Electoral Commission, IFES Electoral Support and Out of Country Voting Programs," 7/5/2010, pp. 14, 16, 21.

399 SIGIR, *Quarterly Report to the United States Congress*, 10/30/2009, p. 77.

400 USAID OIG Audit E-267-12-003, "Audit of USAID/Iraq's Electoral Technical Assistance Program," 3/22/2012, p. 1.

401 SIGIR, *Quarterly Report to the United States Congress*, 4/30/2012, p. 47; USAID OIG Audit E-267-12-003, "Audit of USAID/Iraq's Electoral Technical Assistance Program," 3/22/2012, p. 1.

402 SIGIR Audit 10-012, "Department of State Grant Management: Limited Oversight of Costs and Impact of International Republican Institute and National Democratic Institute Democracy Grants," 1/26/2010, p. 5.

403 CPA, *Achieving the Vision*, 7/23/2003, pp. 4–5; USAID, Bureau for the Middle East, Office of Iraq and Arabian Peninsula Affairs, information provided to SIGIR Audits, 9/30/2012.

404 SIGIR, *Quarterly and Semiannual Report to the United States Congress*, 1/30/2012, p. 57.

405 SIGIR, *Quarterly Report to the United States Congress*, 10/30/2012, p. 43.

406 SIGIR, *Hard Lessons: The Iraq Reconstruction Experience*, 2/2009, p. 238, and *Quarterly Report to the United States Congress*, 4/30/2010, p. 82.

407 SIGIR, *Quarterly Report to the United States Congress*, 4/30/2010, p. 81. For funding sources, see endnote 2.

408 SIGIR, *Quarterly and Semiannual Report to the United States Congress*, 7/30/2007, pp. 35–36. For funding sources, see endnote 2.

409 SIGIR, *Hard Lessons: The Iraq Reconstruction Experience*, 2/2009, p. 295.

410 USAID, Bureau for the Middle East, Office of Iraq and Arabian Peninsula Affairs, information provided to SIGIR Audits, 9/30/2012; NEA-I, response to SIGIR data call, 9/28/2011; U.S. Embassy-Baghdad, responses to SIGIR data calls, 10/5/2011, 1/4/2012, 7/3/2012, and 10/1/2012; SIGIR, *Quarterly and Semiannual Report to the United States Congress*, 1/30/2011, p. 81.

411 SIGIR, *Quarterly Report to the United States Congress*, 4/30/2010, pp. 81–82.

412 SIGIR, *Quarterly and Semiannual Report to the United States Congress*, 7/30/2012, p. 67.

413 SIGIR, *Quarterly and Semiannual Report to the United States Congress*, 7/30/2011, pp. 63–64.

414 SIGIR, *Quarterly Reports to the United States Congress*, 10/30/2011, p. 45, and 4/30/2012, p. 46.

415 USAID, Bureau for the Middle East, Office of Iraq and Arabian Peninsula Affairs, information provided to SIGIR Audits, 9/30/2012; SIGIR Audit 09-003, "Cost, Outcome, and Oversight of Local Governance Program Contracts with Research Triangle Institute," 10/21/2008, p. 1.

416 SIGIR, *Quarterly Report to the United States Congress*, 4/30/2005, p. 84.

417 SIGIR, *Quarterly Reports to the United States Congress*, 10/30/2011, pp. 45–46, and 10/30/2012, p. 45.

418 SIGIR, *Hard Lessons: The Iraq Reconstruction Experience*, 2/2009, pp. 240–241, 271, and *Quarterly and Semiannual Reports to the United States Congress*, 7/30/2006, p. 50, and 1/30/2008, p. 49.

419 USACE, response to SIGIR data call, 10/1/2012.

420 SIGIR, *Quarterly and Semiannual Reports to the United States Congress*, 4/30/2011, p. 75, and 7/30/2012, pp. 33–34; IRMS, *Global Benchmark*, 9/3/2010; USACE, information provided to SIGIR audits, 11/20/2012.

421 SIGIR PA-08-165 & 167, "Missan Surgical Hospital, Al Amarah, Iraq," 7/16/2009, pp. 7–8, and *Quarterly Report to the United States Congress*, 10/30/2012, p. 56.

422 SIGIR, *Quarterly and Semiannual Report to the United States Congress*, 7/30/2010, p. 30.

423 SIGIR Audit 09-011, "Opportunities to Improve Management of the Quick Response Fund," 1/29/2009, pp. i, 1.

424 SIGIR Audit 12-016, "Interim Review of State Department's Progress in Implementing SIGIR Recommendations Addressing Quick Response Fund Management Controls," 4/30/2012, pp. 1–2, and 11-011, "Quick Response Fund: Management Controls Have Improved But Earlier Projects Need Attention," p. 6.

425 NEA-I, response to SIGIR data call, 10/2/2012.

426 USAID OIG Audit E-267-06-003-P, "Audit of USAID/Iraq's Local Governance Activities," 7/10/2006, p. 2.

[427] UN/World Bank, "Joint Iraq Needs Assessment," 10/2003, pp. viii, 21–22, 62–63; USAID OIG Audit E-266-04-001-P, "Audit of USAID's Results Data for Its Education Activities in Iraq," 3/19/2004, pp. 6, 20; SIGIR PA 08-144-148, "Falluja Waste Water Treatment System, Falluja, Iraq," 10/27/2008, p. 2.

[428] IRMS, *USF-I CERP Category Report*, 9/20/2010; NEA-I, responses to SIGIR data calls, 9/20/2012 and 10/2/2012; USACE, response to SIGIR data call, 10/1/2012. For funding sources, see endnote 2.

[429] UN/World Bank, "Joint Iraq Needs Assessment," 10/2003, p. 16; SIGIR PA 08-160, "Basrah Children's Hospital, Basrah, Iraq," 7/28/2009, p.1.

[430] USAID, *Vision for Post-Conflict Iraq*, 2/19/2003, p. 4.

[431] USAID, *Vision for Post-Conflict Iraq*, 2/19/2003, p. 4.

[432] CPA, *Achieving the Vision*, 7/23/2003, p. 17.

[433] IRMS, *USF-I CERP Category Report*, 9/20/2010; USACE, response to SIGIR data call, 10/1/2012; NEA-I, responses to SIGIR data call, 9/20/2012 and 10/2/2012.

[434] SIGIR Audit 09-015, "Construction of Primary Healthcare Centers Reported Essentially Complete, but Operational Issues Remain," 4/29/2009, p. i.

[435] SIGIR Audit 09-015, "Construction of Primary Healthcare Centers Reported Essentially Complete, but Operational Issues Remain," 4/29/2009, p. i, *Quarterly Report to the United States Congress*, 10/30/2009, p. 78, and PA-08-133, "Heet Primary Healthcare Center, Heet, Iraq," 1/23/2009, pp. ii–iii; IRMS, *Global Benchmark*, 9/3/2010.

[436] SIGIR, *Quarterly Report to the United States Congress*, 4/30/2010, p. 89.

[437] SIGIR, *Quarterly Report to the United States Congress*, 10/30/2012, p. 45; USAID, Bureau for Middle East, Office of Iraq and Arabian Peninsula Affairs, information provided to SIGIR audits, 9/30/2012.

[438] DoS/USAID, "Civil Capacity Development in Iraq," 7/14/2011, p. 7.

[439] SIGIR, *Hard Lessons: The Iraq Reconstruction Experience*, 2/2009, p. 237; IRMS, *USF-I CERP Category Report*, 9/20/2010.

[440] SIGIR, *Hard Lessons: The Iraq Reconstruction Experience*, 2/2009, p. 281–282, 295.

[441] SIGIR, *Quarterly and Semiannual Report to the United States Congress*, 7/30/2011, p. 23.

[442] SIGIR, *Hard Lessons: The Iraq Reconstruction Experience*, 2/2009, p. 281, and *Quarterly and Semiannual Report to the United States Congress*, 7/30/2011, p. 23; USAID, Bureau for Middle East, Office of Iraq and Arabian Peninsula Affairs, information provided to SIGIR audits, 9/30/2012.

[443] USAID Iraq, Fact Sheet, "Accomplishments in Iraq," 10/14/2009.

[444] SIGIR, *Quarterly and Semiannual Report to the United States Congress*, 7/30/2011, pp. 26–27.

[445] UN/World Bank, "Joint Iraq Needs Assessment," 10/2003, pp. 14–16; USAID, *Vision for Post-Conflict Iraq*, 2/19/2003, p. 11; USAID OIG, Audit Report E-267-06-001-P, "Audit of USAID/Iraq's Basic Education Activities," 12/20/2005, p. 2.

[446] CPA, *Achieving the Vision*, 7/13/2003, p. 18; USAID, *Vision for Post-Conflict Iraq*, 2/19/2003, p. 11.

[447] IRMS, *Global Benchmark*, 9/3/2010.

[448] USAID OIG Audit E-267-06-001-P, "Audit of USAID/Iraq's Basic Education Activities," 12/20/2005, p. 8.

[449] SIGIR, *Quarterly Report to the United States Congress*, 4/30/2006, p. 54.

[450] SIGIR Audit 11-012, "Commander's Emergency Response Program Obligations are Uncertain," 1/31/2011, p. 6.

[451] SIGIR *Quarterly Report to the United States Congress*, 4/30/2006, p. 54, and PA-08-141, "Al Iqitadar School, Anbar Province, Iraq," 1/26/2009, pp. 1, 3; IRMS, *Global Benchmark*, 9/3/2010.

[452] SIGIR, *Quarterly Report to the United States Congress*, 10/30/2010, p. 111.

[453] IRMS, *Global Benchmark*, 9/3/2010; USACE, Gulf Region Division, Central District, Iraq, "News," 12/2006, pp. 4–5.

[454] SIGIR, *Quarterly and Semiannual Report to the United States Congress*, 1/30/2010, p. 74.

[455] SIGIR, *Quarterly and Semiannual Reports to the United States Congress*, 1/30/2010, p. 74, and 10/30/2010, p. 111.

[456] DoS, "Civil Capacity Development in Iraq," p. 4.

[457] IRMS, *USF-I CERP Category Report*, 9/20/2010; NEA-I, response to SIGIR data call 10/2/2012.

[458] SIGIR, *Quarterly Report to the United States Congress*, 7/30/2011, p. 102

[459] SIGIR, *Quarterly Report to the United States Congress*, 10/30/2012, p. 43.

[460] SIGIR, *Hard Lessons: The Iraq Reconstruction Experience*, 2/2009, pp. 10, 11, 18–20, 325, 341.

[461] SIGIR, *Hard Lessons: The Iraq Reconstruction Experience*, 2/2009, p. 55, and *Quarterly Report to the United States Congress*, 10/30/2012, p. 65.

[462] USAID OIG Audit E-267-08-002-P, "Audit of USAID/Iraq's Management of the Marla Ruzicka Iraqi War Victims Fund," 4/3/2008, pp. 3, 12; NEA-I, response to SIGIR data call, 9/20/2012.

Special Inspector General for Iraq Reconstruction

463 USAID OIG Audit E-267-08-002-P, "Audit of USAID/Iraq's Management of the Marla Ruzicka Iraqi War Victims Fund," 4/3/2008, pp. 1, 3; "USAID/Iraq Community Action Program III, End of Project Performance Evaluation," 8/2012, p. xi; NEA-I, response to SIGIR data call, 9/20/2012.

464 IRMS, *USF-I CERP Category Report*, 9/20/2010, NEA-I, responses to SIGIR data call, 9/20/2012 and 10/1/2012, DoS, response to SIGIR data call, 4/5/2007, and USAID, response to SIGIR data call, 7/8/2010.

465 SIGIR, *Quarterly Report to the United States Congress*, 10/30/2012, pp. 22–23.

466 DoS, *Section 2207 Report*, 1/2004, p. 93; SIGIR, *Quarterly Report to the United States Congress*, 10/30/2012, p. 36.

467 SIGIR, *Quarterly Report to the United States Congress*, 10/30/2012, p. 36; USAID, "Iraq – Complex Emergency, Fact Sheet #1, Fiscal Year (FY) 2012," 10/21/2011, p. 1.

468 SIGIR, *Quarterly Reports to the United States Congress*, 10/30/2011, p. 49, and 10/30/2012, p. 48.

469 SIGIR, *Quarterly Report to the United States Congress*, 10/30/2012, pp. 22–23; USDA, "Food Aid Programs," www.fas.usda.gov/excredits/ foodaid/title%201/pl480ofst.html, accessed 1/2/2013.

470 SIGIR, *Hard Lessons: The Iraq Reconstruction Experience*, 2/2009, pp. 5–6, 30–31, 92, 136; SIGIR analysis of open-source documents.

471 SIGIR, *Hard Lessons: The Iraq Reconstruction Experience*, 2/2009, pp. 86, 90.

472 CPA, *Achieving the Vision: Taking Forward the CPA Strategic Plan for Iraq*, Working Draft, 7/23/2003, p. 2.

473 CPA, *A Vision for Iraq*, 7/11/2003, p. 3.

474 CPA, *Achieving the Vision: Taking Forward the CPA Strategic Plan for Iraq*, Working Draft, 7/23/2003, pp. 4, 28–30.

475 CPA, *Achieving the Vision: Taking Forward the CPA Strategic Plan for Iraq*, Working Draft, 7/23/2003, pp. 29–30.

476 UN/World Bank, "Joint Iraq Needs Assessment," 10/2003, p. 72.

477 UN/World Bank, "Joint Iraq Needs Assessment, 10/2003, pp. 36, 71.

478 For sources of funding data, see endnote 2.

479 SIGIR, *Hard Lessons: The Iraq Reconstruction Experience*, 2/2009, p. 92; GOI, CBI, "About the CBI," www.cbi.iq/index.php?pid=The CBI, accessed 1/29/2013.

480 SIGIR, *Hard Lessons: The Iraq Reconstruction Experience*, 2/2009, p. 92.

481 Trade Bank of Iraq, "2011 Financial Highlights," www.tbiraq.com/en/about/key-financials/2011_financial_highlights/, accessed 12/7/2012, and "Achievements," www.tbiraq.com/en/newsand-achievements/achievements/, accessed 12/7/2012.

482 SIGIR, *Quarterly and Semiannual Report to the United States Congress*, 7/30/2011, p. 92.

483 SIGIR, *Quarterly and Semiannual Reports to the United States Congress*, 7/30/2011, p. 92, and 4/30/2012, p. 48; USAID, "Economic Growth and Trade," 10/23/2012, www.usaid.gov/where-we-work/middle-east/iraq/economic-growth-and-trade, accessed 12/9/2012, and responses to SIGIR data call, 12/26/2011 and 12/27/2011.

484 SIGIR, *Quarterly Reports to the United States Congress*, 10/30/2011, p. 72, and 10/30/2012, p. 79; UN, "8th UNCTAD Debt Management Conference 14–16 November 2011, List of Contributors," p. 2, r0.unctad.org/dmfas/docs/ DMconf2011/Contributorsjist.pdf, accessed 2/1/2013.

485 SIGIR, *Quarterly Report to the United States Congress*, 10/30/2012, p. 3.

486 SIGIR, *Quarterly Report to the United States Congress*, 10/30/2012, p. 3.

487 SIGIR, *Quarterly and Semiannual Reports to the United States Congress*, 7/30/2011, pp. 91–92, and 7/30/2012, pp. 92–93, 100.

488 SIGIR, *Quarterly and Semiannual Reports to the United States Congress*, 7/30/2011, pp. 91–92, and 7/30/2012, p. 100; International Bank, Iraq country representative, information provided to SIGIR, 11/1/2012.

489 SIGIR, *Hard Lessons: The Iraq Reconstruction Experience*, 2/2009, pp. 5, 90.

490 SIGIR, *Quarterly Report to the United States Congress*, 10/30/2010, p. 98; TFBSO, response to SIGIR data call, 1/4/2011.

491 SIGIR, *Quarterly Report to the United States Congress*, 4/30/2012, p. 91.

492 World Bank, Iraq privatization specialist, meeting with SIGIR, 10/10/2012, and information provided to SIGIR, 1/4/2013; SIGIR, *Quarterly Report to the United States Congress*, 4/30/2012, p. 109.

493 USAID, "Fact Sheet: Accomplishments in Iraq," 10/14/2009, pdf.usaid.gov/pdf_docs/ PDACN488.pdf, accessed 1/18/2009, "Capacity Building Programs, Administrative Reform Project," 4/15/2012, iraq.usaid.gov/node/36, accessed 12/11/2012, and "Izdihar: Progress Highlights, Key Accomplishments as of 14 March 2008," 3/14/2008, izdihar-iraq.com/ progress.html, accessed 12/11/2012; SIGIR, *Quarterly and Semiannual Report to the United States Congress*, 7/30/2011, p. 92.

[494] USAID, "Izdihar: Progress Highlights, Key Accomplishments as of 14 March 2008," 3/14/2008, izdihar-iraq.com/progress.html, accessed 12/11/2012, and Bureau for the Middle East, Office of Iraq and Arabian Peninsula Affairs, information provided to SIGIR Audits, 10/23/2012.

[495] USAID, "Fact Sheet: Provincial Economic Growth Program," 11/2011, www.krgmopdcc.com/dcc/resources/PDF/1.%20Tijara%20 Provincial%20Economic%20Growth%20 Fact%20Sheet%20Nov%202011.pdf, accessed 1/18/2013.

[496] USAID, "Izdihar: Progress Highlights, Key Accomplishments as of 14 March 2008," 3/14/2008, izdihar-iraq.com/progress.html, accessed 1/18/2013; SIGIR, *Quarterly Report to the United States Congress*, 4/30/2012, p. 49; CIA, *The World Factbook*, www.cia.gov/library/ publications/the-world-factbook/geos/iz.html, accessed 12/11/2012.

[497] USAID, "Tijara Provincial Economic Growth Program Midterm Evaluation, Final Report," 7/2011, pp. 29–31.

[498] World Bank, IFC, "Doing Business: Economy Rankings," 2012, www.doingbusiness.org/ ranking, accessed 12/11/2012, and *Doing Business in the Arab World 2012*, p. 64.

[499] DAI, "Agricultural Reconstruction and Development Program for IRAQ (ARDI)," dai.com/our-work/projects/iraq%E2%80%94agriculture-reconstructionand-development-program-iraq-ardi, accessed 1/13/2013; USAID, Bureau for the Middle East, Office of Iraq and Arabian Peninsula Affairs, information provided to SIGIR Audits, 9/30/2012.

[500] USAID, "USAID-Inma Agribusiness Program," iraq.usaid.gov/node/166, accessed 1/18/2013, and Bureau for the Middle East, Office of Iraq and Arabian Peninsula Affairs, information provided to SIGIR Audits, 10/23/2012; SIGIR Audit 08-006, "Commander's Emergency Response Program in Iraq Funds Many Large-Scale Projects," 1/25/2008, pp. 2, 7.

[501] U.S. Embassy-Baghdad, USDA team meetings with SIGIR, 2/4/2012 and 5/31/2012.

[502] USAID, "USAID-Inma Agribusiness Program," iraq.usaid.gov/node/96, accessed 1/30/2013; SIGIR, *Quarterly Report to the United States Congress*, 10/30/2012, p. 43.

[503] USAID, "Inma Agribusiness Program Evaluation, Final Draft," 5/6/2010, p. 25.

[504] USAID, Bureau for the Middle East, Office of Iraq and Arabian Peninsula Affairs, information provided to SIGIR Audits, 9/30/2012.

[505] USAID, "Fact Sheet, Accomplishments in Iraq," 10/14/2009, p. 4; USAID OIG Audit E-266-04- 004, "Audit of USAID/Iraq's Economic Reform Program," pp. 5–8.

[506] USAID OIG Audit E-267-09-004-P, "Audit of USAID/Iraq's Economic Governance II Program," 6/3/2009, p. 3; SIGIR, *Quarterly Report to the United States Congress*, 10/30/2011, p. 79.

[507] USAID OIG Audit E-267-09-004-P, "Audit of USAID/Iraq's Economic Governance II Program," 6/3/2009, pp. 1–8

[508] IRMS, *USF-I CERP Category Report*, 9/20/2010.

[509] IRMS, *USF-I CERP Category Report*, 9/20/2010; CENTCOM, press release, "Central Euphrates Farmers' Market Open for Business," 6/17/2009.

[510] IMF, *World Economic Outlook 2012*, p. 81, and *Iraq Program Note*, 10/5/2012; GOI, CBI, "Economic Data," www.cbi.iq/index. php?pid=Home, accessed 1/13/2013.

[511] IMF, Country Report No. 11/75, "Iraq: Second Review Under the Stand-By Arrangement, Request for Waiver of Applicability, Extension of the Arrangement and Rephrasing of Access," 3/2011, p. 22; SIGIR, *Quarterly and Semiannual Reports to the United States Congress*, 7/30/2012, p. 93, and 10/30/2012, p. 84.

[512] IMF, Country Report No. 11/75, "Iraq: Second Review Under the Stand-By Arrangement, Request for Waiver of Applicability, Extension of the Arrangement and Rephrasing of Access," 3/2011, p. 22.

[513] UN, UNCC, "Status of Processing and Payment Claims," 10/25/2012, www.uncc.ch/status.htm, accessed 2/18/2013.

[514] P.L. 110-417, Section 872.

[515] P.L. 109-364, Section 814. In P.L. 110-417, Section 867, this provision was linked to non-Defense award and incentive fees as well.

[516] P.L. 110-252, Section 1402(a).

[517] P.L. 111-32, Section 1106.

[518] P.L. 112-81, Sections 841 and 842.

[519] P.L. 112-239, Section 844.

[520] P.L. 112-239, Section 802.

[521] P.L. 110-417, Section 866.

[522] P.L. 112-239, Section 846.

[523] P.L. 112-239, Section 848.

524 P.L. 112-239, Section 861; House Report 112-705, p. 811.

525 P.L. 112-239, Section 1273; House Report 112- 705, pp. 912–913.

526 DoS, "About S/CRS," 2001-2009.state.gov/s/crs/ c12936.htm, accessed 11/27/2012.

527 P.L. 108-447, Section 408.

528 DoS, *Leading Through Civilian Power: The First Quadrennial Diplomacy and Development Review*, 12/2010.

529 DoD Directive 3000.05, "Military Support for Stability, Security, Transition and Reconstruction (SSTR) Operations,"11/28/2005.

530 DoD Directive 3000.05, "Military Support for Stability, Security, Transition and Reconstruction (SSTR) Operations,"11/28/2005.

531 DoD Instruction 3000.05, "Stability Operations," 9/16/2009.

532 Explanatory Statement related to P. L. 110- 252, printed in Congressional Record (daily edition) at H3969, 5/15/2008. The matter under consideration was the House amendment to the Senate amendment to H.R. 2642, which was eventually enacted into law without further amendment.

533 P.L. 110-417, Section 1214; SIGIR, *Quarterly Report to the United States Congress*, 10/30/2008, p. 206.

534 House Report 111-288 (Conference Report accompanying the National Defense Authorization Act for Fiscal Year 2010); P.L. 111- 84, Section 1222; SIGIR, *Quarterly Report to the United States Congress*, 10/30/2010, p. 173.

535 Dane F. Smith, Jr., *An Expanded Mandate for Peace Building: The State Department Role in Peace Diplomacy, Reconstruction, and Stabilization*, Washington, DC: Center for Strategic and International Studies, 4/30/2009, p. 39.

536 USA, Headquarters, Field Manual 3–07, Stability Operations, 10/2008, p. 13.

537 SIGIR, *Applying Iraq's Hard Lessons to the Reform of Stabilization and Reconstruction Operations*, 2/2010, pp. 6–7.

538 P.L. 110-417. It is similar to an earlier bill, S. 613, introduced by Senator Richard Lugar and then-Senator Joseph Biden, which was reported by the Senate Foreign Relations committee but did not go further, and to H.R. 1084, introduced by Reps. Farr and Saxton, which passed the House on 3/5/2008.

539 OSD, memorandum for the Secretary of State, "Options for Remodeling Security Sector Assistance Authorities," 12/15/2009.

540 DoS, *Leading Through Civilian Power: The First Quadrennial Diplomacy and Development Review*, 12/2010.

541 DoS, *Leading Through Civilian Power: The First Quadrennial Diplomacy and Development Review*, 12/2010. "[O]ne of the elements for consideration in selecting Deputy Chiefs of Mission or Chiefs of Mission must be how well candidates have worked with the interagency or managed multi-agency missions in previous postings."

542 DoS, *Leading Through Civilian Power: The First Quadrennial Diplomacy and Development Review*, 12/2010, pp. 135–136.

543 DoS, *Leading Through Civilian Power: The First Quadrennial Diplomacy and Development Review*, 12/2010, p. xiv.

544 DoS, *Leading Through Civilian Power: The First Quadrennial Diplomacy and Development Review*, 12/2010, p. 136.

545 DoS, *Leading Through Civilian Power: The First Quadrennial Diplomacy and Development Review*, 12/2010, pp. 135–136.

546 DoS, *Leading Through Civilian Power: The First Quadrennial Diplomacy and Development Review*, 12/2010, pp. 134−135.

547 CSO, "Newsletter–September," 9/14/2012, www. state.gov/j/cso/releases/other/197922.htm, accessed 11/28/2012.

548 CSO, "Newsletter–September," 9/14/2012, www. state.gov/j/cso/releases/other/197922.htm, accessed 11/28/2012.

549 SIGIR estimates that an office with a standing capacity of 200 staff would cost approximately $30 mil lion annually. Waste resulting from management failures in Iraq alone is approximately $4 billion–$5 billion (SIGIR estimate).

550 Todd Moss, "Too Big to Succeed? Why (W)Hole-of-Government Cannot Work for U.S. Development Policy," Global Development: Views from the Center, 10/5/2010, blogs.cgdev.org/globaldevelopment/2010/10/too-big-to-succeed-why-whole-of-government-cannot-work-for-u-s-development-policy.php, accessed 2/7/2013.

551 FEMA Publication 592, "Robert T. Stafford Disaster Relief and Emergency Assistance Act, P.L. 93–288, as amended, 42 U.S.C. 5121–5207, and Related Authorities," 6/2007.

[552] CWC, "At What Risk? Correcting Over-reliance on Contractors in Contingency Operations," 2/24/2011, Appendix A.

Sources for Figures

1.1 SIGIR Audits Directorate data.

1.2 SIGIR Inspections Directorate data.

1.3 SIGIR Inspections Directorate data.

1.4 SIGIR Investigations Directorate data.

3.1 SIGIR, *Quarterly and Semiannual Reports to the United States Congress*, 2004–2012.

3.2 USF-I, responses to SIGIR data calls, 1/4/2011, 4/8/2011, 7/1/2011, 10/5/2011, 10/7/2011, and 12/21/2011; refer to sources for Figure 4.4.

3.3 GAO Audit 09-86R, "Provincial Reconstruction Teams in Afghanistan and Iraq," 10/1/2008, pp. 4–5; DoS, *Iraq Status Report*, 8/9/2005, slide 29; SIGIR Audit 07-014, "Status of the Provincial Reconstruction Team Progress Expansion in Iraq," 7/28/2007, p. 2; SIGIR Audit 09-013, "Provincial Reconstruction Teams' Performance Measurement Has Improved," 1/28/2009, p. 2; SIGIR Audit 09-020, "Provincial Reconstruction Teams: Developing a Cost-tracking System Will Enhance Decision-making," 4/28/2009, p. 2; U.S. Embassy-Baghdad, response to SIGIR data call, 7/6/2009; U.S. Embassy-Baghdad, OPA, PRT response to SIGIR data call, 1/4/2010; SIGIR, *Quarterly and Semiannual Reports to the United States Congress*, 1/30/2008, p. 81, 1/30/2010, p. 36, 4/30/2010, p. 82, 7/30/2010, pp. 42–43, 10/30/2010, p. 52, 1/30/2011, p. 42, 7/30/2011, pp. 2–3, and 1/30/2012, p. 37.

3.4 SIGIR Audit 07-008, "Fact Sheet on the Roles and Responsibilities of U.S. Government Organizations Conducting IRRF-Funded Reconstruction Activities," 7/26/2007, p. i.

3.5 GAO Testimony GAO-12-856T, statement of Michael J. Courts, Acting Director International Affairs and Trade, "Mission Iraq: State and DoD Face Challenges in Finalizing Support and Security Capabilities," 6/28/2012, p. 3.

3.6 USAID, Bureau for the Middle East, Office of Iraq and Arabian Peninsula Affairs, information provided to SIGIR Audits, 9/30/2012.

3.7 USACE, information provided to SIGIR Audits, 11/20/2012.

3.8 DoD, OUSD(AT&L), SPOT Program Support, responses to SIGIR data calls, 4/2011–10/2012.

3.9 DSCA, Historical Facts Book, 9/30/2011, www. dsca.osd.mil /programs/biz-ops/factsbook/Historical%20Facts%20Book% 20-%2030%20 September%202011.pdf, accessed 12/28/2012; Major Jared L. Ware, Program Manager, Foreign Military Sales Construction, MNSTC-I, "Foreign Military Sales Construction in Iraq," *DISAM Journal*, 11/2009, pp. 154–158, www. disam.dsca.mil/pubs/INDEXES/Vol%20 31_3/Ware. pdf, accessed 12/28/2012; OSC-I, response to SIGIR data call, 7/15/2012; Larry D. McCaskill, "ACC-RI Now Responsible for Closing Out Contracts in Iraq and Afghanistan," 12/9/2011, www.army.mil, accessed 12/28/2012; SIGIR Audit 12-005, "U.S. Central Command Contracting Command Had Few Contract Terminations That Resulted in Wasted Funds in Iraq," 10/28/2011, and Iraq Reconstruction: Lessons in Contracting and Procurement, 7/2006, pp. 21–22, 36, 51, 53. Under the WERC contract,

248   Special Inspector General for Iraq Reconstruction

27 prequalified construction firms were available to perform construction task orders, with a potential contracting capacity of $10 billion.

3.10 SIGIR, *Iraq Reconstruction: Lessons in Contracting and Procurement*, 7/2006, pp. 57–62.

3.11 CEFMS, *ESF, IRRF: Construction, IRRF: Non-construction, ISFF: Construction*, 4/1/2011, 7/9/2011, 10/6/2011 and 10/2/2012; USAID, responses to SIGIR data calls, 1/22/2010, 12/29/2011, 1/3/2012, and 10/2/2012.

4.1 SIGIR, *Quarterly and Semiannual Reports to the United States Congress*, 1/30/2005–10/30/2012.

4.2 P.L. 108-7; P.L. 108-11; P.L. 108-106; P.L. 108-287; P.L. 109-13; P.L. 109-102; P.L. 109-148; P.L. 109-34; P.L. 109-289; P.L. 110-28; P.L. 110-92; P.L. 110-116; P.L. 110-137; P.L. 110-149; P.L. 110-161; P.L. 110-252; P.L. 111-32; P.L. 111-117; P.L. 111-118; P.L. 111-212; P.L. 112-10, P.L. 112-74; ABO, response to SIGIR data call, 1/18/2012; BBG, response to SIGIR data call, 3/7/2011; DCAA, response to SIGIR data call, 10/4/2011; DoJ, Justice Management Division, response to SIGIR data call, 10/9/2012; PM, response to SIGIR data call, 7/6/2011; DoS, "Congressional Budget Justification: Foreign Assistance," Summary Tables, FY 2009–FY 2011; DoS, "Executive Budget Summary Function 150 & Other International Programs, Fiscal Year 2013," p. 173; DRL, response to SIGIR data call, 7/9/2012; ECA, response to SIGIR data call, 4/14/2010; OMB, response to SIGIR data call, 6/21/2010; INL, response to SIGIR data call, 10/16/2012; USAID, "U.S. Overseas Loans and Grants [Greenbook]," 2008; U.S. Treasury, OTA, "Office of Technical Assistance Overview," 12/30/2005; TFBSO, response to SIGIR data call, 1/4/2011; SIGIR Audit 11-007, "Iraq Relief and Reconstruction Fund 1: Report on Apportionments, Expenditures, and Cancelled Funds," 12/28/2010; USAID, responses to SIGIR data calls, 1/12/2009, 4/8/2009, 10/2/2012, and 10/15/2012; U.S. Embassy-Baghdad, responses to SIGIR data calls, 10/3/2009, 10/5/2011, 1/4/2012, 4/3/2012, 7/3/2012, and 10/1/2012; NEA-I, responses to SIGIR data calls, 10/4/2012, 10/6/2010, 4/15/2011, 9/28/2011, 9/20/2012, 9/27/2012, 9/25/2012, 10/1/2012, 10/2/2012, and 10/10/2012; OUSD(C), "United States Department of Defense Fiscal Year 2012 Budget Request," Overview, 2/2012, p. 6-6; OUSD(C), responses to SIGIR data calls, 10/14/2010 and 10/2/2012; USACE, responses to SIGIR data calls, 10/6/2008 and 10/1/2012; GOI, CoR, "Federal Budget Law for the Fiscal Year/2012, articles 1, 2, 36, 2/23/2012, and "Federal Public Budget Law for the Fiscal Year 2011," 2/23/2011, Article 2; GOI, MOF, information provided to SIGIR, 6/27/2011; "GOI Budget" (as approved by TNA and written into law December 2005); GOI, Presidency of the Iraqi Interim National Assembly, "The State General Budget for 2005," 2005; GOI, MoPDC, "Indicators of the Investment Budget for Year 2010," Table 17, 2011; GOI, "Budget Revenues and Expenses 2003, July–December," 2003; SIGIR, *Quarterly and Semiannual Reports to the United States Congress*, 3/30/2004–4/30/2011; U.S. Treasury, responses to SIGIR data calls, 1/4/2008 and 4/9/2009. NEA-I, responses to SIGIR data calls, 4/5/2011, 4/7/2011, and 7/12/2011; World Bank, "World Bank Operations in Iraq," 12/31/2011; Embassy of Japan in Iraq, press release, "Provision of Yen Loan to Iraq," 5/29/2012.

4.3 P.L. 108-11; P.L. 108-106; P.L. 108-287; P.L. 109- 13; P.L. 109-102; P.L. 109-148; P.L. 109-34; P.L. 109-289; P.L. 110-28; P.L. 110-92; P.L. 110-116; P.L. 110-137; P.L. 110-149; P.L. 110-61; P.L. 110- 252; P.L. 111-32; P.L. 111-117; P.L. 111-118; P.L. 111-212;

P.L. 112-10, P.L. 112-74; INL, response to SIGIR data call, 10/16/2012; ABO, response to SIGIR data call, 1/18/2012; CENTCOM OIG, information provided to SIGIR audits, 1/14/2013; NEA-I, responses to SIGIR data calls, 9/28/2011, 9/20/2012, 9/25/2012, 10/1/2012, and 10/2/2012; USACE, response to SIGIR data call, 10/1/2012; U.S. Embassy-Baghdad, responses to SIGIR data calls, 10/5/2011, 1/4/2012, 4/3/2012, 7/3/2012, 10/1/2012; SIGIR Audit 11-007, "Iraq Relief and Reconstruction Fund 1: Report on Apportionments, Expenditures, and Cancelled Funds," 12/28/2010; OUSD(C), response to SIGIR data call, 10/2/2012.

4.4 SIGIR, *Quarterly and Semiannual Reports to the United States Congress*, 3/30/2004–10/30/2012; CEFMS, *ISFF Funds Execution Reports*, 10/1/2007 and 1/8/2008; DFAS, responses to SIGIR data calls, 1/9/2008–4/10/2009; DoD, Secretary of the Army Updates, 8/31/2007 and 9/30/2007; DoS, response to SIGIR data call, 4/5/2007, and *Section 2207 Reports*, 10/2004–10/2008; GRD, Program Review Board, 3/3/2007, and responses to SIGIR data calls, 4/5/2008–7/18/2009; INL, responses to SIGIR data calls, 1/4/2008–10/16/2012; IRMO, *Weekly Status Reports*, 4/17/2007 and 6/26/2007; IRMS, *ESF Cost to Complete Reports*, 7/5/2007–1/5/2009, and *USF-I CERP Category Report*, 9/20/2010; ITAO, *Essential Indicators Reports*, 10/2/2007–5/14/2009, and responses to SIGIR data calls, 10/10/2007–3/29/2009; NEA-I, responses to SIGIR data calls, 1/6/2010–10/2/2012; OMB, *Section 2207 Reports*, 1/2004–7/2004; OSD, responses to SIGIR data calls, 7/9/2008–10/2/2012; DoD, *Secretary of the Army Finance Reports*, 12/31/2006–7/8/2007; U.S. Treasury, responses to SIGIR data calls, 4/6/2007–4/2/2009; U.S. Embassy-Baghdad, responses to SIGIR data calls, 7/6/2009– 10/1/2012; USACE, responses to SIGIR data calls, 4/7/2007–10/1/2012; USAID, *Activities Report*, 7/12/2007, and responses to SIGIR data calls, 4/6/2007–4/2/2012; USTDA, responses to SIGIR data calls, 10/1/2007–4/2/2009; P.L. 108-11; P.L. 108-106; P.L. 109-13; P.L. 109-102; P.L. 109-234; P.L. 109-289; P.L. 110-5; P.L. 110- 28; P.L. 110-92; P.L. 110-137; P.L. 110-149; P.L. 110-161; P.L. 110-252; P.L. 111-8; P.L. 111-32; P.L. 111-117; P.L. 111-212; P.L. 112-10; P.L. 112-74.

4.5 Refer to sources for Figure 4.4.

4.6 SIGIR, *Hard Lessons: The Iraq Reconstruction Experience*, 2/2009, p. 170; SIGIR Audit 11-013, "Iraq Relief and Reconstruction Fund 2: Report on Apportionments, Expenditures, and Status at End of Fiscal Year 2010," 4/22/2011, p. 16.

4.7 OSD, response to SIGIR data call, 4/18/2011; DoD, "FY 2005 Supplemental Request for Operation Iraqi Freedom (OIF), Operation Enduring Freedom (OEF), and Operation Unified Assistance," 2/2005, pp. 78–79; DoD, "FY 2006 Supplemental Request for Operation Iraqi Freedom (OIF) and Operation Enduring Freedom (OEF)," 2/2006, pp. 60–61; DoD, "Amendment to FY 2007 Emergency Supplemental Request for the Global War on Terror," 3/2007, p. 5; DoD, "FY 2007 Emergency Supplemental Request for the Global War on Terror," 2/2007, pp. 38–49; DoD, "FY 2008 Global War on Terror Request," 2/2007, pp. 34–40; DoD, "FY 2008 Global War on Terror Amendment, Department of Defense," 10/2007, pp. 26–27; DoD, "FY 2009 Global War on Terror Bridge Request," 5/2008, pp. 15–16; DoD, "FY 2009 Supplemental Request," 4/2009, pp. 41–43; DoD, "FY 2011 Budget Request Overview," 2/2010, pp. 6-8–6-9; P.L. 109-13; P.L. 109-234; P.L. 109-252; P.L. 109-289; P.L. 110-161; P.L. 110-28; P.L. 111-212; P.L. 111-32; P.L. 112-10; House Report 109-234, to accompany H.R. 4939, 6/8/2006, pp. 83–84; House Report 109-676, to accompany H.R. 5631, 9/25/2006, p. 365; House

250 Special Inspector General for Iraq Reconstruction

Report 110-107, to accompany H.R. 1591, 4/24/2007, p. 131; Senate Report 111-188, to accompany H.R. 4899, 5/14/2010, p. 25.

4.8 Refer to sources for Figure 4.4.

4.9 Refer to sources for Figure 4.4.

4.10 Refer to sources for Figure 4.4.

4.11 Refer to sources for Figure 4.4.

4.12 P.L. 109-102; House Report 109-265, to accompany H.R. 3057, 11/2/2005, p. 86; P.L. 109-234; House Report 109-494, to accompany H.R. 4939, 6/8/2006, pp. 95–96; P.L. 110-28; House Report 110-107, to accompany H.R. 1591, 4/24/2007, pp. 202–204; P.L. 110-92; P.L. 110-137; P.L. 110-149; P.L. 110-161; House Appropriations Committee, "Consolidated Appropriations Act, 2008, Committee Print: Division J— Department of State, Foreign Operations, and Related Programs Act, 2008," 1/30/2008, pp. 2177–2178, 2208; P.L. 110-252; Senate Explanatory Statement, to accompany H.R. 2642, 6/26/2008; P.L. 111-32; Conference Report 111-151, to accompany H.R. 2346, 6/12/2009, pp. 127– 129; P.L. 111-117; Conference Report 111-366, to accompany H.R. 3288, 12/8/2009, pp. 1466, 1470; DoS, "Foreign Operations Congressional Budget Justification, FY 2006," p. 448; House Document 109-90, "Request for FY 2006 Budget Amendments," 2/28/2006, p. 26; DoS, "Foreign Operations Congressional Budget Justification, FY 2008," pp. 48, 128–129, 138, 490; DoS and USAID, "Supplemental Appropriations Justification, FY 2008," p. 38; DoS, "Foreign Operations Congressional Budget Justification, FY 2009," pp. 542–544; DoS and USAID, "Supplemental Justification, FY 2009," pp. 40–43; DoS, "Foreign Operations Congressional Budget Justification, Annex: Regional Perspectives, FY 2010," pp. 421–426; DoS, "Foreign Operations Congressional Budget Justification, Annex: Regional Perspectives, FY 2011," pp. 471–477; DoS, "Foreign Operations Congressional Budget Justification, Annex: Regional Perspectives, FY 2012," pp. 522– 528; USAID, response to SIGIR data call, 7/7/2011; USACE, response to SIGIR data call, 7/5/2011; NEA-I, responses to SIGIR data calls, 4/12/2011, 4/15/2011, 6/24/2011, 6/27/2011, 7/7/2011, and 7/8/2011; SIGIR Audit 07-005, "Fact Sheet on Sources and Uses of U.S. Funding Provided in Fiscal Year 2006 for Iraq Relief and Reconstruction," 7/27/2007, p. 13.

4.13 Refer to sources for Figure 4.4.

4.14 NEA-I, responses to SIGIR data calls, 9/28/2011, 9/25/2012, 10/1/2012, and 10/2/2012; USACE, response to SIGIR data call, 10/1/2012; U.S. Embassy-Baghdad, responses to SIGIR data calls, 10/5/2011, 1/4/2012, 4/3/2012, 7/3/2012, and 10/1/2012.

4.15 Refer to sources for Figure 4.4.

4.16 ABO, responses to SIGIR data calls, 10/4/2010, 10/8/2010, 12/6/2010, 12/22/2010, 4/5/2011, 4/18/2011, 7/5/2011, 7/14/2011, 10/18/2011, and 1/18/2012; USF-I, response to SIGIR data call, 1/3/2012.

4.17 Refer to sources for Figure 4.4.

4.18 DoS, "Congressional Budget Justification: Foreign Operations, FY 2006," 2/15/2005, p. 449; DoS, "Supplemental Budget Justification, FY 2006," 2/16/2006; P.L. 109-234; House Report 109-494, to Accompany H.R. 4939, "Making Emergency Supplemental Appropriations for the Fiscal Year Ending September 30, 2006, and for Other Purposes," 6/8/2006, p. 36; DoS, "Congressional Budget Justification: Foreign Operations, FY 2007," 2/13/2006; DoS, "Congressional Budget Justification: Foreign Operations, FY 2007," 2/13/2006, p. 460; P.L. 110-5; INL, response to SIGIR data call, 7/2/2010; DoS,

"FY 2007 Global War on Terror (GWOT) Supplemental," 2/14/2007, pp. 132–133; P.L. 110-28; Conference Report 110-107, to accompany H.R. 1591, "Making Emergency Supplemental Appropriations for the Fiscal Year Ending September 30, 2007, and for Other Purposes," 4/24/2007, p. 206; DoS, "Congressional Budget Justification: Foreign Operations, FY 2008," 2/13/2007, p. 75; House Report 109-265, to accompany H.R. 3057, "Making Appropriations for Foreign Operations, Export Financing, and Related Programs for the Fiscal Year Ending September 30, 2006, and for Other Purposes," 11/2/2005, pp. 97–98; House Report 110-197, to accompany H.R. 2764, "State, Foreign Operations, and Related Programs Appropriations Bill, 2008," 6/18/2007, p. 105; P.L. 110-161; DoS, "FY 2008 Global War on Terror (GWOT) Emergency," 2/13/2007, p. 139; P.L. 110-252; Senate Explanatory Statement to accompany H.R. 2642, "Making Appropriations for Military Construction, the Department of Veterans Affairs, and Related Agencies for the Fiscal Year Ending September 30, 2008, and for Other Purposes," 6/26/2008; DoS, "Congressional Budget Justification: Foreign Operations, FY 2009," 2/2008, pp. 54, 542; Senate Report 110-425, to accompany S. 3288, "Department of State, Foreign Operations, and Related Programs Appropriations Bill, 2009," 7/18/2008, pp. 53–54; P.L. 111-8; DoS and USAID, "FY 2009 Supplemental Justification," 5/13/2009, pp. 40–42; P.L. 111-32; House Report 111-151, to accompany H.R. 2346, "Making Supplemental Appropriations for the Fiscal Year Ending September 30, 2009, and for Other Purposes," 6/12/2009, p. 131; DoS, "Guidelines for Government of Iraq Financial Participation in United States Government-Funded Civilian Foreign Assistance Programs and Projects," 4/9/2009; DoS, "Congressional Budget Justification: Foreign Operations, FY 2010," 5/28/2009, p. 47; P.L. 111-117; Conference Report 111-366, to accompany H.R. 3288, "Departments of Transportation and Housing and Urban Development, and Related Agencies Appropriations Act, 2010," 12/8/2009, pp. 1483–1484; DoS and USAID, "Supplemental Budget Justification, FY 2010," 3/2010, pp. 31–32; P.L. 111-212; Senate Report 111-188, to accompany H.R. 4899, "Making Emergency Supplemental Appropriations for Disaster and Relief and Summer Jobs for the Fiscal Year Ending September 30, 2010, and for Other Purposes," pp. 64–65; DoS, "Congressional Budget Justification: Foreign Operations, FY 2011," 3/10/2010, pp. 471–476; DoS, "Congressional Budget Justification: Foreign Operations, FY 2012," 4/8/2011, p. 188.

4.19 DoS, response to SIGIR data call, 4/5/2007; INL, response to SIGIR data call, 10/16/2012; IRMS, *USF-I CERP Category Report*, 9/20/2010; U.S. Embassy-Baghdad, responses to SIGIR data calls, 10/5/2011, 1/4/2012, 4/3/2012, 7/3/2012, and 10/1/2012; U.S. Treasury, response to SIGIR data call, 4/2/2009; USTDA, response to SIGIR data call, 4/2/2009; USACE, response to SIGIR data call, 10/1/2012; USAID, response to SIGIR data call, 7/8/2010; OSD, responses to SIGIR data calls, 4/10/2009 and 10/2/2012; NEA-I, responses to SIGIR data calls, 9/28/2011, 9/20/2012, 9/25/2012, 10/1/2012, and 10/2/2012. Figure does not account for unobligated funds, including $521 million of the IRRF, $625 million of the ISFF, $556 million of the ESF, $391 million of the CERP, and $157 million of the INCLE.

5.1 For sources of funding data, see endnote 2.

5.2 IRMS, *USF-I CERP Category Report*, 9/20/2010; NEA-I, response to SIGIR data call, 9/20/2012; OSD, response to SIGIR data call, 4/10/2009; USACE, response to SIGIR data call, 10/1/2012; USAID, response to SIGIR data call, 7/8/2010.

5.3 USACE, information provided to SIGIR Audits, 11/20/2012.

5.4 EIA, *International Energy Annual 2006*; ITAO/ ESD, *Electric Daily Performance Reports*, 6/1/2006-6/30/2011; DoS, *Iraq Status Reports*, 10/25/2006, slide 11, and 5/9/2007, slide 11; U.S. Embassy-Baghdad, responses to SIGIR data calls, 1/22/2012, 4/13/2012, 7/3/2012, and 10/1/2012; GOI, NMC, "Status of the Ministry of Electricity," selected reports, 9/1/2012– 9/30/2012, nmc.gov.iq/default.aspx, accessed various dates.

5.5 U.S. Energy Information Administration, "World Crude Oil Production, 1960-2008," www.eia.doe.gov, accessed 12/30/2009; GOI, Ministry of Oil, "Domestic Consumption," www.oil.gov.iq, accessed 1/4/2013.

5.6 NEA-I, responses to SIGIR data calls, 7/6/2010, 1/11/2011, 4/5/2011, 7/7/2011, 10/17/2011, and 1/6/2012; GOI, Ministry of Oil, "Crude Oil Exports," www.oil.gov.iq, accessed 1/30/2013.

5.7 U.S. Treasury, responses to SIGIR data calls, 4/10/2009, 2/25/2010, 4/12/2011, 1/10/2012, and 10/16/2012.

5.8 SIGIR, *Quarterly and Semiannual Reports to the United States Congress*, 7/30/2006, p. 81, 4/30/2007, p. 69, 4/30/2008, p. 135, 4/30/2009, p. 81, 1/30/2010, p. 63, 7/30/2010, p. 101, 10/30/2010, p. 22, and 1/30/2012, p. 90.

5.9 SIGIR, *Quarterly and Semiannual Reports to the United States Congress*, 7/30/2008, p. 93, and 1/30/2011, p. 66.

5.10 Refer to sources for Figure 4.4.

5.11 DoS, response to SIGIR data call, 4/5/2007; INL, response to SIGIR data call, 10/16/2012; IRMS, *USF-I CERP Category Report*, 9/20/2010; OSD, response to SIGIR data call, 10/2/2012; USACE, response to SIGIR data call, 10/1/2012; NEA-I, responses to SIGIR data calls, 9/20/2012 and 9/25/2012.

5.12 Refer to sources for Figure 4.4.

5.13 Refer to sources for Figure 4.4.

5.14 NEA-I, response to SIGIR data call, 9/20/2012; OSD, response to SIGIR data call, 10/2/2012; INL, response to SIGIR data call, 10/16/2012; IRMS, *USF-I CERP Category Report*, 9/20/2010.

5.15 DoD, *Measuring Stability and Security in Iraq*, 2005–2008.

5.16 DSCA, response to SIGIR data call, 10/4/2012.

5.17 INL, response to SIGIR data call, 10/16/2012; IRMS, *USF-I CERP Category Report*, 9/20/2010; DoS, response to SIGIR data call, 4/5/2007; NEA-I, responses to SIGIR data call, 9/20/2012 and 9/25/2012.

5.18 Transparency International, *Corruption Perception Index*, www.transparency.org/research/cpi/overview, accessed 2/1/2013. **Note:** In its 2012 report, Transparency International revised the methodology used to construct its *Corruption Perception Index*. In doing so, it changed the index scale from 0–10 to 0–100. To show how Iraq's ranking *relative to other countries* has changed from year to year, SIGIR converted the 2012 data to the scale used in previous years. The absolute scores shown for 2012 should not be compared with scores in previous years.

5.19 For sources of funding data, see endnote 2.

5.20 DoS, response to SIGIR data call, 4/5/2007; IRMS, *USF-I CERP Category Report*, 9/20/2010; U.S. Embassy-Baghdad, responses to SIGIR data calls, 10/5/2011, 1/4/2012, 4/3/2012, 7/3/2012, and 10/1/2012; USACE, response to SIGIR data call, 10/1/2012;

USAID, response to SIGIR data call, 7/8/2010; NEA-I, responses to SIGIR data calls, 9/28/2011, 9/20/2012, 9/25/2012, 10/1/2012, and 10/2/2012.

5.21 SIGIR, *Quarterly and Semiannual Reports to the United States Congress*, 2004–2012.

5.22 DoS, response to SIGIR data call, 4/5/2007; IRMS, *USF-I CERP Category Report*, 9/20/2010; USAID, responses to SIGIR data calls, 7/8/2010 and 10/15/2012; NEA-I, responses to SIGIR data calls, 10/6/2010, 9/20/2012, 10/1/2012, 10/10/2012.

5.23 IRMS, *USF-I CERP Category Report*, 9/20/2010; U.S. Treasury, response to SIGIR data call, 4/2/2009; USTDA, response to SIGIR data call, 4/2/2009; USAID, response to SIGIR data call, 7/8/2010; NEA-I, responses to SIGIR data call, 9/20/2012, 9/25/2012, and 10/2/2012.

5.24 For sources of funding data, see endnote 2.

5.25 The World Bank, IFC, *Doing Business in the Arab World 2012*, p. 64.

5.26 World Bank, "Doing Business: Economy Rankings," www.doing business.org/rankings, accessed 1/16/2013.

5.27 UNCC, "Status of Processing and Payment of Claims," 10/25/2012, www.uncc.ch/status.htm, accessed 12/20/2012.

Sources for Tables

1.1 SIGIR data.

4.1 P.L. 108-11; P.L. 108-106; P.L. 108-287; P.L. 109-13; P.L. 109-102; P.L. 109-148; P.L. 109-34; P.L. 109-289; P.L. 110-28; P.L. 110-92; P.L. 110-116; P.L. 110-137; P.L. 110-149; P.L. 110-61; P.L. 110-252; P.L. 111-32; P.L. 111-117; P.L. 111-118; P.L. 111-212; P.L. 112-10, P.L. 112-74; ABO, response to SIGIR data call, 1/18/2012; BBG, response to SIGIR data call, 3/7/2011; DCAA, response to SIGIR data call, 10/4/2011; DoJ, Justice Management Division, response to SIGIR data call, 10/9/2012; DoS, PM, response to SIGIR data call, 7/6/2011; DoS, "Congressional Budget Justification: Foreign Assistance," Summary Tables, FY 2009–FY 2011; DoS, "Executive Budget Summary Function 150 & Other International Programs, Fiscal Year 2013," p. 173; DRL, response to SIGIR data call, 7/9/2012; ECA, response to SIGIR data call, 4/14/2010; OMB, response to SIGIR data call, 6/21/2010; INL, response to SIGIR data call, 10/16/2012; USAID, "U.S. Overseas Loans and Grants [Greenbook]," 2008; U.S. Treasury, OTA, "Office of Technical Assistance Overview," 12/30/2005; TFBSO, response to SIGIR data call, 1/4/2011; SIGIR Audit 11-007, "Iraq Relief and Reconstruction Fund 1: Report on Apportionments, Expenditures, and Cancelled Funds," 12/28/2010; USAID, responses to SIGIR data calls, 1/12/2009, 4/8/2009, 10/2/2012, and 10/15/2012; U.S. Embassy-Baghdad, responses to SIGIR data calls, 10/3/2009, 10/5/2011, 1/4/2012, 4/3/2012, 7/3/2012, and 10/1/2012; NEA-I, responses to SIGIR data calls, 10/4/2012, 10/6/2010, 4/15/2011, 9/28/2011, 9/20/2012, 9/27/2012, 9/25/2012, 10/1/2012, 10/2/2012, and 10/10/2012; OUSD(C), "United States Department of Defense Fiscal Year 2012 Budget Request," Overview, 2/2012, p. 66, and responses to SIGIR data calls, 10/14/2010 and 10/2/2012; USACE, responses to SIGIR data calls, 10/6/2008 and 10/1/2012.

4.2 NEA-I, response to SIGIR data call, 9/20/2012; OSD, response to SIGIR data call, 4/10/2009; DoS, response to SIGIR data call, 4/5/2007; USTDA, response to SIGIR data call, 4/2/2009; U.S. Treasury, response to SIGIR data call, 4/2/2009; USAID, response to

254 Special Inspector General for Iraq Reconstruction

SIGIR data call, 7/8/2010; SIGIR Audit 11-007, "Iraq Relief and Reconstruction Fund 1: Report on Apportionments, Expenditures, and Cancelled Funds," 12/28/2010.

4.3 OUSD(C), response to SIGIR data call, 10/2/2012.

4.4 NEA-I, responses to SIGIR data calls, 9/28/2011, 9/25/2012, 10/1/2012, and 10/2/2012; USACE, response to SIGIR data call, 10/1/2012; U.S. Embassy-Baghdad, responses to SIGIR data calls, 10/5/2011, 1/4/2012, 4/3/2012, 7/3/2012, and 10/1/2012.

4.5 ABO, responses to SIGIR data calls, 10/4/2010, 10/8/2010, 12/6/2010, 12/22/2010, 4/5/2011, 4/18/2011, 7/5/2011, 7/14/2011, 10/18/2011, and 1/18/2012; USF-I, response to SIGIR data call, 1/3/2012.

4.6 INL, response to SIGIR data call, 10/16/2012.

4.7 DoS, "Executive Budget Summary Function 150 and Other Internal Programs, Fiscal Year 2013," p. 173; OSC-I Chief, meeting with SIGIR, 9/21/2012; **NRRRF:** USACE, GRD, response to SIGIR data call, 10/6/2008; **IFF:** OSD, responses to SIGIR data calls, 10/2/2009 and 4/14/2010; **OHDACA:** DSCA, "Overseas Humanitarian, Disaster, and Civic Aid: Fiscal Year 2010 Budget Estimates," 5/2009; OSD, response to SIGIR data call, 4/15/2010; **MRA and ERMA:** DoS, PRM, response to SIGIR data call, 4/14/2010; **Democracy Fund:** DoS, DRL, responses to SIGIR data call, 4/2/2010 and 4/9/2010; **NADR:** USAID, "U.S. Overseas Loans and Grants [Greenbook]," 2008; DoS, "Foreign Operations Congressional Budget Justification, Fiscal Year 2010," 5/2009, pp. 49, 55; **IMET:** DoS, "Foreign Operations Congressional Budget Justification, Fiscal Year 2010," 5/2009, p. 88; DoS, response to SIGIR data call, 3/17/2010; **ECA:** NEA-I, response to SIGIR data call, 10/2/2009; DoS, ECA, response to SIGIR data call, 4/14/2010; **IDA/IDFA:** USAID, response to SIGIR data call, 4/14/2010; **P.L. 480:** USDA, Foreign Agricultural Service, "Fact Sheet: Food Assistance," 4/2009; NEA-I, response to SIGIR data call, 4/2/2010; **CSH:** NEA-I, response to SIGIR data call, 4/2/2010; **International Affairs Technical Assistance:** U.S. Treasury, OTA, "Office of Technical Assistance Overview," 12/30/2005; U.S. Embassy-Baghdad, response to SIGIR data call, 10/3/2009.

5.1 DoS, response to SIGIR data call, 4/5/2007; INL, response to SIGIR data call, 10/16/2012; IRMS, *USF-I CERP Category Report*, 9/20/2010; U.S. Embassy-Baghdad, responses to SIGIR data calls, 10/5/2011, 1/4/2012, 4/3/2012, 7/3/2012, 10/1/2012; U.S. Treasury, response to SIGIR data call, 4/2/2009; USTDA, response to SIGIR data call, 4/2/2009; USACE, response to SIGIR data call, 10/1/2012; USAID, response to SIGIR data call, 7/8/2010; OSD, responses to SIGIR data calls, 4/10/2009 and 10/2/2012; NEA-I, responses to SIGIR data calls, 9/28/2011, 9/20/2012, 9/25/2012, 10/1/2012, 10/2/2012.

5.2 IRMS, *Global Benchmark*, 9/3/2010; USACE, information provided to SIGIR audits, 11/20/2012; USAID, Bureau for the Middle East, Office of Iraq and Arabian Peninsula Affairs, information provided to SIGIR Audits, 10/23/2012; SIGIR Audit 07-009, "Review of Bechtel's Spending under Its Phase II Iraq Reconstruction Contract," 7/24/2007.

5.3 IRMS, *Global Benchmark*, 9/3/2010; USACE, information provided to SIGIR audits, 11/20/2012; USAID, Bureau for the Middle East, Office of Iraq and Arabian Peninsula Affairs, information provided to SIGIR Audits, 10/23/2012; SIGIR Audit 07-009, "Review of Bechtel's Spending under Its Phase II Iraq Reconstruction Contract," 7/24/2007, Audit 08- 018, "Review of Outcome, Cost, and Oversight of Water Sector Reconstruction Contract with FluorAMEC, LLC, 7/15/2008, PA-08-143, "Sadr City R3

Water Treatment Plant," 10/29/2008, and *Quarterly and Semiannual Report to the United States Congress*, 7/30/2008, p. 128.

5.4 IRMS, *Global Benchmark*, 9/3/2010; USACE, information provided to SIGIR audits, 11/20/2012; USAID, Bureau for the Middle East, Office of Iraq and Arabian Peninsula Affairs, information provided to SIGIR Audits, 10/23/2012; SIGIR PA-05-10, "Al Fatah Pipe River Crossing," 3/7/2006, and Audit 09-008, "Cost, Outcome, and Oversight of Iraq Oil Reconstruction Contract with Kellogg Brown & Root Services, Inc.," 1/13/2009.

5.5 IRMS, *Global Benchmark*, 9/3/2010; USACE, information provided to SIGIR audits, 11/20/2012, and response to SIGIR data call, 7/12/2012; USAID, Bureau for the Middle East, Office of Iraq and Arabian Peninsula Affairs, information provided to SIGIR Audits, 10/23/2012; SIGIR Audit 07-002, "Status of the Advanced First Responder Network," 4/25/2007, Audit 07-009, "Review of Bechtel's Spending under Its Phase II Iraq Reconstruction Contract," 7/24/2007, and *Quarterly and Semiannual Reports to the United States Congress*, 7/30/2010, p. 79, and 1/30/2012, p. 91.

5.6 SIGIR, *Quarterly and Semiannual Report to the United States Congress*, 1/30/2012, p. 68.

5.7 IRMS, *Global Benchmark*, 9/3/2010; USACE, information provided to SIGIR audits, 11/20/2012; USAID, Bureau for the Middle East, Office of Iraq and Arabian Peninsula Affairs, information provided to SIGIR Audits, 10/23/2012; SIGIR Audit 08-019, "Outcome, Cost, and Oversight of the Security and Justice Contract with Parsons Delaware, Inc.," 7/28/2008, Audit 09-027, "Developing a Depot Maintenance Capability at Taji Hampered by Numerous Problems," 7/30/2009, Audit 10-001, "Iraqi Security Forces Facilities: Environmental Chemical Corporation Projects Achieved Results, but with Significant Cost Increases and Schedule Delays," 10/22/2009, PA-06-087 and PA-06-088, "Tallil Military Base Camp Ur," 4/25/2007, PA-07-098, "Al Rasheed Brigade Set," 7/17/2007, PA-07-102, "Ministry of Defense Headquarters Building," 7/17/2007.

5.8 IRMS, *Global Benchmark*, 9/3/2010; USACE, information provided to SIGIR audits, 11/20/2012; USAID, Bureau for the Middle East, Office of Iraq and Arabian Peninsula Affairs, information provided to SIGIR Audits, 10/23/2012; SIGIR Audit 08-019, "Outcome, Cost, and Oversight of the Security and Justice Contract with Parsons Delaware, Inc.," 7/28/2008, PA-08-152, "Anbar Rule of Law/ Judicial Complex, Ramadi, Iraq," 1/27/2009, and PA-09-177, "Renovate and Expand Chamchamal Correctional Facility, Chamchamal, Iraq," 10/22/2009.

5.9 IRMS, *Global Benchmark*, 9/3/2010; USACE, information provided to SIGIR audits, 11/20/2012, and response to SIGIR data call, 7/12/2012; USAID, Bureau for the Middle East, Office of Iraq and Arabian Peninsula Affairs, information provided to SIGIR Audits, 10/23/2012; SIGIR Audit 06-011, "Management of the Primary Healthcare Centers Construction Projects," 4/29/2006, Audit 06-026, "Review of the U.S. Agency for International Development's Management of the Basrah Children's Hospital Project," 7/31/2006, Audit 09-015, "Construction of Primary Healthcare Centers Reported Essentially Complete, but Operational Issues Remain," 4/29/2009, Audit 10-015, "Health Center Sustainment Contract Resulted in Some Repairs, but Iraqi Maintenance Capability Was Not Achieved," 4/29/2010, PA-08-165 & 167, "Missan Surgical Hospital under the Economic Support Fund, Al Amarah, Iraq," 7/16/2009, and *Quarterly and Semiannual Report to the United States Congress*, 7/30/2012, pp. 33–34.

5.10 Bank financial statements provided to USAID, Private Banking Industry Survey, Iraq Financial Development Project, 4/2011, p. 45. Cash/ Deposits measures the ability of a bank to meet sudden demands by depositors to withdraw funds. The near one-to-one relationship is strongly indicative of a system that is not performing its role as financial intermediary. In banking environments where there is a responsive, active interbank market (and a Central Bank willing to serve as lender of last resort), the Cash/Deposits ratio is normally extremely low. JPMorgan Chase data is current as of 2/24/2010.

B.1 SIGIR, *Quarterly and Semiannual Reports to the United States Congress*, 7/30/2004–10/30/2012.

B.2 SIGIR, *Quarterly and Semiannual Reports to the United States Congress*, 7/30/2004–10/30/2012; USACE, information provided to SIGIR audits, 11/20/2012.

B.3 P.L. 108-11; P.L. 108-106; P.L. 108-287; P.L. 109-13; P.L. 109-102; P.L. 109-148; P.L. 109-34; P.L. 109-289; P.L. 110-28; P.L. 110-92; P.L. 110- 116; P.L. 110-137; P.L. 110-149; P.L. 110-61; P.L. 110-252; P.L. 111-32; P.L. 111-117; P.L. 111-118; P.L. 111-212; P.L. 112-10, P.L. 112-74; ABO, response to SIGIR data call, 1/18/2012; BBG, response to SIGIR data call, 3/7/2011; DCAA, response to SIGIR data call, 10/4/2011; DoJ, Justice Management Division, response to SIGIR data call, 10/9/2012; DoS, PM, response to SIGIR data call, 7/6/2011; DoS, "Congressional Budget Justification: Foreign Assistance," Summary Tables, FY 2009–FY 2011; DoS, "Executive Budget Summary Function 150 & Other International Programs, Fiscal Year 2013," p. 173; DRL, response to SIGIR data call, 7/9/2012; ECA, response to SIGIR data call, 4/14/2010; OMB, response to SIGIR data call, 6/21/2010; INL, response to SIGIR data call, 10/16/2012; USAID, "U.S. Overseas Loans and Grants [Greenbook]," 2008; U.S. Treasury, OTA, "Office of Technical Assistance Overview," 12/30/2005; TFBSO, response to SIGIR data call, 1/4/2011; SIGIR Audit 11-007, "Iraq Relief and Reconstruction Fund 1: Report on Apportionments, Expenditures, and Cancelled Funds," 12/28/2010; USAID, responses to SIGIR data calls, 1/12/2009, 4/8/2009, 10/2/2012, and 10/15/2012; U.S. Embassy-Baghdad, responses to SIGIR data calls, 10/3/2009, 10/5/2011, 1/4/2012, 4/3/2012, 7/3/2012, and 10/1/2012; NEA-I, responses to SIGIR data calls, 10/4/2012, 10/6/2010, 4/15/2011, 9/28/2011, 9/20/2012, 9/27/2012, 9/25/2012, 10/1/2012, 10/2/2012, and 10/10/2012; OUSD(C), "United States Department of Defense Fiscal Year 2012 Budget Request," Overview, 2/2012, p. 66, and responses to SIGIR data calls, 10/14/2010 and 10/2/2012; USACE, responses to SIGIR data calls, 10/6/2008 and 10/1/2012.

B.4 OSD, response to SIGIR data call, 4/18/2011; DoD, "FY 2005 Supplemental Request for Operation Iraqi Freedom (OIF), Operation Enduring Freedom (OEF), and Operation Unified Assistance," 2/2005, pp. 78–79; DoD, "FY 2006 Supplemental Request for Operation Iraqi Freedom (OIF) and Operation Enduring Freedom (OEF)," 2/2006, pp. 60–61; DoD, "Amendment to FY 2007 Emergency Supplemental Request for the Global War on Terror," 3/2007, p. 5; DoD, "FY 2007 Emergency Supplemental Request for the Global War on Terror," 2/2007, pp. 38–49; DoD, "FY 2008 Global War on Terror Request," 2/2007, pp. 34–40; DoD, "FY 2008 Global War on Terror Amendment, Department of Defense," 10/2007, pp. 26–27; DoD, "FY 2009 Global War on Terror Bridge Request," 5/2008, pp. 15–16; DoD, "FY 2009 Supplemental Request," 4/2009, pp. 41–43; DoD, "FY 2011 Budget Request Overview," 2/2010, pp. 6-8–6-9; P.L. 109-13; P.L. 109-234; P.L. 109-252; P.L. 109-289; P.L. 110-161; P.L. 110-28; P.L. 111-212; P.L. 111-32; P.L. 112-10; House Report 109-234, to accompany H.R. 4939, 6/8/2006, pp. 83–84; House Report 109-676, to accompany H.R. 5631, 9/25/2006, p. 365; House

Report 110-107, to accompany H.R. 1591, 4/24/2007, p. 131; Senate Report 111-188, to accompany H.R. 4899, 5/14/2010, p. 25.

B.5 P.L. 109-102; House Report 109-265, to accompany H.R. 3057, 11/2/2005, p. 86; P.L. 109-234; House Report 109-494, to accompany H.R. 4939, 6/8/2006, pp. 95–96; P.L. 110-28; House Report 110-107, to accompany H.R. 1591, 4/24/2007, pp. 202–204; P.L. 110-92; P.L. 110-137; P.L. 110-149; P.L. 110-161; House Appropriations Committee, "Consolidated Appropriations Act, 2008, Committee Print: Division J— Department of State, Foreign Operations, and Related Programs Act, 2008," 1/30/2008, pp. 2177–2178, 2208; P.L. 110-252; Senate Explanatory Statement, to accompany H.R. 2642, 6/26/2008; P.L. 111-32; Conference Report 111-151, to accompany H.R. 2346, 6/12/2009, pp. 127– 129; P.L. 111-117; Conference Report 111-366, to accompany H.R. 3288, 12/8/2009, pp. 1466, 1470; DoS, "Foreign Operations Congressional Budget Justification, FY 2006," p. 448; House Document 109-90, "Request for FY 2006 Budget Amendments," 2/28/2006, p. 26; DoS, "Foreign Operations Congressional Budget Justification, FY 2008," pp. 48, 128–129, 138, 490; DoS and USAID, "Supplemental Appropriations Justification, FY 2008," p. 38; DoS, "Foreign Operations Congressional Budget Justification, FY 2009," pp. 542–544; DoS and USAID, "Supplemental Justification, FY 2009," pp. 40–43; DoS, "Foreign Operations Congressional Budget Justification, Annex: Regional Perspectives, FY 2010," pp. 421–426; DoS, "Foreign Operations Congressional Budget Justification, Annex: Regional Perspectives, FY 2011," pp. 471–477; DoS, "Foreign Operations Congressional Budget Justification, Annex: Regional Perspectives, FY 2012," pp. 522– 528; USAID, response to SIGIR data call, 7/7/2011; USACE, response to SIGIR data call, 7/5/2011; DoS, NEA-I, responses to SIGIR data calls, 4/12/2011, 4/15/2011, 6/24/2011, 6/27/2011, 7/7/2011, and 7/8/2011; SIGIR Audit 07-005, "Fact Sheet on Sources and Uses of U.S. Funding Provided in Fiscal Year 2006 for Iraq Relief and Reconstruction," 7/27/2007, p. 13.

B.6 DoS, "Congressional Budget Justification: Foreign Operations, FY 2006," 2/15/2005, p. 449; DoS, "Supplemental Budget Justification, FY 2006," 2/16/2006; P.L. 109-234; House Report 109-494, to Accompany H.R. 4939, "Making Emergency Supplemental Appropriations for the Fiscal Year Ending September 30, 2006, and for Other Purposes," 6/8/2006, p. 36; DoS, "Congressional Budget Justification: Foreign Operations, FY 2007," 2/13/2006; DoS, "Congressional Budget Justification: Foreign Operations, FY 2007," 2/13/2006, p. 460; P.L. 110-5; INL, response to SIGIR data call, 7/2/2010; DoS, "FY 2007 Global War on Terror (GWOT) Supplemental," 2/14/2007, pp. 132–133; P.L. 110- 28; Conference Report 110-107, to accompany H.R. 1591, "Making Emergency Supplemental Appropriations for the Fiscal Year Ending September 30, 2007, and for Other Purposes," 4/24/2007, p. 206; DoS, "Congressional Budget Justification: Foreign Operations, FY 2008," 2/13/2007, p. 75; House Report 109-265, to accompany H.R. 3057, "Making Appropriations for Foreign Operations, Export Financing, and Related Programs for the Fiscal Year Ending September 30, 2006, and for Other Purposes," 11/2/2005, pp. 97–98; House Report 110-197, to accompany H.R. 2764, "State, Foreign Operations, and Related Programs Appropriations Bill, 2008," 6/18/2007, p. 105; P.L. 110-161; DoS, "FY 2008 Global War on Terror (GWOT) Emergency," 2/13/2007, p. 139; P.L. 110-252; Senate Explanatory Statement to accompany H.R. 2642, "Making Appropriations for Military Construction, the Department of Veterans Affairs, and Related Agencies for the Fiscal Year Ending September 30, 2008, and for Other

Purposes," 6/26/2008; DoS, "Congressional Budget Justification: Foreign Operations, FY 2009," 2/2008, pp. 54, 542; Senate Report 110-425, to accompany S. 3288, "Department of State, Foreign Operations, and Related Programs Appropriations Bill, 2009," 7/18/2008, pp. 53–54; P.L. 111-8; DoS and USAID, "FY 2009 Supplemental Justification," 5/13/2009, pp. 40–42; P.L. 111-32; House Report 111-151, to accompany H.R. 2346, "Making Supplemental Appropriations for the Fiscal Year Ending September 30, 2009, and for Other Purposes," 6/12/2009, p. 131; DoS, "Guidelines for Government of Iraq Financial Participation in United States Government-Funded Civilian Foreign Assistance Programs and Projects," 4/9/2009; DoS, "Congressional Budget Justification: Foreign Operations, FY 2010," 5/28/2009, p. 47; P.L. 111-117; Conference Report 111-366, to accompany H.R. 3288, "Departments of Transportation and Housing and Urban Development, and Related Agencies Appropriations Act, 2010," 12/8/2009, pp. 1483–1484; DoS and USAID, "Supplemental Budget Justification, FY 2010," 3/2010, pp. 31–32; P.L. 111-212; Senate Report 111-188, to accompany H.R. 4899, "Making Emergency Supplemental Appropriations for Disaster and Relief and Summer Jobs for the Fiscal Year Ending September 30, 2010, and for Other Purposes," pp. 64–65; DoS, "Congressional Budget Justification: Foreign Operations, FY 2011," 3/10/2010, pp. 471–476; DoS, "Congressional Budget Justification: Foreign Operations, FY 2012," 4/8/2011, p. 188.

In: Iraq: Reconstruction Lessons, Politics and Governance   ISBN: 978-1-62618-707-8
Editor: Connor E. Smits   © 2013 Nova Science Publishers, Inc.

Chapter 2

IRAQ: POLITICS, GOVERNANCE, AND HUMAN RIGHTS[*]

Kenneth Katzman

SUMMARY

Accelerating violence and growing political schisms call into question whether the fragile stability left in place in Iraq after the U.S. withdrawal from Iraq will collapse. Iraq's stability is increasingly threatened by a revolt—with both peaceful and violent aspects—by Sunni Arab Muslims who resent Shiite political domination. Sunni Arabs, always fearful that Prime Minister Nuri al-Maliki would seek unchallenged power, accuse him of attempting to marginalize them politically by arresting or attempting to remove key Sunni leaders. Sunni demonstrations have grown since late December 2012 over Maliki's moves against leading Sunni figures. Iraq's Kurds are increasingly aligned with the Sunnis, based on their own disputes with Maliki over territorial, political, and economic issues. The Shiite faction of Moqtada Al Sadr has been leaning to the Sunnis and Kurds and could hold the key to Maliki's political survival. Adding to the schisms is the physical incapacity of President Jalal Talabani, a Kurd who has served as a key mediator, who suffered a stroke in mid-December 2012. The growing rifts raise the potential for early national elections, originally due for 2014 but which could be advanced to coincide with provincial elections in April 2013.

The violent component of revolt is spearheaded by Sunni insurgents linked to Al Qaeda in Iraq (AQ-I), perhaps emboldened by the Sunni-led uprising in Syria. They have conducted numerous complex attacks against Shiite religious pilgrims and neighborhoods and Iraqi Security Force (ISF) members. The attacks are intended to reignite all-out sectarian conflict, but have failed to do so to date. There are concerns whether the ISF— which numbers nearly 700,000 members— can counter the violence now that U.S. troops are no longer in Iraq; U.S. forces left in December 2011 in line with a November 2008 bilateral U.S.-Iraq Security Agreement. The Iraqis refused to extend the presence of U.S. troops in Iraq, believing Iraq could handle violence on its own and seeking to put behind it the period of U.S. occupation and political and military tutelage.

---

[*] This is an edited, reformatted and augmented version of Congressional Research Service, Publication No. RS21968, dated January 15, 2013.

Since the U.S. pullout, U.S. training for Iraq's security forces through an Office of Security Cooperation—Iraq (OSC-I) and a State Department police development program have languished. However, the Administration—with increasing Iraqi concurrence—has asserted that the escalating violence necessitates that Iraq rededicate itself to military cooperation with and assistance from the United States. Since August 2012, Iraqi officials have requested expedited delivery of U.S. arms and joint exercises and in December 2012 signed a new defense cooperation agreement with the United States.

Although recognizing that Iraq wants to rebuild its relations in the Arab world and in its immediate neighborhood, the United States is seeking to prevent Iraq from falling under the sway of Iran. The Maliki government is inclined toward close relations with the Islamic Republic, but the legacy of Iran-Iraq hostilities, and Arab and Persian differences, limit Iranian influence. Still, Iraq has aligned with Iran's support for Bashar Al Assad's regime in Syria and may be allowing Iranian arms supply flights to reach Syria by transiting Iraqi airspace. Some see Iraq instead to reestablish its historic role as a major player in the Arab world. Iraq took a large step toward returning to the Arab fold by hosting an Arab League summit on March 27-29, 2012.

OVERVIEW OF THE POST-SADDAM POLITICAL TRANSITION

During the 2003-2011 presence of U.S. forces, Iraq completed a transition from the dictatorship of Saddam Hussein to a plural political system in which varying sects and ideological and political factions compete in elections. A series of elections began in 2005, after a one-year occupation period and a subsequent seven-month interim period of Iraqi self-governance. There has been a consensus among Iraqi elites since 2005 to give each community a share of power and prestige to promote cooperation and unity. Still, disputes over the relative claim of each community on power and economic resources permeated almost every issue in Iraq and were never fully resolved. The constant infighting among the major factions over their perceived share of power and resources has not dramatically hampered the basic functions of governing but has produced popular frustration over a failure of government to improve services.

Initial Transition and Construction of the Political System

After the fall of Saddam Hussein's regime in April 2003, the United States set up an occupation structure, reportedly based on concerns that immediate sovereignty would favor major factions and not produce democracy. In May 2003, President Bush, reportedly seeking strong leadership in Iraq, named Ambassador L. Paul Bremer to head a "Coalition Provisional Authority" (CPA), which was recognized by the United Nations as an occupation authority. Bremer discontinued a tentative political transition process and instead appointed (July 13, 2003) a non-sovereign Iraqi advisory body, the 25-member "Iraq Governing Council" (IGC). During that year, U.S. and Iraqi negotiators, advised by a wide range of international officials and experts, drafted a "Transitional Administrative Law" (TAL, interim constitution), which became effective on March 4, 2004.[1]

After about one year of occupation, the United States, following a major debate between the CPA and various Iraqi factions over the modalities and rapidity of a resumption of Iraqi sovereignty, handed sovereignty to an appointed Iraqi interim government on June 28, 2004. That date was two days ahead of the TAL-specified date of June 30, 2004, for the handing over of Iraqi sovereignty and the end of the occupation period, which also laid out the elections roadmap discussed below. The interim government was headed by a prime minister, Iyad al-Allawi, leader of the Iraq National Accord (INA), a secular, non-sectarian faction. Allawi is a Shiite Muslim but his supporters are mostly Sunni Arabs, including some former members of the Baath Party. The president was Sunni tribalist Ghazi al-Yawar.

This interim government was weak and heavily influenced by parties and factions that had long campaigned to oust Saddam. These included longstanding anti-Saddam Shiite Islamist parties, such as the Da'wa Party and the Islamic Supreme Council of Iraq (ISCI), as well as a Shiite Islamist faction loyal to radical cleric Moqtada Al Sadr that gelled as a cohesive party after Saddam's ouster and also formed an armed faction called the Mahdi Army. Also influential were the long-established Kurdish parties the Kurdistan Democratic Party (KDP) headed by Masoud Barzani, son of the late, revered Kurdish independence fighter Mullah Mustafa Barzani, and the Patriotic Union of Kurdistan (PUK) headed by Jalal Talabani.

Interim Government Formed and New Coalitions Take Shape

Iraqi leaders of all factions agreed that elections should determine the composition of Iraq's new power structure. The beginning of the elections process was set for 2005 to produce a transitional parliament that would supervise writing a new constitution, a public referendum on a new constitution, and then the election of a full term government under that constitution.

In accordance with the dates specified in the TAL, the first post-Saddam election was held on January 30, 2005. The voting was for a 275-seat transitional National Assembly (which would form an executive), four-year-term provincial councils in all 18 provinces, and a Kurdistan regional assembly (111 seats). The election for the transitional Assembly was conducted according to the "proportional representation/closed list" election system, in which voters chose among "political entities" (a party, a coalition of parties, or people). A total of 111 entities were on the national ballot, of which 9 were multi-party coalitions.

Still restive over their displacement from power in the 2003 U.S. invasion, Sunni Arabs (20% of the overall population) boycotted, winning only 17 Assembly seats, and only 1 seat on the 51-seat Baghdad provincial council. That council was dominated (28 seats) by representatives of the ISCI, then led by Abd al-Aziz al-Hakim. (In August 2003, when Abd al-Aziz's brother, Mohammad Baqr al-Hakim, was assassinated in a bombing outside a Najaf mosque, Abd al-Aziz succeeded his brother as ISCI leader. After Abd al-Aziz al-Hakim's death from lung cancer in August 2009, his son Ammar, born in 1971, succeeded him.)

Radical Shiite cleric Moqtada Al Sadr, whose armed faction was then at odds with U.S. forces, also boycotted, leaving his faction poorly represented on provincial councils in the Shiite south and in Baghdad. The resulting transitional government placed Shiites and Kurds in the highest positions—Patriotic Union of Kurdistan (PUK) leader Jalal Talabani was president and Da'wa (another Shiite Islamist party) leader Ibrahim al-Jafari was prime minister. Sunnis were Assembly speaker, deputy president, a deputy prime minister, and six ministers, including defense. Another significant longtime anti-Saddam faction was the Iraqi National Congress (INC) of Ahmad Chalabi, which had lobbied since the early 1990s for the United States to take steps to overthrow Saddam Hussein.

Permanent Constitution[2]

The elected Assembly was to draft a permanent constitution by August 15, 2005, to be put to a referendum by October 15, 2005, subject to veto by a two-thirds majority of voters in any three provinces. On May 10, 2005, a 55-member drafting committee was appointed, but with only two Sunni Arabs (15 Sunnis were later added as full members and 10 as advisors). In August 2005, the talks produced a draft, providing for:

- The three Kurdish-controlled provinces of Dohuk, Irbil, and Sulaymaniyah to constitute a legal "region" administered by the Kurdistan Regional Government (KRG), which would have its own elected president and parliament (Article 113).
- a December 31, 2007, deadline to hold a referendum on whether Kirkuk (Tamim province) would join the Kurdish region (Article 140).
- designation of Islam as "a main source" of legislation.
- all orders of the U.S.-led occupation authority (Coalition Provisional Authority, CPA) to be applicable until amended (Article 126), and a "Federation Council" (Article 62), a second chamber with size and powers to be determined in future law (not adopted to date).
- a 25% electoral goal for women (Article 47).
- families to choose which courts to use for family issues (Article 41); making only primary education mandatory (Article 34).
- having Islamic law experts and civil law judges on the federal supreme court (Article 89). Many Iraqi women opposed this and the previous provisions as giving too much discretion to male family members.
- two or more provinces to join together to form new autonomous "regions"— reaffirmed in passage of an October 2006 law on formation of regions.
- "regions" to organize internal security forces, legitimizing the fielding of the Kurds' *peshmerga* militia (Article 117). This continue a TAL provision.
- the central government to distribute oil and gas revenues from "current fields" in proportion to population, and for regions to have a role in allocating revenues from new energy discoveries (Article 109). Disputes over these concepts continue to hold up passage of national hydrocarbons legislation. Sunnis dominate areas of Iraq that have few proven oil or gas deposits, and favor centralized control of oil revenues, whereas the Kurds want to maintain maximum control of their own burgeoning energy sector.

These provisions left many disputes unresolved, particularly the balance between central government and regional and local authority. With this basic question unresolved, Sunnis registered in large numbers (70%-85%) to try to defeat the constitution, prompting a U.S.-mediated agreement (October 11, 2005): a panel would propose amendments within four months after a post-December 15 election government took office (Article 137), and the amendments would be voted on within another two months —under the same rules as the October 15 referendum. Despite that stipulation, the Sunni provinces of Anbar and Salahuddin had a 97% and 82% "no" vote, respectively, but the constitution was adopted because Nineveh province voted 55% "no," missing the threshold for three provinces to vote "no" by a two-thirds majority.

December 15, 2005, Elections

The December 15, 2005, elections were for a full-term (four-year) national government (also in line with the schedule laid out in the TAL). Under the voting mechanism used for that election, each province contributed a predetermined number of seats to a "Council of Representatives" (COR)—a formula adopted to attract Sunni participation. Of the 275-seat body, 230 seats were allocated this way, with 45 "compensatory" seats for entities that would have won additional seats had the constituency been the whole nation. There were 361 political "entities," including 19 multi-party coalitions, competing in a "closed list" voting system (in which party leaders choose the people who will actually sit in the Assembly). As shown in Table 5, voters chose lists representing their sects and regions, and the Shiites and Kurds again emerged dominant. The COR was inaugurated on March 16, 2006, but political infighting caused the Shiite bloc "United Iraqi Alliance (UIA)" to replace Jafari with another Da'wa figure, Nuri Kamal al-Maliki, as Prime Minister.

On April 22, 2006, the COR approved Talabani to continue as president. His two deputies were Adel Abd al-Mahdi (incumbent) of ISCI and Tariq al-Hashimi, leader of the Iraqi Islamic Party (IIP). Another Sunni figure, the hardline Mahmoud Mashhadani (National Dialogue Council party), became COR speaker. Maliki won COR approval of a 37-member cabinet (including two deputy prime ministers) on May 20, 2006. Three key slots (Defense, Interior, and National Security) were not filled permanently until June 2006, due to infighting. Of the 37 posts, there were 19 Shiites; 9 Sunnis; 8 Kurds; and 1 Christian. Four were women.

2006-2011: SECTARIAN CONFLICT AND U.S.-ASSISTED RECONCILIATION

The 2005 elections were, at the time, considered successful by the Bush Administration but did not resolve the Sunni-Arab grievances over their diminished positions in the power structure. However, later events suggested that the elections in 2005 might have worsened the violence by exposing and reinforcing the political weakness of the Sunni Arabs. With tensions high, the bombing of a major Shiite shrine within the Sunni-dominated province of Salahuddin in February 2006 set off major sectarian unrest, characterized in part by Sunni insurgent activities against government and U.S. troops, high-casualty suicide and other bombings, and the empowerment of Shiite militia factions to counter the Sunni acts. The sectarian violence was so serious that many experts, by the end of 2006, were considering the U.S. mission as failing, an outcome that an "Iraq Study Group" concluded was a significant possibility absent a major change in U.S. policy.[3]

Benchmarks and a Troop Surge

As assessments of possible overall U.S. policy failure multiplied, in August 2006, the Administration and Iraq agreed on a series of "benchmarks" that, if adopted and implemented, might achieve political reconciliation. Under Section 1314 of a FY2007 supplemental appropriation (P.L. 110-28), "progress" on 18 political and security benchmarks—as assessed in Administration reports due by July 15, 2007, and then

September 15, 2007—was required for the United States to provide $1.5 billion in Economic Support Funds (ESF) to Iraq. President Bush exercised the waiver provision. The law also mandated an assessment by the GAO, by September 1, 2007, of Iraqi performance on the benchmarks, as well as an outside assessment of the Iraqi security forces (ISF).

In early 2007, the United States began a "surge" of about 30,000 additional U.S. forces (bringing U.S. troop levels from their 2004-2006 baseline of about 138,000 to about 170,000 at the height of the surge) intended to blunt insurgent momentum and take advantage of growing Sunni Arab rejection of extremist groups. The Administration cited as partial justification the Iraq Study Group's recommending such a step. As 2008 progressed, citing the achievement of many of the major Iraqi legislative benchmarks and a dramatic drop in sectarian violence that was attributed to surge, the Bush Administration asserted that political reconciliation was advancing. However, U.S. officials maintained that its extent and durability would depend on the degree of implementation of adopted laws, on further compromises among ethnic groups, and on continued attenuated levels of violence. For Iraq's performance on the benchmarks, see Table 7.

Iraqi Governance During the Troop Surge: 2008-2009

The passage of Iraqi laws in 2008 considered crucial to reconciliation, continued reductions in violence accomplished by the U.S. surge, and the continued turn of many Sunni militants away from violence, facilitated political stabilization. A March 2008 offensive ordered by Maliki against the Sadr faction and other militants in Basra and environs ("Operation Charge of the Knights") pacified the city and caused many Sunnis and Kurds to see Maliki as even-handed— willing to take on radical groups even if they were Shiite. This contributed to a decision in July 2008 by the Sunni-led Accord Front to end its one-year boycott of the cabinet. During the period in which the Accord Front, the Sadr faction, and the bloc of former Prime Minister Iyad al-Allawi were boycotting, there were 13 vacancies out of 37 cabinet slots.

Empowering Local Governance: Provincial Powers Law and January 31, 2009, Provincial Elections

The first provincial elections, held January 31, 2009, continued Iraq's political stabilization. The provincial elections followed adoption in 2008 of a "provincial powers law" intended to decentralize governance by setting up powerful provincial councils that could decide local allocation of resources. The provincial councils in Iraq choose the province's governor and governing administrations. Some central government funds are given as grants directly to provincial administrations for their use, although most of Iraq's budget is controlled centrally. There have been efforts in 2012 in some provinces to consult with district and municipal level officials to assure a fair distribution of provincial resources.

The provincial elections had been planned for October 1, 2008, but were delayed when Kurdish restiveness over integrating Kirkuk into the KRG caused a presidential council veto of the July 22, 2008, election law needed to hold these elections. That draft provided for equal division of power in Kirkuk (among Kurds, Arabs, and Turkomans) until its status is finally resolved, a proposal strongly opposed by the Kurds because it would dilute their political dominance there. On September 24, 2008, the COR passed an election law, providing for the provincial elections by January 31, 2009, but putting off provincial elections in Kirkuk and the three KRG provinces.[4]

In the elections, about 14,500 candidates vied for the 440 provincial council seats in the 14 Arab-dominated provinces of Iraq. About 4,000 of the candidates were women. The average number of council seats per province was about 30,[5] down from a set number of 41 seats per province (except Baghdad) in the 2005-2009 councils. The Baghdad provincial council has 57 seats. This yielded an average of more than 30 candidates per council seat. However, the reduction in number of seats also meant that many incumbents were not reelected.

The provincial elections were conducted on an "open list" basis—voters were able to vote for a party slate, or for an individual candidate (although they also had to vote for that candidate's slate). This procedure encouraged voting for slates and strengthened the ability of political parties to choose who on their slate will occupy seats allotted for that party. This election system was widely assessed to favor larger, well-organized parties, because smaller parties might not meet the vote threshold to obtain any seats on the council in their province.[6] This was seen as likely to set back the hopes of some Iraqis that the elections would weaken the Islamist parties, both Sunni and Shiite, that have dominated post-Saddam politics.

About 17 million Iraqis (any Iraqi 18 years of age or older) were eligible for the vote, which was run by the Iraqi Higher Election Commission (IHEC). Pre-election-related violence was minimal, although five candidates were killed. There were virtually no major violent incidents on election day. Turnout was about 51%, somewhat lower than some expected. Some voters complained of being turned away at polling places because their names were not on file; others had been displaced by sectarian violence and were unable to vote in their new areas of habitation.

The vote totals were finalized on February 19, 2009, and were certified on March 29, 2009. Within 15 days of that (by April 13, 2009) the provincial councils began to convene under the auspices of the incumbent provincial governor, and to elect a provincial council chairperson and deputy chairperson. Within another 30 days after that (by May 12, 2009) the provincial councils selected (by absolute majority) a provincial governor and deputy governors. The term of the provincial councils is four years from the date of their first convention.

Outcomes: Maliki Strongest among Shiites, and Sunni Tribalists Enter Politics

The hopes of some Maliki opponents that the provincial elections would empower local authorities were dashed somewhat when Maliki's "State of Law Coalition" (a coalition composed of his Da'wa Party plus other Shiite and a few non-Shiite allies) was the clear winner of the provincial elections. With 28 out of the 57 total seats, the Maliki slate gained control of the Baghdad provincial council, and ran very strong in most of the Shiite provinces of the south, including Basra, where it won an outright majority (20 out of 35 seats). ISCI, which ran under a separate slate, won only 3 seats on the Baghdad province council, down from the 28 it held previously, and only 5 in Basra. Some observers believe that the poor showing for ISCI was a product of its perceived close ties to Iran and interest in political and economic gain for its supporters.

Although Maliki's State of Law coalition fared well, subsequent efforts to form provincial administrations demonstrated that he still needed to strike bargains with rival factions, including Sadr, ISCI, and various Sunni parties such as the IIP and the National

Dialogue Council. Aside from the victory of Maliki's slate, the unexpected strength of secular parties, such as that of former Prime Minister Allawi, corroborated the view that voters favored slates committed to Iraqi nationalism and strong central government. The provincial administrations that took shape are discussed in Table 5.

Another important trend outcome of the 2009 provincial elections was the entry of into the political process of Sunni tribal leaders ("Awakening Councils") who had recruited the "Sons of Iraq" fighters and who were widely credited for turning Iraqi Sunnis against Al Qaeda-linked extremists in Iraq. Sunni tribalists had largely stayed out of the December 2005 elections because their attention was focused primarily on the severe violence in the Sunni provinces, particularly Anbar, and because of Al Qaeda in Iraq's admonition that Sunnis stay out of the political process. However, in the 2009 provincial elections, as violence was ebbing, tribalists offered election slates and showed strength at the expense of the mostly urban Sunni parties (IIP and National Dialogue Council. The main "Iraq Awakening" tribal slate came in first in Anbar Province. In Diyala Province, hotly contested among Shiite and Sunni Arab and Kurdish slates, the provincial version of the (Sunni Arab) Accord Front edged out the Kurds for first place and subsequently led the provincial administration there.

THE MARCH 7, 2010, ELECTIONS: SHIITES FRACTURE AND SUNNIS COHERE

After his slate's strong showing in the provincial elections, Maliki was the favorite to retain his position in the March 7, 2010, COR elections. The elected COR chooses the full-term government. Maliki derived further political benefit from the U.S. implementation of the U.S.- Iraq "Security Agreement" (SA), discussed below in the section on the U.S. military mission.

However, as 2009 progressed, Maliki's image as protector of law and order was tarnished by several high-profile attacks. Realizing the potential for security lapses to reduce his chances to remain prime minister, Maliki ordered several ISF commanders questioned for lapses in connection with the major bombings in Baghdad on August 20, 2009, in which almost 100 Iraqis were killed and the buildings housing the Ministry of Finance and of Foreign Affairs were heavily damaged. Makeshift Ministry of Finance buildings were attacked again on December 7, 2009.

Politically, sensing Maliki's weakness and a more open competition for prime minister, Shiite unity broke down and a rival Shiite slate took shape as a competitor to State of Law. The "Iraqi National Alliance (INA)" formed as a coalition of ISCI, the Sadrists (faction of Moqtada Al Sadr), and other Shiite figures. The INA coalition believed that each of its component factions would draw support from their individual constituencies to produce an election victory.

To Sunni Arabs, the outwardly cross-sectarian Iraq National Movement ("Iraqiyya") of former transitional Prime Minister Iyad al-Allawi had strong appeal. There was an openly Sunni slate, leaning Islamist, called the Accordance slate led by IIP figures, but it was not expected to fare well compared to Allawi's less sectarian bloc. Some Sunni figures joined Shiite slates in order to improve their chances of winning a seat.

Table 1. Major Coalitions for 2010 National Elections

State of Law Coalition (slate no. 337)	Led by Maliki and his Da'wa Party. Included Anbar Salvation Front of Shaykh Hatim al-Dulaymi, which is Sunni, and the Independent Arab Movement of Abd al-Mutlaq al-Jabbouri. Appealed to Shiite sectarianism during the campaign by backing the exclusion of candidates with links to outlawed Baath Party.
Iraqi National Alliance (slate no. 316)	Formed in August 2009, was initially considered the most formidable challenger to Maliki's slate. Consisted mainly of his Shiite opponents and was perceived as somewhat more Islamist than the other slates. Included ISCI, the Sadrist movement, the Fadilah Party, the Iraqi National Congress of Ahmad Chalabi, and the National Reform Movement (Da'wa faction) of former Prime Minister Ibrahim al-Jafari. This slate was considered close to Ayatollah Sistani, but did not receive his formal endorsement.
Iraqi National Movement ("Iraqiyya"—slate no. 333)	Formed in October 2009. Led by former Prime Minister Iyad al-Allawi who is Shiite but his faction appeals to Sunnis, and Sunni leader Saleh al-Mutlaq (ex-Baathist who leads the National Dialogue Front). The coalition included the IIP and several powerful Sunni individuals, including Usama al-Nujaifi and Rafi al-Issawi.
Kurdistan Alliance (slate no. 372)	Competed again in 2010 as a joint KDP-PUK Kurdish list. However, Kurdish solidarity was shaken by July 25, 2009, Kurdistan elections in which a breakaway PUK faction called Change (Gorran) did unexpectedly well. Gorran ran its own separate list for the March 2010 elections. PUK's ebbing strength in the north did not jeopardize Talabani's continuation as president, although Sunnis sought that position.
Unity Alliance of Iraq (slate no. 348)	Led by Interior Minister Jawad Bolani, a moderate Shiite who has a reputation for political independence. Bolani was not previously affiliated with the large Shiite parties such as ISCI and Dawa, and was only briefly aligned with the Sadr faction (which has been strong in Bolani's home town of Amarah, in southeastern Iraq). Considered non-sectarian, this list included Sunni tribal faction led by Shaykh Ahmad Abu Risha, brother of slain leader of the Sunni Awakening movement in Anbar. The list included first post-Saddam defense minister Sadun al-Dulaymi.
Iraqi Accordance (slate no. 338)	A coalition of Sunni parties, including some breakaway leaders of the IIP. Led by Ayad al-Samarrai, then-speaker of the COR. Was viewed as a weak competitor for Sunni votes against Allawi's Iraqiyya.

Sources: Carnegie Endowment for International Peace; various press.

Election Law Dispute and Final Provisions

While coalitions formed to challenge Maliki, disputes emerged over the ground rules for the election. The holding of the elections required passage of an election law setting out the rules and parameters of the election. Under the Iraqi constitution, the elections were to be held by January 31, 2010, in order to allow 45 days before the March 15, 2010, expiry of the current COR's term. Iraq's election officials had ideally wanted a 90-day time frame between the election law passage and the election date, in order to facilitate the voter registration process.

Because the provisions of the election law (covering such issues as voter eligibility, whether to allot quota seats to certain constituencies, and the size of the next COR) shape the election outcome, the major Iraqi communities were divided over its substance and the COR repeatedly missed self-imposed deadlines to pass it. One dispute was over the election system, with many COR members leaning toward a closed list system that gives the slates the power to determine who occupies COR seats after the election. Others, backed by Grand Ayatollah Sistani, called for an open list vote, which allows voters to also vote for candidates as well as coalition slates. Each province served as a single constituency and a fixed number of seats for each province (see Table 2, for the number of seats per province).

There was also a dispute over how to apply the election in disputed Tamim (Kirkuk) province, where Kurds feared that the election law drafts would cause Kurds to be underrepresented. The version of the election law passed by the COR on November 8, 2009 (141 out of 195 COR deputies voting), called for using current food ration lists as representative of voter registration. The Kurds had sought this provision, opposing the use instead of 2005 voter lists that contained fewer Kurds. A compromise in that version of the law allowed for a process to review, for one year, complaints about fraudulent registration, thus easing Sunni and Shiite Arab fears about an excessive Kurdish vote in Kirkuk.

However, this version guaranteed only a small quota of seats for Iraqis living abroad or who are displaced—and Sunnis believed they would therefore be undercounted because it was mainly Sunnis who had fled Iraq. On this basis, deputy president Tariq al Hashimi vetoed the law on November 18, 2009, sending it back to the COR. A new version was adopted on November 23, 2009, but it was viewed as even less favorable to Sunni Arabs than the first version, because it eliminated any reserved seats for Iraqis in exile. Hashimi again threatened a veto, which he was required to exercise within 10 days. As that deadline was about to lapse, the major factions, at the urging of U.S. diplomats, adopted a new law on December 6, 2009.

Election Parameters

The compromise version, not vetoed by any member of the presidency council, provided for

- Expansion of the size of the COR to 325 total seats. Of these, 310 were allocated by province, with the constituency sizes ranging from Baghdad's 68 seats to Muthanna's 7. The COR size, in the absence of a recent census, was based on taking 2005 population figures and adding 2.8% per year growth.[7]
- The remaining 15 seats to be minority reserved seats (8) and "compensatory seats" (7)—seats allocated from "leftover" votes; votes for parties and slates that did not meet a minimum threshold to achieve any seats outright.
- No separate electoral constituency for Iraqis in exile, so Iraqis in exile had their votes counted in the provinces where these voters originated.
- An open list election system.
- An election date set for March 7, 2010.

Flashpoint: De-Baathification and Disqualification of Some Prominent Sunnis

The electoral process was at least partly intended to bring Sunni Arabs further into the political structure and to turn them away from violence and insurgency. As noted, Sunnis boycotted the January 2005 parliamentary and provincial elections but they did participate to some extent in the December 2005 parliamentary elections. This trend was jeopardized by a major dispute over candidate eligibility for the March 2010 elections. Although a Sunni boycott of the elections did not materialize, there was a Sunni Arab perception that the election might be unfair because of this dispute. The acute phase of this political crisis began in January 2010 when the Justice and Accountability Commission (JAC, the successor to the "De-Baathification Commission" that worked since the fall of Saddam to purge former Baathists from government) invalidated the candidacies of 499 individuals (out of 6,500 candidates running), spanning many different slates. The JAC was headed by Ali al-Lami, a Shiite who had been in U.S. military custody during 2005- 2006 for alleged assistance to

Iranian agents active in Iraq. He was perceived as answerable to or heavily influenced by Ahmad Chalabi, who had headed the De-Baathification Commission. Both were part of the Iraqi National Alliance slate and both are Shiites, leading many to believe that the disqualifications represented an attempt to exclude prominent Sunnis from the vote.

The JAC argued that the disqualifications were based on law and not based on sect, even though most of the candidates disqualified were Shiites. The IHEC reviewed and backed the invalidations on January 14, 2010; disqualified candidates had three days to file an appeal in court. Apparently due in part to entreaties from Vice President Joseph Biden (during a visit to Iraq on January 22, 2010) and partner countries —all of which feared a return to instability— the appeals court ruled that disqualified candidates could run in the election and clear up questions of Baathist affiliation afterwards. However, about 300 disqualified candidates had already been replaced by other candidates on their respective slates. The slate most affected by the disqualifications was Iraqiyya, because two of its leading candidates, National Dialogue Front party leader Saleh al-Mutlaq and Dhafir al-Ani, both Sunnis, were replaced on their slates. Still, the slate campaigned vigorously, hoping to use high turnout to achieve political results. Even the JAC's disqualification of an additional 55 mostly Iraqiyya candidates the night before the election did not prompt a Sunni boycott.

The crisis appeared to prompt the February 16, 2010, comments by General Ray Odierno, then the top U.S. commander in Iraq (who was replaced as of September 1, 2010, by his deputy, General Lloyd Austin), that Iran was working through Chalabi and al-Lami to undermine the legitimacy of the elections. General Odierno specifically asserted that the two were working with Iraqi allies of General Qasem Soleimani, commander of the Qods Force unit of Iran's Islamic Revolutionary Guard Corps (IRGC).[8] Chalabi's successful efforts to turn the election into a campaign centered on excluding ex-Baathists—which Sunnis view as a codeword for their sect— caused particular U.S. alarm. (Lami was assassinated on May 26, 2011, presumably by Sunnis who viewed him as an architect of the perceived discrimination. Chalabi, a member of parliament as of the 2010 elections, initially replaced Lami as manager of the JAC, but Maliki dismissed Chalabi, appointing instead the minister for human rights to serve in that role concurrently.)

Election and Results

About 85 total coalitions were accredited for the March 7, 2010, election. There were about 6,170 total candidates running on all these slates and, as noted, Iraqis were able to vote for individual candidates as well as overall slates. The major blocs are depicted in Table 1. All available press reports indicated that campaigning was vibrant and vigorous. Total turnout was about 62%, according to the IHEC, although somewhat lower than that in Baghdad because of the multiple insurgent bombings that took place just as voting was starting.

The final count was announced on March 26, 2010, by the IHEC. As noted in Table 2, Iraqiyya won a plurality of seats, winning a narrow two-seat margin over Maliki's State of Law slate. The Iraqi constitution (Article 73) mandates that the COR "bloc with the largest number" of members gets the first opportunity to form a government.

On that basis, Allawi, leader of the Iraqiyya slate, demanded the first opportunity to form a government. However, on March 28, 2010, Iraq's Supreme Court ruled that a coalition that forms after the election could be deemed to meet that requirement, essentially denying Allawi the first opportunity to form a government.

The vote was to have been certified by April 22, 2010, but factional disputes delayed the certification. On March 21, 2010, before the count was final, Prime Minister Maliki issued a statement, referring to his role as armed forces commander-in-chief, demanding the IHEC respond to requests from various blocs for a manual recount of all votes.

The IHEC responded that a comprehensive recount would take an extended period of time. Several international observers, including then-U.N. Special Representative for Iraq Ad Melkert (and head of the U.N. Assistance Mission—Iraq, UNAMI), indicated that there was no cause to suggest widespread fraud. (Melkert was replaced in September 2011 by Martin Kobler.)

After appeals of some of the results, Iraq's Supreme Court certified the results on June 1, 2010, triggering the following timelines:

- Fifteen days after certification (by June 15, 2010), the new COR was to be seated and to elect a COR speaker and deputy speaker. (The deadline to convene was met, although, as noted, the COR did not elect a leadership team and did not meet again until November 11, 2010.)
- After electing a speaker, but with no deadline, the COR is to choose a president (by a two-thirds vote). (According to Article 138 of the Iraqi constitution, after this election, Iraq is to have a president and at least one vice president—the "presidency council" concept was an interim measure that expired at the end of the first full-term government.)
- Within another 15 days, the largest COR bloc is tapped by the president to form a government. (The selection of a president occurred on November 11, 2010, and Maliki was formally tapped to form a cabinet on November 25, 2010.)
- Within another 30 days (by December 25, 2010), the prime minister-designate is to present a cabinet to the COR for confirmation (by majority vote).

Post-Election Government

In accordance with timelines established in the Constitution, the newly elected COR convened on June 15, 2010, but the session ended after less than a half hour without electing a COR leadership team. Under Article 52 of the Constitution, the "eldest member" of the COR (Kurdish legislator Fouad Massoum) became acting COR speaker. During the period when no new government was formed, the COR remained inactive, with most COR members in their home provinces while still collecting their $10,000 per month salaries. The resentment over this contributed to the popular unrest in February 2011.

Allawi's chances of successfully forming a government appeared to suffer a substantial setback in May 2010 when Maliki's slate and the rival Shiite INA bloc formed a broader "National Alliance." However, this coalition was not able to immediately agree to a prime minister selectee and the COR aborted its second meeting scheduled for July 27, 2010. The various factions made little progress through August 2010, as Maliki insisted he remain prime minister for another term and remained in a caretaker role.

With the end of the U.S. combat mission on August 31, 2010, approaching, the United States reportedly stepped up its involvement in political talks. Some discussions were held between Maliki and Allawi's bloc on a U.S.-proposed formulas under which Allawi, in return for supporting Maliki, would head a new council that would have broad powers as a check and balance on the post of prime minister. Alternate proposals had Allawi being given the presidency, although the Kurds refused to cede that post to another community, fearing loss of leverage on other demands. An expectation that the August 10-September 11, 2010, Ramadan period would enable the blocs to reach an agreement was not met.

Part of the difficulty forming a government was the close result, and the dramatic implications of gaining or retaining power in Iraq, where politics is often seen as a "winner take all" proposition. Others blamed Allawi for the impasse, claiming that he was insisting on a large, powerful role for himself even though he could not assemble enough COR votes to achieve a majority there.

Agreement on a New Government Reached ("Irbil Agreement")

On October 1, 2010, Maliki received the backing of most of the 40 COR Sadrist deputies. The United States reportedly was alarmed at the prospect that Maliki might be able to form a government primarily by allying with Sadrist, but they, Allawi, and the Sunni Arab regional states acquiesced to a second Maliki term. The key question that remained was whether Maliki would agree to form a broad based government that met the demands of Iraqiyya for substantial Sunni Arab inclusion. Illustrating the degree to which the Kurds reclaimed their former role of "kingmakers," Maliki, Allawi, and other Iraqi leaders met in the capital of the Kurdistan Regional Government-administered region in Irbil on November 8, 2010, to continue to negotiate on a new government. (Sadr did not attend the meeting in Irbil, but ISCI/Iraq National Alliance slate leader Ammar Al Hakim did.)

On November 10, 2010, with reported direct intervention by President Obama, the "Irbil Agreement" was reached in which (1) Allawi agreed to support Maliki and Talabani to remain in their offices for another term; (2) Iraqiyya would be extensively represented in government—one of its figures would become COR Speaker, another would be defense minister, and another (presumably Allawi himself) would chair the enhanced oversight body discussed above, though renamed the "National Council for Strategic Policies;"[9] and (3) amending the de-Baathification laws that had barred some Iraqis, such as Saleh al-Mutlaq, from holding political positions. Observers praised the agreement because it included all major factions and was signed with KRG President Masoud Barzani and then U.S. Ambassador to Iraq James Jeffrey in attendance. The agreement did not specify concessions to the Sadr faction.

2010-2014 Government Formed[10]

At the November 11, 2010, COR session to implement the agreement, Iraqiyya figure Usama alNujaifi (brother of controversial Nineveh Governor Atheel Nujaifi) was elected COR speaker, as agreed. However, Allawi and most of his bloc walked out after three hours over the refusal of the other blocs to readmit the three Iraqiyya members who had been disqualified from running for the COR (see above). The remaining COR members were sufficient for a quorum and Talabani was re-elected president after two rounds of voting. Fears were further calmed on November 13, 2010, when most of Allawi's bloc attended the COR session and continued to implement the settlement agreement; Allawi himself did not attend. On November 25, 2010, Talabani formally tapped Maliki as the prime minister-designate, giving him 30 days (until December 25, 2010) to name and achieve majority COR confirmation for a new cabinet.

Governmental formation advanced on December 19, 2010, when Allawi reaffirmed his intent to join the government. His cooperation came when the COR voted (with barely a quorum achieved after a Shiite walkout) to reinstate to politics the three barred members of his bloc, discussed above. Mutlaq was subsequently named one of three deputy prime ministers.

On December 21, 2010, in advance of the December 25, 2010, deadline, Maliki presented a cabinet to the COR (42 seats, including the posts of prime minister, 3 deputy prime ministers, and 38 ministries and ministers of state) receiving broad approval. No permanent appointments were named for seven ministries. Still, the government formed was inclusive of all major factions. Among major outcomes were the following:

- As for the State of Law list, Maliki remained prime minister, and retained for himself the Defense, Interior, and National Security (minister of state) posts pending permanent nominees for those positions. The faction took seven other cabinet posts, in addition to the post of first vice president (Khudair al Khuzai of the Da'wa Party) and deputy prime minister for energy issues (Hussein Shahristani, previously the oil minister).
- For Iraqiyya, in addition to Mutlaq becoming a deputy prime minister, Tariq al-Hashimi remained a vice president (second of three). The bloc also obtained nine ministerial posts, including the key Finance Ministry (Rafi al-Issawi, previously a deputy prime minister).
- For the Iraqi National Alliance, a senior figure, Adel Abdul Mahdi, remained a vice president (third of three). The alliance also obtained 13 cabinet positions, parceled out among its various factions. An INA technocrat, Abd al Karim Luaibi, was appointed oil minister. A Fadilah party member, Bushra Saleh, became minister of state without portfolio and the only woman in the cabinet until the February 13, 2011, naming of Ibtihal Al Zaidy as minister of state for women's affairs (not an INA member). Another Fadila activist was named minister of justice.
- Of the 13 INA cabinet seats, Sadr faction members headed eight ministries, including Housing, Labor and Social Affairs, Ministry of Planning (Ali Abd alNabi, appointed in April 2011), and Tourism and Antiquities. A Sadrist also became one of two deputy COR speakers. The Sadrists received additional influence when one of its members subsequently became governor of Maysan Province.
- The Kurdistan Alliance received major posts. Talabani stayed President; and the third deputy prime minister is Kurdish figure (PUK faction) Rows Shaways, who has served in various central and KRG positions since the fall of Saddam. Arif Tayfour is second deputy COR speaker. Alliance members had six other cabinet seats, including longtime Kurdish (KDP) stalwart Hoshyar Zebari remaining as foreign minister (a position he's held since the transition governments that followed the fall of Saddam). Khairallah Hassan Babakir, was named trade minister in a February 13, 2011, group of ministerial appointments.

POST-U.S. WITHDRAWAL POLITICAL UNRAVELING

The agreements that led to the 2010 government formation did not resolve the underlying differences among the major communities. Subsequent disputes, particularly between Maliki and the Iraqiyya bloc of Iyad al-Allawi tarnished the U.S. assessment that Iraqi factions would continue to share power. The unraveling of the Irbil Agreement in the immediate aftermath of the December 18, 2011, U.S. withdrawal cast some doubt on President Obama's assertion, marking the U.S. withdrawal, that Iraq is now "sovereign, stable, and self-reliant." The sections below also discuss the various disagreements and their causes.

Disputes over Maliki's Attempts to Monopolize Power

The central assertion of Maliki's opponents is that he seeks to centralize power in his own and his faction's hands. His attempts to purge leading Sunni Arabs from government are discussed below in the context of the post-U.S. withdrawal political crisis, but Sunnis are not the only group criticizing Maliki on this basis. The criticisms are discussed below.

- *Security Ministerial Appointments.* Maliki's critics accuse him of monopolizing control of the major security posts. Maliki refuted Allawi's interpretation of the Irbil Agreement as requiring appointment of an Iraqiyya official as defense minister, asserting that the appointee could be any Sunni Arab, not necessarily a member of the Iraqiyya faction. With this dispute unresolved, Maliki appointed allies and associates as acting ministers of Defense, of Interior, and of National Security. Sadun Dulaymi—a Sunni Arab member of the Iraq Unity Alliance, not Iraqiyya—is acting Defense Minister. Falih al-Fayad, a Shiite in the faction of former Prime Minister Ibrahim al-Jafari, is acting Minister of State for National Security. Adnan al-Asadi, another Shiite aligned with Maliki, is acting interior minister. No permanent choices for any of these posts have been nominated to date.
- *Direct Control Over Security Forces.* Maliki's critics have long asserted that he has sought to exercise direct control over the security forces and to use them for political purposes. In 2008, he began to restructure security organs to report to his office rather than the Defense or Interior ministries. Through his Office of the Commander-in-Chief, he commands direct command of the National Counterterrorism Force (about 10,000 personnel) as well as the Baghdad Brigade, responsible for security in the capital. Reports quoting U.S. commanders in Iraq in June 2011 said that lower-level commanders routinely bypass the official chain of command and report directly to Maliki's office. On at least one occasion, he has ordered tanks deployed around the homes and offices of an opponent. In August 2012, Maliki formed a "Tigris Operations Command" composed of Arab troops in the north which the Kurds viewed as a Maliki attempt to exercise control over Kurd-Arab disputed areas.
- *National Council for Strategic Policies.* Another issue, although raised seldom as of early 2013, was stalemate over the formation of the National Council for Strategic Policies—a key provision of the Irbil Agreement. Proposals from those sympathetic to Allawi called for the council to include the prime minister, president, their deputies, and a representative of all major blocs—and for decisions of the council to be binding if they achieve support of 80% of the council members. Allawi refused to chair the body unless it was given significant authorities. Maliki and his supporters wanted this council to have as few powers as possible, and the concept was not voted on by the COR.

- *Blockage of Sunni Moves to Form Separate Regions.* In late 2011, local Sunni leaders attempted to use legal mechanisms to reduce central government control. The provincial council of the mostly Sunni province of Salahuddin (which contains Tikrit) voted on October 28, 2011, to start the process of forming a separate "region." Overwhelmingly Sunni Anbar province followed suit. The mixed province of Diyala took a similar step on December 12, 2011, setting off protests by Shiites in the province who might have been instigated by the Shiite-dominated central government. Previously, the mostly Shiite provinces of Basra and Wasit had begun similar processes, although doing so requires parliamentary concurrence and a popular referendum of approval. The Maliki government has essentially ignored these votes and did not task the Independent Higher Election Commission (IHEC), which is a central government body, to organize the referenda needed as part of the region formation process. The IHEC is subject to Maliki's control, giving him a de-facto veto over the region formation process.
- *Exercise of Control Over Independent Bodies.* Maliki's critics assert that he has tried to put under his executive control several independent bodies. In late 2010, he requested that Iraq's Supreme Court rule that several independent commissions— including the Independent Higher Election Commission and the anti-corruption commission—be supervised by the cabinet. The court ruled in Maliki's favor on January 23, 2011, although the court also said in its ruling that the institutions must remain free of political interference.[11] In March 2012, Maliki also asserted governmental control over another institution that was to be independent—the Central Bank. In October 2012, Maliki fired the Central Bank governor for allegedly allowing unauthorized bulk transfers of foreign currency out of the country.

Political Crisis Begins Immediately after U.S. Withdrawal Completion

The political disputes discussed above intensified as U.S. forces drew down until the final withdrawal on December 18, 2011. As the last U.S. forces were exiting, and even as Maliki visited Washington, DC, on December 12, 2011, to meet with President Obama, the carefully constructed political power-sharing arrangements broke down. As a part of what Sunni Iraqis— and also KRG President Barzani—have called a clear power grab by Maliki, Iraq has been experiencing its worst political crisis since the U.S. invasion of 2003. Still, Iraqi factions have, in the past, cobbled together agreements when faced with the alternative of political collapse.

As the U.S. withdrawal completion approached, fears of some Sunnis were inflamed in October and November 2011 by a series of arrests by security forces. About 600 Sunnis were arrested, ostensibly for involvement in a coup plot alleged by the new leaders of Libya. Some Sunnis were reportedly purged from the security forces, and 140 faculty members from the University of Tikrit (Saddam's home town) were removed for alleged Baathist associations. Many of the latter have since been reinstated. These sentiments continue to plague post-U.S. presence Iraq.

The day of the final U.S. withdrawal (December 18, 2011), Maliki asked the COR to vote no confidence against Deputy Prime Minister Saleh al-Mutlaq, a senior Sunni Iraqiyya figure. That day, Iraqiyya parliamentarians walked out of the COR and most of the Iraqiyya members of the cabinet suspended their work. On December 19, 2011, the government announced an arrest warrant against Vice President Tariq al-Hashimi, another major Iraqiyya figure, accusing him of ordering his security staff to commit acts of assassination. Three such guards were shown on television "confessing" to assassinating rival politicians at Hashimi's behest. Hashimi fled to the KRG region for meetings with President Talabani and refused to return to face trial in Baghdad, as is demanded by the judiciary, unless his conditions for a fair trial there were met. His trial in absentia began in Baghdad in May 2012 and the court convicted and sentenced him to death on September 9, 2012, for the killing of two Iraqis. There was not an international outcry over the verdict and sentence suggesting that Maliki succeeded, to some extent, in convincing international servers that there is evidence to support the allegations. Hashimi remains in Turkey, where he eventually fled, meaning there is virtually no chance the death sentence will ever be implemented. During January 19-20, 2012, security forces raided the homes of two Sunni politicians in Diyala province and arrested the Sunni vice chairman of the Baghdad provincial council.

Mid-2012: The Crisis Produces Failed Attempt to Vote out Maliki

Sensing possible political unraveling, U.S. officials intervened diplomatically during 2012, initially succeeding in containing the crisis. Iraqiyya COR deputies resumed their duties in late January 2012 and Iraqiyya ministers returned to their offices on February 8, 2012. For his part, Maliki arranged the release of some of the Baathists arrested in early 2012 and he agreed to legal amendments to give provinces more autonomy over their budgets and the right of consent when national security forces are deployed.[12]

By March 2012, the factions tentatively agreed to hold a "national conference," to be chaired by President Talabani, the purpose of which would be to achieve durable solutions to the outstanding fundamental Sunni-Shiite-Kurdish issues. A "preparatory committee" was named to establish an agenda and format, but the committee repeatedly failed to meet. However, March 20, 2012 comments by KRG President Barzani, accusing Maliki of a "power grab" by harnessing control of the security forces dimmed prospects for holding the conference. On April 1, 2012, Maliki nonetheless formally issued invitations to the major factions to convene on April 5, 2012. Barzani kept intact his plans to visit the United States at that time and the conference was not held, nor was a new date for it set.

With attempts to repair the rifts failing, during April 27-28, Maliki critics met in the KRG region at the invitation of Barzani. Also attending the meetings were Iraqiyya leader Allawi, Iraqiyya member and COR speaker Osama Nujaifi, and Moqtada Al Sadr, in what reportedly was his first ever visit to the Kurdish north. At the conclusion of the meetings, the four reportedly issued a letter to Maliki threatening a vote of no-confidence within 15 days unless he adheres to the "principles and framework" of a more democratic approach to governance.

During late May and early June 2012, the Maliki opponents obtained the signature of 176 deputies requesting a no-confidence vote. Under Article 61 of the constitution, signatures of only 20% of the 325 COR deputies (65 signatures) are needed to trigger a vote, but President Talabani, who is required to present a valid request to the COR to hold the vote, determined that factions must demonstrate they have enough support to win such a vote. On June 10, 2012, Talabani stated that there were only 160 valid signatures, after some deputies asked their signatures be removed. On that basis he declined to ask the COR to go forward with the no-confidence vote. Some experts attributed the signature withdrawals to pressure by Iran, through the Sadr faction, to keep Maliki in office.[13] Some Maliki opponents may have been dissuaded from continuing the effort by Maliki's counter-threat to call early national elections, suggesting that the crisis might have bolstered Maliki's popularity with his Shiite base. On the other hand, one rival Shiite leader, ISCI's leader Ammar al-Hakim, proved an able and successful mediator, perhaps in an effort to position himself for national leadership in the future elections.

In part to cause the no-confidence vote effort to falter, or to calm the political situation in general, Maliki reached out to Sunni leaders. Deputy Prime Minister Saleh al-Mutlaq resumed his duties, signaling an end to another of Maliki's efforts against Sunni leadership figures. And, Iraqi news sources said that Maliki was able to at least temporarily win the support of two other senior Iraqiyya figures in early September 2012—COR Speaker Nujaifi and Finance Minister Rafi alIssawi. On the other hand, Minister of Communications Mohammad al-Allawi, an Iraqiyya member, resigned in late August 2012 in protest of what he said was Maliki's interference in the work of his ministry.

Crisis Intensifies as 2013 Begins, Triggered by Move against Another Key Sunni

As many experts predicted, Maliki's outreach to Sunni leaders was either temporary or insincere, and a new crisis flared immediately after the widely respected political mediator President Talabani suffered a stroke on December 18, 2012. The day he was flown out of Iraq for treatment on December 20, 2012, Maliki again moved against his perceived Sunni adversaries with the arrest of ten bodyguards of Finance Minister Rafi al-Issawi. That move again ignited broad Sunni fears and touched off immediate anti-Maliki demonstrations—some large—in the major Sunnis cities of Anbar, Salahuddin, and Nineveh provinces, as well as in Baghdad. Although the thrust of the unrest was based on perceived discrimination against Sunnis by the Maliki-dominated central government, some demonstrators used the protests to express their grievances over continued shortfalls in government services. Some protesters carried pictures of ousted dictator Saddam Hussein, prompting Maliki to warn that "former regime" elements might take advantage of the protests and to threaten measures to end the protests. On January 7, 2013, ISF members fired into the air to disperse protests. The demonstrator have essentially blocked the roads leading from Iraq to Jordan. Violent Sunni elements have taken advantage of the unrest, for example by organizing a breakout of AQ-I and other Sunni insurgent figures from a prison at Taji on January 11, 2013.

Politically, the new Sunni unrest sparked by the Issawi bodyguard arrests may jeopardize Maliki's prime ministership. Allawi and Saleh al-Mutlaq have called on Maliki to resign and, in a potentially ominous sign for Maliki, Moqtada Al Sadr has shown cracks in Shiite solidarity by supporting the demonstrators. In the COR, as of January 9, 2013, more than the required twenty five deputes had signed on to a formal request for Maliki to appear before the COR to answer questions about the unrest. As part of his political attempts to calm the demonstrations and divide his opponents, Maliki has raised the possibility of calling elections earlier than the planned 2014 timeframe—perhaps concurrent with the April 2013 provincial elections (which are discussed below).[14] Maliki has tried to mollify the protesters by releasing some imprisoned Sunnis, including 300 released on January 14, 2013.

Also unresolved—and perhaps adding to the unrest—is the incapacity of President Talabani. Because first vice president al-Hashimi has been convicted and sentenced, second vice president Khudayr Khuzai, a Shiite has become acting president while Talabani recovers. This has raised fears that Maliki will try to engineer (through allies in the COR) the permanent replacement of Talabani, a Kurd, with a Shiite (Khuzai). Doing so would upend the informal factional and ethnic balance in the top tiers of government, and add substantial

Kurdish unrest to that in the Sunni community. And, Talabani's incapacity has removed from the scene his substantial capacity to mediate resolutions among the major factions.

The Crisis and Upcoming Elections

The political crisis threatened to have adverse effects on several upcoming elections in Iraq. The mandate of the current nine-member IHEC expired at the end of April 2012. The April 12, 2012, arrest of the IHEC chairman, Faraj al-Haidari, threatened to complicate the naming of a new panel, but he was released and had resumed his duties by April 15, 2012. In late April, the IHEC's mandate was extended by three months, and the COR confirmed a new panel in September 2012. The IHEC is needed to run the upcoming elections scheduled or possible.

April 2013 Provincial Elections

As noted above, the terms of the provincial councils are four years, mandating the elections in the central government controlled provinces in early 2013. On October 30, 2012, the Iraqi cabinet set a date for these elections as April 21, 2013. They will not be held in the KRG-controlled provinces. The deadline for party registration expired on November 25, 2012, and the IHEC subsequently published a list of 261 political entities that registered to run. The registrants suggest that both the large Sunni as well as Shiite coalitions— including Maliki's—have fractured somewhat and their constituent parties are running separately. Candidate registration is due by December 25, 2012. The seat distribution per province has changed little from the 2009 election, but there is still an institutional dispute over the electoral law that will govern these elections.

KRG Elections

Provincial elections in the KRG-controlled provinces were not held during the January 2009 provincial elections in the other areas of Iraq, nor were they held during the March 7, 2010, COR vote. These elections had been scheduled for September 27, 2012, but a June 2012 KRG announcement postponement them indefinitely because the IHEC ruled that Christian voters could only vote for Christian candidates, a ruling the Kurds said restricted the rights of minorities living in the KRG. The Iraqi National Assembly has not enacted an election law to govern these KRG elections and no date for them is scheduled.

Kirkuk Referendum

There is also to be a vote on a Kirkuk referendum at some point, if a negotiated settlement is reached. However, a settlement does not appear within easy reach as of early 2012 and no referendum is scheduled.

District and Sub-District Elections

District and sub-district elections throughout Iraq were previously slated for July 31, 2009. However, those have been delayed as well, and no date has been announced.

Constitutional Amendments

There could also be a vote on amendments to Iraq's 2005 constitution if and when the major factions agree to finalize the recommendations of the constitutional review commission

(CRC). There has been no movement on this issue for at least three years, and no indication such a referendum will be held in the near future.

Next COR Elections

The term of the existing COR expires no later than early 2014. That schedule could change if the political crisis leads to early elections, as discussed above. If there were a decision to hold the COR elections concurrent with the April 2013 provincial elections, the COR would need to act quickly on an election law governing the COR vote.

Broader Sunni Community Grievances and Escalating Violence

The 2012-2013 Sunni unrest has again exposed the simmering, unresolved sense among Sunnis that they are now "second-class citizens" in Iraq. The political disputes are discussed above, but there is also a violent component to the Sunni grievances.

Sunni Insurgent Violence/Al Qaeda in Iraq (AQ-I) and Naqshabandis

The continuing Sunni resentment of the distribution of power might account for some of the high-profile attacks that continue in Iraq, including those carried out by Al Qaeda in Iraq (AQ-I). U.S. officials estimated in November 2011 that there might be 800-1,000 people in Al Qaeda-Iraq's network, of which many are involved in media or finance of operations.[15] An antecedent of AQ-I was named by the United States as a Foreign Terrorist Organization (FTO) in March 2004 and the designation applies to AQ-I.

Since then, AQ-I and other Sunni insurgent groups have escalated their attacks with numerous high-profile suicide and other attacks. The primary targets have been Shiite religious pilgrims and Shiite neighborhoods, as well as members and installations of the Iraqi Security Forces (ISF). These attacks are perceived as an effort by Sunni insurgents and AQ-I to undermine Maliki's leadership; to retaliate against his perceived actions against Sunnis; to undermine the confidence of the ISF; and to possibly reignite sectarian conflict. The attacks have not, to any significant extent, accomplished those objectives to date. Some assert that AQ-I and other Sunni insurgent groups have been emboldened by the civil conflict in Syria, in which Sunni insurgents are challenging the Assad regime, which is linked to Shiite Iran. In sympathy with the Sunni-led "Free Syrian Army" armed opposition in Syria, some Iraqi groups have begun referring to themselves as the "Free Iraqi Army."

As examples of escalating violence, on February 7, 2012, the AQ-I affiliate Islamic State of Iraq claimed responsibility for two attacks on Shiites—January 5 and January 14, 2012—that killed 78 and 53 Shiite pilgrims, respectively. On February 23, March 20, April 19, June 12, and July 4, 2012, AQ-I conducted multiple-city, complex attacks that killed 50, 40, 35, 65, and 50 people, respectively.

Attacks later in the summer of 2012 were even more deadly. On July 23, 2012, AQ-I conducted numerous attacks in several cities, killing about 115 Iraqis; the attacks came a day after AQ-I leader Abu Bakr Al Baghdadi announced a "Breaking Down Walls" offensive against government targets. Shortly thereafter, Iraqi insurgents downed an Iraqi helicopter. In late July 2012, the AQ-I offensive compelled 15 Diyala Province "*mukhtars*"—chosen community liaisons with the central government—to resign, claiming the government is not able to protect them. In mid-August, AQ-I insurgents briefly captured a local government building in Haditha (Anbar Province) and raised an Al Qaeda battle flag over it. On August 17, 2012, 93 Iraqis, mostly in Shiite areas, were killed in a wide range of attacks around Iraq. On September 9, 2012, bombings in numerous cities, and attributed to AQ-I, again killed more than 100 Iraqis. Another 26 Iraqis were killed on September 30, 2012, a few days after insurgents attacked a jail in the Sunni-inhabited town of Tikrit (Saddam Hussein's home town) and freed 47 suspected AQ-I militants. Observers say that more Iraqis (more than 200) were killed in militant attacks in September 2012 than any time in the past two years. On November 6, 2012, a blast at a military base in Taji, north of Baghdad, killed more than two dozen persons seeking to be recruited into the ISF. On November 30, 2012, and despite optimism over relative calms during the Shiite commemoration of Ashura one week earlier, bombings in several cities killed 48 persons, mostly Shiites. A total of 32 Shiite pilgrims were killed in multiple incidents around Iraq on January 4, 2013. A member of the COR was killed by a suicide bomber on January 15, 2013.

Prior to the spate of major attacks in summer of 2012, U.S. officials asserted that, by U.S. measures of "security incidents" (attacks against diplomats, the government, or civilians) levels of violence had not increased since the U.S. pullout, and remained roughly at a post-2003 low of about 100 such incidents per week. However, the intensity of the summer 2012 attacks produced a reassessment of that analysis. A visit to Iraq by Chairman of the Joint Chiefs of Staff Martin Dempsey on August 21, 2012, appeared intended to respond to Iraqi overtures to re-engage of some of the U.S. military and police training programs that have languished throughout 2012— overtures motivated by increasing Iraqi nervousness about the ability of the Iraq Security Forces (ISF) to prevent further such incidents. This issue is discussed further below.

Many Iraqi Sunnis do not want the AQ-I campaigns to succeed and are inclined to work with the government against AQ-I. In early 2012, more than 60 leaders of tribes in Sunni-dominated areas of Iraq—with the concurrence of local government and security officials—reached agreement to authorize tribal leaders to enforce strict codes of justice against insurgents and their accomplices. Suggesting that the attacks may be intended to dissuade moderate Sunnis from engaging with the government, one such moderate Sunni cleric, Shaykh Mahdi al-Sumaidaie, was seriously injured in a bomb attack against his convoy on August 19, 2012.

Since early 2012, there have been indications that AQ-I might be intervening in the unrest in Syria.[16] Director of National Intelligence James Clapper testified on February 16, 2012, that it might have been responsible for several suicide bombings against security targets in Damascus.

Iraq's position on the Syria unrest is discussed in greater detail below. In July 2012, Iraqi Foreign Minister Hoshyar Zebari corroborated the U.S. accusations about AQ-I movement into Syria. Other press reports indicate that, in late October 2012, Jordanian authorities disrupted a plot by AQ-I to bomb multiple targets in Amman, Jordan, possibly including the U.S. Embassy there. On December 11, 2012, the United States designated a Syrian jihadist rebel group, the Al Nusrah Front, as a Foreign Terrorist Organization (FTO), asserting that it is an alias of AQ-I.

Another Sunni group, linked to ex-Baathists, is the Naqshabandi faction, based in northern Iraq. Former Ambassador-nominee to Iraq Brett McGurk said in his June 6, 2012, confirmation hearings that the Naqshabandis are responsible for most of the attacks on U.S. diplomatic facilities in northern Iraq (particularly Kirkuk), although such attacks number only about 2-3 per week, a relatively low level compared to periods at the height of the U.S. military mission in Iraq. The attacks might have contributed to the State Department decision in mid-2012 to close the Kirkuk consulate.

Sons of Iraq Fighters

Another Sunni grievance has been the slow pace with which the Maliki government implemented its pledge to fully integrate the approximately 100,000 "Sons of Iraq" fighters (former insurgents who ended their fight and cooperated with U.S. forces against Al Qaeda in Iraq and other militants) into the Iraqi Security Forces (ISF) or provide them with government jobs. During 2009 and 2010, there were repeated reports that some Sons of Iraq had been dropped from payrolls, harassed, arrested, or sidelined, and that the Maliki government might want to strangle the program. However, according to Ambassador-nominee Brett McGurk in confirmation hearings on June 6, 2012, about 70,000 have been integrated into the ISF or given civilian government jobs, while 30,000 continue to man checkpoints in Sunni areas and are paid about $300 per month by the government.

KRG-Central Government Disputes[17]

Since the end of the U.S.-led war to liberate Kuwait in early 1991, the United States has played a role of protecting Iraq's Kurds from the central government. Iraq's Kurds have tried to preserve this "special relationship" with the United States and use it to their advantage. Iraq's Kurdish leaders have long said they do not seek outright independence or affiliation with Kurds in neighboring countries, but the Iraqi Kurds seek to preserve and expand on the autonomy they have achieved. The issues dividing the KRG and Baghdad include not only KRG autonomy but also disputes over territory and resources, particularly the ability of the KRG to export its oil. That difference underpins KRG-Baghdad disagreements over proposed national oil laws. The KRG has a directly elected President, Masoud Barzani, and elected Kurdistan National Assembly, and an appointed Prime Minister. Since January 2012, the KRG Prime Minister has been Nechirvan Barzani (Masoud's nephew), who returned to that post after three years in which the post was held by PUK senior figure Barham Salih.

To ensure their autonomy, the two main Kurdish factions (Patriotic Union of Kurdistan, PUK, and Kurdistan Democratic Party, KDP) continue to field their own force of *peshmerga* (Kurdish militiamen) numbering perhaps 75,000 fighters. They are generally lightly armed. Kurdish leaders continue to criticize Maliki for opposing paying the *peshmerga* out of the national budget, leaving the KRG to fund its operations. KRG President Barzani, during his U.S. visit in April 2012, discussed the reform of the *peshmerga* into a smaller but more professional and well trained force.

The increasing disillusionment of Kurdish leaders with Maliki could produce lasting political realignment. During 2012, Kurdish leaders have adopted the Sunni Arab criticisms of Maliki. KRG President Masoud Barzani, who was directly elected by the residents of the Kurdish region in July 2009, hinted at a potential break with Maliki on March 20, 2012, accusing him of monopolizing power. Following a visit to Washington, DC, in early April 2012, Barzani indirectly threatened to allow a vote on Kurdish independence unless Maliki resolves the major issues with the KRG. [18] In June 2012, the Kurds in the COR joined Iraqiyya in an unsuccessful to oust Maliki through a no confidence vote. This joint effort came despite Iraqi Kurdish hesitancy to side with the Sunni Arabs because of the legacy of repression of the Kurds by Saddam Hussein and other Sunni Iraqi leaders in the past.

In late 2012, the growing KRG-Baghdad animosity nearly produced all-out violent conflict between the KRG and Baghdad. In August 2012, as noted above, Maliki formed a Tigris Operational Command out of ISF units in the north. In mid-November 2012, a commercial dispute between an Arab and Kurd in Tuz Khurmatu, a town straddling the Baghdad-KRG territorial border, caused a clash and a buildup of ISF and Kurdish troops facing off. Several weeks of U.S. and intra-Iraq mediation resulted in a tentative agreement on December 6, 2012, for both sides to pull back their forces and for local ethnic groups to form units to replace ISF and *peshmerga* units along the Baghdad-KRG frontier. The agreement has not been implemented, although tensions seem to have calmed somewhat as 2013 began.

Territorial Issues/"Disputed Internal Boundaries"

The November 2012 KRG-peshmerga clash also relates to the lack of any progress in recent years in resolving the various territorial disputes between the Kurds and Iraq's Arabs. The most emotional of which is the Kurdish insistence that Tamim Province (which includes oil-rich Kirkuk) is "Kurdish land" and must be formally affiliated to the KRG. There was to be a census and referendum on the affiliation of the province by December 31, 2007, in accordance with Article 140 of the Constitution, but the Kurds have agreed to repeated delays in order to avoid jeopardizing overall progress in Iraq. Nor has the national census that is pivotal to any such referendum been conducted; it was scheduled for October 24, 2010, but then postponed until at least December 2010 to allow time for a full-term government to take office. It still has not begun, in part because of the broader political crisis (discussed below) as well as differences over how to account for movements of populations into or out of the Kurdish controlled provinces.

In the absence of movement on formally integrating Kirkuk into the KRG, the Kurds have attempted to steadily assert control in the province. The current governor of Kirkuk is Najmaddin Karim, a longtime Kurdish activist in the United States before he moved back to Iraq following the fall of Saddam Hussein. The Property Claims Commission that is adjudicating claims from the Saddam regime's forced resettlement of Arabs into the KRG region is functioning. Of the 178,000 claims received, nearly 26,000 were approved and 90,000 rejected or ruled invalid, as of the end of 2011, according to the State Department human rights report for 2011. Since 2003, more than 28,000 Iraqi Arabs settled in the KRG area by Saddam have relocated from Kirkuk back to their original provinces.

Nineveh Province, which is mostly Arab but includes many villages where Kurds predominate, is a component of the dispute. In the provincial elections of 2009, Sunni Arabs wrested back control of the Nineveh (Mosul) provincial council from the Kurds. The Kurds had won control of that council in the 2005 election because of the broad Sunni Arab boycott of that election. A Sunni list (al-Hadba'a) won a clear plurality of the 2009 Nineveh vote and subsequently took control of the provincial administration there. Al-Hadba'a is composed of hardline Sunni Arabs who openly oppose Kurdish encroachment in the province and who are committed to the "Arab and Islamic identity" of the province. A member of the faction, Atheel al-Nufaiji, is the governor (brother of 2010-2014 COR speaker Usama al-Nujaifi), and the Kurds have been preventing his visitation of areas of Nineveh where the Kurds' *peshmerga* militia operates. In October 2011, the central government ordered the Kurdish flags taken down from public buildings in Khanaqin, a Kurdish town in the province; the Kurdish police in the city disobeyed the order.

Attempts to Resolve or Mitigate the Dispute

Attempting to resolve this dispute has been part of the work of the U.N. Assistance Mission—Iraq (UNAMI), which has been consultations with all parties for several years.[19] The mandate of UNAMI—which is also to facilitate national reconciliation and civil society, and assisting vulnerable populations—was established in 2003 and has been renewed every year since. U.N. Security Council Resolution 2061 of July 25, 2012, renewed the mandate for another year (until July 24, 2013).

During the U.S. military presence, the United States had set up mechanisms to prevent the tensions from flaring into conflict, but these mechanisms may be deteriorating now that all U.S. troops are out of Iraq. In August 2009 then-top U.S. commander in Iraq General Raymond Odierno developed a plan to partner U.S. forces with *peshmerga* units and with ISF units in the province to build confidence along the frontier between the two forces. The process was also intended to reassure Kurdish, Arab, Turkomen, and other province residents. Implementation of this "combined security mechanism" (CSM) began in January 2010, consisting of joint (ISF-U.SKurdish) patrols, maintenance of 22 checkpoints, and U.S. training of participating ISF and *peshmerga* forces. The mechanism has been administered through provincial level Combined Coordination Centers, and disagreements were referred to a Senior Working Group and a High Level Ministerial Committee.[20]

U.S. military involvement in the mechanism declined as U.S. forces withdrew from Iraq during 2011, but the United States continues to participate in it despite the absence of U.S. combat forces from Iraq. Through Office of Security Cooperation—Iraq (OSC-I) facilities in Nineveh Province, some U.S. military personnel attached to that office, assisted by U.S. diplomats and contractors, help coordinate the joint patrols and checkpoints. Previously, some experts have advanced alternatives to U.S. force participation in the CSM, including giving the U.S. role to a United Nations force, NATO, or civilians (Iraqi or international). It is not clear that any of these alternative ideas are supported by Iraqi factions.

KRG Oil Exports/Oil Laws

The KRG and Baghdad have had repeated disputes over the ability of the Kurds to export oil that is discovered and extracted in the KRG region. The Kurds view it as their right to develop their resources, whereas Baghdad fears that Kurdish oil exports can potentially enable the Kurds to set up an economically-viable independent state. Baghdad calls the KRG's separate energy development deals with international firms "illegal" but still allows KRG oil exports to proceed. Under a Baghdad-KRG agreement, revenues from KRG oil exports go into central government accounts, which distributes proceeds to the KRG and pays the international oil companies working in the KRG.

Oil exports from the KRG have been repeatedly suspended, for varying periods of time, over central government withholding of payments to the international energy firms. A recent suspension of oil exports through the national oil grid began in April 2012 after the KRG accused Baghdad of falling $1.5 billion in arrears to the companies extracting oil in the KRG region. At the time of the suspension, KRG oil exports had reached about 175,000 barrels of crude oil per day. The dispute escalated in July 2012 when the KRG began exporting crude oil by road to Turkey, some of which is being refined and returned as gasoline to the KRG region. The dispute was defused temporarily and Kurdish exports through the national grid resumed on August 9, 2012, amid a KRG threat to conduct another halt by September 15, 2012 if the international companies were not paid. A Baghdad-KRG agreement of September 14, 2012, headed off another shutdown—the pact provided for the Kurds to raise exports to 200,000 barrels per day as of October 1, 2012, to increase that to 250,000 barrels per day for 2013, and for Baghdad to pay about $900 million in arrears due the international firms. The agreement held for several months, but the KRG slashed its oil exports in late November 2012 because of slow Baghdad payments to the oil firms involved as well as the broader KRG-Baghdad problems discussed above. KRG oil exports ceased again entirely on December 26, 2012. If this issue is permanently resolved, the KRG has the potential to increase exports to 500,000 barrels per day by the end of 2013, and 1 million barrels per day by 2019.[21]

The September 2012 KRG-Baghdad agreement had boosted hope for resolving their differences over national oil laws. The KRG adopted its own oil laws in 2007. The Kurds opposed oil laws adopted by the Iraqi cabinet in late August 2011, and sent on to the COR for ratification, as favoring a centralized energy sector that would impinge on KRG control of its energy resources. In connection with the visit to the United States of then KRG Prime Minister Barham Salih, Kurdish representatives said on November 8, 2011, that it is likely that the oil laws would be taken up by the COR by the end of 2011.[22] In part due to the political crisis, the issue did not progress. The Baghdad-KRG agreement in September 2012 included a provision to set up a six member committee to review the different versions of the oil laws under consideration and decide which version to submit to the COR for formal consideration.

In the absence of adoption of national oil laws, the issue of foreign firm involvement in the KRG energy sector also remains unresolved. The October 2011 KRG signing of an energy development deal with U.S. energy giant Exxon-Mobil represents a further dimension of the energy row with Baghdad. The central government denounced the deal as illegal, in part because the oil fields involved are in or very close to disputed territories. The KRG has sought to defuse this consideration by saying that if the territory of the oil fields is subsequently judged to be part of central government-administered territory, then the revenues would be reallocated accordingly. Still, the central government threatened to cancel the firm's existing contract to develop the West Qurna oil field near Basra, which was signed with the central government. On February 13, 2012, the central government announced its sanction against the firm as a prohibition on bidding for work on unexplored fields to be tendered later in 2012. On March 17, 2012, Baghdad claimed that Exxon-Mobil had frozen the KRG contract, but the KRG denies the company has stopped work in the KRG region. Energy industry observers corroborate the KRG view and say Exxon will likely begin production in the KRG in late 2012.[23] Further disputes occurred over a July 2012 KRG deal with Total SA of France; in August 2012 the central government told Total SA to either terminate its arrangement with the KRG or give up work on the central government Halfaya field.

Turkish Involvement
The growing relationship between Turkey and the KRG energy sector introduces additional tensions into the issue and has raised tensions between Turkey and Baghdad. The KRG and Turkey are reportedly discussing a broad energy deal that would include Turkish

investment in drilling for oil and gas in the KRG-controlled territory as well as construct a separate oil pipeline linking KRG-controlled fields to the Turkish border. [24] That would reduce the KRG dependence on the national oil export grid—the key source of Baghdad's leverage over the KRG. To try to head off such a deal, the Iraqi government has blacklisted Turkey's state energy pipeline firm (TPAO) from some work in southern Iraq. In December 2012, Iraq turned back a plane carrying Turkey's energy minister to a conference in the KRG capital of Irbil. However, Turkey and the KRG continue to negotiate to finalize the large deal.

Intra-Kurdish Divisions

Further complicating the political landscape are widening divisions within the Kurdish community. The KRG elections (conducted concurrently with the March 2010 national elections throughout Iraq), to some extent, shuffled the political landscape. A breakaway faction of President Talabani's PUK, called "Change" ("Gorran"), won an unexpectedly high 25 seats (out of 111) in the Kurdistan national assembly, embarrassing the PUK and weakening it relative to the KDP. KRG President Masoud Barzani, leader of the KDP, easily won reelection as President against weak opposition. Gorran ran its own list in the March 2010 elections and constituted a significant challenge to the Kurdistan Alliance in Sulaymaniyah Province, according to election results. As a result, of the 57 COR seats held by Kurds, 14 are held by parties other than the Kurdistan Alliance. Gorran has 8, the Kurdistan Islamic Union has 4, and the Islamic Group of Kurdistan has 2.

These divisions may also have played a role in the popular demonstrations that occurred in Sulaymaniyah in early 2011. The demonstrations reflected frustration over jobs and services but possibly also over the monopolization of power in the KRG by the Barzani and Talabani clans. Some of these were suppressed by *peshmerga.*

More recently, the health of Iraq's President and PUK leader Jalal Talabani is said to be failing. Barham Salih, mentioned above, is said to be pressing to replace him in that position. Another PUK stalwart, Kosrat Rasoul, is said to be lining up support to succeed Talabani as PUK leader should Talabani leave the scene. Talabani's son, Qubad, had headed the KRG representative office in Washington, DC, until July 2012, when he returned home to become more involved in Kurdish and PUK politics as his father's health fades. Talabani's wife, Hero Ibrahim Ahmad Talabani, is also a major figure in PUK politics.

The Sadr Faction's Continuing Ambition and Agitation

Within the broader Shiite community, the faction of Shiite cleric, Moqtada Al Sadr sees itself as the main representative for Iraq's Shiites, particularly the majority of Shiites who are poor or working class. The large Sadrist constituency has caused an inherent rivalry with Maliki and other Shiite leaders in Iraq. Although Sadr was part of the anti-Maliki Shiite coalition (Iraqi National Alliance) for the March 2010 national elections, he reached a political arrangement with Maliki that paved the way for Maliki's achieving another term, as noted above.

Suggesting that Sadr often shifts so as to maximize his faction's leverage, in May 2012 Sadr himself participated in meetings in the KRG region with other anti-Maliki factions to put pressure on Maliki to increase power sharing. In June 2012, Sadrist deputies in the COR joined the effort to vote no-confidence against Maliki, discussed above, only to abandon that effort under Iranian pressure, by many accounts. Sadr appears to have again shifted against Maliki in the context of the late 2012-early 2013 Sunni unrest. Sadr's shifts against Maliki represent a continuation of a high level of activity he has exhibited since he returned to Iraq, from his studies in Iran, in January 2011. After his return, he gave numerous speeches that, among other themes, insisted on full implementation of a planned U.S. withdrawal by the end of 2011. Sadr's position on the U.S. withdrawal appeared so firm that, in an April 9, 2011, statement, he threatened to reactivate his Mahdi Army militia if U.S. forces remained in Iraq beyond the December 31, 2011, deadline. His followers conducted a large march in Baghdad on May 26, 2011, demanding a full U.S. military exit. The threats were pivotal to the Iraqi decision not to retain U.S. troops in Iraq beyond 2011. Sadr's threats to instigate violence were considered not idle. In June and July 2011, U.S. officials accused Shiite militia offshoots of Sadr's Mahdi Army militia of causing an elevated level of U.S. troop deaths in June 2011 (14 killed, the highest in any month in over one year). These militias operate under names including Asa'ib Ahl al-Haq (AAH, League of the Righteous), Khata'ib Hezbollah (Hezbollah Battalions), and Promised Day Brigade. In June 2009, Khata'ib Hezbollah was named by the United States as a Foreign Terrorist Organization (FTO). U.S. officials accused Iran of arming these militias with upgraded rocket-propelled munitions, such as Improvised Rocket Assisted Munitions (IRAMs), in an effort to ensure a full U.S. withdrawal and to claim credit for forcing that withdrawal. U.S. officials reportedly requested that the ISF act against these militias and to prevail on Iran to stop aiding the militias, actions that subsequently, but temporarily, quieted the Shiite attacks on U.S. forces in Iraq. Some rocket attacks continued against the U.S. consulate in Basra, which has nearly 1,000 U.S. personnel (including contractors). However, Ambassador-nominee McGurk stated at his confirmation hearings on June 6, 2012, that AAH, Khata'ib Hezbollah, and Promised Day Brigade had all become less active since the U.S. military withdrawal because the U.S. exit removed their justification for armed activity. Sadr's Mahdi Army has integrated into the political process in the form of a charity and employment network called *Mumahidoon* or "those who pave the way." Still, on November 8, 2012, the Treasury Department designated several Khata'ib Hezbollah operatives, and their Iranian Revolutionary Guard—Qods Force mentors as terrorism supporting entities under Executive Order 13224.

GOVERNANCE AND HUMAN RIGHTS ISSUES

The continuing political crises discussed above have dashed most hopes that Iraq will become a fully functioning democracy with well-established institutions and rule of law.

National Oil Laws and Other Pending Laws

Adopting national oil laws has been considered key to establishing rule of law and transparency in a key sector. Substantial progress appeared near in August 2011 when both the COR and the cabinet drafted the oil laws long in the works to rationalize the energy sector and clarify the rules for foreign investors. However, there were differences in their individual versions: the version drafted by the Oil and Natural Resources Committee was presented to the full COR on August 17, 2011. The cabinet adopted its separate version on August 28, 2011; there was some expectation that the COR would take up the issue when it reconvened on September 6, 2011, after the Eid alFitr celebration marking the end of Ramadan. It was unclear which version would form the basis of final legislation, amid opposition from the Kurds to what they see as an overly centralized energy industry encapsulated in the cabinet's draft law. The opposition and the presence of two competing versions of the oil laws accounted for the postponement of further COR action until at least the end of 2011, and the political crisis prevented movement on it subsequently. However, as discussed above, in concert with a temporary KRG-Baghdad agreement on some aspects of their dispute over the KRG energy sector, a six member panel has been working since September 2012 to decide which version of draft oil legislation the COR will consider. Also not passed are laws addressing the environment, other elections, consumer protections, intellectual property rights, building codes, and the permanent rules for de-Baathification. Others say that the failure to adopt new laws governing investment, taxation, and property ownership account for the slow pace of building a modern, dynamic economy, although others say the success of Iraq's energy sector is overriding these adverse factors. On the other hand, on April 30, 2012, the COR enacted a law to facilitate elimination of trafficking in persons, both sexual and labor-related.

Energy Sector Development

The continuing deadlock on oil laws has not, however, prevented progress in the crucial energy sector, which provides 90% of Iraq's budget. Iraq possesses a proven 143 billion barrels of oil, and increasing exports enabled Iraq's GDP to grow by about 12% in 2012, according to the World Bank. After long remaining below the levels achieved prior to the ouster of Saddam Hussein, Iraq's oil exports recovered to about 2.1 million barrels per day by March 2012, roughly the level achieved during Saddam's rule. Production reached the milestone 3 million barrels per day mark in February 2012, which Iraqi leaders trumpeted as a key milestone in Iraq's recovery, and expanded further to about 3.2 million barrels per day in September 2012. Iraqi leaders say they want to increase production to over 10 million barrels per day by 2017. The International Energy Agency estimates more modest but still significant gains: it sees Iraq reaching 6 mbd of production by 2020 if it attracts $25 billion in investment per year, and potentially 8 mbd by 2035. What is helping the Iraqi production is the involvement of foreign firms, including BP, Exxon-Mobil, Occidental, and Chinese firms. U.S. firms assisted Iraq's export capacity by developing single-point mooring oil loading terminals to compensate for deterioration in Iraq's existing oil export infrastructure in Basra and Umm Qasr. The growth of oil exports appears to be fueling a rapid expansion of the consumer sector. Press reports in 2012 have noted the development of several upscale malls and other consequences of positive economic progress.

Corruption

The State Department human rights report for 2011 contains substantial detail on the continuing lack of progress in curbing governmental corruption. That assessment was corroborated by the quarterly report of the Special Inspector General for Iraq Reconstruction

(SIGIR), released October 30, 2012, which said that corruption is one of the main obstacles to democratic progress and development in Iraq. The reports assess that political and other factors that have caused anticorruption institutions, such as the Commission on Integrity (COI) and the Joint Anti-Corruption Council, to be regularly thwarted or hampered in attempts to investigate and prosecute corruption. The Joint Anti-Corruption Council is tasked with implementing the government's 2010-14 Anti-Corruption Strategy.

Another body is the Supreme Board of Audits, which monitors the use of government funds. The COR has its own Integrity Committee that oversees the executive branch and the governmental anti-corruption bodies. And, the KRG has its own separate anti-corruption institutions, including an Office of Governance and Integrity in the KRG council of ministers.

The State Department report states, in a three month period in 2011, over 200 corruption investigations were halted on the authority of Iraqi ministers—presumably because they did not want their departments or political allies investigated.

However, in September 2012, there was some cause for optimism on this issue because the Supreme Board of Audits discovered that about 80% of the $1 billion in weekly government foreign currency purchases was being transferred out of the country under false pretenses. As a result of the discovery, Maliki removed longtime Central Bank governor Sinan al-Shabibi.

General Human Rights Issues

The State Department's report on human rights for 2011 released May 24, 2012, largely repeated the previous years' criticisms of Iraq's human rights record and the attribution of deficiencies in human rights practices to the overall security situation and sectarian and factional divisions.[25]

The State Department report cited a wide range of human rights problems committed by Iraqi government security and law enforcement personnel, including some unlawful killings; torture and other cruel punishments; poor conditions in prison facilities; denial of fair public trials; arbitrary arrest; arbitrary interference with privacy and home; limits on freedoms of speech, assembly, and association due to sectarianism and extremist threats; lack of protection of stateless persons; wide scale governmental corruption; human trafficking; and limited exercise of labor rights.

Many of these same abuses and deficiencies are discussed in the Human Rights Watch World Report for 2012, released January 22, 2012.

Use of Coercive Force against Arab Spring-Related Demonstrations
Iraq's government, although flawed, is the product of democratic choices. Therefore, many experts were surprised when protests—inspired by the uprisings taking place elsewhere in the Arab world and distinct from the unresolved ethno-sectarian conflicts discussed above—began in several provinces of Iraq on February 6, 2011. The protesters expressed frustrated by what they perceive as a nearly exclusive focus of the major factions on politics rather than governing or improving services. Many protesters expressed particular outrage at the still severe shortages of electricity in Iraq, as well as the lack of job opportunities and perceived elite corruption. Iraqis who cannot afford their own generators (or to share a generator with a few others) face repeated power outages every day. Twenty Iraqis were

killed by security forces in the large February 25, 2011, "Day of Rage" demonstrations called by Iraqi activists.

Unrest in the KRG region appeared to reflect deep frustrations and was more intense than in the rest of Iraq. The unrest in Sulaymaniyah resulted in the deaths of at least three protestors at the hands of *peshmerga* and Kurdish intelligence (*Asayesh*), and was said to rattle the top Kurdish leaders, who fear the KRG's image as an oasis of stability and prosperity was clouded.

The government measures in addition to repression to calm the unrest. In February 2011, Maliki announced a voluntary cut in his salary (from about $350,000 per year to half that) and indicated he would not seek a third term when his current term expires in 2014. On February 27, 2011, he announced that his new cabinet would have "100 days" to prove its effectiveness or face replacement. That deadline expired on June 7, 2011, without significant incident, although U.S. diplomats say the government began public works projects and provided some fuel supplies as part of its efforts to show results by that time. In addition, on May 31, 2011, third deputy president Adel Abdul Mahdi resigned in an effort to show that the government is committed to cutting its bloated bureaucracy. To reinforce that commitment, the COR voted on July 30, 2011, to back Maliki's plan to reduce the number of cabinet posts from the current 42 to 29.

Another component of the response was to appoint several technocrats to permanently fill cabinet slots in ministries that deliver services to the public. In a wave of appointments on February 13, 2011, an Iraqiyya technocrat, Raad Shallal, was appointed minister of electricity and power. In addition, Municipality and Public Works Minister Adel Mohder was named, as were appointments to be ministers of state for tribal affairs, civilian community affairs, and national reconciliation. Shallal was removed in August 2011, most likely as a scapegoat for continued electricity shortages, although the stated cause of his removal was a failure to follow proper procedures in signing $1.7 billion worth of power plant construction contracts with Canadian and German firms.

In early June 2011, in advance of the June 7 "100 day" deadline, the government detained several dozen activists in order to preempt protests. Additional steps were taken subsequently to curb protests, including tolerating pro-government thugs to beat demonstrators on June 10, 2011.

Trafficking in Persons

The State Department's Trafficking in Persons report for 2012, released on June 19, 2012, places Iraq in "Tier 2 Watch List" for the fourth year in a row. This is one rank short of Tier 3, the lowest ranking. For 2012, Iraq received a waiver from automatic downgrading to Tier 3 (which happens if a country is "watchlisted" for three straight years) because it has a plan to make significant efforts to meet minimum standards for the elimination of trafficking and is devoting significant resources to that plan.

Media and Free Expression

While State Department and other reports attribute most of Iraq's human rights difficulties to the security situation and factional infighting, apparent curbs on free expression appear independent of such factors. One issue that troubles human rights activists is a law, passed by the COR in August 2011, called the "Journalist Rights Law." The law purports to protect journalists but left many of the provisions of Saddam-era libel and defamation laws in place. For example, the new law leaves in place imprisonment for publicly insulting the government. The State Department human rights report for 2011 noted continuing instances of harassment and intimidation of journalists who write about corruption and the lack of government services. Much of the private media that operate is controlled by individual factions or powerful personalities. There are no overt government restrictions on access to the Internet.

In March 2012, some observers reported a setback to free expression, although instigated by militias or non-governmental groups, not the government. There were reports of 14 youths having been stoned to death by militiamen for wearing Western-style clothes and haircuts collectively known as "Emo" style. In late June 2012, the government ordered the closing of 44 new organizations that it said were operating without a license. Included in the closure list were the BBC, Voice of America, and the U.S.-funded Radio Sawa. The COR is also considering an "Information Crimes Law" to regulate the use of information networks, computers, and other electronic devices and systems. Human Rights Watch said in July 2012 that the draft law "violates international standards protecting due process, freedom of speech, and freedom of association."[26]

Labor Rights
A 1987 (Saddam era) labor code remains in effect, restricting many labor rights, particularly in the public sector. Although the 2005 constitution provides for the right to strike and form unions, the labor code virtually rules out independent union activity. Unions have no legal power to negotiate with employers or protect workers' rights through collective bargaining.

Religious Freedom/Situation of the Christian Religious Minority
The Iraqi constitution provides for religious freedom and the government generally respected religious freedom, according to the State Department's report on International Religious Freedom for 2011, released July 30, 2012. However, reflecting the conservative Islamic attitudes of many Iraqis, conservative Shiite and Sunni clerics seek to enforce aspects of Islamic law and customs, sometimes coming into conflict with Iraq's generally secular traditions as well as constitutional protections. On September 13, 2012, hundreds— presumably Shiites—took to the streets in predominantly Shiite Sadr City to protest the "Innocence of Muslims" video that was produced in the United States and set off protests throughout the Middle East in September 2012.

Concerns about religious freedom in Iraq tends to center on government treatment of religious minorities. A major concern is the safety and security of Iraq's Christian and other religious minority populations which are concentrated in northern Iraq as well as in Baghdad. These other groups include most notably the Yazidis, which number about 500,000-600,000; the Shabaks, which number about 400,000-500,000; the Sabeans, who number about 4,000; the Baha'i's that number about 2,000; and the Kakai's of Kirkuk, which number about 24,000. Since the 2003 U.S. intervention, more than half of the 1 million-1.5 million Christian population that was there during Saddam's time have left. Recent estimates indicate that the Christian population of Iraq is less than 500,000.

The State Dept. report details abuses or restrictions on the freedoms of religious minorities, both by Baghdad as well as the KRG. In the past, violent attacks on members of the community have occurred in waves. The body of Chaldean Catholic archbishop Faraj

Rahho was discovered in Mosul on March 13, 2008, two weeks after his reported kidnapping. An attack on the Yazidis in August 2007, which killed about 500 people, appeared to exemplify the precarious situation for Iraqi minorities. In the run-up to the January 2009 provincial elections, about 1,000 Christian families reportedly fled the province in October 2008, although Iraqi officials report that most families returned by December 2008. The issue faded in 2009 but then resurfaced late in that year when about 10,000 Christians in northern Iraq, fearing bombings and intimidation, fled the areas near Kirkuk during October-December 2009. On October 31, 2010, a major attack on Christians occurred when a church in Baghdad (Sayidat al-Najat Church) was besieged by militants and as many as 60 worshippers were killed. The siege shook the faith of the Christian community in their security. Many Christian families fled their homes after the church attack, often going to live with relatives in Christian-inhabited locations around Iraq. Partly as a result, Christian celebrations of Christmas 2010 were said to be subdued—following three years in which Christians had felt confident enough to celebrate that holiday openly. Several other attacks appearing to target Iraqi Christians have taken place since.

Some Iraqi Christians blame all the various attacks on them on Al Qaeda in Iraq, which is still somewhat strong in Nineveh Province and which associates Christians with the United States. Some human rights groups allege that it is the Kurds who are committing abuses against Christians and other minorities in the Nineveh Plains, close to the KRG-controlled region. Kurdish leaders deny the allegations, and the State Department human rights report for 2010 says the KRG has permitted Christians fleeing violence in Baghdad to relocate into KRG-controlled areas. Some Iraqi Christian groups advocate a "Nineveh Plains Province Solution," in which the Nineveh Plains would be turned into a self-administering region, possibly its own province but affiliated or under KRG control. Supporters of the idea claim such a zone would pose no threat to the integrity of Iraq, but others say the plan's inclusion of a separate Christian security force could set the scene for violence and confrontation. Even at the height of the U.S. military presence in Iraq, U.S. forces did not specifically protect Christian sites at all times, partly because Christian leaders do not want to appear closely allied with the United States. The State Dept. report said that during 2011, U.S. Embassy Baghdad designated a "special coordinator" to oversee U.S. funding, program implementation, and advocacy to address minority concerns.

Specific Funding for Religious Minorities in Iraq

The FY2008 consolidated appropriation earmarked $10 million in ESF from previous appropriations to assist the Nineveh Plain Christians. A supplemental appropriation for 2008 and 2009 (P.L. 110-252) earmarked another $10 million for this purpose. The Consolidated Appropriations Act of 2010 (P.L. 111-117) made a similar provision for FY2010, although focused on Middle East minorities generally and without a specific dollar figure mandated for Iraqi Christians. In the 112th Congress, a bill, H.R. 440, which would establish a post of Special Envoy to promote religious freedom in the Middle East and South Central Asia, passed the House on July 29, 2011, by a vote of 402-20. Ambassador-designate to Iraq, Robert Stephen Beecroft, testified at his Senate Foreign Relations Committee confirmation hearings on September 19, 2012, that the State Department has spent $72 million total to protect religious minorities in Iraq.

Women's Rights

Iraq has a tradition of secularism and liberalism, and women's rights issues have not been as large a concern for international observers and rights groups as they have in Afghanistan or the Persian Gulf states, for example. Women serve at many levels of government, as discussed above, and are well integrated into the work force in all types of jobs and professions. By tradition, many Iraqi women wear traditional coverings but many adopt Western dress. On October 6, 2011, the COR passed legislation to lift Iraq's reservation to Article 9 of the Convention on the Elimination of All Forms of Discrimination Against Women.

Executions

The death penalty is legal in Iraq. In June 2012, Amnesty International condemned the "alarming" increase in executions, which had by then put 70 persons to death. U.N. High Commissioner for Human Rights Navi Pillay also expressed shock in 2012 over the high number of executions in Iraq. On August 28, 2012, the government executed 21 people, including three women, convicted of terrorism-related charges.

Mass Graves

As is noted in the State Department report on human rights for 2010, the Iraqi government continues to uncover mass graves of Iraqi victims of the Saddam regime. This effort is under the authority of the Human Rights Ministry. On April 15, 2011, a mass grave of more than 800 bodies became the latest such discovery. The largest to date was a mass grave in Mahawil, near Hilla, that contained 3,000 bodies; the grave was discovered in 2003, shortly after the fall of the regime.

REGIONAL DIMENSION

Iraq's neighbors, as well as the United States, have high interest in Iraq's stability and its friendship. Iraq's post-Saddam leadership has affinity for Iran, which supported them in years of struggle against Saddam. Yet, Iraq also seeks to reintegrate into the Arab fold—of which Iran is not a part—after more than 20 years of ostracism following Iraq's invasion of Kuwait in August 1990. That motive mitigates, to some extent, Iranian influence in Iraq because the Arab world is primarily composed of Sunni Muslims and much of the Arab world is either at odds with or highly suspicious of Iran.

Iraq's reintegration into the Arab fold took a large step forward with the holding of an Arab League summit in Baghdad during March 27-29, 2012. Iraq hailed the gathering as a success primarily because of the absence of major security incidents during the gathering. However, only 9 heads of state out of the 22 Arab League members attended, and only one Persian Gulf leader, Amir Sabah al-Ahmad Al Sabah of Kuwait, attended. Building on that success, and on its relations with both the United States and Iran, on May 23-24, 2012, Iraq hosted nuclear talks between Iran and the six negotiating powers (United States, Britain, France, Germany, Russia, and China).

Iraq is also sufficiently confident to begin offering assistance to other emerging Arab democracies. Utilizing its base of expertise in chemical weaponry during the Saddam Hussein regime, Iraq has provided some technical assistance to the post-Qadhafi authorities in Libya to help them clean up chemical weapons stockpiles built up by the Qadhafi regime. It has also donated $100,000 and provided advisers to support elections in Tunisia after its 2011 revolution.[27]

Iran

The United States remains at odds with Iran and seeks to limit Iranian influence over the Iraqi political structure. Some argue that the withdrawal of all U.S. troops from Iraq represented a success for Iranian strategy and that Iranian influence in Iraq is preponderant. Others argue that it was U.S. policy that created this opportunity for Iran by bringing to power Iraqi Shiite Islamist politicians long linked to Iran. To counter the impression that Iran might benefit from the complete U.S. pullout, Secretary of State Clinton said on October 23, 2011, that:

> I think Iran should look at the region. We may not be leaving military bases in Iraq, but we have bases elsewhere. We have support and training assets elsewhere. We have a NATO ally in Turkey. The United States is very present in the region.

That theme was echoed by Secretary of Defense Leon Panetta that same day, saying that the United States, even without U.S. troops present in Iraq, would be able to counter any threat from Iranian influence or from Iran-backed Iraqi Shiite militias. These militias have been perceived as a threat particularly to U.S. personnel in southern Iraq, although that threat abated in 2012.

Prime Minister Maliki has tried to calm fears that Iran exercises undue influence over post-U.S. military Iraq. In so doing, he has stressed themes that are advanced by many experts that Iraqi nationalism is resisting Iranian influence. Experts also note lingering distrust of Iran from the 1980-1988 Iran-Iraq war, in which an estimated 300,000 Iraqi military personnel (Shiite and Sunni) died. In his December 5, 2011, op-ed in the *Washington Post*, entitled "Building a Stable Iraq," Maliki wrote:

Iraq is a sovereign country. Our foreign policy is rooted in the fact that we do not interfere in the affairs of other countries; accordingly, we oppose foreign interference in Iraqi affairs.

Defense and security ties between Iran and Iraq have been discussed but little has materialized. In an interview with CNN broadcast on October 23, 2011, Iran's President Mahmoud Ahmadinejad said Iran planned a closer security relationship with Iraqi forces after U.S. troops depart. After the U.S. withdrawal that was completed December 18, 2011, Iran announced it would welcome closer defense ties to Iraq, including training Iraqi forces, although no such training has been reported to date.

Iraq's Shiite clerics also resist Iranian interference and take pride in Najaf as a more prominent center of Shiite theology and history than is the Iranian holy city of Qom. In late 2011, representatives of Ayatollah Mahmud Shahrudi, an Iraqi cleric long resident in Iraq, opened offices in Najaf, Iraq. This was widely seen as an effort to promote Shahrudi as a possible successor as *marja taqlid* ("source of inspiration,"—the most senior Shiite cleric) to the increasingly frail Grand Ayatollah Ali al-Sistani. During an April 22-23, 2012, visit to Iran, Maliki met with Shahrudi, in addition to meeting senior Iranian figures. However, observers say the offices have not created a wave of support for Shahrudi as successor to Sistani.

Some assess that evidence of Iranian influence can be seen in Iraq's alignment, in general, with Iranian policy that seeks to keep Bashar Al Assad in power in Syria. This has put Iraq in a difficult position between its two allies, the United States and Iran, in that the United States seeks Assad's ouster and is demanding Iraq not cooperate with any Iranian efforts to keep Assad in power. This is discussed further below.

There are indications the Shiite-led government of Iraq has sought to shield pro-Iranian militants who committed past acts of violence against U.S. forces. In May 2012, Iraqi courts acquitted and Iraq released from prison a purported Hezbollah commander, Ali Musa Daqduq, although he subsequently remained under house arrest. He had been in U.S. custody for alleged activities against U.S. forces but, under the U.S.-Iraq Security Agreement (discussed below) he was transferred to Iraqi custody in December 2011. In July 2012, U.S. officials asked Iraqi leaders to review the Daqduq case or extradite him to the United States, but Iraq released him in November 2012 and he returned to Lebanon, despite U.S. efforts to persuade Iraq to keep him there.

Still others see Iranian influence as less political than economic, raising questions about whether Iran is using Iraq to try to avoid the effects of international sanctions. Some reports say Iraq is enabling Iran's efforts by allowing it to interact with Iraq's energy sector and its banking system. In July 2012, the Treasury Department imposed sanctions on the Elaf Islamic Bank of Iraq for allegedly conducting financial transactions with the Iranian banking system that violated the Comprehensive Iran Sanctions, Accountability, and Divestment Act of 2010 (CISADA, P.L. 111- 195). On the other hand, Iraq is at least indirectly assisting U.S. policy toward Iran by supplying oil customers who, in cooperation with U.S. sanctions against Iran, are cutting back buys of oil from Iran.

Observers also report that Iran is heavily promoting brands of its products, such as yogurt and jams, in Iraqi shops primarily in southern Iraq. Some Iraqi businessmen are said to resent what they believe is Iranian dumping of cheap products in Iraq, which is depressing the development of Iraqi industries. Iranian officials said in mid-September 2012 that Iran's exports to Iraq will reach about $10 billion from March 2012-March 2013, a large increase from the $7 billion in exports in the prior one year.

Iranian Opposition: People's Mojahedin/Camp Ashraf and PJAK

The Iraqi government treatment of the population of Camp Ashraf, a camp in which over 3,500 Iranian oppositionists (People's Mojahedin Organization of Iran, PMOI) have resided, is an indicator of the government's close ties to Iran. The residents of the camp accuse the government of repression and of scheming to expel the residents or extradite them to Iran, where they might face prosecution or death. An Iraqi military redeployment at the camp on April 8, 2011, resulted in major violence against camp residents in which 36 of them were killed.

In November 2011, Maliki insisted that camp will close at the end of 2011, and the U.N. High Commissioner for Refugees, the European Union, and other organizations worked to broker a solution that avoids violence or forcible expulsion. In late December 2011 Maliki signed an agreement with the United Nations on December 26, 2011, to relocate the population to former U.S. military base Camp Liberty. The PMOI later accepted the agreement, dropping demands that U.S. troops guard the residents during any relocation, and all but a residual 200 Ashraf residents have completed their relocation to a former U.S. base, Camp Liberty (renamed Camp Hurriya). There, each case is being evaluated by the U.N. High Commissioner for Refugees for the potential for relocation outside Iraq. The relocation was a major factor in the U.S. decision, formalized on September 28, 2012, to take the PMOI off the U.S. list of Foreign Terrorist Organizations. Still, the PMOI alleges that Iraq is denying some services to the residents of Camp Liberty and that these residents are suffering in the conditions there.

Iran has periodically acted against other Iranian opposition groups based in Iraq. The Free Life Party (PJAK) consists of Iranian Kurds, and it is allied with the Kurdistan Workers' Party that opposes the government of Turkey. Iran has shelled purported camps of the group on several occasions. Iran is also reportedly attempting to pressure the bases and offices in Iraq of such Iranian Kurdish parties as the Kurdistan Democratic Party of Iran (KDP-I) and Komaleh.

Syria

Iraq has disagreed with U.S. policy toward Syria—which is to oust President Bashar Al Assad— in large part because Maliki's government perceives that post-Assad Syria would be run by Sunni Arabs. A Sunni-led Syria would then likely align with Saudi Arabia, Turkey, and Jordan, and not with Shiite-led Iraq. During March 2011-August 2011, Iraq, as did Iran, refrained from sharp criticism of Assad for using military force against protests, and Maliki received several high-level business and other delegations from Syria. In September 2011, Iraq backed Iran's calls for Assad to make major reforms, but opposed the 22-country Arab League move in November 2011 to suspend Syria's membership. Iraq formally abstained on the vote, with Yemen and Lebanon the only two "no" votes. Perhaps to ensure Arab participation at the March 2012 Arab League summit in Baghdad, Iraq voted for a January 22, 2012, Arab League plan for a transition of power in Syria. As an indication of Iraq's policy of simultaneously engaging with the United States on the Syria issue, Foreign Minister Hoshyar Zebari has attended U.S.-led meetings of "Friends of Syria" countries that are seeking Assad's ouster.

A major issue that has erupted between Iraq and the United States since August 2012 has been Iraq's reported permission for Iranian arms supplies to overfly Iraq en route to Syria.[28] Iraq had been preventing them as of March 2012 but the flights reportedly resumed in August 2012. Following high level U.S. demands that Iraq request the Iranian flights land in Iraq for inspection, Iraq stopped a North Korean flight to Syria on September 21, 2012, and announced on September 30, 2012, that it would conduct random searches of Iranian overflights. The first such search of an Iranian flight was conducted on October 2, 2012, but it was allowed to proceed when no arms were found aboard. Iraq again compelled an Iranian cargo flight to land for inspection on October 29, 2012, and again allowed it to proceed after determining no contraband was aboard. Some press reports say that many more Iranian flights to Syria overfly Iraq and are inspected by Iraq only upon their return, after their cargo has been offloaded in Syria.

Aside from official Iraqi policy, the unrest in Syria has generated a scramble among Iraqi factions to affect the outcome there. As discussed above, AQ-I members have reportedly entered Syria to help the mostly Sunni opposition to President Assad and, as noted, on

December 11, 2012, the United States designated the Al Nusrah Front rebel group as an alias of AQ-I, thereby listing it as an FTO. At the same time, there have been numerous reports that Iraqi Shiite militiamen have entered Syria to fight on behalf of the Assad regime; it is not clear that the Iraqi government has sought to prevent these fighters from going there.

The KRG appears to be assisting the Syrian Kurds, who joined the revolt against Assad in July 2012. KRG President Barzani has hosted several meetings of Syrian Kurds to promote unity and a common strategy among them, and the KRG reportedly has been training Syrian Kurdish militia forces to prepare them to secure an autonomous Kurdish area if and when Assad falls. On November 6, 2012, Barzani warned the two major Syrian Kurdish factions—the Democratic Union Party (PYD) and the Kurdish National Council—to avoid discord after the two had been clashing inside Syria.

Turkey

Turkey's concerns have historically focused mostly on the Kurdish north of Iraq, which borders Turkey. Turkey has historically been viewed as concerned about the Iraqi Kurdish insistence on autonomy and Iraqi Kurds' ethnically based sympathies for Kurdish oppositionists in Turkey. The anti-Turkey Kurdistan Workers' Party (PKK) has long maintained camps inside Iraq, along the border with Turkey. Turkey continues to conduct periodic bombardments and other military operations against the PKK encampments in Iraq. For example, in October 2011, Turkey sent ground troops into northern Iraq to attack PKK bases following the killing of 24 Turkish soldiers by the PKK. However, suggesting that it has built a pragmatic relationship with the KRG, Turkey has emerged as the largest outside investor in northern Iraq and is building an increasingly close political relationship with the KRG as well.

As Turkey's relations with the KRG have deepened, relations between Turkey and the Iraqi government have worsened. Turkey's provision of refuge for Vice President Tariq al-Hashimi has been a source of tension; Maliki sought his extradition for trial, but Turkey has not turned him over. On August 2, 2012, Turkish Foreign Minister Ahmet Davotoglu visited the city of Kirkuk, prompting a rebuke from Iraq's Foreign Ministry that the visit constituted inappropriate interference in Iraqi affairs. And, tensions have been aggravated by their differing positions on Syria: Turkey is a prime backer of the mostly Sunni rebels there where. And, as noted above, Baghdad has sought to block Turkey's attempts to broaden energy relations with the KRG.

Gulf States

Iraq also has unresolved disputes with several of the Sunni-led Persian Gulf states who have not fully accommodated themselves to the fact that Iraq is now dominated by Shiite factions. However, Iraq has tried, with some success, to settle some of these issues to encourage maximum Gulf participation in the March 27-29, 2012, Arab League summit in Baghdad. All the Gulf states were represented at the summit but, among Gulf rulers, only Amir Sabah of Kuwait attended. Qatar sent a very low-level delegation which it said openly was meant as a protest against the Iraqi government's treatment of Sunni Arab factions.

Saudi Arabia had been widely criticized by Iraqi leaders because it has not opened an embassy in Baghdad, a move Saudi Arabia pledged in 2008 and which the United States has long urged. This issue was mitigated on February 20, 2012, when Saudi Arabia announced that it had named its ambassador to Jordan, Fahd al-Zaid, to serve as a non-resident ambassador to Iraq concurrently. However, it did not announce the opening of an embassy in Baghdad. The Saudi move came after a visit by Iraqi national security officials to Saudi Arabia to discuss greater cooperation on counterterrorism and the fate of about 400 Arab prisoners in Iraqi jails. The other Gulf countries have opened embassies and all except the UAE have appointed full ambassadors to Iraq.

The government of Bahrain, which is mostly Sunni, also fears that Iraq might work to empower Shiite oppositionists who have demonstrated for a constitutional monarchy during 2011. Ayatollah Sistani is revered by many Bahraini Shiites, and Iraqi Shiites have demonstrated in solidarity with the Bahraini opposition, but there is no evidence that Iraq has had any direct role in the Bahrain unrest.

Kuwait

The relationship with Kuwait has always been considered difficult to resolve because of the legacy of the 1990 Iraqi invasion. However, a possible indication of greater acceptance of the Iraqi government by the state it once occupied (1990-1991) came when Kuwait's then prime minister visited Iraq on January 12, 2011. Maliki subsequently visited Kuwait on February 16, 2011, and, as noted above, the Amir of Kuwait attended the Arab League summit in Baghdad in March 2012.

These key exchanges took place after the U.N. Security Council on December 15, 2010, passed three resolutions (1956, 1957, and 1958) that had the net effect of lifting most Saddam-era sanctions on Iraq, although the U.N.-run reparations payments process remains intact (and deducts 5% from Iraq's total oil revenues). As of the end of December 2012, a U.N. Compensation Commission set up under Security Council Resolution 687 has paid $38.8 billion to claimants from the 1990-91 Iraqi occupation of Kuwait, with an outstanding balance of $13.6 billion to be paid by April 2015.

A U.N. envoy, Gennadi Tarasov, remains empowered by the Security Council to clear up the issues of Kuwaitis and other nationals missing from the Iraqi invasion of Kuwait, and the issue of the missing Kuwaiti national archives that Iraq allegedly took out of Kuwait. Very little progress on these issues has been made in recent years, as was made clear in a Security Council statement of December 15, 2011 (SC/10490) as well as in Security Council documents issued December 14, 2012 (S/2012/931 and S/2012/932). The remains of 236 of the approximately 605 missing Kuwaitis have been found, but efforts to find 369 missing Kuwaitis have been unsuccessful, despite continued research and investigation of possible burial sites. On the other hand, the U.N. reports of December 14, 2012 indicated that Iraq had, in 2012, found and returned to Kuwait some Kuwaiti media archives, as well as keys to safes from the Central Bank of Kuwait. Still, the Kuwaiti national archives remain missing. Other mutual suspicions persist—in August 2011 Iraqi politicians accused Kuwait of intruding on Iraq's oil through slant drilling at the border.

Some other bilateral issues moved forward during the March 15, 2012, visit of Maliki to Kuwait. After Maliki's meetings, the two announced that Iraq had agreed to pay its share of compensation to maintain border markings between the two. Iraq agreed to pay $300 million to the Kuwaiti government and to invest $200 million in a joint venture of the two as settlement for Kuwait Airways' claim for $1.2 billion in compensation for planes and parts allegedly stolen by Iraq during the 1990-1991 occupation. These agreements paved the way for Amir Sabah to attend the Arab League summit in Baghdad. Subsequently, Iraq-Kuwait direct flights resumed, and an agreement was reached for Iraq to pay its share of the costs of maintaining border markings.

U.S. MILITARY WITHDRAWAL AND POST-2011 POLICY

A complete U.S. military withdrawal from Iraq by the end of 2011 was a specific stipulation of the November 2008 U.S.-Iraq Security Agreement (SA), which took effect on January 1, 2009. Following the SA's entry into force, President Obama, on February 27, 2009, outlined a U.S. troop drawdown plan that provided for a drawdown of U.S. combat brigades by the end of August 2010, with a residual force of 50,000 primarily for training the Iraq Security Forces, to remain until the end of 2011. An interim benchmark in the SA was the June 30, 2009, withdrawal of U.S. combat troops from Iraq's cities. These withdrawal deadlines were strictly adhered to.

Question of Whether U.S. Forces Would Remain Beyond 2011

During 2011, with the deadline for a complete U.S. withdrawal approaching, continuing high-profile attacks, fears of expanded Iranian influence, and perceived deficiencies in Iraq's nearly 700,000 member security forces caused U.S. officials to seek to revise the SA to keep some U.S. troops in Iraq after 2011. Some U.S. experts feared the rifts among major ethnic and sectarian communities were still wide enough that Iraq could still become a "failed state" unless some U.S. troops remained. U.S. officials emphasized that the ongoing ISF weaknesses centered on lack of ability to defend Iraq's airspace and borders. Iraqi comments, such as an October 30, 2011, statement by Iraqi Army Chief of Staff Lieutenant General Babaker Zebari that Iraq would be unable to execute full external defense until 2020-2024, reinforced those who asserted that a U.S. force presence was still needed.[29] Renegotiating the SA to allow for a continued U.S. troop presence required discussions with the Iraqi government and a ratification vote of the Iraqi COR.

Several high-level U.S. visits and statements urged the Iraqis to consider extending the U.S. troop presence. Maliki told visiting Speaker of the House John Boehner, during an April 16, 2011, visit to Baghdad, that Iraqi forces were capable of securing Iraq after 2011, but that Iraq would welcome U.S. training and arms after that time.[30] Subsequent to Boehner's visit, Maliki, anticipating that a vote of the COR would be needed for any extension, stated that a request for U.S. troops might be made if there were a "consensus" among political blocs, which he defined as at least 70% concurrence.[31] This appeared to be an effort to isolate the Sadr faction, the most vocal opponent of a continuing U.S. presence.

In his first visit to Iraq as Defense Secretary on July 11, 2011, Leon Panetta urged Iraqi leaders to make an affirmative decision, and quickly. On August 3, 2011, major factions gave Maliki their backing to negotiate an SA extension, and Secretary Panetta said on August 20, 2011, that it was likely that Iraq would request a continued U.S. presence primarily to train the ISF. In September 2011, a figure of about 15,000 remaining U.S. troops, reflecting recommendations of the U.S. military, was being widely discussed.[32] However, the issue became a subject of substantial debate when the *New York Times* reported on September 7, 2011, that the Administration was considering proposing to Iraq to retain only about 3,000-4,000 forces, mostly in a training role.[33] Many experts criticized that figure as too low to carry out the intended missions.

President Obama Announces Decision on Full Withdrawal

The difficulty in the negotiations—primarily a function of strident Sadrist opposition to a continued U.S. presence—became clearer on October 5, 2011, when Iraq issued a statement that some U.S. military personnel should remain in Iraq as trainers but that Iraq would not extend the legal protections contained in the existing SA. That stipulation failed to meet the requirements of the Defense Department, which feared that trying any American soldier under the Iraqi constitution could lead to serious crises at some stage.

On October 21, 2011, President Obama announced that the United States and Iraq had agreed that, in accordance with the November 2008 Security Agreement (SA) with Iraq, all U.S. troops would leave Iraq at the end of 2011. With the formal end of the U.S. combat mission on August 31, 2010, U.S. forces dropped to 47,000, and force levels dropped steadily from August to December 2011. The last U.S. troop contingent crossed into Kuwait on December 18, 2011.

The withdrawal—and perhaps the political crisis that broke out immediately after the completion of the withdrawal—caused some to argue that U.S. gains were jeopardized and that the Administration should have pressed Iraqi leaders harder to allow a U.S. contingent to remain. Those who support the Administration view say that political crisis was likely no matter when the United States withdrew and that it is the responsibility of the Iraqis to resolve their differences.

Structure of the Post-Troop Relationship

After the withdrawal announcement, senior U.S. officials stated that the United States would be able to continue to help Iraq secure itself using programs commonly provided for other countries. Administration officials stressed that the U.S. political and residual security-related presence would be sufficient to exert influence and leverage to ensure that Iraq remained stable, allied to the United States, continuing to move toward full democracy, and economically growing and vibrant.

At the time of the withdrawal, there were about 16,000 total U.S. personnel in Iraq, about half of which were contractors. Of the contractors, most are security contractors protecting the U.S. Embassy and consulates, and other State Department and Office of Security Cooperation-Iraq facilities throughout Iraq. However, staff cuts discussed below have left the total number of U.S. personnel in Iraq at about 12,500 at the end of 2012.

Office of Security Cooperation-Iraq (OSC-I)

The Office of Security Cooperation—Iraq (OSC-I), operating under the authority of the U.S. Ambassador to Iraq, is the primary Iraq-based U.S. institution that continues to train and mentor the Iraqi military, as well administer the Foreign Military Sales (FMS) programs (U.S.

arms sales to Iraq). OSC-I, funded with the Foreign Military Financing (FMF) funds discussed in the aid table below, is the largest U.S. security cooperation office in the world. It works out of the U.S. Embassy in Baghdad and five other locations around Iraq (Kirkuk Regional Airport Base, Tikrit, Besmaya, Umm Qasr, and Taji), but OSC-I plans to transfer its facilities to the Iraqi government by the end of 2013.

The total OCS-I personnel numbers over 3,500, but the vast majority are security and support personnel, most of which are contractors. Of the staff, about 175 are U.S. military personnel and an additional 45 are Defense Department civilians. About 46 members of the staff administers the Foreign Military Sales (FMS) program and other security assistance programs such as the International Military Education and Training (IMET) program. Since 2005, DOD has administered 231 U.S.-funded FMS cases totaling $2.5 billion, and 201 Iraq-funded cases totaling $7.9 billion. There are a number of other purchase requests initiated by Iraq that, if they all move forward, would add bring the estimated value of all Iraq FMS cases to over $19 billion.[34]

The largest FMS case is the sale of 36 U.S.-made F-16 combat aircraft to Iraq, notified to Congress in two equal tranches, the latest of which was made on December 12, 2011 (Transmittal No. 11-46). The total value of the sale of 36 F-16s is up to $6.5 billion when all parts, training, and weaponry are included. Iraq has paid $2.5 billion of that amount, to date. The first deliveries of the aircraft are scheduled for September 2014.

Another large part of the arms sale program to Iraq is for 140 M1A1 Abrams tanks. Deliveries began in August 2010 and the last of them were delivered in late August 2012. the tanks cost about $860 million, of which $800 million was paid out of Iraq's national funds. Iraq reportedly is also seeking to buy up to 30 Stryker armored vehicles equipped with gear to detect chemical or biological agents—a purchase that, if notified to Congress and approved and finally agreed with Iraq, would be valued at about $25 million. On December 23, 2012, the U.S. Navy delivered two support ships to Iraq, which will assist Iraq's fast-attack and patrol boats that secure its offshore oil platforms and other coastal and offshore locations.

In addition to administering arms sales to Iraq, OSC-I's mission—involving about 160 personnel— is to conduct train and assist programs for the Iraq military. Because the United States and Iraq have not agreed on a Status of Forces Agreement (SOFA) document (which would grant legal immunities to U.S. military personnel), the personnel involved in these programs are mostly contractors. They train Iraq's forces on counterterrorism and naval and air defense. Some are "embedded" with Iraqi forces as trainers not only tactically, but at the institutional level by advising Iraqi security ministries and its command structure. If a SOFA is agreed, some of these missions could be performed by U.S. military personnel, presumably augmenting the effectiveness of the programs. In some cases, not limited to OSC-I personnel, Iraq has been detaining U.S. security contractors at checkpoints, complicating not only the U.S. security assistance effort but also the U.S. effort to protect its own personnel and facilities.

On October 2, 2012, OSC-I officials said they planned to review their operations because the Continuing Appropriations for FY2013 (P.L. 112-175), did not reauthorize for FY2013 (that began October 1, 2012) U.S. funding to train the ISF. Defense Department spokespersons subsequently said they had identified other funding to continue OSC-I training activities in Iraq through the end of 2012.

Police Development Program

A separate program is the Police Development Program, which is the largest program that has transitioned from DOD to State Department lead. An October 2011 audit by the SIGIR (Special Inspector General for Iraq Reconstruction) identified deficiencies in the U.S.-funded training program for the Iraqi police forces (Police Development Program, PDP) as that responsibility was transferred from DOD to State on October 1, 2011.[35] That program draws on International Narcotics and Law Enforcement (INCLE) funds. However, Iraq's drive to emerge from U.S. tutelage has produced apparent Iraqi disinterest in the PDP. It now consists of only 36 advisers, about 10% of what was envisioned as an advisory force of 350. Two facilities built with over $200 million in U.S. funds (Baghdad Police College Annex and part of the U.S. consulate in Basra) are to be turned over the Iraqi government by December 2012. Some press reports say there is Administration consideration of discontinuing the program entirely.[36]

Late 2012: Iraq Rededicating to U.S. Security Programs?

Heightened AQ-I and other insurgent activity since mid-2012 has apparently shaken the Iraqi leadership's confidence in the ISF somewhat, and apparently prompted the Iraqi government to re-emphasize security cooperation with the United States. On August 19, 2012, en route to a visit to Iraq, Chairman of the Joint Chiefs of Staff General Martin Dempsey said that "I think [Iraqi leaders] recognize their capabilities may require yet more additional development and I think they're reaching out to us to see if we can help them with that."[37]

General Dempsey's August 21, 2012, visit focused on the security deterioration, as well as the Iranian overflights to Syria discussed above, according to press reports. Regarding U.S.-Iraq security relations, Iraq reportedly expressed interest in expanded U.S. training of the ISF, joint exercises, and accelerated delivery of U.S. arms to be sold, including radar, air defense systems, and border security equipment.[38] Some refurbished air defense guns are being provided gratis as excess defense articles (EDA), but Iraq was said to lament that the guns would not arrive until June 2013. Iraq reportedly argued that the equipment was needed to help it enforce insistence that Iranian overflights to Syria land in Iraq for inspection.

After the Dempsey visit, reflecting the Iraqi decision to re-engage intensively with the United States on security, it was reported that, at the request of Iraq, a unit of Army Special Operations forces had recently deployed to Iraq to advise on counterterrorism and help with intelligence, presumably against AQ-I.[39] (These forces presumably are operating under a limited SOFA or related understanding crafted for this purpose.) Iraq pressed its attempts to speed up weapons deliveries during a visit by Deputy Defense Secretary Ashton Carter on October 18, 2012.

Reflecting an acceleration of the Iraqi move to re-engage militarily with the United States, during December 5-6, 2012, Under Secretary of Defense for Policy James Miller and acting Under Secretary of State for International Security Rose Gottemoeller visited Iraq and a Memorandum of Understanding (MOU) was signed with acting Defense Minister Sadoun Dulaymi. The five year MOU provides for:

- high level U.S.-Iraq military exchanges
- professional military education cooperation
- counter-terrorism cooperation

- the development of defense intelligence capabilities
- joint exercises

The MOU appears to address many of the issues that have hampered OSC-I from performing the its mission to its full potential. The MOU also reflects some of the more recent ideas, such as joint exercises, that were advanced during the August 2012 Dempsey visit. There are no indications to date, however, that the apparent phase-out of the State Department-run Police Development Program is being slowed or reversed. However, it is possible that the United States and Iraq might agree to continue to phase it out and perhaps replace it with a DoD-led program with similar objectives.

Still, Iraq seeks to diversify its arms supplies. Maliki visited Russia on October 8, 2012, and signed deals for Russian arms worth about $4.2 billion. The arms are said to include 30 MI-28 helicopter gunships and air defense missiles, including the Pantsir. However, a few days later, Iraq said it was reviewing the deal because of allegations that corruption was involved in its negotiation.

It is not clear where the deal stands as of December 2012. Iraq might also buy MiG fighter jets in the future, according to press reports. In mid-October 2012, Iraq agreed to buy 28 Czech-made military aircraft, a deal valued at about $1 billion.[40]

Regional Reinforcement Capability

In conjunction with the withdrawal, Defense Secretary Panetta stressed that the United States would retain a large capability in the Persian Gulf region, presumably to be in position to assist the ISF were it to falter, and to demonstrate continuing U.S. interest in Iraq's security as well as to deter Iran.

The United States has about 50,000 military personnel in the region, including about 15,000 mostly U.S. Army forces in Kuwait, a portion of which are, as of mid-2012, combat ready rather than purely support forces. There are also about 7,500 mostly Air Force personnel in Qatar; 5,000 mostly Navy personnel in Bahrain; and about 3,000 mostly Air Force and Navy in the UAE, with very small numbers in Saudi Arabia and Oman. The remainder are part of at least one aircraft carrier task force in or near the Gulf at any given time. The forces are in the Gulf under bilateral defense cooperation agreements with all six Gulf Cooperation Council (GCC) states that give the United States access to their military facilities and, in several cases, to station forces and preposition even heavy armor.

The Diplomatic and Economic Relationship

In his withdrawal announcement, President Obama stated that, through U.S. assistance programs, the United States would be able to continue to develop all facets of the bilateral relationship with Iraq and help strengthen its institutions."[41] The bilateral civilian relationship was the focus of a visit to Iraq by Vice President Biden in early December 2011, just prior to the December 12, 2011, Maliki visit to the United States, which reportedly focused on these issues but also exposed some U.S.-Iraq disagreements, such as over policy toward Syria.

The cornerstone of the bilateral relationship is the Strategic Framework Agreement (SFA). The SFA, signed and entered into effect at the same time as the SA, presents a framework for longterm U.S.-Iraqi relations, and is intended to help orient Iraq's politics and its economy toward the West and the developed nations, and reduce its reliance on Iran or other regional states.

The SFA provides for the following (among other provisions):

- U.S.-Iraq cooperation "based on mutual respect," and that the United States will not use Iraqi facilities to launch any attacks against third countries, and will not seek permanent bases.
- U.S support for Iraqi democracy and support for Iraq in regional and international organizations.
- U.S.-Iraqi dialogue to increase Iraq's economic development, including through the Dialogue on Economic Cooperation and a Trade and Investment Framework Agreement.
- Promotion of Iraq's development of its electricity, oil, and gas sector.
- U.S.-Iraq dialogue on agricultural issues and promotion of Iraqi participation in agricultural programs run by the U.S. Department of Agriculture and USAID.
- Cultural cooperation through several exchange programs, such as the Youth Exchange and Study Program and the International Visitor Leadership Program.

State Department-run aid programs are intended to fulfill the objectives of the SFA, according to State Department budget documents. These programs, implemented mainly through the Economic Support Fund account, and based on the State Department budget justification for foreign operations for FY2013, are intended to:

- Promote Iraqi political reconciliation and peaceful dispute resolution.
- Strengthen the ability of COR deputies to represent their constituents.
- Make the electoral institutions, such as the IHEC, more effective.
- Strengthen the delivery of services to citizens.
- Improve primary education.
- Assist local governing bodies, such as the provincial councils.
- Promote Iraqi economic growth and the development of the private sector, particularly the financial sector.
- Continue counterterrorism operations (NADR funds).
- Institute anti-corruption initiatives.

U.S. officials stress that the United States does not bear the only burden for implementing the programs above, in light of the fact that Iraq is now a major oil exporter. For programs run by USAID in Iraq, Iraq matches dollar for dollar the U.S. funding contribution.

The State Department as Lead Agency

Virtually all of the responsibility for conducting the bilateral relationship falls on the State Department, which became the lead U.S. agency in Iraq as of October 1, 2011. With the transition completed, the State Department announced on March 9, 2012, that its "Office of the Iraq Transition Coordinator" has closed. In concert with that closure, the former coordinator, Ambassador Pat Haslach, assumed a senior post in another State Department bureau. Of the total U.S. personnel in Iraq, about 1,200 are U.S. diplomats or other civilian employees of the U.S. government.[42]

In July 2011, as part of the transition to State leadership in Iraq, the United States formally opened consulates in Basra, Irbil, and Kirkuk. An embassy branch office was considered for Mosul but cost and security issues kept the U.S. facility there limited to a diplomatic office. The Kirkuk consulate close at the end of July 2012 in part due to security concerns and to save costs.

Not only have U.S. plans for some consulates been altered, but the size and cost of the U.S. civilian presence in Iraq is undergoing reduction. In part this is because Iraqi leaders chafed at continued U.S. tutelage and were less welcoming of frequent U.S. diplomatic exchanges.

Press reports say the Iraqis are increasingly displacing foreign firms and contractors from the International Zone (Green Zone) in favor of Iraqi institutions, and U.S. diplomats have had trouble going outside the Zone for official appointments because of security concerns.

Former Ambassador-nominee to Iraq Brett McGurk stated in his June 6, 2012, confirmation hearings that the U.S. Embassy in Baghdad, built at a cost of about $750 million, is too large and carries too much staff relative to the needed mission. He said the State Department plan is to cut the staff at the embassy by about 25% by the end of 2013. The process of reducing staff in part accounts for the fall in the total number of U.S. personnel in Iraq to about 12,500 as of the end of 2012 from nearly 17,000 at the time of the completion of the U.S. withdrawal at the end of 2011.

As shown in Table 3 below (in the note), the State Department request for operations (which includes costs for the Embassy as well as other facilities and all personnel in Iraq) is about $2.7 billion for FY2013, down from $3.6 billion requested for FY2012—with FY2012 considered a "transition year" to State Department leadership, and requiring high start-up costs. In addition, press reports say the Central Intelligence Agency is planning to reduce its staff to about 40% of the 700 personnel it had in Iraq at the height of the U.S. military presence there.[43]

The debate over staff is separate from but related to the debate over whether the State Department, using security contractors, can fully secure its personnel in Iraq. No U.S. civilian personnel in Iraq have been killed or injured since the troop withdrawal.

Status of the Ambassador Post. As noted above, Brett McGurk was nominated and had his Senate confirmation hearings on June 6, 2012. Shortly thereafter, he withdrew after revelations of an extramarital relationship with an Iraq-based U.S. journalist during his prior service at the U.S. Embassy in Baghdad.

The Administration subsequently named deputy chief of mission in Iraq, Robert Stephen Beecroft, as Ambassador-Designate. His confirmation hearings were held by the Senate Foreign Relations Committee on September 19, 2012; he was confirmed three days later and is serving in Baghdad.

No Sanctions Impediments

As the U.S.-Iraq relationship matures, some might focus increasingly on U.S.-Iraq trade and U.S. investment in Iraq. After the fall of Saddam Hussein, all U.S. economic sanctions against Iraq were lifted. Iraq was removed from the "terrorism list," and the Iraq Sanctions Act (Sections 586- 586J of P.L. 101-513), which codified a U.S. trade embargo imposed after Iraq's invasion of Kuwait, was terminated.

As noted above in the section on the Gulf states, in December 2010, a series of U.N. Security Council resolutions removed most remaining "Chapter VII" U.N. sanctions against Iraq, with the exception of the reparations payments to Kuwait. The lifting of U.N. sanctions allows any country to sell arms to Iraq.

However, Iraq still is required to comply with international proliferation regimes—meaning that it is generally barred from reconstituting Saddam era weapons of mass destruction programs. On October 24, 2012, Iraq demonstrated its commitment to compliance with these restrictions by signing the "Additional Protocol" of the Nuclear Non-Proliferation Treaty. Because sanctions have been lifted, there are no impediments to U.S. business dealings with Iraq.

Table 2. March 2010 COR Election: Final, Certified Results by Province

Province	Elected Seats in COR	Results
Baghdad	68	Maliki: 26 seats; Iraqiyya: 24 seats; INA: 17 seats; minority reserved: 2 seats
Nineveh (Mosul)	31	Iraqiiya: 20; Kurdistan Alliance: 8; INA: 1; Accordance: 1; Unity (Bolani): 1; minority reserved: 3
Qadisiyah	11	Maliki: 4; INA: 5; Iraqiyya: 2
Muthanna	7	Maliki: 4; INA: 3
Dohuk	10	Kurdistan Alliance: 9; other Kurdish lists: 1; minority reserved: 1
Basra	24	Maliki: 14 ; INA: 7; Iraqiyya: 3
Anbar	14	Iraqiyya: 11; Unity (Bolani): 1; Accordance: 2
Karbala	10	Maliki: 6; INA: 3; Iraqiyya: 1
Wasit	11	Maliki: 5; INA: 4; Iraqiyya: 2
Dhi Qar	18	Maliki: 8; INA: 9; Iraqiyya: 1
Sulaymaniyah	17	Kurdistan Alliance: 8; other Kurds: 9
Kirkuk (Tamim)	12	Iraqiyya: 6; Kurdistan Alliance: 6
Babil	16	Maliki: 8; INA: 5; Iraqiyya: 3
Irbil	14	Kurdistan Alliance: 10; other Kurds: 4
Najaf	12	Maliki: 7; INA: 5
Diyala	13	Iraqiyya: 8; INA: 3; Maliki: 1; Kurdistan Alliance: 1
Salahuddin	12	Iraqiyya: 8; Unity (Bolani): 2; Accordance: 2
Maysan	10	Maliki: 4; INA: 6
Total Seats	325	Iraqiyya: 89 + 2 compensatory = 91
	(310 elected + 8 minority reserved + 7 compensatory)	Maliki: 87 + 2 compensatory = 89 INA: 68 + 2 compensatory = 70 (of which about 40 are Sadrist) Kurdistan Alliance: 42 +1 compensatory = 43
		Unity (Bolani): 4
		Accordance: 6
		other Kurdish: 14
		minority reserved: 8

Source: Iraqi Higher Election Commission, March 26, 2010.

Notes: Seat totals are approximate and their exact allocation may be subject to varying interpretations of Iraqi law. Total seat numbers include likely allocations of compensatory seats. Total seats do not add to 325 total seats in the COR due to some uncertainties in allocations.

Table 3. U.S. Assistance to Iraq: FY2003-FY2013
(appropriations/allocations in millions of $)

	FY '03	04	05	06	07	08	09	10	11	12	Total 03-12	FY'13 Request
IRRF	2,475	18,389	—	10	—	—	—	—	—	—	20,874	
ESF	—	—	—	1,535.4	1,677	429	541.5	382.5	325.7	299	5,190	262.9
Democracy Fund	—	—	—	—	250	75	—	—	—	—	325	
IFTA (Treasury Dept. Asst.)	—	—	—	13.0	2.8	—	—	—	—	—	15.8	
NADR	—	—	3.6	—	18.4	20.4	35.5	30.3	29.8	32	170	30.3
Refugee Accounts (MRA and ERMA)	39.6	.1	—	—	78.3	278	260	316	280	—	1,252	
IDA	22	—	7.1	.3	45	85	51	42	17	—	269	
Other USAID Funds	470	—	—	—	—	23.8	—	—	—	—	494	
INCLE	—	—	—	91.4	170	85	20	702	114.6	500	1,683	850
FMF										850	850	900
IMET	—	1.2	—	—	1.1	—	2	2	1.7	2	10	2
DOD—ISF Funding	—	—	5,391	3,007	5,542	3,000	1,000	1,000	1,500	—	20,440	
DOD—Iraq Army	51.2	—	210	—	—	—	—	—	—	—	261	
DOD—CERP	—	140	718	708	750	996	339	263	44.0	—	3,958	
DOD—Oil Repair	802	—	—	—	—	—	—	—	—	—	802	
DOD—Business Support	—	—	—	—	50.0	50.0	74.0	—	—	—	174	
Total	3,859	18,548	6,329	5,365	8,584	5,042	2,323	2,738	2,313	1,683	56,768	2,045.2

Sources: State Department FY2013 Executive Budget Summary, February 2012; SIGIR Report to Congress, January 30, 2012; and CRS calculations. FY2012 appropriations in Consolidated Appropriation, P.L. 112-74.

Notes: Table prepared by Curt Tarnoff, Specialist in Foreign Affairs, on February 17, 2012.

This table does not contain agency operational costs, including CPA, State Department, and PRTs, except where these are embedded in the larger reconstruction accounts. Estimated operational costs to date are an additional $9.3 billion, including $3.6 billion estimated for FY2012. Approximately $2.7 billion is requested by State Department for these costs in FY2013.

Possible cuts in staff at the U.S. embassy and other locations is addressed in this report. IG oversight costs estimated at $417 million. IMET=International Military Education and Training; IRRF=Iraq Relief and Reconstruction Fund; INCLE=International Narcotics and Law Enforcement Fund; ISF=Iraq Security Force; NADR=Nonproliferation, Anti-Terrorism, Demining and Related: ESF=Economic Support Fund; IDA=International Disaster Assistance; FMF=Foreign Military Financing; ISF= Iraqi Security Forces.

Table 4. Recent Democracy Assistance to Iraq
(in millions of current $)

	FY2009	FY2010 (act.)	FY2011	FY2012
Rule of Law and Human Rights	32.45	33.3	16.5	29.75
Good Governance	143.64	117.40	90.33	100.5
Political Competition/Consensus-Building	41.00	52.60	30.00	16.25
Civil Society	87.53	83.6	32.5	55.5
Totals	**304.62**	**286.9**	**169.33**	**202.0**

Source: Congressional Budget Justification, March 2011. Figures for these accounts are included in the overall assistance figures presented in the table above.

Table 5. January 31, 2009, Provincial Election Results (Major Slates)

Baghdad—55 regular seats, plus one Sabean and one Christian set-aside seat	State of Law (Maliki)—38% (28 seats); Independent Liberals Trend (pro-Sadr)—9% (5 seats); Accord Front (Sunni mainstream)—9% (9 seats); Iraq National (Allawi)— 8.6%; Shahid Mihrab and Independent Forces (ISCI)—5.4% (3 seats) ; National Reform list (of former P.M. Ibrahim al-Jafari)—4.3% (3 seats)
Basra—34 regular seats, plus one Christian seat	State of Law—37% (20); ISCI—11.6% (5); Sadr—5% (2); Fadhila (previously dominant in Basra)—3.2% (0); Allawi—3.2% (0); Jafari list—2.5% (0). Governor : Shiltagh Abbud (Maliki list); Council chair: Jabbar Amin (Maliki list)
Nineveh—34 regular seats, plus one set aside each for Shabaks, Yazidis, and Christians	Hadbaa—48.4%; Fraternal Nineveh—25.5%; IIP—6.7%; Hadbaa took control of provincial council and administration. Governor is Atheel al-Nujaifi (Hadbaa).
Najaf—28 seats	State of Law—16.2% (7); ISCI—14.8% (7); Sadr—12.2% (6); Jafari—7% (2); Allawi— 1.8% (0); Fadhila—1.6% (0). Council chairman: Maliki list
Babil—30 seats	State of Law—12.5% (8); ISCI—8.2% (5); Sadr—6.2% (3); Jafari—4.4% (3); Allawi— 3.4%; Accord Front—2.3% (3); Fadhila—1.3%. New Council chair: Kadim Majid Tuman (Sadrist); Governor—Salman Zirkani (Maliki list)
Diyala—29 seats	Accord Front list—21.1%; Kurdistan Alliance—17.2%; Allawi—9.5%; State of Law— 6 %. New council leans heavily Accord, but allied with Kurds and ISCI.
Muthanna—26 seats	State of Law—10.9% (5); ISCI—9.3% (5); Jafari—6.3% (3); Sadr—5.5% (2); Fadhila— 3.7%.
Anbar—29 seats	Iraq Awakening (Sahawa-Sunni tribals)—18%; National Iraqi Project Gathering (established Sunni parties, excluding IIP)—17.6%;; Allawi—6.6%; Tribes of Iraq—4.5%.
Maysan—27 seats	State of Law—17.7% (8); ISCI—14.6% (8); Sadr—7; Jafari—8.7% (4); Fadhila—3.2%; Allawi—2.3%. New Governor: Mohammad al-Sudani (Maliki); Council chair: Hezbollah Iraq
Dhi Qar—31 seats	State of Law—23.1% (13); pro-Sadr—14.1% (7); ISCI—11.1% (5); Jafari—7.6% (4); Fadhila—6.1%; Allawi—2.8%. Governor—Maliki list; Council chair: Sadrist
Karbala—27 seats	List of Maj. Gen. Yusuf al-Habbubi (Saddam-era local official)—13.3% (1 seat); State of Law—8.5% (9); Sadr—6.8% (4); ISCI—6.4% (4); Jafari—2.5% ; Fadhila—2.5%.
Salah Ad Din—28 seats	IIP-led list—14.5%; Allawi—13.9%; Sunni list without IIP—8.7%; State of Law—3.5%; ISCI—2.9%. Council leans Accord/IIP
Qadissiyah—28 seats	State of Law—23.1% (11); ISCI—11.7% (5); Jafari—8.2% (3); Allawi—8%; Sadr— 6.7% (2); Fadhila—4.1%. New governor: Salim Husayn (Maliki list)
Wasit—28 seats	State of Law—15.3% (13); ISCI—10% (6); Sadr—6% (3); Allawi—4.6%; Fadhila— 2.7%. Governor: Shiite independent; Council chair: ISCI

Source: UNAMI translation of results issued February 2, 2009, by the Independent Higher Election Commission of Iraq; Vissar, Reidar. The Provincial Elections: The Seat Allocation Is Official and the Coalition-Forming Process Begins. February 19, 2009.

Iraq: Politics, Governance, and Human Rights

Table 6. Election Results (January and December 2005)

Bloc/Party	Seats (Jan. 05)	Seats (Dec. 05)
United Iraqi Alliance (UIA, Shiite Islamist). 85 seats after departure of Fadilah (15 seats) and Sadr faction (28 seats) in 2007. Islamic Supreme Council of Iraq of Abd al-Aziz al-Hakim has 30; Da'wa Party (25 total: Maliki faction, 12, and Anizi faction, 13); independents (30).	140	128
Kurdistan Alliance—KDP (24); PUK (22); independents (7)	75	53
Iraqis List (secular, Allawi); added Communist and other mostly Sunni parties for Dec. vote.	40	25
Iraq Accord Front. Main Sunni bloc; not in Jan. vote. Consists of Iraqi Islamic Party (IIP, Tariq al-Hashimi, 26 seats); National Dialogue Council of Khalaf Ulayyan (7); General People's Congress of Adnan al-Dulaymi (7); independents (4).	—	44
National Iraqi Dialogue Front (Sunni, led by former Baathist Saleh al-Mutlak) Not in Jan. 2005 vote.	—	11
Kurdistan Islamic Group (Islamist Kurd) (votes with Kurdistan Alliance)	2	5
Iraqi National Congress (Chalabi). Was part of UIA list in Jan. 05 vote	—	0
Iraqis Party (Yawar, Sunni); Part of Allawi list in Dec. vote	5	—
Iraqi Turkomen Front (Turkomen, Kirkuk-based, pro-Turkey)	3	1
National Independent and Elites (Jan)/Risalyun (Message, Dec) pro-Sadr	3	2
People's Union (Communist, non-sectarian); on Allawi list in Dec. vote	2	—
Islamic Action (Shiite Islamist, Karbala)	2	0
National Democratic Alliance (non-sectarian, secular)	1	—
Rafidain National List (Assyrian Christian)	1	1
Liberation and Reconciliation Gathering (Umar al-Jabburi, Sunni, secular)	1	3
Ummah (Nation) Party. (Secular, Mithal al-Alusi, former INC activist)	0	1
Yazidi list (small Kurdish, heterodox religious minority in northern Iraq)	—	1

Notes: Number of polling places: January: 5,200; December: 6,200; Eligible voters: 14 million in January election; 15 million in October referendum and December; Turnout: January: 58% (8.5 million votes)/ October: 66% (10 million)/December: 75% (12 million).

Table 7. Assessments of the Benchmarks

Benchmark	July 12, 2007, Admin. Report	GAO (Sept. 07)	Sept. 14, 2007, Admin. Report	Subsequent Actions and Assessments—May 2008 Administration report, June 2008 GAO report, International Compact with Iraq Review in June 2008, and U.S. Embassy Weekly Status Reports (and various press sources)
1. Forming Constitutional Review Committee (CRC) and completing review	(S) satisfactory	unmet	S	CRC filed final report in August 2008 but major issues remain unresolved and require achievement of consensus among major faction leaders.
2. Enacting and implementing laws on De-Baathification	(U) unsatisfact.	unmet	S	"Justice and Accountability Law" passed Jan. 12, 2008. Allows about 30,000 fourth ranking Baathists to regain their jobs, and 3,500 Baathists in top three party ranks would receive pensions. Could allow for judicial prosecution of all ex-Baathists and bars ex-Saddam security personnel from regaining jobs.

Table 7. (Continued)

				De-Baathification officials used this law to try to harm the prospects of rivals in March 2010 elections.
3. Enacting and implementing oil laws that ensure equitable distribution of resources	U	unmet	U	Framework and three implementing laws long stalled over KRG-central government disputes, but draft legislation still pending in COR. Revenue being distributed equitably, including 17% revenue for KRG. Kurds also getting that share of oil exported from fields in KRG area.
4. Enacting and implementing laws to form semi-autonomous regions	S	partly met	S	Regions law passed October 2006, with relatively low threshold (petition by 33% of provincial council members) to start process to form new regions, took effect April 2008. November 2008: petition by 2% of Basra residents submitted to IHEC (another way to start forming a region) to convert Basra province into a single province "region. Signatures of 8% more were required by mid-January 2009; not achieved. Najaf, Diyala, Salahuddin, and Anbar have asked for a referendum to become a region.
5. Enacting and implementing: (a) a law to establish a higher electoral commission, (b) provincial elections law; (c) a law to specify authorities of provincial bodies, and (d) set a date for provincial elections	S on (a) and U on the others	overall unmet; (a) met	S on (a) and (c)	Draft law stipulating powers of provincial governments adopted February 13, 2008, took effect April 2008. Implementing election law adopted September 24, 2008, provided for provincial elections by January 31, 2009. Those elections were held, as discussed above.
6. Enacting and implementing legislation addressing amnesty for former insurgents	no rating	unmet	Same as July	Law to amnesty "non-terrorists" among 25,000 Iraq-held detainees passed February 13, 2008. Most of these have been released. 19,000 detainees held by U.S. were transferred to Iraqi control under SA.
7. Enacting and implementing laws on militia disarmament	no rating	unmet	Same as July	March 2008 Basra operation, discussed above, viewed as move against militias. On April 9, 2008, Maliki demanded all militias disband as condition for their parties to participate in provincial elections. Law on militia demobilization stalled.
8. Establishing political, media, economic, and services committee to support U.S. "surge"	S	met	met	No longer applicable; U.S. "surge" has ended and U.S. troops now out of Iraq.

Iraq: Politics, Governance, and Human Rights

9. Providing three trained and ready brigades to support U.S. surge	S	partly met	S	No longer applicable. Eight brigades were assigned to assist the surge when it was in operation.
10. Providing Iraqi commanders with authorities to make decisions, without political intervention, to pursue all extremists, including Sunni insurgents and Shiite militias	U	unmet	S to pursue extremists U on political interference	No significant change. Still some U.S. concern over the Office of the Commander in Chief (part of Maliki's office) control over appointments to the ISF—favoring Shiites. Some politically motivated leaders remain in ISF. But, National Police said to include more Sunnis in command jobs and rank and file than one year ago.
11. Ensuring Iraqi Security Forces (ISF) providing even-handed enforcement of law	U	unmet	S on military, U on police	U.S. interpreted March 2008 Basra operation as effort by Maliki to enforce law even-handedly. Widespread Iraqi public complaints of politically-motivated administration of justice.
12. Ensuring that the surge plan in Baghdad will not provide a safe haven for any outlaw, no matter the sect	S	partly met	S	No longer applicable with end of surge. Ethno-sectarian violence has fallen sharply in Baghdad.
13. (a) Reducing sectarian violence and (b) eliminating militia control of local security	Mixed. S on (a); U on (b)	unmet	same as July 12	Sectarian violence has not re-accelerated outright, although there are fears the political crisis in December 2011 could reignite sectarian conflict.
14. Establishing Baghdad joint security stations	S	met	S	Over 50 joint security stations operated in Baghdad at the height of U.S. troop surge. Closed in compliance with June 30, 2009, U.S. pull out from the cities.
15. Increasing ISF units capable of operating independently	U	unmet	U	ISF now securing Iraq under the SA. Iraqi Air Force not likely to be able to secure airspace and DOD has approved potential sale to Iraq of F-16s and other major equipment.
16. Ensuring protection of minority parties in COR	S	met	S	No change. Rights of minority parties protected by Article 37 of constitution. Minorities given a minimum seat allocated in 2010 election law.
17. Allocating and spending $10 billion in 2007 capital budget for reconstruction.	S	partly met	S	About 63% of the $10 billion 2007 allocation for capital projects was spent.
18. Ensuring that Iraqi authorities not falsely accusing ISF members	U	unmet	U	Some governmental recriminations against some ISF officers still observed.

Source: Compiled by CRS.

End Notes

[1] Text, in English, is at: http://www.constitution.org/cons/iraq/TAL.html

[2] Text of the Iraqi constitution is at: http://www.washingtonpost.com/wp-dyn/content/article /2005/10/12/AR2005101201450.html.

[3] "The Iraq Study Group Report." Vintage Books, 2006. The Iraq Study Group was funded by the conference report on P.L. 109-234, FY2006 supplemental, which provided $1 million to the U.S. Institute of Peace for operations of an Iraq Study Group. The legislation did not specify the Group's exact mandate or its composition.

[4] The election law also stripped out provisions in the vetoed version to allot 13 total reserved seats, spanning six provinces, to minorities. An October 2008 amendment restored six reserved seats for minorities: Christian seats in Baghdad, Nineveh, and Basra; one seat for Yazidis in Nineveh; one seat for Shabaks in Nineveh; and one seat for the Sabean sect in Baghdad.

[5] Each provincial council has 25 seats plus one seat per each 200,000 residents over 500,000.

[6] The threshold for winning a seat is the total number of valid votes divided by the number of seats up for election.

[7] Analysis of Iraq expert Reidar Visser. "The Hashemi Veto." http://gulfanalysis.wordpress.com /2009/11/18/the-hashemi-veto/.

[8] Gertz, Bill. "Inside the Ring." *Washington Times*, February 18, 2010.

[9] Fadel, Leila and Karen DeYoung. "Iraqi Leaders Crack Political Deadlock." *Washington Post*, November 11, 2010.

[10] The following information is taken from Iraqi news accounts presented in http://www.opensource.gov.

[11] Parker, Ned and Salar Jaff. "Electoral Ruling Riles Maliki's Rivals." *Los Angeles Times*, January 23, 2011.

[12] Tim Arango. "Iraq's Prime Minister Gains More Power After Political Crisis." *New York Times*, February 28, 2012.

[13] "Embattled Iraqi PM Holding On To Power for Now." Associated Press, June 12, 2012.

[14] Zaid Sabah. "Iraq's al-Maliki Proposes Early Elections, al-Sumaria Reports. *Bloomberg News*, December 30, 2012.

[15] Michael Schmidt and Eric Schmitt. "Leaving Iraq, U.S. Fears New Surge of Qaeda Terror." *New York Times*, November 6, 2011.

[16] Sahar Issa. "Iraq Violence Dips Amid Rise in Syria." Philadelphia Inquirer, February 21, 2012.

[17] For more information on Kurd-Baghdad disputes, see CRS Report RS22079, *The Kurds in Post-Saddam Iraq*, by Kenneth Katzman.

[18] Interview with Masoud Barzani by Hayder al-Khoie on Al-Hurra television network. April 6, 2012.

[19] Meeting with congressional staff, February 24, 2011.

[20] "Managing Arab-Kurd Tensions in Northern Iraq After the Withdrawal of U.S. Troops." Rand Corporation, 2011.

[21] Jane Arraf. "Iraq's Unity Tested by Rising Tensions Over Oil-Rich Kurdish Region." *Christian Science Monitor*, May 4, 2012.

[22] Author conversation with then KRG Washington, DC, representative Qubad Talabani, November 8, 2011.

[23] Iraq Oil Report. Exxon to Start Drilling in Disputed Kurdish Blocks. October 18, 2012.

[24] International Crisis Group. "Iraq and the Kurds: The High-Stakes Hydrocarbons Gambit." April 19, 2012.

[25] http://www.state.gov/j/drl/rls/hrrpt/humanrightsreport/index.htm?dynamic_load_id =186428# wrapper

[26] Human Rights Watch. "Iraq's Information Crimes Law: Badly Written Provisions and Draconian Punishments Violate due Process and Free Speech." July 12, 2012.

[27] Tim Arango. "Iraq Election Official's Arrest Casts Doubt on Prospects for Fair Voting." *New York Times*, April 17, 2012.

[28] Kristina Wong, " Iraq Resists U.S. Prod, Lets Iran Fly Arms to Syria." *Washington Times*, March 16, 2012.

[29] "Iraq General Says Forces Not Ready 'Until 2020.'" Agence France Presse, October 30, 2011.

[30] Prashant Rao. "Maliki Tells US' Boehner Iraqi Troops Are Ready." *Agence France Presse*, April 16, 2011.

[31] Aaron Davis. "Maliki Seeking Consensus on Troops." *Washington Post*, May 12, 2011.

[32] Author conversations with Iraq experts in Washington, DC, 2011.

[33] Eric Schmitt and Steven Lee Myers. "Plan Would Keep Military in Iraq Beyond Deadline." September 7, 2011.

[34] Iraq Signs Arms Deals Worth $4.2 Billion. *Washington Post*, October 10, 2012; Tony Capaccio. "Iraq Seeks Up to 30 General Dynamics Stryker Vehicles." Bloomberg News, November 19, 2012.

[35] http://www.sigir.mil/files/audits/12-006.pdf#view=fit.

[36] Tim Arango. "U.S. May Scrap Costly Efforts to Train Iraqi Policy." *New York Times*, May 13, 2012.

[37] "U.S. Hopes For Stronger Military Ties With Iraq: General" Agence France-Presse, August 19, 2012.

[38] Dan De Luce. "U.S. 'Significant' in Iraq Despite Troop Exit: Dempsey." Agence France-Presse, August 21, 2012.

[39] Tim Arango. "Syrian Civil War Poses New Peril For Fragile Iraq." New York Times, September 25, 2012.

[40] Adam Schreck. "Iraq Presses US For Faster Arms Deliveries." Yahoo.com, October 18, 2012.

[41] Remarks by the President on Ending the War in Iraq." http://www.whitehouse.gov, October 21, 2011.

[42] Tim Arango. "U.S. Plans to Cut Its Staff by Half at Iraq Embassy." *New York Times*, February 8, 2012.

[43] Siobhan Gorman and Adam Entous. "CIA Prepares Iraq Pullback." Wall Street Journal, June 5, 2012.

INDEX

#

9/11, 123

A

abuse, 3, 4, 8, 11, 17, 37, 55, 158, 181, 210
access, 14, 109, 111, 115, 121, 122, 125, 130, 136, 156, 166, 171, 172, 176, 189, 210, 289, 301
accountability, 17, 54, 56, 63, 70, 142, 189, 198, 199, 209, 218
accounting, 89, 103, 113, 201, 207
adaptability, 44
adaptation, 43
administrative support, 161
adverse effects, 277
advisory body, 260
advocacy, 210, 290
Afghanistan, vii, 1, 2, 4, 11, 18, 36, 41, 42, 43, 45, 47, 48, 61, 63, 70, 72, 102, 110, 183, 186, 187, 188, 190, 195, 222, 224, 232, 235, 247, 291
age, 121, 172, 177, 265
agility, 188
agricultural sector, 173, 177
agriculture, 24, 111, 112, 209, 218, 219, 220
Air Force, 80, 86, 133, 144, 146, 222, 230, 301, 309
airports, 23, 130, 132
air-traffic, 210
Al Qaeda, viii, 259, 266, 278, 279, 280, 290
ambassadors, 296
American Samoa, 198
anchoring, 157
appointments, 202, 207, 208, 272, 288, 303, 309
appropriations, 3, 55, 63, 89, 91, 95, 96, 97, 98, 102, 105, 107, 111, 130, 194, 197, 203, 217, 219, 220, 232, 235, 290, 305
Appropriations Act, 251, 258
Appropriations Committee, 221, 233, 250, 257

Arab League, viii, 260, 291, 294, 295, 296, 297
Arab League summit, viii, 260, 291, 294, 295, 296, 297
Arab world, viii, 260, 287, 291
Arabian Peninsula, 229, 241, 242, 243, 245, 247, 254, 255
architect, 269
armed forces, 270
arms sales, 299
arrest(s), 15, 34, 174, 274, 276, 277, 287, 293
assassination, 28, 153, 275
assault, 148
assessment, 12, 23, 32, 68, 77, 151, 200, 201, 208, 264, 273, 286
assets, 19, 70, 92, 102, 132, 143, 176, 202, 292
asylum, 158
ATF, 137
atmosphere, 161
attitudes, 209, 289
Attorney General, 58
attribution, 287
audit(s), vii, 1, 2, 3, 4, 5, 6, 7, 8, 9, 10, 11, 16, 18, 20, 23, 28, 59, 62, 68, 70, 77, 89, 98, 103, 113, 134, 135, 150, 151, 155, 157, 158, 159, 163, 165, 174, 179, 188, 194, 195, 198, 203, 207, 208, 231, 233, 239, 242, 243, 249, 254, 255, 256, 300, 310
automobiles, 85
autonomy, 162, 275, 280, 295
awareness, 17

B

backlash, 158
bacteria, 121
Bahrain, 296, 301
balance sheet, 191
Bangladesh, 186
banking, 172, 173, 174, 175, 176, 210, 256, 293

banking industry, 174
banking sector, 173, 174, 175, 176
banks, 111, 172, 174
base, 85, 143, 149, 191, 221, 276, 279, 291, 293
basic needs, 24
basic services, 27, 112, 115
benchmarks, 112, 163, 219, 263, 264
benefits, vii, 2, 27, 31, 43, 47, 163, 187, 189, 193, 195, 209, 220
bias, 190
bilateral relationship, 301, 302
blame, 26, 33, 290
blogs, 246
blood, 23, 43, 63
bomb attack, 279
bonuses, 217
border security, 136, 150, 300
bribes, 15, 85
Britain, 291
building code, 286
Bureau of Alcohol, Tobacco, Firearms, and Explosives, 210
bureaucracy, 95, 111, 176, 184, 288
Burma, 187
burn, 119
business education, 174
businesses, 169, 176, 203, 210
buyers, 173

C

campaigns, 279
candidates, 246, 265, 267, 268, 269, 277
CAP, 163, 218, 219, 220, 222, 227
capacity building, 52, 81, 97, 99, 106, 200, 206, 221
capital projects, 115, 183, 309
Capitol Hill, 39
career development, 170
cash, 9, 15, 18, 19, 41, 70, 109, 172, 173, 174
catalyst, 152
caucuses, 161
causal relationship, 170
CBP, 210, 222
ceasefire, 238
cell phones, 50
Central Asia, 290
ceramic, 167
certification, 210, 219, 270
chain of command, 48, 273
challenges, vii, 1, 3, 4, 7, 16, 32, 40, 54, 59, 63, 89, 136, 144, 158, 170, 182, 186, 194, 232
chaos, 36, 67, 72, 153, 171
charities, 165

chemical(s), 125, 291, 299
Chief Justice, 21, 27, 28
Chief of Staff, 15, 22, 35, 37, 44, 45, 196, 231, 297
children, 121, 166, 167, 170, 196
China, 291
Chinese firms, 286
Christians, 290, 306
CIA, 34, 245, 311
city(s), 27, 58, 72, 121, 123, 167, 169, 170, 219, 238, 254, 276, 278, 289, 297, 309
citizens, 2, 163
civil law, 262
civil servants, 163
civil society, 97, 99, 109, 159, 160, 163, 200, 209, 219, 220, 282
civil war, 4, 136
Civil War, 311
Civilian Response Corps, 187
clarity, 191
classification, 202, 207
cleanup, 165, 167
climate, 34, 173
closure, 158, 169, 289, 302
CNN, 292
Coast Guard, 210, 226
coherence, 193
collaboration, 146
collective bargaining, 289
colleges, 201
combustion, 117, 118, 119
command economy, 172
commander-in-chief, 270
commercial, 130, 132, 133, 167, 172, 173, 174, 176, 179, 219, 281
commercial bank, 172, 173, 174, 176
Committees on Appropriations, 184, 197
commodity, 177
common rule, 74
Commonwealth of the Northern Mariana Islands, 198
communication, 29, 61, 130, 135, 163
communication systems, 163
community(s), 20, 142, 165, 171, 190, 197, 209, 219, 220, 260, 267, 271, 272, 277, 278, 284, 288, 289, 297
community conflict, 220
compensation, 180, 203, 296
competition, 11, 69, 81, 266
complement, 38, 143, 167, 204
complexity, 44, 78
compliance, 210, 304, 309
complications, 48
composition, 261, 310

computer, 27, 156
conditioning, 170
conference, 217, 218, 275, 284, 310
Conference Report, 184, 218, 219, 220, 232, 233, 246, 250, 251, 257
conflict, viii, 44, 64, 109, 110, 125, 140, 157, 164, 182, 185, 186, 187, 189, 200, 201, 204, 219, 220, 259, 278, 281, 282, 289, 309
conflict prevention, 186, 187
conflict resolution, 164, 219
confrontation, 290
Congressional Budget Office, 74
consensus, 260, 297, 306, 307, 310
consent, 200, 205, 275
Consolidated Appropriations Act, 233, 250, 257, 290
consolidation, 190
conspiracy, 15, 85
constituents, 302
Constitution, 161, 210, 270, 281
construction, vii, 1, 3, 6, 10, 13, 14, 15, 23, 31, 59, 69, 77, 79, 81, 82, 86, 87, 89, 98, 99, 117, 121, 131, 134, 135, 149, 151, 153, 155, 156, 166, 167, 169, 170, 179, 185, 193, 219, 220, 221, 240, 248, 288
consumer protection, 286
contingency, 6, 10, 17, 42, 46, 48, 52, 55, 62, 63, 182, 183, 184, 186, 188, 189, 190, 193
controversial, 22, 33, 66, 271
controversies, 33
convention, 265
convergence, 193
conversations, 310
conviction, 85, 158
cooperation, viii, 5, 23, 27, 33, 38, 47, 152, 200, 260, 271, 293, 296, 299, 300, 301, 302
cooperative agreements, 66, 81, 227
coordination, 6, 8, 27, 30, 34, 36, 39, 47, 61, 72, 77, 84, 184, 186, 187, 188, 189, 193, 200, 201, 202, 209
corruption, 25, 27, 28, 29, 30, 31, 32, 33, 41, 111, 150, 153, 155, 157, 158, 159, 180, 193, 209, 221, 274, 286, 287, 289, 301, 302
cost, 4, 11, 12, 23, 25, 27, 31, 36, 41, 48, 50, 61, 63, 68, 69, 77, 86, 103, 108, 113, 116, 123, 134, 143, 144, 155, 166, 183, 184, 188, 193, 217, 218, 230, 246, 299, 303
Council of Ministers, 33, 58, 159, 174, 222
counterterrorism, 77, 146, 148, 296, 299, 300, 302
covering, 10, 13, 15, 78, 267
CPI, 158, 222
cracks, 276
crimes, 34, 85, 210
criminal justice system, 221

criminals, 6
crises, 200, 285, 298
critical infrastructure, 84, 111, 115, 142
criticism, 58, 294
crop, 178
crude oil, 119, 125, 128, 129, 157, 179, 240, 282
cultural conditions, 43
cultural heritage, 109
culture, 34, 36, 47, 144, 159, 164, 195, 218
currency, 157, 274, 287
curricula, 188
curriculum, 170, 188
customers, 135, 293
Customs and Border Protection, 210, 222
cycles, 186

D

danger, 123
DART, 66, 222
database, 9, 84, 89, 103, 113, 183, 194
death penalty, 291
deaths, 5, 74, 75, 121, 285, 288
decentralization, 164
decision-making process, 189
defamation, 288
defects, 5, 15
deficiency(s), 10, 11, 14, 15, 113, 123, 135, 155, 165, 169, 287, 297, 300
degradation, 218
democracy, 10, 21, 23, 30, 58, 81, 90, 97, 99, 109, 160, 161, 163, 218, 219, 227, 260, 285, 298, 302
democratic elections, 162
Democratic Party, 34, 261, 280, 294
demonstrations, viii, 259, 276, 284, 288
denial, 287
Department of Agriculture, 40, 82, 210
Department of Commerce, 82, 210
Department of Defense, 4, 34, 36, 63, 79, 90, 108, 109, 110, 151, 181, 197, 198, 199, 200, 203, 205, 222, 223, 230, 231, 232, 234, 235, 240, 248, 249, 253, 256
Department of Health and Human Services, 82, 210
Department of Homeland Security, 82, 210
Department of Justice, 5, 14, 28, 58, 82, 91, 135, 209, 210, 213, 223
Department of Labor, 223
Department of the Treasury, 82, 109, 209, 210, 226
Department of Transportation, 82, 210, 223
deployments, 188
deposits, 262
destruction, 109, 171
detainees, 156, 308

detection, 8
detention, 156, 157, 221
developed nations, 301
development assistance, 78
DHS, 210
diffusion, 69
diplomacy, 40, 78, 186, 189, 209
disability, 202
disaster, 32, 66, 114, 198, 199
disaster relief, 66
disclosure, 202, 208
discrimination, 269, 276
disease rate, 121
diseases, 121
disorder, 16
displacement, 171, 261
disposition, 30, 77, 103, 113
dissatisfaction, 181
distribution, 11, 45, 110, 117, 121, 153, 162, 184, 264, 277, 278, 308
District of Columbia, 198
divergence, 193
dominance, 264
draft, 161, 162, 182, 187, 235, 262, 264, 286, 289, 308
drinking water, 50, 125
drugs, 221
due process, 289
dumping, 293
durability, 264

E

earnings, 179
economic development, 51, 67, 69, 97, 99, 205, 210, 302
economic empowerment, 209
economic growth, 47, 81, 111, 112, 174, 176, 220, 302
economic institutions, 220
economic performance, 179
economic problem, 30
economic progress, 286
economic resources, 260
education, 17, 30, 43, 90, 109, 111, 115, 164, 165, 170, 171, 220, 262, 300, 302
educational institutions, 165
Egypt, 51, 209
El Salvador, 187
elected leaders, 47, 161
election, 22, 25, 161, 162, 163, 220, 261, 262, 263, 264, 265, 266, 267, 268, 269, 270, 277, 278, 281, 284, 307, 308, 309, 310

electricity, vii, 1, 4, 26, 27, 30, 31, 43, 46, 50, 56, 67, 69, 90, 93, 94, 110, 112, 116, 117, 118, 119, 120, 121, 125, 136, 165, 287, 288, 302
embargo, 111, 303
embassy, 296, 302, 303, 305
emergency, 171, 189, 198, 202, 204, 206
Emergency Assistance, 246
emergency relief, 171
employees, 59, 128, 131, 150, 158, 188, 198, 203, 204, 207, 208, 210, 302
employers, 289
employment, 94, 134, 169, 170, 172, 179, 194, 202, 203, 208, 218, 219, 220, 285
empowerment, 263
enemies, 55, 112
energy, 120, 262, 272, 282, 283, 285, 286, 293, 295
enforcement, 5, 17, 80, 120, 153, 220, 221, 309
engineering, 89
entrepreneurs, 176
environment(s), 4, 26, 39, 40, 41, 44, 46, 47, 63, 64, 112, 131, 140, 142, 157, 167, 176, 192, 205, 209, 217, 256, 286
equipment, 11, 13, 70, 73, 77, 81, 90, 96, 123, 125, 133, 134, 140, 141, 142, 143, 148, 149, 156, 166, 167, 169, 170, 177, 207, 210, 217, 218, 239, 300, 309
erosion, 123
ESD, 224, 236, 252
ethnic groups, 264, 281
ethnicity, 142
Europe, 49
European Union, 293
evidence, 25, 27, 103, 150, 156, 170, 275, 293, 296
evolution, 142
exclusion, 25, 225, 267
execution, 1, 8, 23, 33, 51, 58, 59, 82, 102, 119, 162, 164, 167, 184, 187, 189, 191, 199, 200, 201, 209, 210, 220
executive branch, 8, 287
Executive Order, 285
exercise, 61, 89, 148, 150, 202, 207, 268, 273, 287
exile, 22, 268
expenditures, 4, 20, 23, 70, 89, 90, 93, 95, 96, 97, 98, 101, 102, 103, 106, 113, 140, 141, 142, 143, 145, 146, 155, 160, 170, 179, 182, 189, 190, 201, 202, 235
expertise, 9, 32, 82, 161, 191, 203, 291
exporter, 302
exports, 59, 99, 112, 126, 128, 129, 146, 173, 180, 209, 240, 282, 286, 293
exposure, 62
expulsion, 293
extradition, 295

Index

317

extremists, 5, 266, 309

F

faith, 196, 290
families, 110, 120, 262, 290
family members, 262
famine, 109
farmers, 210
FBI, 210
fear(s), 268, 274, 276, 282, 288, 292, 296, 297, 309
federal agency, 195
Federal Emergency Management Agency, 189, 223
federal government, 162, 220
Federal Housing Finance Agency, 206
Federal Register, 202
Federal Reserve, 19
felon, 15
FEMA, 189, 223, 246
fertilizers, 173
financial, vii, 2, 5, 8, 10, 17, 20, 24, 28, 70, 84, 103, 109, 111, 172, 173, 174, 180, 190, 195, 196, 199, 201, 209, 210, 217, 219, 220, 244, 255, 293, 302
financial crimes, 209, 210
financial data, 103
financial institutions, 174
financial reports, 103
financial sector, 173, 302
financial system, 109
firearms, 70, 153
fires, 64
first responders, 134, 135
flexibility, 44
flight(s), viii, 32, 62, 132, 260, 294, 297
food, 109, 110, 115, 171, 173, 177, 209, 268
food security, 115, 209
force, 8, 24, 25, 32, 43, 44, 74, 109, 126, 142, 143, 146, 148, 149, 150, 158, 217, 225, 238, 280, 282, 290, 291, 294, 297, 298, 300, 301
foreign affairs, 202, 208
foreign aid, 49
foreign assistance, 209
foreign exchange, 179
foreign firms, 286, 303
foreign policy, 186, 189, 292
formation, 148, 210, 262, 271, 272, 273, 274
formula, 44, 64, 263
foundations, 172
France, 283, 291, 310, 311
fraud, 3, 4, 5, 8, 11, 14, 15, 16, 17, 19, 55, 85, 89, 113, 149, 158, 165, 180, 181, 240, 270
free trade, 176, 177
freedom, 209, 289, 290

friction, 193
friendship, 291

G

gangs, 33
GAO, 223, 235, 236, 237, 247, 264, 307
GDP, 173, 176, 179, 223, 286
general election, 22
Georgia, 62
Germany, 291
global economy, 176
global markets, 210
goods and services, 68, 85
governance, vii, 1, 6, 33, 43, 45, 47, 50, 67, 73, 78, 81, 111, 112, 130, 159, 160, 162, 163, 164, 173, 179, 195, 209, 218, 219, 260, 264, 275
government funds, 264, 287
governments, 45, 73, 109, 164, 165, 200, 217, 272, 308
governor, 264, 265, 272, 274, 281, 287, 306
grants, 9, 20, 68, 77, 161, 163, 165, 169, 176, 227, 264
Grievances, 278
gross domestic product, 172, 223
growth, 25, 28, 59, 103, 128, 152, 153, 163, 172, 176, 177, 179, 224, 244, 268, 286
guidance, 10, 17, 74, 162, 180, 183, 187
guidelines, 125, 184, 193

H

harassment, 289
health, 23, 43, 50, 90, 109, 110, 112, 115, 121, 165, 166, 167, 220, 284
health care, 43, 50, 90, 110, 115, 165, 166, 220
health information, 166
health services, 166
height, 264, 280, 290, 303, 309
Hezbollah, 285, 293, 306
hiring, 5, 17, 227
history, 6, 27, 60, 66, 182, 184, 188, 191, 193, 199, 292
homes, 34, 273, 275, 290
host, 6, 9, 39, 41, 43, 45, 63, 183, 184, 189, 193, 195
hostilities, viii, 260
House, 53, 56, 57, 58, 59, 60, 61, 62, 103, 196, 197, 221, 223, 228, 233, 234, 246, 249, 250, 256, 257, 290, 297
House of Representatives, 196, 197, 228, 234
House Report, 233, 234, 246, 249, 250, 256, 257
housing, 3, 115, 266

Housing and Urban Development, 251, 258
hub, 85, 134, 151
human, 2, 17, 150, 153, 159, 199, 200, 209, 210, 219, 220, 221, 269, 281, 286, 287, 288, 290, 291
human capital, 17
human right(s), 153, 159, 200, 209, 219, 220, 221, 269, 281, 286, 287, 288, 290, 291
humanitarian aid, 66, 109
humanitarian crises, 64, 171
Hungary, 186
Hunter, 198
husband, 15
hydrocarbons, 219, 262
hygiene, 209

I

IAO, 223
identification, 208
identity, 281
image, 159, 266, 288
imbalances, 199
IMF, 179, 180, 223, 245
Immigration and Customs Enforcement, 210
imports, 119, 173, 177
imprisonment, 289
improvements, 21, 45, 69, 74, 123, 135, 139, 164
in transition, 200
income, 157, 172
incumbents, 265
independence, 156, 174, 261, 267, 280
India, 147
individuals, 14, 24, 74, 85, 110, 158, 169, 204, 267, 268
industry(s), 24, 43, 180, 283, 286, 293
inflation, 179
information sharing, 146
information technology, 150, 188
initiation, 67
inmates, 210
insecurity, 30, 111
inspections, vii, 1, 2, 5, 6, 7, 13, 14, 18, 20, 35, 43, 59, 119, 195, 210
inspectors, 2, 5, 6, 8, 14, 34, 54, 55, 57, 123, 158, 194, 210
institutions, 25, 29, 30, 33, 43, 50, 72, 111, 153, 157, 159, 160, 172, 174, 176, 195, 201, 210, 217, 219, 220, 274, 285, 287, 301, 302, 303
insurgency, 39, 45, 47, 50, 51, 69, 112, 136, 150, 157, 167, 169, 171, 268
integration, 47, 182, 187, 221
integrity, 28, 33, 112, 183, 221, 290
intellectual property, 286

intellectual property rights, 286
intelligence, 33, 142, 143, 146, 197, 198, 201, 235, 288, 300, 301
interagency coordination, 19, 38, 60, 63, 199, 208
interbank market, 256
interest rates, 179
interference, 33, 172, 274, 276, 287, 292, 295, 309
Internal Revenue Service, 210
internally displaced, 109, 110, 171, 209, 223
International Energy Agency, 121, 286
international law, 5
International Monetary Fund, 223
International Narcotics Control, 20, 90, 91, 105, 211, 223
International Ship and Port Facility Security, 210
international standards, 209, 220, 289
international trade, 111, 176, 179
intervention, 140, 200, 271, 289, 309
intimidation, 289, 290
investment(s), 19, 34, 39, 44, 56, 75, 111, 118, 123, 130, 139, 140, 170, 172, 173, 195, 210, 218, 284, 286, 303
investment bank, 39
investors, 285
Iran, viii, 111, 119, 151, 260, 265, 269, 275, 278, 285, 291, 292, 293, 294, 301, 310
Iranian influence, viii, 260, 291, 292, 293, 297
Iraq War, 111
Iraqi airspace, viii, 130, 260
Iraqi leaders, vii, 1, 2, 20, 21, 30, 66, 193, 261, 271, 281, 286, 293, 296, 297, 298, 300, 303
Iraqi Security Forces, vii, 1, 28, 44, 45, 143, 144, 195, 217, 218, 224, 240, 255, 278, 280, 305, 309
IRI, 161, 218, 224
irrigation, 122, 173, 177
ISF, viii, 69, 75, 77, 79, 80, 95, 139, 140, 141, 142, 143, 144, 146, 217, 218, 219, 224, 238, 239, 259, 264, 266, 276, 278, 279, 280, 281, 282, 285, 297, 298, 299, 300, 301, 305, 309
Islam, 262
Islamic law, 262, 289
isolation, 51
issues, vii, viii, 2, 5, 10, 12, 48, 52, 56, 67, 123, 130, 153, 162, 167, 169, 180, 183, 187, 190, 210, 259, 262, 267, 272, 275, 280, 291, 295, 296, 301, 302, 303

J

Japan, 231, 248
jihadist, 279
job creation, 176, 220
job training, 219

Index 319

Jordan, 132, 209, 276, 279, 294, 296
journalists, 288
judicial branch, 28
judiciary, 28, 209, 221, 275
jurisdiction, 42, 49, 198, 204
justification, 264, 285, 302
juveniles, 156

K

Kenya, 187
kidnapping, 180, 290
knees, 172
Korea, 49
Kurd(s), viii, 34, 35, 136, 140, 259, 261, 262, 263, 264, 266, 268, 271, 273, 276, 277, 280, 281, 282, 283, 284, 286, 290, 294, 295, 304, 306, 307, 308, 310
Kuwait, 66, 85, 132, 180, 181, 280, 291, 295, 296, 298, 301, 303

L

lack of confidence, 186
landscape, 284
law enforcement, 89, 136, 221, 287
laws, 2, 130, 173, 201, 221, 264, 271, 280, 283, 285, 286, 288, 307, 308
lead, 3, 4, 31, 42, 63, 64, 68, 73, 75, 144, 181, 182, 183, 185, 196, 199, 298, 300, 302
leadership, vii, 2, 3, 5, 20, 38, 42, 45, 62, 66, 67, 72, 75, 111, 164, 174, 186, 187, 196, 260, 270, 276, 278, 291, 300, 302, 303
learning, 51, 170
Lebanon, 209, 293, 294
legal protection, 298
legislation, 54, 55, 93, 94, 130, 157, 172, 189, 219, 262, 286, 291, 308, 310
lender of last resort, 256
lending, 172, 174, 210, 219
letters of credit, 173
liberalism, 291
light, 11, 121, 302
limited liability, 210
literacy, 170
literacy rates, 170
living environment, 167
loans, 6, 20, 92, 173, 174, 176, 177, 210
local authorities, 265
local community, 165
local government, 45, 51, 72, 159, 164, 165, 218, 219, 220, 278, 279

locus, 182, 187, 191
logistics, 116, 142, 144, 146, 150, 217, 218, 220
love, 196
LPG, 224
lung cancer, 261

M

Macedonia, 49
magnitude, 157, 195
major issues, 280, 307
majority, 55, 65, 80, 87, 93, 105, 128, 133, 134, 136, 153, 164, 179, 262, 265, 270, 271, 284, 299
malnutrition, 167, 171
man, 64, 280
management, 6, 8, 9, 10, 17, 31, 39, 44, 54, 58, 59, 60, 63, 68, 69, 74, 77, 79, 82, 86, 89, 116, 144, 163, 164, 165, 178, 179, 180, 181, 182, 184, 186, 187, 188, 190, 194, 199, 204, 210, 218, 219, 220, 221, 230, 246
man-made disasters, 64
manpower, 43
Marine Corps, 19, 226
market economy, 112, 179
market structure, 172
marketing, 177
mass, 140, 291
materials, 27, 123, 170
matter, 14, 221, 246, 298, 309
measles, 167
measurement, 49
media, 210, 219, 220, 278, 289, 296, 308
mediation, 281
medical, 31, 79, 166, 167
medical care, 31
medicine, 210
melon, 178
membership, 25, 43, 59, 294
memory, 23
mental health, 210
mentor, 80, 156, 221, 298
mentoring, 90, 151, 158, 162
mentorship, 156
metaphor, 193
meter, 31, 81
methodology, 252
Middle East, 1, ii, iii, 51, 52, 59, 81, 117, 125, 135, 166, 170, 177, 179, 219, 223, 229, 241, 242, 243, 245, 247, 254, 255, 289, 290
military aid, 30
military exchanges, 300

militia(s), 5, 25, 33, 72, 139, 140, 142, 149, 150, 217, 238, 262, 263, 281, 285, 289, 292, 295, 308, 309
Ministry of Education, 36
minorities, 219, 277, 289, 290, 310
mission(s), vii, 1, 2, 3, 4, 7, 8, 20, 42, 43, 46, 49, 52, 54, 56, 58, 61, 66, 70, 72, 74, 77, 78, 141, 142, 148, 149, 159, 172, 182, 185, 186, 187, 188, 190, 191, 195, 196, 197, 209, 217, 232, 246, 263, 266, 270, 280, 298, 299, 301, 303
Missouri, 55
misuse, 8
mobile phone, 130, 134, 135
models, 43
modernization, 135, 173, 218
momentum, 172, 264
monetary policy, 172
money laundering, 15, 28, 32, 33, 174
Moqtada Al Sadr, viii, 259, 261, 266, 275, 276, 284
mortality, 167
mortality rate, 167
motivation, 41
mumps, 167
Muslims, viii, 259, 289, 291
mutual respect, 302

N

naming, 272, 277
narcotics, 210
narratives, 103
National Defense Authorization Act, 10, 17, 55, 184, 186, 198, 203, 224, 246
national income, 129
national security, 39, 136, 146, 182, 191, 199, 202, 208, 275, 296
National Security Council, 110, 184, 187, 188, 195, 238
National Strategy, 238
nationalism, 266, 292
nation-building, 50, 51
NATO, 42, 224, 282, 292
natural disaster, 198
natural gas, 119, 129
NDI, 161, 218, 224
negative effects, 51
neglect, 12, 23, 50, 111, 114, 126, 130, 166
negotiating, 291
negotiation, 301
nervousness, 279
NGOs, 109
Nigeria, 186
nominee, 279, 280, 285, 303

nonprofit organizations, 165
North Africa, 177, 179
North Atlantic Treaty Organization, 224
North Korea, 294
nuclear talks, 291

O

Obama, 192
obstacles, 287
OCS, 299
Office of Management and Budget, 17, 37, 67, 93, 188, 205, 225
Office of the Inspector General, 206, 216
officials, viii, 9, 12, 13, 19, 22, 26, 27, 28, 33, 36, 46, 48, 56, 63, 70, 73, 78, 110, 116, 121, 125, 151, 156, 158, 159, 164, 165, 167, 174, 183, 204, 210, 233, 260, 264, 267, 275, 278, 279, 285, 290, 293, 296, 297, 298, 299, 302, 308
oil, 19, 30, 43, 45, 46, 50, 59, 64, 79, 93, 99, 109, 111, 112, 119, 125, 126, 127, 128, 129, 146, 153, 172, 173, 174, 179, 180, 220, 237, 240, 252, 262, 272, 280, 281, 282, 283, 284, 285, 286, 293, 296, 299, 302, 308
oil production, 125, 126, 127, 172
oil revenues, 43, 173, 180, 262, 296
OMB, 217, 225, 227, 230, 231, 232, 234, 235, 248, 249, 253, 256
OPA, 225, 247
open economy, 172
open markets, 172
operating costs, 70
Operation Enduring Freedom, 232, 249, 256
Operation Iraqi Freedom, 19, 42, 44, 232, 238, 249, 256
operational independence, 217
opportunities, 33, 34, 54, 67, 85, 171, 191, 287
optimism, 45, 279, 287
organizational culture, 164
organize, 80, 262, 274
organs, 273
orthopedic surgeon, 24
OSC, viii, 77, 78, 96, 108, 215, 225, 229, 232, 234, 239, 247, 254, 260, 282, 298, 299, 301
outreach, 156, 210, 220, 276
overhead costs, 27, 163
Overseas Private Investment Corporation, 82, 210, 225
ownership, 11, 61, 286

Index

321

P

Paris Club, 20, 227
Parliament, 24
participants, 6, 153
peace, 34, 56, 192, 210
peacekeeping, 210
penalties, 16, 210
Pentagon, 36, 39, 185
performance indicator, 184
permission, 294
permit, 56, 208
perseverance, 196
Persian Gulf, 291, 295, 301
personal relations, 26
personal relationship, 26
personnel costs, 108
petroleum, 70, 125, 129, 180, 224, 225
Philadelphia, 310
Philippines, 186
pipeline, 128, 129, 153, 225, 240, 284
plants, 19, 27, 36, 50, 118, 121
platform, 185
pleasure, 195
PM, 225, 230, 231, 232, 234, 235, 248, 253, 256, 310
PMOI, 293
Poland, 49
police, viii, 3, 20, 27, 32, 45, 64, 77, 79, 80, 84, 90, 95, 106, 136, 139, 140, 141, 142, 143, 146, 148, 149, 150, 151, 153, 209, 218, 220, 221, 238, 260, 279, 282, 300, 309
policy, 4, 5, 17, 33, 36, 43, 52, 64, 111, 164, 173, 180, 187, 189, 210, 219, 246, 293, 294, 301
policy initiative, 173
political crisis, 268, 273, 274, 277, 278, 281, 283, 286, 298, 309
political instability, 30
political participation, 161
political parties, 28, 33, 219, 220, 265
political power, 274
political system, 260
politics, 265, 271, 272, 284, 287, 301
polling, 265, 307
poor performance, 135
population, 26, 47, 51, 121, 130, 136, 166, 198, 261, 262, 268, 289, 293
portfolio, 272
power generation, 23, 132
power plants, 116, 117, 118, 119, 121
power sharing, 284
precedent, 195
predicate, 160

prejudice, 217
preparation, 61, 74, 163, 190, 197, 198, 201
presidency, 268, 270, 271
president, 261, 262, 263, 267, 268, 270, 271, 272, 273, 276, 288
President Clinton, 37
President Jalal Talabani, viii, 35, 37, 73, 259
President Obama, 37, 77, 196, 271, 273, 274, 297, 298, 301
prestige, 260
prevention, 8, 167, 182, 210, 220
primary school, 170
primary school enrollment, 170
Prime Minister Nuri al-Maliki, viii, 21, 22, 37, 259
principles, 163, 275
prisoners, 296
prisons, 12, 79, 140, 156, 210, 220, 221
private banks, 174
private investment, 210
private sector, 179, 198, 218, 302
privatization, 173, 176, 244
procurement, 17, 68, 89, 166, 219, 221
producers, 118, 177
professionalism, 109, 164, 196, 220
professionals, 170
programming, 187, 219
proliferation, 304
proposition, 271
prosperity, 28, 176, 179, 224, 288
protection, 74, 80, 153, 155, 156, 191, 210, 217, 220, 221, 287, 309
prototype, 180
provincial councils, 47, 220, 261, 264, 265, 277, 302
public awareness, 167
public health, 121
public investment, 110
public life, 24
public opinion, 121
public safety, 134, 165
public sector, 111, 164, 289
public service, 24, 25, 31, 34, 54, 78, 159, 160, 165
Puerto Rico, 198
PVC, 11

Q

qualifications, 203
quality assurance, 14
quality control, 14, 150
query, 58

R

radar, 300
radio, 134
Ramadan, 271, 286
ratification, 283, 297
RE, 205
real estate, 18, 85
reality, 177
recognition, 204
recommendations, 7, 11, 53, 55, 69, 186, 277, 298
reconciliation, 5, 72, 218, 219, 220, 263, 264, 282, 288, 302
reconstruction operation, vii, 1, 2, 6, 7, 8, 18, 21, 31, 41, 46, 47, 48, 53, 54, 55, 56, 58, 59, 60, 63, 64, 66, 85, 181, 182, 189, 190, 191, 197, 198, 199, 200, 201, 202, 203, 204, 205, 206, 208, 225
recovery, 5, 45, 63, 67, 85, 110, 111, 125, 171, 209, 286
recruiting, 142, 143
redundancy, 199
reelection, 284
reform(s), vii, 2, 6, 7, 18, 22, 39, 53, 55, 57, 59, 60, 63, 101, 155, 160, 164, 157, 170, 172, 173, 174, 175, 176, 179, 181, 182, 184, 186, 188, 189, 190, 191, 197, 200, 210, 219, 220, 221, 225, 239, 244, 245, 246, 267, 280, 294, 306
refugees, 109, 110, 171, 209, 220
regulations, 2, 15, 43, 85, 102, 172, 188, 190, 193, 200, 201, 210
regulatory framework, 218
rehabilitation, 23, 52, 93, 117, 119, 136, 167, 170, 219
reimburse, 217
rejection, 264
relatives, 290
relief, 7, 14, 21, 31, 63, 66, 67, 82, 89, 90, 92, 101, 107, 109, 110, 111, 112, 113, 141, 160, 171, 184, 185, 188, 189, 198, 204
remediation, 123
repair, 52, 53, 115, 117, 122, 125, 130, 133, 165, 167, 275
repression, 52, 281, 288, 293
reputation, 267
requirements, 17, 68, 81, 86, 89, 101, 141, 142, 143, 176, 180, 184, 188, 197, 210, 218, 298
resentment, 270, 278
reserves, 59, 119, 125, 129
resettlement, 210, 281
resistance, 162
resolution, 162, 302
resource management, 115
resources, 3, 9, 17, 25, 33, 34, 43, 49, 63, 68, 110, 113, 136, 140, 157, 158, 164, 177, 181, 182, 184, 186, 190, 194, 199, 200, 208, 245, 260, 264, 280, 282, 283, 288, 308
response, 58, 62, 68, 82, 96, 109, 125, 139, 150, 178, 186, 197, 198, 208, 226, 229, 230, 231, 232, 233, 234, 236, 237, 238, 239, 240, 241, 242, 243, 244, 247, 248, 249, 250, 251, 252, 253, 254, 255, 256, 257, 288
responsiveness, 163, 220
restitution, 15, 16, 85
restoration, 31, 78, 125
restrictions, 63, 109, 172, 289, 304
restructuring, 172, 190, 210
retail, 174
revenue, 19, 112, 220, 308
Revolutionary Guard, 269, 285
RIE, 117, 225
rights, 129, 150, 197, 209, 277, 287, 288, 289, 290, 291
risk(s), 62, 73, 75, 167, 183, 200, 210
Romania, 186
root, 8
rotations, 67
rubella, 167
rule of law, 43, 47, 90, 111, 136, 140, 153, 159, 193, 218, 220, 221, 285
rules, 51, 62, 109, 193, 200, 201, 262, 267, 285, 289
rural development, 112
rural population, 166
Russia, 20, 291, 301

S

sabotage, 116, 134
Saddam Hussein, 3, 50, 56, 110, 157, 159, 161, 180, 260, 261, 276, 279, 281, 286, 291, 303
safe haven, 309
safety, 173, 289
SAMHSA, 210
sanctions, 23, 52, 111, 114, 120, 125, 130, 166, 170, 172, 175, 293, 296, 303, 304
satellite service, 134
Saudi Arabia, 294, 296, 301
savings, 5, 10, 188, 190, 199
school, 23, 79, 112, 170, 171, 174
scope, 3, 6, 78, 86, 89, 125, 150
second-class citizens, 278
Secretary of Defense, 36, 37, 38, 41, 63, 64, 84, 109, 110, 148, 184, 185, 186, 189, 190, 195, 200, 204, 205, 225, 227, 292, 300
sectarianism, 150, 195, 267, 287
secularism, 291

security assistance, 77, 95, 96, 299

security forces, viii, 4, 10, 43, 45, 56, 64, 74, 77, 80, 90, 112, 136, 142, 149, 150, 153, 198, 260, 262, 264, 273, 274, 275, 288, 297

security guard, 180

security threats, 14

seed, 173

self-esteem, 24

Senate, 45, 53, 59, 186, 196, 197, 200, 221, 225, 233, 239, 246, 250, 251, 257, 290, 303

Senate Foreign Relations Committee, 53, 239, 290, 303

sensing, 266

September 11, 110, 271

septic tank, 121

servers, 27, 275

services, 11, 46, 47, 67, 70, 74, 79, 81, 89, 109, 112, 114, 122, 125, 130, 131, 146, 150, 159, 160, 165, 167, 171, 176, 189, 198, 203, 207, 210, 219, 227, 230, 240, 260, 276, 284, 287, 288, 289, 294, 302, 308

sewage, 23, 27, 165

shape, 21, 190, 266, 267

shelter, 171

Shiite factions, 295

Shiites, 261, 263, 265, 266, 269, 274, 278, 279, 284, 289, 296, 309

shock, 291

shortfall, 27, 30, 111

showing, 112, 265, 266

signs, 155

skilled personnel, 208

skin, 60

Slovakia, 186

smuggling, 128, 210

soccer, 169

social services, 220

society, 24, 43, 53, 153, 195

software, 27, 209

SOI, 139, 152, 153, 225

solidarity, 267, 276, 296

solution, 18, 49, 119, 180, 182, 184, 187, 190, 191, 293

Somalia, 187

sovereignty, 3, 67, 68, 110, 136, 161, 195, 260, 261

specifications, 14, 15, 48

speech, 287, 289

spending, 3, 5, 20, 22, 27, 31, 35, 44, 49, 61, 95, 98, 115, 140, 142, 145, 153, 156, 164, 182, 190, 207, 217, 309

Spring, 287

stability, viii, 24, 41, 47, 59, 72, 109, 174, 185, 186, 198, 220, 259, 288, 291

stabilization, vii, 1, 2, 6, 7, 8, 13, 18, 21, 31, 42, 45, 46, 47, 48, 53, 54, 55, 56, 58, 59, 60, 63, 64, 85, 139, 167, 181, 182, 184, 185, 186, 188, 189, 190, 191, 197, 198, 199, 200, 201, 202, 203, 204, 205, 206, 207, 208, 220, 225, 264

staff members, 78

staffing, 64, 68, 240

Stafford Act, 189

stakeholders, 190

state(s), 32, 45, 111, 112, 122, 133, 134, 136, 153, 166, 172, 173, 174, 180, 189, 210, 225, 246, 271, 272, 282, 284, 287, 288, 291, 295, 296, 297, 301, 303, 310

state-owned banks, 210

state-owned enterprises, 111, 172, 173

stimulus, 173

storage, 129, 144

stress, 302

stroke, viii, 64, 259, 276

strong force, 38

structural reforms, 186

structure, 3, 4, 27, 31, 45, 48, 57, 58, 59, 64, 103, 142, 149, 150, 178, 179, 182, 187, 188, 260, 261, 263, 268, 292, 299

style, 289

subscribers, 130, 135

succession, 30, 63

Sudan, 187

suicide, 85, 263, 278, 279

Sunni Arabs, viii, 259, 261, 262, 263, 266, 268, 273, 281, 294

Sunnis, viii, 4, 45, 55, 72, 152, 162, 259, 261, 262, 263, 264, 266, 267, 268, 269, 273, 274, 276, 278, 279, 309

supervision, 148, 189, 190, 200, 201, 207

support services, 84

Supreme Council, 261, 307

Supreme Court, 269, 270, 274

survival, viii, 15, 259

suspensions, 16

sustainability, 9, 13, 14, 41, 52, 56, 169, 193, 206

sympathy, 278

synchronization, 45

Syria, viii, 51, 187, 209, 259, 260, 278, 279, 293, 294, 295, 300, 301, 310

T

talent, 187

tanks, 81, 143, 145, 273, 299

target, 5, 12, 43, 49, 290

Task Force, 47, 79, 80, 85, 106, 117, 126, 156, 175, 209, 210, 222, 224, 225

Index

tax base, 210
taxation, 210, 286
taxes, 61
TBI, 173, 225
teachers, 170, 171
team members, 193
teams, 3, 5, 6, 8, 13, 51, 58, 72, 80, 111, 149
technical assistance, 69, 84, 125, 173, 176, 220, 291
technical support, 79, 156
techniques, 156, 164, 177
technology, 170
telecommunications, 23, 93, 111, 112, 115, 130, 134, 135
telephone, 130, 134, 135
tempo, 142
tension(s), 48, 69, 102, 129, 263, 281, 282, 283, 295
tenure, 30, 33, 59, 67, 70, 111, 160, 195, 230
terminals, 132, 286
territorial, viii, 112, 259, 281
territory, 136, 162, 198, 280, 283, 284
terrorism, 23, 28, 91, 112, 213, 224, 285, 291, 300, 303
terrorist attack, 110
terrorists, 32, 308
testing, 135
textbooks, 170
theft, 15, 125
threats, 142, 149, 285, 287
time constraints, 66
time frame, 267
Title I, 91, 109, 212
Title II, 91, 109, 212
tones, 22
top-down, 178
torture, 153, 287
total costs, 148
trade, 23, 173, 176, 209, 226, 244, 272, 303
traditions, 289
trafficking, 210, 286, 287, 288
trafficking in persons, 286
trainees, 142
training programs, 44, 140, 186, 209, 220, 279
trajectory, 66
tranches, 299
transactions, 17, 28, 293
transfer payments, 70
translation, 306
transmission, 117, 134
transparency, 28, 218, 252, 285
transport, 14, 115, 131, 178, 218
transportation, 93, 96, 111, 112, 130, 131, 132, 133, 141, 143, 173, 210, 220, 221
transportation infrastructure, 130

Treasury, 20, 36, 187, 205, 210, 225, 226, 231, 248, 285, 293, 305
treatment, 19, 23, 27, 36, 79, 125, 156, 166, 207, 226, 276, 289, 293, 295
trial, 157, 158, 275, 295
trust fund, 173
Turkey, 34, 209, 240, 275, 282, 283, 292, 294, 295, 307
turnout, 269
turnover, 56, 59, 67, 181

U

U.N. Security Council, 282, 296, 303
U.S. Army Corps of Engineers, 43, 46, 51, 63, 99, 111, 153, 226, 229
U.S. assistance, 21, 95, 187, 301
U.S. Department of Agriculture, 226, 302
U.S. history, 1, 126, 195
U.S. policy, vii, 1, 62, 263, 292, 293, 294
U.S. reconstruction, vii, 1, 17, 18, 19, 22, 23, 25, 26, 27, 28, 30, 32, 33, 36, 41, 48, 49, 50, 52, 54, 55, 56, 59, 62, 64, 70, 80, 82, 92, 105, 113, 132, 157, 171, 174, 176, 177, 180
U.S. Treasury, 109, 210, 226, 227, 230, 231, 232, 234, 235, 237, 248, 249, 251, 252, 253, 254, 256
U.S. troop presence, 297
UN, 170, 180, 226, 228, 235, 237, 243, 244, 245
UNDP, 209, 226
unemployed individuals, 24
UNHCR, 226
uniform, 6, 41, 43, 113, 193
unions, 289
unit cost, 218
United Nations, 19, 81, 107, 111, 121, 125, 130, 161, 173, 174, 180, 195, 209, 226, 260, 282, 293
United Nations Development Program, 226
United Nations Development Programme, 226
universities, 112, 201
urban, 121, 166, 266
urban areas, 121
urban population, 121
USA, 226, 246
USDA, 210, 226, 244, 245, 254

V

vacancies, 264
vacuum, 25, 35, 178, 238
vehicles, 4, 15, 18, 70, 143, 156, 192, 299
versatility, 44
vessels, 143, 146

Index

veto, 262, 264, 268, 274, 310
Vice President, 192, 269, 274, 295, 301
victims, 109, 163, 291
Vietnam, 53, 62
violence, viii, 5, 30, 43, 58, 72, 94, 116, 136, 139, 152, 153, 164, 167, 169, 170, 199, 209, 217, 219, 238, 259, 260, 263, 264, 265, 266, 268, 278, 279, 285, 290, 293, 309
vision, 26, 37, 38, 186
vocational education, 219
vocational training, 169
voluntary organizations, 109
vote, 159, 262, 265, 267, 268, 269, 270, 274, 275, 276, 277, 278, 280, 281, 285, 290, 294, 297, 307
voters, 261, 262, 263, 265, 266, 267, 268, 277, 307
voting, 261, 263, 265, 268, 269, 271

W

wages, 217
waiver, 163, 264, 288
war, 12, 16, 33, 37, 50, 56, 63, 64, 66, 109, 110, 111, 112, 125, 126, 130, 135, 136, 153, 163, 170, 175, 192, 195, 209, 280, 292
War on Terror, 232, 249, 251, 256, 257
Washington, 34, 46, 57, 58, 64, 66, 67, 79, 117, 123, 222, 246, 274, 280, 284, 292, 310
waste, 3, 4, 8, 11, 14, 17, 23, 41, 54, 55, 59, 61, 79, 89, 149, 156, 158, 180, 182, 188, 190, 193, 240
wastewater, 36, 90, 121, 125, 226
water, vii, 1, 19, 23, 27, 46, 50, 67, 69, 79, 85, 90, 93, 94, 110, 112, 115, 120, 121, 122, 125, 136, 165, 171, 209, 218
water quality, 121, 125
water resources, 93, 218
weakness, 35, 41, 54, 60, 73, 111, 164, 182, 263, 266

wealth, vii, 1, 30, 59
weapons, 27, 32, 111, 136, 143, 209, 217, 292, 300, 304
weapons of mass destruction, 136, 209, 304
wear, 291
welfare, 176
well-being, 116
wellness, 167
West Bank, 51
White House, 34, 37, 67, 186
WHO, 226
wholesale, 25
Wisconsin, 3
withdrawal, viii, 5, 37, 56, 75, 77, 84, 218, 259, 273, 274, 285, 292, 297, 298, 301, 303
witnesses, 156, 221
WMD, 112
workers, 128, 175, 289
workforce, 17, 172, 173
working class, 284
working groups, 153
World Bank, 130, 170, 173, 176, 178, 231, 235, 237, 243, 244, 245, 248, 253, 286
World Health Organization, 125, 226
World Trade Organization, 173, 226
World War I, 49
worldwide, 96, 99, 151, 184, 200
wrongdoing, 8
WTO, 176, 226

Y

Yale University, 48
Yemen, 294
yield, 63
youth unemployment, 176